THE BOOK OF DA

by

André Lacocque

Translated by David Pellauer
English edition revised by the Author

Foreword by Paul Ricoeur

JOHN KNOX PRESS
ATLANTA

First published in French as
Le Livre de Daniel by
Delachaux & Niestlé S.A., Neuchatel—Paris
© Delachaux & Niestlé S.A., Neuchatel (Suisse)—Paris, 1976

Published simultaneously in the United States by John Knox Press
and in Great Britain by SPCK.

Translation © 1979 The Society for Promoting Christian Knowledge.

Library of Congress Cataloging in Publication Data

Lacocque, André.
  The book of Daniel.

  Translation of Le livre de Daniel.
  Bibliography: p. 253
  Includes index.
  1. Bible. O. T. Daniel—Commentaries. I. Title.
BS1555.3.L313   224´.5´077   78-2036
ISBN 0-8042-0090-4

Printed in Great Britain by
William Clowes & Sons Limited, London, Beccles and Colchester

John Knox Press
Atlanta, Georgia

For Claire

Contents

CONTENTS

CONTENTS

CHAPTERS 10—12: The Great Final Vision

CHAPTER 11: Historical Retrospective

CHAPTER 12: Resurrection and Eschatology

INDEXES

Abbreviations

ANET	Pritchard, J. B., *The Ancient Near Eastern Texts relating to the O.T.* Princeton.
Ant. Bibl.	Kisch, G., *Liber Antiquitatum Biblicarum of Pseudo-Philo.*
ARM	*Archives royales de Mari.* Paris.
ATD	*Das Alte Testament Deutsch.* Göttingen.
BASOR	*Bulletin of the American Schools of Oriental Research.* New Haven.
Bib.	*Biblica.* Rome.
BJRL	*Bulletin of the John Rylands Library.* Manchester.
BLea	Bauer, H., and Leander, P., *Historische Grammatik der Hebräischen Sprache des A.T.* Halle 1922 = Hildesheim 1962.
BZ	*Biblische Zeitschrift.* Paderborn.
CBQ	*Catholic Biblical Quarterly.* Washington.
CIS	*Corpus Inscriptionum Semiticarum.*
C.T.A.	Virolleaud, C., *Textes en Cunéiformes* . . . . Paris.
EB	*Encyclopaedia Biblica.* New York.
Ency. Bibl.	*Encyclopedia Mikraït* (Hebrew). Jerusalem.
ETL	*Ephemerides Theologicae Lovanienses.* Louvain.
E.T.	*The Expository Times.* Edinburgh.
Ges.-Kau.	Gesenius-Kautzsch, *Hebräische Grammatik.* Leipzig. 1909 = *Gesenius' Hebrew Grammar*, ed. E. Kautzsch, 2nd Eng. edn, A. E. Cowley. Oxford 1910.
Ges.St.z.A.T.	Noth, M., *Gesammelte Studien zum A.T.* Munich.
HAT	*Handbuch zum Alten Testament.* Tübingen.
HUCA	*Hebrew Union College Annual.*
ICC	*International Critical Commentary.* Edinburgh.
IDB	*Interpreter's Dictionary of the Bible.* Nashville.
Jastrow, *Dict.*	Jastrow, M., *A Dictionary of the Targumin, the Talmud Babli and Yerushalmi, and the Midrashic Literature*, 2 vols. New York.
JBL	*Journal of Biblical Literature.* New Haven.
JNES	*Journal of Near Eastern Studies.* Beirut.
Journ. of Phil.	*Journal of Philosophy.* New York.

JTS	*Journal of Theological Studies.* London; Oxford; n.s., Oxford.
KAT	*Kommentar zum Alten Testament,* ed. E. Sellin. Leipzig.
MGWJ	*Monatschrift zur Geschichte und Wissenschaft des Judentums.* Breslau.
Migne, *PG*	*Patrologia Graeca,* ed. J.-P. Migne. Paris.
Migne, *PL*	*Patrologia Latina,* ed. J.-P. Migne. Paris.
NRTh	*Nouvelle Revue Théologique.* Louvain.
OTL	Old Testament Library. Philadelphia.
OTS	Oudtestamentische Studien. Leyden.
RB	*Revue Biblique.* Paris.
RES	*Répertoire d'épigraphie sémitique.*
RHPR	*Revue d'histoire et de philosophie religieuses.* Strasbourg; Paris.
RQ	*Revue de Qumran.* Paris.
Schrader *KB*	Schrader, E., *Keilinschriftliche Bibliotheek,* 6 vols. 1889–1901.
Str. Bill.	Strack, H. L., & Billerbeck, P., *Kommentar zum N.T. aus Talmud und Midrasch,* 5 vols. Munich.
Syria	*Revue d'art oriental et d'archéologie.* Paris.
ThR	*Theologische Rundschau.* Tübingen.
ThZ	*Theologische Zeitschrift.* Basle.
T.O.B.	Lacocque, A. and Grelot, P., *La Traduction Oecuménique de la Bible, Daniel.*
T.S.K.	*Theologische Studien und Kritiken.* Stuttgart–Gotha–Berlin.
TWNT	*Theologisches Wörterbuch zum Neuen Testament,* ed. G. Kittel and G. Friedrich. Stuttgart.
V. Dom.	*Verbum Domini.* Rome.
VT	*Vetus Testamentum* (and Supplements = *SVT*). Leyden.
ZATW	*Zeitschrift für die Alttestamentliche Wissenschaft.* Giessen; Berlin.
ZDMG	*Zeitschrift der Deutschen Morgenländischen Gesellschaft.* Leipzig; Wiesbaden.
ZDPV	*Zeitschrift des Deutschen Palästina-Vereins.* Leipzig; Wiesbaden.
ZNTW	*Zeitschrift für die Neutestamentliche Wissenschaft.* Giessen; Berlin.
ZSTh	*Zeitschrift für Systematische Theologie.* Gütersloh; Berlin.
ZThK	*Zeitschrift für Theologie und Kirche.* Tübingen.

INTERTESTAMENTAL LITERATURE

Add. Dan.	Additions to Daniel
Apoc. Ab.	Apocalypse of Abraham
Asc. Is.	Ascension of Isaiah
Ass. Mos.	Assumption of Moses
1, 2 En.	1, 2 Enoch
Jub.	Jubilees
1, 2, 3, 4 Macc.	1, 2, 3, 4 Maccabees
Odes of Sol.	Odes of Solomon
Or. Sib.	Sibylline Oracles
Ps. Sol.	Psalms of Solomon
Test. XII Pat.	Testaments of the Twelve Patriarchs
T. Benj.	Testament of Benjamin
T. Jos.	Testament of Joseph
T. Jud.	Testament of Judah
T. Napht.	Testament of Naphtali
T. Reu.	Testament of Reuben
T. Sim.	Testament of Simeon
T. Zab.	Testament of Zabulon
Vit. Ad. et Ev.	Life of Adam and Eve

THE DEAD SEA SCROLLS

Q	Qumran
CD (C)	The Damascus Document
1 QS	Manual of Discipline
1 QS b	Supplement to the Manual of Discipline
1 QM	War of the Sons of Light and the Sons of Darkness
1 QH	Hymns of Thanksgiving
1 Qp Hab.	*Pesher*, Habakkuk
1 Q Is.	Isaiah Scroll
1 Q Gen. Ap.	Genesis Apocryphon
3 Q 4	An Isaiah Text
4 Q or. Nab.	The Prayer of Nabonidus

4 Q p Nah.	*Pesher*, Nahum
4 Q p Mic.	*Pesher*, Micah
4 Q p Is.	*Pesher*, Isaiah
4 Q Dib. Ham.	*Dibre ha-Me'oroth*; prayer of intercession
6 Q Dan.	Fragments of manuscript of Daniel found in Qumran Cave 6
11 Q Ps.	A Psalms Text

THE TEXT

A	Aquila
Θ	Theodotion
Σ	Symmachus
Kt	Ketib
Lu	Lucianic recension of the LXX
LXX	Septuagint
MT	Masoretic Text
NT	New Testament
OT	Old Testament
Pesh	Peshitta
Qr	Qere
RSV	Revised Standard Version
Samar.	Samaritan
Targ.	Targum
Targ. Jon.	Targum Jonathan
Targ. Onk.	Targum Onkelos
Vss.	Versions
Vul.	Vulgate

RABBINIC LITERATURE

Talm.	Talmud
Mid.	Midrash
m.	Mishnah
b.	Babylonian
j.	Jerusalem
R.	Rabba (Gen R = Genesis Rabba; etc.)
Tanḥ.	Tanḥuma (midrash)
Psik R	Pesikta Rabbati (midrash)
ARN	Aboth of Rabbi Nathan
AZ	Abodah Zarah
BB	Baba Bathra
Ber.	Berachobh
Hag.	Hagigah

Kidd.	Kiddushin
Maaser Sh.	Maaser Sheni
Meg.	Megillah
Ned.	Nedarim
PA(both)	Pirke Aboth
Pes.	Pesachim
RhSh	Rosh ha-Shanah
Sanh.	Sanhedrin
Shab.	Shabbat
Sheq.	Sheqalin
Taan.	Taanith
Yebam.	Yebamoth

Acknowledgements

Thanks are due to the following for permission to quote from copyright sources:

T. & T. Clark Limited: *A Critical and Exegetical Commentary on the Book of Daniel* by J. A. Montgomery

Oxford University Press: *The Apocrypha and Pseudepigrapha of the Old Testament* edited and translated by R. H. Charles.

Thanks are also due to Carol P. Wilson for compiling the indexes.

Foreword

It was certainly not because I have any particular competence in the field of biblical studies—and especially that concerning Judaism—that my friend André Lacocque asked me to write this foreword. He wanted me instead to continue the conversations we have been having for a number of years in Chicago about the modes of discourse brought into play by the biblical writings.

The Book of Daniel, in effect, poses in an especially sharp way most of the problems raised in reading the other books of the Bible. I have selected from his Introduction and Commentary some features upon which I will attempt to reflect, as a reader who has lost his naiveté and who has been instructed by Lacocque's exegesis.

First, the simple fact that Daniel A (chapters 1—6) and Daniel B (chapters 7—12) reveal two different genres within one genre which encompasses them—usually called 'apocalyptic'—immediately poses the question of identifying these genres and their function in the production of the text. In Daniel A, we have six stories, which are in fact *midrashim* and which stem from an edifying parenetic and apologetic kind of literature. Daniel is here designated in the third person. In Daniel B, we have four 'visions' in which Daniel, now speaking in the first person, is himself the seer who receives the aid of an angel in interpreting his visions. So the reader is invited to a divided reading of the same book. What is more, he is invited to a bilingual reading if he takes into account the substitution of Aramaic for Hebrew and the return to Hebrew which, as our exegete demonstrates, accords with the fundamental structures of the book (p. 13).

Second, the book as a whole presents itself as a writing constructed upon other writings. On the one hand, the *midrash* of Daniel A develops and expands upon texts well known to the original reader. On the other hand, as regards the apocalypse properly speaking, it, too, assumes that the reader knows the prophetic writings which it 'reuses', according to a frequent expression of A.L. and which, he adds, it replaces by a trans-historic speculation based upon contemporary events. The fact that the visions are not introduced by the messenger's clause—the *Botenformel*—'Thus says the Lord', constitutes a particularly sure clue for the exegete that the apocalypse is not an original oracle and does not pretend to be one. Besides, the Hebrew Bible placed this book among the 'Writings' and not among the 'Prophets', in opposition to the Canon of Alexandria. It is this 'reuse' which poses a baffling hermeneutical problem. An important key for any reading might be to track down and dislodge the models reactivated in this indirect manner, and, in fact, a good part of the Commentary is devoted to this work of discernment.[1] The result is that the expert reading which we possess through this exegesis itself tends to become an *indirect* reading which re-actualizes these very texts.

A third feature will also attract our attention. It concerns the pseud-epigraphic character of the work, the fact that it is antedated and pseudonymous, the name Daniel designating at the same time, we are told, an incomparably wise archaic hero and one of the Judean exiles in Babylon. This problem of pseudonyms, known to modern readers through Kierkegaard, brings into play, or rather into question, what we take as most assured concerning the notion of an author. The explanation offered by A.L. in his Introduction deserves our attention. We can distinguish there three explanatory levels of decreasing generality. In the background we find the conviction that every veridical teaching, in Israel, finds a fundamental unity in Moses which makes the respective individuality of each presumed author unessential; next comes the apocalypticists' conviction of belonging to a distinct line which confers a collective personality upon them whereby the continuity of inspiration is assured; finally, detached from this double foundation is the conviction of the exhaustion of the prophetic spirit in the time when the author is writing his work. This last motif more directly accounts for the need to give oneself over to some fictional author from the past who thereby becomes what Wayne Booth, in *The Rhetoric of Fiction*, calls the 'implied author'. But we must pay attention to what happens to the reading and the reader when we know this. We are guided by the exegete through a reading not only divided and indirect, as we said above, but also, if we may say so, stereoscopic. We are invited to imagine a writer of the time of Antiochus IV Epiphanes hidden behind a fictional author. The paradox is that the real author is never more than presumed obliquely across the fictional author of a real text.[2]

---

[1] Thus Daniel, the interpreter of the king's dreams in Dan. 2 and 4, is a replica of Joseph who was also called upon to interpret the dreams of a pagan king; at the same time, by means of this analogy of roles, a more global judgement is implied or at least suggested about every great profane civilization. Daniel 2 thus appears as a *midrash* on Gen. 41. In Daniel 9, it is from a text of Jeremiah that the author draws what A.L. calls a midrashic actualization. And the great prayer of confession which prepares Daniel for understanding the vision in the same chapter turns out to be a mosaic of citations. Finally, the fourth vision, which extends over chapters 10—12, is a complete *midrash* on Isaiah. One commentary cited by A.L. even calls this text 'the oldest interpretation of the suffering servant', which does not exclude that the same text continues by reusing Ezekiel.

[2] One exegete cited by A.L. even expressly defines 'apocrypha' by this criterion: 'a volume of alleged antiquity that had been purposely "hidden away" until the emergency arrived for publication' (J. A. Montgomery, cited below, p. 4).

The next step leads to the point where identifying the literary genre is no longer distinguished from the very comprehension of its meaning. The theme of pseudonymity, remarks the exegete, adjoins that of the *esoteric*. But what does it mean to read an *esoteric* writing? We cannot limit ourselves to the surface of the text or to what I call a phenomenology of the manifest text, that is, to the simple description of the situation where someone reports a dream which an interpreter deciphers, or where a seer reports a vision which a celestial being interprets. The idea of supernatural communication of uncommunicable secrets by natural means certainly does furnish a good phenomenal criterion of the apocalyptic genre (from Isaiah 24—7 and Ezekiel 38—9 to the Apocalypse of John). This criterion may even be completed by the very special role played in a whole group of related writings by what Gerhard von Rad calls 'historical summaries' (*Wisdom in Israel*, pp. 263–83) and which appear in our text in the form of a periodization divided into four great episodes: Babylonian, Median, Persian, and Macedonian. It is one of the objects of the vision to reveal the succession of historical epochs from the time of the legendary author to the crisis experienced by the real author; furthermore, the law of this genre requires that the past should be presented as something still to come and as predicted in its unfolding.[3] This phenomenology of the manifest text is complete when this fictional prophetic periodization, which is finally retrospective, issues in the true message of the author, real prophecy, which he *presents as a vision* of the final victory of the righteous.[4] We will return to the meaning of this message later. For the moment, let us go back to our question: what does it mean to read an esoteric text when we know that it is esoteric?

One response which appears to be unavoidable is that to read an esoteric text is to replace its apparent meaning by the meaning reconstructed by exegesis in retrieving the *Sitz im Leben*. In other words, to understand, here, is to know to what *situation* the text responds or corresponds.

That we should begin in such a manner is not to be doubted. On this point, A.L. is correct when he says that the recourse to the original situation of the real author—the *Sitz im Leben*—is our principal defence

---

[3] This is why the practised eye of the exegete is required to spot the moment when the author passes from prophecy *post eventum* to actual prophecy, as in Dan. 11.40. ('Here', notes A.L., 'the history properly speaking ends and the "prophecy" begins.' p. 232.) But, precisely, the process of reuse permits the continual passing beyond prophecy, which is fictitious for the fictitious author, about an history that the real author knows as real, to real prophecy which takes what precedes as a model.

[4] Jean Steinmann's definition (*Daniel* (1961) p. 24), cited by A.L. in his Introduction (p. 6, n. 22), brings together all the elements of what I call a phenomenological definition of apocalyptic writing, i.e., the meaning which *appears* to a first reading.

against the pretension of a modern reader to draw from the Book of Daniel prophecies concerning his own future. This reuse of a reuse is no longer possible once exegesis has taught us to see in apocalyptic writings the anticipations of writers who belong to our past and who themselves depend upon 'historical summaries' dressed up as prophecies *post eventum*.

We must begin therefore by reconstituting the *Sitz im Leben* of the apocalyptic writing. But where does this inquiry lead? What do we learn when we practise it rigorously as does A.L.? We set out to study the author and his epoch, the redactional milieu and the primitive audience. We thereby come upon the persecution of Antiochus IV[5] and a particular milieu closely associated with the Hassidim or Asideans. And we form the hypothesis of an Asidean Daniel (p. 229). By this we mean that the meaning of the text is to say something to the Jews persecuted by Antiochus. The meaning of the text is the message deciphered as a function of its *Sitz im Leben*.

For the most part, the Commentary you are about to read fulfils this methodological rule. But I wonder whether the author does not lead us further, not in spite of, but thanks to this deliberately 'historicizing' treatment of the text. It is evident that we 'understand something' when we learn that the destruction of the single statue which represents the four great Babylonian, Median, Persian, and Macedonian empires *signified to* a reader in the second century BC that a miracle was going to resolve his situation of distress. It is the same for the miracle of the three young men saved from the crematory oven in Daniel 3. A.L. says, 'It is within the context of the persecution of the Jews by Antiochus and the installation of the abomination of desolation in the Temple that our chapter gets all its meaning. It is an exhortation to martyrdom' (p. 58). The same assertion recurs concerning the similar episode reported in chapter six (Daniel in the Lions' Den): 'The story gets all its meaning from the fact that in 169, Antiochus IV wanted to force the Jews to worship the dynastic god Baal Shamem (identified with the Olympian Zeus) whose epiphany he considered himself to be' (pp. 107–8). And again: 'Daniel's message to a persecuted people is that their innocence will save them from the "lion's pit" where they have been thrown by Antiochus Epiphanes' (p. 119). Antiochus is also the 'little arrogant horn' of Daniel 7. And as regards the fourth vision of Daniel 10—12, it is said to attain its ultimate goal in 11.44–5 which prophesies the death of Antiochus: '. . . he will meet his end with no one to help him.' The martyrdom of the Asideans becomes *the* meaning of the symbol of the suffering servant from second Isaiah as Daniel 10—12 reuses it. It is this

---

[5] This unity, says A.L. in his Introduction (p. 15), 'is assured by the omnipresent shadow of Antiochus Epiphanes, as much in the first part as in the second.'

accentuation of the original audience that allows A.L. to form what he calls straight away 'the hypothesis of an Asidean Daniel'.

Is it true, nevertheless, that the meaning is exhausted by this ciphered message addressed to those persecuted in the second century BC? One thing is certain in any case. Whatever supplementary meaning we might look for, it is built upon this 'historical' meaning. If we have not understood what the great refusal of the Jews with regard to every attempt at levelling, at absorption through pan-Hellenic syncretism, can signify, no more universal meaning can emerge. In effect, it is this great refusal—of the author writing under Antiochus IV—which is retroactively projected into the similar resistance of the fictional heroes confronted by a similar syncretism in the Babylonian and Persian periods. This reaction to Hellenism constitutes both the *Sitz im Leben* and the 'historical' meaning at the same time. The singularity of the apocalyptic vision becomes more precise if we note, as we have already done above from another point of view, that the transference into a fictional past accords with a time when the hope of Israel is disappointed, when the eschatological dream is collapsing. The text then takes on a function which today we would call a 'performative' one: *to give courage* to the Jews persecuted by Antiochus Epiphanes who reigned from 175–164 BC. The parenetic function of Daniel A and the exhortative function of Daniel B are brought together in this englobing performative function. This therefore is the certain basis assured by the rigorous application of the historical method. For it, the meaning is the *function* of the text in a singular situation.

To the request that hermeneutics may raise for a meaning which would be the *meaning of the text*, open to interpretations situated in another present than that of the author and his original audience, the exegete as exegete may reply that that is not his task, declaring that his work is completed when he has established an intelligible correlation between a certain type of discourse and a certain historical situation. The same exegete may even declare, somewhat brusquely, that any 'application' or 'actualization' of the meaning in the present of the reader concerns the preacher, not the exegete.

I am ready to believe that the historical–critical exegete has finished his task at the point mentioned. But is this true for all exegesis? It seems to me that the exegesis of A.L. *does something else*, to the extent that it first does *that*, that is, when it 'completely historicizes' the message. What it disengages beyond this I suggest we may call, following Max Weber, the *ideal-type* of apocalyptic writing.

The very functioning of meaning in apocalyptic literature pushes the exegete in this direction. We have seen how the author proceeds to a fictional transference of his heroes into another time in order to express the spirit of resistance to the present persecution, that of Antiochus Epiphanes. In so doing, the author constitutes the past as the model for his own time and prophecy *post eventum* is transformed according to a schematic rule into new prophecy. He has therefore reduced his time and the past to their respective singularity in order to apprehend them as types of situations. The establishment of an analogical relation between one situation and the other thus underlies the very operation of apocalyptic discourse. The symbolization of the intended events contributes to this process. The statue which the three young men of chapter three refuse to worship is just as much the golden calf as it is any other idol. In chapter two, the statue in the king's dream, whose different levels allegorically represent four empires, virtually signifies every empire and all hubris by any political-religious power because the statue brings them together in a single reign covering four empires. The king of chapter four, condemned to graze like a beast, is Adam and every other Master whose inhumanity leads back to a bestial condition.

It is true that in Daniel B (chapters 7ff.), this symbolic *expansion* appears to be thwarted by the very nature of the message to be deciphered. Interpretation here seems to fix upon the identification of individual personages and unique historical situations. In fact, all the energy of some exegetes seems to be given over to a term by term and detail by detail translation: for this beast, this empire; for that horn, that petty king! This little detective game, similar to that offered by *romans à clef*, is in full flower in the commentary on chapters 8, 9, and 11. It is up to each exegete, to decipher his own little enigma! The game even continues to the point where the exegete catches the author in the act of unfulfilled prophecy when the apocalypticist ventures to prophesy the death of an evil king who really died in another manner than that predicted (11.44–5)! And yet, even in the case of those figures calling for an unequivocal decipherment, the very fact that the discourse remains *allusive* leaves a margin of free play. The author seems to be saying, 'Understand, the beasts are empires and their horns are kings, but guess their names!' The symbolic expansion here finds a narrow piece of manoeuvring room.

This space seems to me considerably larger in the case of a figure such as the 'son of man' of Daniel 7.13. The very expression 'one like a son of man coming with the clouds of heaven', seems to want to preserve a space of hesitation. In this regard, I want to resist somewhat the tendency of A.L. to determine in too univocal a fashion for my taste this figure who becomes Israel itself considered in its 'transcendent dimension' (p. 128), or at least the 'haughty saints' of Israel, which is to say, a well-determined circle of believers and righteous people. Was there not already a 'fourth man' in the furnace whom we should not be too hasty to identify? And 'the man clothed in linen and girded with a gold belt', who gives the meaning of the vision in Daniel 10, must he be identified? Even if Israel is signified by the transcendental figure of the son of man, does he not lose a little of his precise historical contours by becoming a figure? The exchanges, noted by A.L., which take place between the three figures of Daniel, the 'son of man', and the archangel Michael, do these not restore to each figure the symbolic expansion which the little detective game risks cutting off? Does he not say (p. 133), that the figure of the son of man is so inclusive that even the angel Michael is one of its aspects? The exegete himself notes that a certain 'remythologization' is at work here in the political bestiary which arises from the primordial waters. Also, from a simple literary point of view, the occurrence of the figure of the 'son of man' is expressly a poetic occurrence, as is moreover the theophany of He-Who-Endures several verses earlier, which is so evocative of the visions of Isaiah and Ezekiel 1.[6] This is why perhaps we should not be too hasty *to identify* the son of man, promoted to divine stature, and to discern there in too univocal a fashion a personification of the Jewish people, the perfect image of the righteous individual (p. 146). A too assured and too exclusive assimilation to the Israelite saints of divine stature would risk, at its limit, giving rise to a religious hubris symmetrical to that of the fallen kings. This is why perhaps it is wise to leave *a bit of play* to this figure, to allow several concurrent identifications *play*, from the *Urmensch* to the Jewish people and up to such and such a sect or righteous individual.[7]

Hence it is the historical-critical method itself which leads the exegete to surpass his historicism. It contributes to the revealing of a mode of discourse which aims at particular situations, but *only* across a process of symbolization which does not limit itself to concealing them, but which also tends to typify them. This analogical assimilation, which we have seen at work in several instances, is part of the text's meaning, even according to the criteria of historical-critical exegesis. The text itself, not the reader, proposes the analogy.

This movement of analogical assimilation, this process of symbolization, which the author spontaneously practises, may be taken into account—and systematized by the exegete—he thereby forms what I have called the *ideal-type* of apocalyptic, that is, one possible model of response to a certain type of challenge. A text of Adolphe Lods, cited by

---

[6] A.L. writes, 'The text which has been in prose up to this point, changes over to poetry in verses 9–10. The same thing happens also in verses 13–14 and 23–7' (p. 142).

[7] The existence of 'corporate personalities' (Israel represented by the four companions of chapter one standing up to the royal court of the greatest empire), moreover, confirms the *over-determined* character of the central figure of a 'son of man'. The fourth personage at the side of the three young men in the crematory oven extends this communal reality to its absent members.

xxiii

A.L. (p. 11), is a good indication of the meaning of this operation: 'The attitude recommended by Daniel is in no way armed struggle, but expectation (12.12), patience even unto death if necessary: God reserves the resurrection for martyrs. . . . The author awaits the destruction of the oppressor solely by a miracle; the tyrant will perish and the kingdom of the saints will be established, without the intervention of any human hand (2.44–5; 8.25).'

Not only is this *typology*, capable of balancing pure and simple research into the *Sitz im Leben*, not excluded by the exegesis of A.L., but the indications his commentary gives are sufficient to rectify in a very sensible fashion the more systematic reconstruction of von Rad in his *Old Testament Theology* (I, 407ff.; II, 99ff.) and especially in his *Wisdom in Israel* (pp. 263; 268–83).

According to von Rad, 'the ideal of a primeval, divine pre-determination of specific events and destinies' (*WI*, p. 263) constitutes a theological determinism profoundly different from the historical vision of the prophets based upon the notion of the favourable time, on new divine decisions arriving unexpectedly in history, on the unexpected eruption of the Word. The conception of history particularly implied by the apocalypses' historical summaries, incorporated in their turn as detailed prophecies into the discourse-testament of a man of the distant past, is that of an absolute determinism. Even the clairvoyance of the seer is incorporated as a landmark for the completion of history. Because events are irrevocably fixed in advance, the apocalyptic inventory is possible. 'How else, in such a distant past, could a whole chain of consecutive events have been foretold?' (ibid., p. 269). It is not events immanent in history which are preparing the salvation of those who have been elected since the beginning: 'Rather the end erupts abruptly into a world of history which is growing darker and darker . . .' (ibid., p. 273). Von Rad goes so far as to speak of a 'characteristic theological or, to be more precise, soteriological depletion of history' (ibid.). Even 'the content of "Israel" begins to disintegrate' (ibid.) with the idea of a salvation reserved for an elect group, such as the Hassidim, or an isolated individual. The division of history into numerical periods has replaced the soteriological institutions. In short, apocalyptic requires a 'complete change in the way of looking at history' (ibid., p. 277), the 'refusal to recognize in events orders immanent in history' (ibid.). Nothing in the present is significant any more: 'There has emerged a way of looking at history which does not include praise for God's historical indications of salvation. Praise emerges only in anticipation of the apocalyptic end' (ibid.). In short, the maturation of history through new events and new interventions of God and his Word is succeeded by an idea of a history which has reached the next to the last hour, where

God is the master of the passing to the last hour, which is certain because it was fixed from the beginning.[8]

It helps to have clear cut oppositions. Thinking according to ideal-types requires such discontinuities between the global meaning of one epoch or culture and the global meaning of another one. So we understand by differentiation.

It seems to me, however, that the exegesis of A.L. allows us to correct von Rad's 'model' of apocalyptic by introducing several paradoxes into it.

Certainly, the little stone which strikes the colossus of chapter two was touched by no hand; the miracles of the crematory oven and the lion pit are exterior to their actors; the three words 'counted', 'fixed', and 'divided' announce a destiny ruled from afar; and salvation always does irrupt amid the full paroxysm of abomination; yet a little while and God will reverse the situation: the enemies of Israel will be judged, the people restored, and messianic era will arrive. All this is certain because the seer sees it as *already having arrived* as he prophesies what has already taken place. Yet what always comes to rectify this determinist schema is the very speech act constituted by the publication of a pretended ancient book, held to be previously hidden. This speech act does something. It exhorts, it calls for martyrdom, and it gives courage. The 'performative' function of prophecy comes to be inserted between the next to the last hour and the last hour in an efficacious fashion. The clairvoyance of the visionary, his 'understanding', joined to the vision, become themselves landmarks and factors in the completion of history. Even the personage of Daniel and his companions signifies that something is still to come: the refusal to worship the statue, the courage under torture, the patience during persecution, the accomplishment of acts of piety—'turned toward Jerusalem . . .'—whatever they may cost, the supplication with ashes and sackcloth, and the great prayer of confession before receiving the interpretation of the vision. As for those powers whose end is signified, their condemnation stems from their hubris; the three fatal words which appear on the palace wall are also the projection of the spirit of those who receive them.[9]

The relation between radical extrinsic deliverance and the movement

---

[8] This predetermined character of the end presumably explains why apocalyptic impatience would always be constrained by its own system to calculate the date of the coming Kingdom. In fact, notes A.L. (p. 249), 'the book gives four ciphers for the time of the End'.

[9] On this very occasion, A.L. notes: 'Here is the whole argument of the Book of Daniel: history is the bearer of God's judgement. History is theophany and verdict' (p. 105). A propos the relation between Daniel 3 and 6, he writes: 'The faithful of Israel are miraculously saved while their persecutors are devoured by their evil undertakings (p. 107).

of history is therefore more paradoxical than it had appeared to be. Because the apocalypse, as an act of discourse, is itself an intervention *in* history which responds to a still *open* question for all those who have not received the vision and known the interpretation. This question asks: How long will tribulation continue? Is God weak? Indifferent? Malicious? What is the meaning of suffering?[10] It is to this existential situation, at the hinge of the next to the last hour and the last hour, that apocalyptic speech wants to respond, with the *penultimate efficacity* of a call to passive resistance. It is right that henceforth this resistance, with its suffering, should be a part of salvation. For in the final analysis this very resistance, thanks to the word of comfort, knows itself to be situated *between* what is next to last and what is the Last.

PAUL RICOEUR

[10] The commentary on chapter 12 (p. 234) is very enlightening in this regard, to the extent that on the level of revealed events, 'the Book of Daniel has attained its ultimate goal with 11.44–5 with the description of the tyrant's end'. However the task of speech is not ended—one question remains in suspense: How much longer? Who will be the beneficiaries of the parousia?

Introduction

In the wide variety of literature which makes up Scripture, the Book of Daniel occupies a unique place.[1] Its twelve chapters—in its present form—are divided into two major parts: the first six are '*midrashim*' and the last five are 'apocalypses', while chapter seven serves as a transition between these two genres and participates in both of them.

Manifestly, with the Book of Daniel we are in a period of exploitation of 'canonized' material (or, in any case, material which is considered as having authority) and not in a time of pure creation. '*Midrash*' is an expansion of a known text, a series of variations on a central and fundamental biblical theme. 'Apocalypse' is a prolongation of prophecy and, in a way, its replacement by a transhistorical speculation on the basis of contemporary events. In both cases, it is clear that one biblical period has ended and that a new era has begun. The first has laid the foundation for the second, which refers to it as recognized and uncontested authority, something unique and divine *in relation to which* it situates itself. It is not an accident that Daniel was not placed among the 'Prophets' by Jewish tradition, but among the 'Writings', that is, in the collection of books which the Synagogue considers as a third series resting upon the group of *Nebiim*, which were themselves founded upon the Torah.[2]

The problems the Book of Daniel poses to the critic are incredibly numerous and complex. Not only is apocalyptic language intentionally obscure and its historical allusions deliberately cryptic, but, what is more, the work is pseudepigraphic, antedated, bilingual, and affected by literary and spiritual influences of diverse foreign origins, as well as being represented by Greek versions of greater amplitude and often of a divergent character in relation to the Semitic text, etc. As for the message, it is presented in a form full of traps and snares for the reader. The Author uses already existing material which he reworks to make it fit his own purpose. He wants to be both obscure—for that is how he conceives the

---

[1] Despite the numerous parallels with other literary genres known from the Bible, including the use of anthology. See G. von Rad, *Theology of the Old Testament*, vol. 2 (New York 1965), p. 314, n. 29: 'Might not the presentation in Dan. II [i.e., part 2 of the Book] actually be described as a *pesher* of Isaiah?' The same opinion is found in J. L. Seeligmann, 'Midraschexegese', *Suppl. VT* I, p. 171.

[2] See the judgement of Maimonides in his *Guide for the Perplexed*, III, ch. 45. There are, he says, eleven degrees of prophecy of which the lowest is a (simple) communication from the Spirit of the Lord. 'Daniel is placed among the Hagiographa, and not among the prophets, because he was only inspired by the spirit of the Lord which often manifests itself through dreams, proverbs, psalms, etc . . ., even if the authors call themselves prophets, using the term in a general sense.'

We also note that Daniel never employs the prophets' authoritative formula: 'Thus says the Lord. . . .'

prophetic form—and comprehensible at the same time, in view of the urgency for Israel to grasp the lesson of a history that is about to arrive at its end. He is a man of his time who sees himself, as a religious thinker, compelled to opt for the proclamation of a 'prophetic' message,[3] but also as constrained to speak a language appropriate to the culture of his contemporaries. In one sense, the passage from Hebrew to Aramaic and then back to Hebrew again is already an indication of the difficulties the Author experienced on a technical level. Should he speak the holy language at the risk of appearing artificial, or the vernacular at the risk of imitating foreign writings?[4]

'Daniel' faced still more decisive alternatives. Does history have a meaning, as the prophets believed? Why then did contemporary events seem to deny this assurance? Is the signification of history jealously guarded by God, with the result that human freedom is negated and we are playthings in his hands? Or—dizzying thought—is God himself capable of being defied by self-divinized human tyrants?[5] Is Israel, in the second century BCE, the powerless victim of a cosmic battle between two contrary and opposed powers? Were the prophets mistaken in protesting against Babylonian dualism?[6] And if they were correct, what role then does evil play in the dialogue between God and his People? How long will God use it? How will he lead us out of this tunnel? Is the end of our tribulations in sight? In what form? Eschatological? Messianic? A new life after death?

As one can see, the whole problematic of the Book of Daniel is influenced by the epoch of its redaction. Here, more than ever, the *Sitz im Leben* question must be resolved and its solution must serve as a constant point of reference for any reading of this document throughout its twelve chapters. By having not been aware of this elementary approach, ancient and modern commentators (but not exegetes) have attempted to speculate about the pretended previsions of a mysterious future contained in this book. They have given themselves over to calculations as vain as they are extravagant in order to know the date of the 'end of time'.

The Name Daniel

Daniel is the name of a mythical personage mentioned along with Noah

[3] In the sense indicated above of fidelity to models such as Isaiah, Jeremiah, Ezekiel, or Habakkuk.
[4] The Author lifts himself out of this impasse by suggesting that the discourse of the 'Chaldeans' is in Aramaic. See Dan. 2.4. We consider the phrase 'in Aramaic' authentic and not a gloss. See below, p. 39.
[5] See Dan. 8.10.
[6] See Isa. 45.7.

and Job in Ezek. 14.14 and 20.[7] He is counted among the wisest men the world has known (Ezek. 28.3).[8] We know now, thanks to the Canaanite literature from Ugarit, that there existed a popular hero, King Dan(i)el.[9] He reappears (with his name spelled without *yod*) in Enoch 6, 7, and 69.2.[10]

It is true that Daniel is a relatively frequent name in the Bible.[11] See 1 Chron. 3.1 (a son of David and Abigail); in Ezra 8.2 and Neh. 10.7, it is the name of a priest who returns to Jerusalem from exile. The punctuation or vocalization is uniformly strange for it obscures the divine element in the name.[12] In Hebrew, it signifies 'God is the defender of my right' (see Gen. 30.6).[13] It seems evident that the Author of our book has taken something from the legends circulating about the incomparably wise hero Daniel, while making 'Daniel' one of the Judean exiles at Babylon in the sixth century BCE.

This pseudonymic process responds to two conditions. On the one hand, the conviction that the prophetic spirit was exhausted after Haggai, Zachariah, and Malachi, a conviction which has been maintained up to this day in Rabbinic Judaism.[14] According to Ecclus. 49.10, for example, 'the twelve prophets' constitute a closed category.

[7] Always spelled without the *yod* in Ezekiel. But it was read 'Daniel' however; see the Greek transcription and the attestation of a Mari text of the 18th cent. (ARM, VII, No. 263, col. III, 23. Communicated to me by Prof. E. Lipinski of Louvain.)

[8] See Martin Noth, 'Noah, Daniel und Hiob in Ezekiel XIV', *VT*, 1 (1951), pp. 251–60.

[9] See *Syria*, 12 (1931), pp. 21–2, 77, 193; W. Albright, *JBL*, 51 (1932), pp. 99–100; *BASOR*, 46 (1932), p. 19; ibid., 63 (1936), p. 27.

[10] For Norman W. Porteous, *Daniel* (Philadelphia 1965), p. 17, we should perhaps think less of the Daniel of Ras Shamra-Ugarit (the poem Aqhat) and more of the Danel of the Book of Jubilees (4.20): Enoch (the first sage) married Edmu, 'the daughter of Danel'. The association of Daniel with Enoch the Sage would add credence to G. von Rad's contention that Apocalypsa derives from Wisdom (see below).

[11] According to C. D. Ginsburg, the word appears 81 times, of which 30 are in Hebrew. *Introduction to the Massoretico-Critical Edition of the Hebrew Bible* (New York 1966), p. 397.

[12] But it is in accord with the Masoretic rule according to which 'the *tsere* must be under the *yod*, following the celebrated codex from the country of Eden'. See *Orient* 2350, fol. 27a, British Museum; Ginsburg, op. cit., p. 397 and n. 2.

[13] It must be distinguished from the Babylonian 'Da-ni-li' which means 'My God is powerful'.

[14] See 1 Macc. 9.27; Prayer of Azariah in the Greek text of Daniel, 3.28; 1 Macc. 4.46; Josephus, *C. Apion.*, 1.8; *Pirke Aboth* 1.1. See *Meg.* 3a: 'They (Haggai, Zechariah and Malachi) are prophets, but he (Daniel) is not a prophet.' Rashi comments: 'They are prophets because they prophesied to Israel as God's envoys, but he was not sent to Israel for the sake of prophecy.' According to *Meg.* 14a and *Seder Olam R.*, chs. 20—1, there were forty-eight prophets and seven prophetesses in Israel. When the last prophet died, the Spirit withdrew from Israel (see *Tos. Sotah* 13.2: *Sanh.* 11a). Y. Kaufmann, *History of Israel's Faith* (Tel Aviv 1956 (in Hebrew)), vol. 8, pp. 409ff., comments that Daniel kept his revelations to himself (7.28) until the occurrence of the events (8.26; 12.4, 9). He performed no miracles. Daniel is an extraordinary human being, but only because of his *wisdom* (1.17, 20). In chapters 1—6, he does not dream. In 2.19, he only re-experiences the king's dream. Even in chapters 7—12,

On the other hand, following the mentality of the ancient Near East, Israel always considered it perfectly legitimate to put writings which expressed—even if fictionally—her own thought under the name of a hero from the distant past.[15] We have here one of the most important literary phenomena for biblical criticism. The later Jewish tradition will say, in the same spirit, that any true teaching of a 'disciple of sages' can only repeat what Moses received in the revelation on Mt. Sinai.[16] This is an ancient principle. It explains why, for example, it is possible to have two or three works by different authors brought together under the name Isaiah or Zechariah. Above all, it affirms the unity of divine inspiration in authors of various epochs.

The process of pseudonymity implies a certain esotericism. The eschatological secrets have never been known during the course of history except by a few particularly enlightened saints. They are only now revealed ($\dot{\alpha}\pi o\kappa\alpha\lambda\dot{\nu}\pi\tau\epsilon\iota\nu$) openly and publicly to work, among humanity and the People, the final sorting of the elect and the damned. In this sense, the revelation remains 'hidden', impenetrable to those whose eyes have not been opened (see Dan. 8.26; 12.4, 9).[17] This is what makes Daniel, not only an apocalypse (see *infra*), but also the first known example of apocrypha, if we thereby understand, following the definition given this word by Montgomery, 'a volume of alleged antiquity that had been purposely "hidden away" until the emergency arrived for publication'.[18]

The Apocalyptic Genre in the Book of Daniel

Use of the term 'apocalypse' ($\dot{\alpha}\pi o\kappa\dot{\alpha}\lambda\nu\psi\iota s$) to designate the literary character of a book has its origin in the Greek name for the last book in the New Testament. The term has been extended to cover a whole type of literature whose existence stretches, broadly speaking, over the

---

he is seeking understanding (בינה), see 7.16; 8.15; 9.22–3; 10.1, 11–12. There is no parallel in biblical prophecy. Kaufmann concludes that classical prophecy ends in Mal. 3 and that apocalyptic prophecy begins in Dan. 7. The stories reported in chapters 1—6 constitute the transition between the two genres.

[15] See D. S. Russell, *The Method and Message of Jewish Apocalyptic* (London 1964), pp. 127–39. The author accepts the opinion of H. H. Rowley, who says the Apocalypticists were aware of belonging to a line of descent, or a corporate personality, which included Enoch, Moses, Ezra, and Daniel. They were its heir and representatives.

[16] See *Ber.* 26b; *Dt.* R. VIII, 6 (on Deut. 30.12); j. *Meg.* 1, 7, 70d; b. *Hullin* 124a; *B.M.* 58b; *Ex.* R. XXVIII, 4 (cited by S. Baron, *A Social and Religious History of the Jews* (New York 1952), vol. 2, p. 383 n. 14.

[17] According to 4 Esdras 14, it appears that the apocryphal books were more excellent than the canonical ones. They were destined only for an élite. See J. B. Frey, 'Apocalyptique', *Supplément au Dictionnaire de la Bible*, vol. 1 (Paris 1928).

[18] J. A. Montgomery, *A Critical and Exegetical Commentary on the Book of Daniel*, (ICC) (New York 1927), p. 76.

period from the fifth century BCE through the first century CE. These works generally consist of a compendium of visions which an angel interprets for the visionary, who is often a hero from antediluvian times, or from the beginnings of history. The vision bears upon the succession of historical epochs from the time of the legendary author up to the moment of crisis experienced by the real author. When the authentically historical character of the text fades away, it is the sign that the author is moving from chronological retrospection to mystical speculation.[19]

What does the word $\dot{a}\pi o\kappa\dot{a}\lambda v\psi\iota\varsigma$ signify within the context of Daniel? Theodotion[20] understood God as $\dot{a}\pi o\kappa a\lambda\acute{v}\pi\tau\omega\nu\ \mu v\sigma\tau\acute{\eta}\rho\iota a$. He clearly understood the Aramaic root גל׳א as signifying 'the manifestation by God of secrets unknowable by natural means' (see $\varTheta$ Dan. 2.19, 28, 30, 47; 10.1). This conception is found in all the Apocrypha. The Testaments of the XII Patriarchs, for example, feature the intervention of angels as interpreters of divine mysteries (see Test. of Reuben 3.15; Test. of Joseph 6.6); see also Enoch 1.2; 72.1; 74.2; 75.3; 79.2–6; 81.1. In Enoch 46.3 this role is assumed by the Son of Man.[21]

Such revelations bear on the divisions of history:

—*The Past*: great events are presented as still to come and their unfolding is predicted. See Jubilees 2ff.; Enoch 85–90; Slavonic Enoch 23–5; Baruch 53; 56–69; Sibylline Oracles III.819ff.; Apocalypse of Abraham 23–38.

—*The Present*: visions concerning superterrestrial things. See Enoch 14.8—36.4; 64–9; Test. of Levi 2.7—3.8; Baruch 2.17; etc.

—*The Future* (eschatology): Messianic events, the final victory of the righteous, the conversion of surviving Gentiles, the New Jerusalem, the

---

[19] See G. F. Moore, *Judaism in the First Centuries of the Christian Era* (Cambridge, Mass., 1958), vol. 2, pp. 279ff.

[20] Theodotion ($\varTheta$) was once thought to date from the second century CE, but D. Barthélemy has demonstrated that he should be placed before Aquila, which is to say, before 50, and is to be identified with Jonathan ben Uzziel, a disciple of Hillel. The substitution of the $\varTheta$ text of Daniel for that of the LXX took place between 30 and 50 (*Les Devanciers d'Aquila, Suppl. VT*, vol. 10 (Leyden 1963), pp. 148ff.). Barthélemy's position has been contested by Armin Schmitt, 'Stammt der sogenammte "$\varTheta$"-Text bei Daniel wirklich von Theodotion?', in *Nachrichten der Akademie der Wissenschaften*, I, no. 8 (Göttingen 1966). The author responds negatively to his question.

It should be noted that one papyrus of the LXX in the Chester Beatty Collection differs substantially from the version of Theodotion and is very close to the M. T. Justin Martyr, in his *Dialogue with Trypho* (about 150 CE), uses a Greek version of Dan. 7.9–28 which coincides with neither the LXX nor Theodotion. See P. J. de Menasce, 'Daniel', *Bible de Jérusalem* (Paris 1954), p. 19.

[21] For these citations, see J. B. Frey, 'Apocalyptique'. We have borrowed the following development on the object of apocalyptic revelations from this article (col. 329).

resurrection, the individual judgement, the dividing of the righteous and the wicked, the end of the world.[22]

It is therefore a veritable theology of history that apocalyptic seeks to depict. It is a question of showing that every event since the 'beginning' is perfectly embedded in a majestic and, in a word, divine construction. Nothing there is superfluous and nothing is lacking.

Before Daniel, other apocalyptic texts had been written which are retained in the biblical canon: Ezekiel 38—9; Zechariah (1—8); 9—14; Joel 3; and Isaiah 24—7. Most apocalypses, however, were left out of the sacred Writings because they were considered with suspicion by the Pharisees who were responsible for the fixation of the Canon during the first century of our era. According to Rabbi Akiba, consulting an apocalypse would cost the reader his part in the world to come. Hence, some books, though written in Aramaic or even in Hebrew, and for some written before 70 CE,[23] were rejected as 'not defiling one's hands'.[24] But this did not prevent the production of other apocalypses after the year 70.[25]

There is therefore a veritable apocalyptic literature which saw the light of day during the Hellenistic period of the Near East. Being situated in that culture is a fundamental element of the *Sitz im Leben* of the apocalyptic of the time. It is, in effect, a negative reaction to Hellenism, in which Judaism[26] has always seen the most grave menace to its history. Inaugurated by Alexander the Great and his astonishing conquests in the fourth century BCE, the Macedonian dream of a worldwide empire enjoying a unity of culture was widely prevalent in the Mediterranean world. The existence of Judea, especially given its geographical position at the nexus of areas encompassing Ptolemaic Egypt and Seleucid Syria, created political unrest. It was unthinkable by general agreement that any population would persist in having particular, not to say particularist, laws and customs. The οἰκουμένη could suffer no exceptions. At the moment one heard 'the sound of the horn, the flute, the lyre, the sambuca, the bagpipe, and of every sort of instrument', every people of

---

[22] See Jean Steinmann, *Daniel* (Paris 1961), p. 24: 'An apocalypse is a pseudonymous collection of allegorical visions depicting the destiny of the world in the form of a struggle between evil powers, a struggle which is cleared up abruptly by an impromptu triumph of God in a catastrophe which ends the world. The inauguration of this divine reign is accompanied by a general judgement of men and the resurrection of the righteous.'

[23] E.g., the Book of Enoch (from after 163 BCE), the Book of Jubilees (about 163–105 BCE), etc.

[24] A rabbinic expression indicating that the character of the book is not sacred, so there is no need to wash one's hands ritually before reading it.

[25] E.g., 4 Esdras, Baruch, The Apocalypse of John (Revelation).

[26] We can speak of Judaism as beginning with Ezekiel, or certainly with Haggai and Zechariah.

every nation and language had to prostrate themselves and worship the golden statue erected by the universal sovereign.[27] There was no other choice for the central power, invested as it was with the most noble of missions, since it was the most generally human and humanist force, than to throw into a crematory oven any one who would not prostrate himself and worship.[28]

Chronology of the Book

The Book of Daniel opens with a chronological indication: 'In the third year of the reign of Jehoiakim,[29] king of Juda, Nebuchadnezzar, king of Babylon, came to Jerusalem and besieged it' (1.1). Yet already in the third century of our era, the pagan critic Porphyry[30] attacked the authenticity of this chronology. He saw in Daniel the work of a forger writing at the time of Antiochus IV Epiphanes (175–164 BCE).

His solution may lack nuance, but it is correct. Numerous elements prove it. We will consider them rapidly: Not only was the book not received as belonging among the Prophets,[31] but it is necessary to go all the way to the Sibylline Oracles (Book III) to find any trace of it (between 145 and 140 BCE). 1 Macc. 1.54, which is even later (134–104), offers one text which parallels Dan. 9.27 and 11.31. We also find Daniel mentioned in the Book of Jubilees (written about 110 BCE). It is not named in Ben Sira (190–180), even though we would expect to find it, for example, in 48.22 or in 49.7, 8, 10. And it is only in the most recent literary strata of the Book of Enoch that we find any certain traces of it; see 104.2 (end of the first century BCE) and the 'Book of Parables' (which is still later).

External criticism is confirmed by internal criticism. The vision of chapters 10—11 leads us step by step up to the events of 165 (11.39), but before those of 164. The Author knows of the profanation of the

---

[27] See Dan. 3.5; 4. E. Bickerman writes: 'From its beginning Greek culture was supranational, because the Greeks never constituted a unified State . . . their culture was Panhellenic, and was the same on the Nile as on the Euphrates. . . . Greek culture, like modern European culture, was based upon education. A man became a 'Hellene' without at the same time forsaking his gods and his people, but merely by adopting Hellenic culture' (*The Maccabees* (New York 1947), pp. 22–3).

[28] See Dan. 3.6.

[29] That is, in 606; unless Jehoiachin must be substituted, which would place us around 594.

[30] Saint Augustine called him 'the most learned of philosophers'. Despising Judaism and Christianity, this Neoplatonist put forth the theory that Ezra rather than Moses was the author of the Pentateuch. He also declared that the Old Testament recognized the existence of other gods as proved by the Judeo-Christian belief in angels. This last point cannot fail to be of interest to the reader of Daniel! See S. W. Baron, *A Social and Religious History* . . ., vol. 2, pp. 158–9.

[31] According to Y. Kaufmann, op. cit., pp. 405–8, this indicates that the canon of the *Nebiim* was formed before the appearance of pseudonymous prophecy.

Temple at Jerusalem by Antiochus IV (7 December, 167; see Dan. 11.31). He alludes to the revolt of the Maccabees and the first victories of Judas (166). But he is unaware of the death of Antiochus (autumn 164; see Dan. 11.40ff.) and the purification of the Temple by Judas on 14 December 164. We can at least situate the second part of the Book of Daniel (chapters 7—12), therefore, with a very comfortable certainty, in 164 BCE. As for chapters 1—6, they are of another type of composition and belong to the literary genre Midrash. However, their final redaction cannot, for any good reason, be situated much before that of the other chapters. We find in them allusions to the problems of Judaism during the second century BCE, such as respect for the Levitic dietary prescriptions (see Dan. 1.5–8; cf. 2 Macc. 6.18–31), resistance to idolatry, imposed by coercion (Dan. 3.1–12), divinization of a human king (6.6– 10),[32] and martyrdom (3.19–21; 6.17–18). We are not surprised therefore to find throughout the book the theme of feverish expectation of the tyrant's death: 5.22, 30; 7.11, 24–6; 8.25; 9.26–7; 11.45.

The terrain seems sufficiently clear now for us to turn to the question of the origin of the materials employed by the author. This problem is complex for they are of highly different natures. A first distinction must be drawn between chapters 1—6, on the one hand, and 7—12, on the other. The former are edifying stories, parenetic and apologetic homilies, in short, *agadoth*.[33] The latter chapters are eschatological visions or apocalypses also presented with an exhortative goal in mind.

Literary Composition

For Y. Kaufmann, Daniel A (chapters 1—6) is a mirror of exilic Judaism. The Jews are apparently living in peace in the midst of pagan and idolatrous nations. Some of them even become princes at the Babylonian royal court. However, beneath this surface, there is an incompatibility between Judaism and the idolatry of the nations. It is with this inevitable collision that the Book of Daniel opens. Its result is visible in advance: no adversary can successfully oppose the living God,[34] even if it is one of the powerful Babylonian or Medo-Persian kings. This is the motif for the six stories (*History of Israel's Faith* (in Hebrew) p. 432). The kings are forced to recognize that they owe their sovereignty to the

[32] The reader will recall that the title 'Epiphanes' means 'manifestation of God'. To ridicule him his adversaries called him Antiochus 'Epimanes' (the fool or madman).

[33] *Agadoth*, or with singular *agadah*. In contrast to the *halachoth* (laws, ordinances) in traditional Jewish literature, the *agadoth* designate everything that does not arise from the codification of rules. They are legends, stories, parables, sermons, exhortations, proverbs, and hagiography. They are closely related to the *midrashim*, although the *midrash* is based on a text of Scripture which it explicates, comments upon, amplifies, and actualizes.

[34] See Dan. 6.20.

8

'living God' of Israel (Dan. 6.26). There is no parallel in the Bible to the optimism of these chapters concerning the nations.[35]

The atmosphere is totally different in Daniel B (chapters 7—12). The initiative in events, which belonged to the Jews in the first part of the book, now passes over to the enemies of their faith and nation. It is no longer a question of the apparently tranquil existence of the Jews in the midst of pagans, but of religious persecution and martyrdom. The sovereigns no longer benefit from prophetic dreams, now Daniel himself has visions of a divine origin. There is, however, one common point with Daniel A: the final triumph is assured. This element permits a rereading which actualizes the popular tales about the hero Daniel. Above all, what is now seen is his triumph over the idolaters. This process of reinterpretation of the *agadoth* reported in Daniel 1—6 is confirmed in 1 Macc. 2.58–9, where Mattathias recalls these stories to galvanize resistance against the Seleucids. Thus Daniel A and Daniel B were bound into a single book with a precise goal in mind: to render courage to the Jews persecuted by Antiochus Epiphanes.

There is no consensus among critics regarding the unity of the Book of Daniel. Y. Kaufmann, for example,[36] rejects the opinion of H. H. Rowley[37] that there is a fundamental unity to the book. True, he says, the same literary circle is responsible for the final redaction of the two parts of the book, but their differences remain more important than the elements they have in common. The change in atmosphere between Daniel A and Daniel B is too pronounced to be ignored.

Finally, the decisive argument probably pertains to the comparison of chapters 2 and 7. If the kingdoms in both chapters are the same and are presented in the same chronological succession, there is a strong presumption in favour of a single author and date for the whole book. In fact, the majority of modern critics discern in both cases the following four kingdoms: Babylon, Media, Persia, Greece. As Y. Kaufmann himself says, it is remarkable that in chapter 2, the four kingdoms taken ensemble have a single symbol (the statue) and the ruin of the fourth kingdom brings about the ruin of the others. Consequently, there is only one empire, considered in four different epochs, a 'universal kingdom' (op. cit., p. 423).

Our conclusion is that in the second half of the second century BCE,

---

[35] Ch. 1: triumph of the young Jews; ch. 2: Nebuchadnezzar falls on his face; ch. 3: he testifies to the glory of the living God; ch. 4: the same conclusion; ch. 5: Belshazzar receives the prediction of his death with humility; ch. 6: Darius glorifies Daniel's God.

[36] Op. cit.

[37] See 'The Unity of the Book of Daniel,' in *HUCA*, 23 part 1 (1951), pp. 233–72. Reprinted in *The Servant of the Lord and Other Essays* (London 1952), pp. 237–68.

the redactor and veritable Author of Daniel availed himself of the tales belonging to a popular cycle about Daniel. His project was to galvanize the spiritual resistance of the Pious against the persecution of Antiochus IV and the Hellenists. He therefore gave a twist appropriate to his own ends to the *agadoth* associated with the name of Daniel. These are chapters 1—6 or 'Daniel A'. Chapters 7—12 are a more original work of this Author. Here the genre is apocalyptic and the message is more directly conceived with the martyrs of 167–164 in mind.

As such, the book presents a 'dualistic' composition which raises problems for the critic and exegete. However, we should not conclude that two originally independent works were more or less artificially juxtaposed. In itself, it is true, *agadah* is not apocalyptic, nor is apocalyptic necessarily agadic. Yet as we wrote with Professor P. Grelot in our introduction to the Book of Daniel for *La Traduction Oecuménique de la Bible*,[38] 'The literary form of a text is always the consequence of two elements: the function it fulfilled in the community for which it was written, and the conventions in use in its cultural milieu. Seen within the context of its time, the Book of Daniel presents an original combination of two genres which Jewish literature favoured at that time: the didactic story (*agadah*) and the apocalypse.'

The Formative Milieu of the Apocalypses

To paraphrase S. Schechter, it is clear that it is among the sects separated from the great body of Judaism that we must seek the origin of works such as Daniel, not in the Judaism of the Pharisees.[39] The question is then to know which Jewish sect gave birth to a religious philosophy of history where universal events have their assigned place in God's cosmic design,[40] and where the present time, which is always dramatic, is the summit of this history, for it constitutes the birthplace of a 'Son of Man' whose empire will not pass away.[41]

One may think of the Essenes. We know of their speculations about angels and the other world, their tendency toward magic, their asceticism, and their esoteric[42] teachings. But another milieu is more probable,

---

[38] Henceforth referred to as *T.O.B.*
[39] See S. Schechter, *Documents of Jewish Sectaries* (Cambridge 1910), vol. 1; see pp. xxvi–xxix.
[40] Cf. the lyrical declaration of M. J. Lagrange in *Le Judaïsme avant Jésus-Christ* (Paris 1931), p. 72: Daniel 'was the first to envisage world history . . . as preparation for the reign of God, to soberly probe this splendid dawn of the hopes of Israel, and to extend God's plan for men to the threshold of eternity.'
[41] See Dan. 8.19; 11.36; 8.17; 11.40; 8.25; 11.45; also Dan. 7.
[42] See our discussion, *infra*, on Daniel and Qumran. Cf. A. Hilgenfeld, *Die jüdische Apocalyptik in ihrer geschichtlichen Entwickelung* (Jena 1857), pp. 253ff.; J. E. H. Thomson, 'Apocalyptic Literature', in *International Standard Bible Encyclopaedia*, vol. 1 (Chicago 1915), pp. 161–78.

that of the 'Ασιδαῖοι (the Asideans, the Hassidim, the pious, the faithful), or also the *Anawim*, the poor of Israel who were assimilated to the perfect and righteous ones (see Ps. 34.3, 16; 37.11, 17, 18, 29, 37).[43] Like the Essenes, they also seem to have lived in confraternities to resist the pressure of Hellenism (see 1 Macc. 2.42: συναγωγὴ 'Ασιδαίων).[44] These monasteries were of a military type (see Ps. 149).[45] There were numerous scribes among the members (1 Macc. 7.12–13) and, as is to be expected, they were very attached to the priesthood (ibid.). Like them, Daniel shows his faithfulness to the Levitic rites (see Daniel 1 and 6). What is more, we can see in the 'anointed chief' of 9.25 the personage of the High Priest of the Restoration, Joshua. This is probably the best interpretation of this allusive text for in the following verse another High Priest, probably Onias III, is also designated (similarly in 11.22). It is evidently not by accident that for the Author history is punctuated by supreme pontiffs.[46]

The decisive detail from our perspective is Daniel's attitude toward the Maccabees. The participation of the Asideans (Hassidim) in the resistance against the Seleucids was strictly limited to the conquest of religious freedom (see 1 Macc. 6.59). In the same way, for Daniel all human help appears as 'little' (11.34). In Adolphe Lods' terms, 'The attitude recommended by Daniel is in no way armed struggle, but expectation (12.12), patience even unto death if necessary: God reserves the resurrection for martyrs. . . . The author awaits the destruction of the oppressor solely by a miracle; the tyrant will perish and the kingdom of the saints will be established, without the intervention of any human hand (2.44–5; 8.25).'[47] Following the peace of Lysias (163 BCE), the Hassidim left it to the Hasmoneans to win the nation's independence without them (see 1 Macc. 7.4–18).[48]

[43] This is the opinion, for example, of J. A. Montgomery, op. cit., p. 87, and A. Lods, *Histoire de la littérature hébraïque et juive* (Paris 1950), p. 846. We do not press this issue, however, as the documentary evidence is fragmentary on the Hassidim (see 1 Macc. 2.42; 7.12–13; 2 Macc. 14.6). Daniel uses rather the term *maskil* but it is hardly the name of a party (cf. Dan. 11.33 and comm., 11.35; 12.3, 10).

[44] It should be noted that in this text from 1 Maccabees, the Asideans are called ἑκουσιαζόμενοι (devotees of the law), the LXX term corresponding to the Hebrew words from the root נד"ב characteristic of QS (see 1.7, 11; 5.1, 6, 8, 10, 21, 22; 6.13) which uses this term to designate 'the members of the Community willingly and generously engaged in the service of the Torah' (see M. Delcor, *Le Livre de Daniel* (Paris 1971), p. 17).

[45] Only in the Masoretic Text where the term *Hassidim* appears in the plural absolute without a pronominal suffix.

[46] See our commentary on chapters 7—12.

[47] Op. cit., p. 846.

[48] See G. von Rad, op. cit., vol. 2, p. 315: 'Without any doubt, the writer of Daniel sides with those who endure persecution rather than those who take up arms against it, and in so doing he is only being true to his own basic conviction that what must be will be. He is far removed from the Maccabees and their policy of active resistance. . . .'

The similarities to Qumran are numerous and enlightening. It is certain that Daniel was much read among the sectarians. Seven different manuscripts of the book have been recovered. One of these seems to have been written only a half century after the completion of the original work. However, it is not certain that it was considered as a canonical text. The format of the columns of writing and, sometimes, the material employed (Caves 1 and 6) are different from that habitually employed by the Essene library for biblical books.[49]

The points of spiritual and literary contact between the sectarians and Daniel are interesting. The Judean recluses called themselves 'the men of the vision' (I QH 14.7), or 'those who see the angels of holiness, whose ears are open, and who hear profound things' (I QM 10.10–11). I QM 1.3–7 is visibly inspired by Daniel 11.40–5. What is more, in a work from Cave IV, three fragments are 'supposed to account for the revelations of Daniel'.[50] Also, five fragments from Cave IV form 'The Prayer of Nabonidus' which parallels Daniel 3.31—4.34. Daniel is here presented as an anonymous Jewish exorcist.

The Place of Daniel in the Canon

In the Hebrew Bible, the Book of Daniel found its place among the 'Writings', instead of in the 'Prophets' as in the Alexandrian Canon. The latter is responsible for an unfortunate confusion. The Book of Daniel is not oracular, nor does it pretend to be.[51] Moreover, it is easy to differentiate Daniel with respect to the prophets. What for them was preaching calling the people to repentance here becomes a visionary description of the coming of the divine Kingdom. What had been based upon the 'memory' of God's saving acts in history is now turned toward an imminent future. What had had the purpose of influencing the divine plan is now the revelation of God's unalterable plot, whether in its final end (Daniel) or its totality (Enoch).[52]

[49] See D. Barthélemy and J. T. Milik, *Discoveries in the Judean Desert*, vol. 1 (Oxford 1955), 'Qumran Cave I', Appendix III, no. 71, 'Daniel (Premier Exemplaire)' 1.10–17; 2.2–6. Cf. M. Baillet, J. T. Milik, and R. de Vaux, ibid., III, 'Les petites grottes de Qumrân' (Oxford 1962). Fragments of Daniel 8.20–1(?); 11.33–6, 38.

[50] J. Dupont-Sommer, *Les Ecrits Esséniens Découverts près de la Mer Morte* (Paris 1959), p. 336.

[51] Note the absence of the *Botenformel* 'thus says the Lord', so characteristic of prophecy.

[52] '(Daniel) did not only prophesy of future events, as did the other prophets, but he also determined the time of their accomplishment; and while the prophets used to foretell misfortunes, and on that account were disagreeable both to the kings and to the multitude, Daniel was to them a prophet of good things, and this to such a degree, that, by the agreeable nature of his predictions, he procured the good-will of all men; and by the accomplishment of them, he procured the belief of their truth, and the opinion of a sort of divinity for himself, among the multitude. He also wrote and left behind him what made manifest the accuracy and undeniable veracity of his predictions....' (*Josephus' Complete Works*, trans. William Whiston (Grand Rapids 1960), p. 227).

Differing from the Masoretic text, the Alexandrian version includes five additions:[53]

1. The Prayer of Azariah
2. The Song of the Three Young Men
3. Susanna
4. Bel
5. The Dragon.

It should also be noted that Daniel is the only biblical book in whose case the Greek of the LXX has been replaced by that of 'Theodotion'. These two versions represent two different phases in the history of the Alexandrian Bible. The LXX precedes the redaction of 1 Maccabees (about the end of the second century BCE; 1 Macc. 1.54 = LXX Dan. 9.27) and is a paraphrase. 'Theodotion', on the contrary, closely follows the Hebrew and Aramaic text. That his text contains the five additions mentioned above seems to indicate that they were inserted in the book at an early age, before the first century of our era. The following commentary will adhere solely to the Masoretic text.

Bilingualism in the Book of Daniel

One of the more difficult problems encountered by anyone who studies the Book of Daniel is the unexpected shift from Hebrew to Aramaic at 2.4 and then back again to Hebrew at 8.1. The Aramaic passages are certainly not translated from Hebrew; on the contrary, it seems likely that the Hebrew depends on an original Aramaic version. This point is crucial. If it is not recognized, one ends up in an impasse.

For Otto Plöger,[54] the languages correspond to the book's fundamental structures. The 'Aramaic' mentioned in Daniel 2.4b, at the place where the book abandons Hebrew, symbolizes the foreign language Daniel learned at the royal court. The kinship of chapters 2 and 4, 3 and 6, and 2 and 7, indicates why these chapters were written in a common tongue. True, chapter 7 is intimately linked to chapter 8, but in the latter, for the first time really, Israel moves into the foreground and therefore the use of Hebrew is legitimate.

We think that this solution by Otto Plöger combined with results of H. L. Ginsberg's *Studies in Daniel*,[55] is a good one. It explains by which criteria the opening of the book (1—2.4a) and its second part (8—12)

[53] Inserted or placed at 3.24–90; 13, 14. See J. Ziegler, *Septuaginta*, vol. xvi pars 2, 'Susanna. Daniel. Bel et Draco' (Göttingen 1954), pp. 119–32; 80–91; 215–23.
[54] 'Das Buch Daniel', *KAT* (Gütersloh 1965), p. 26.
[55] *Studies in Daniel* (New York 1948).

were translated into Hebrew from an Aramaic original.[56] We will indicate in the course of our critical notes mistakes made in the translation and transmission of the Hebrew texts of Daniel.

One will recall that Aramaic became an international language beginning in the eighth century BCE in the Near East from India to southern Egypt (Elephantine) and from Asia Minor to the north of Arabia, which included the Assyrian and Persian empires. Other passages of the Bible, outside Dan. 2.4b–7, are in Aramaic: Ezra 4.8—6.18; 7.12–26; Jer. 10.11; and Gen. 31.47 (two words).

The Plan of the Book of Daniel

We saw above that the Book of Daniel is divided into two parts, each of a different genre. In the first half there are six stories or *agadoth* (= Daniel A). Daniel is there spoken of in the third person singular.[57]

Ch. 1: The arrival of Daniel and three other young Judeans at the court of the Babylonian king, Nebuchadnezzar. Their education to prepare them for official service.

Ch. 2: Nebuchadnezzar's dream—the statue made of materials with a decreasing value. Daniel's interpretation.

Ch. 3: The erection of a statue by the same king which serves as an idol for the whole empire. Daniel's three companions are thrown into a fiery furnace. Their miraculous survival.

Ch. 4: A new dream of Nebuchadnezzar: the tree which is struck down. Its interpretation by Daniel.

Ch. 5: King Belshazzar's banquet in Babylon. The inscription 'Mene, Tekel, Parsin', on the wall. Daniel's interpretation.

Ch. 6: On the order of King Darius 'the Mede', Daniel is thrown into a lions' den.

The second part of the book consists of four apocalyptic visions (= Daniel B). Here Daniel is designated in the first person singular. He is no longer the interpreter of other people's dreams, but is himself the dreamer and visionary. He needs the help of an angel to understand what he sees.

Ch. 7: The increasing bestiality of the empires and God's judgement delegated to 'someone like a son of man'.

---

[56] On the contrary, the argument, advanced to satiety, that the beginning and end of the book are in Hebrew to legitimate its insertion into the Canon of Scriptures—as though the 'inspectors' or customs officials would content themselves with a cursory examination of the merchandise—is a farce. Even H. L. Ginsberg falls into this trap, op. cit., pp. 38–9.

[57] Except in chapter 3, where Daniel is not mentioned.

Ch. 8: The ram and the he-goat.
Ch. 9: Daniel's prayer of intercession.
   —The explication of Jeremiah's prophecy of the seventy years.
Ch. 10: The man clothed in linen.
   —The apparition of the angel.
Ch. 11: Historical recapitulation from the Median-Persian empire up to Antiochus Epiphanes.
Ch. 12: Resurrection and final retribution.

The unity of the book is assured by the omnipresent shadow of Antiochus Epiphanes, as much in the first part as in the second. He who monstrously incarnates the ungodly empire will be judged and chastised (7.9–11, 26; 8.25; 11.45). At the zenith of his power, he will suddenly be overthrown and this will be the signal for God's universal triumph (2.44; 7.13, 14, 18, 22, 27). The 'seventy weeks' (of years) have elapsed (= 490 years): 9.24–7. There only remains a half-week before the end. The final crisis will certainly be appalling, but it will suffice to have been inscribed in the Book. Then the resurrection will come (12.1ff.).

A Chronological Tableau of Daniel's Epoch

The historical situation in the second century BCE was conducive to the birth of apocalyptic. The Jewish population at the time of the return from the Exile numbered only a few thousand souls,[58] but this did not prevent it from already using in that day a messianic language.[59] However, such hopes went unfulfilled,[60] and the Persian dominance continued for two more centuries without the eschatological dream being realized. On the contrary, the more time passed, the more the advent of the messianic era was felt to be far off rather than something which was drawing near.

This is one excellent reason why an apocalypticist of the second century would choose to place us in his book in the Babylonian and Persian period. It was a question of looking more closely at whether and

[58] The lists in Ezra 2 and Nehemiah 7 give a total population of about 50,000. W. Albright, *The Biblical Period from Abraham to Ezra* (New York 1963), p. 49, estimates that it was not more than 20,000. John Bright, *The Kingdom of God* (Nashville 1953), p. 165, writes that the community might have thought of itself as the prophetic 'Remnant' after 'a purge of monstrous proportions had occurred, leaving but a cut-down stump of David's house and a pitifully chastened people.'

[59] With regard to Zerubbabel, for example (see Zech. 6.12b–13; cf. 3.8; Hagg. 2.21–3). According to K. Galling, 'The Gola List According to Ezra 2 = Nehemiah 7', *JBL*, 70 (1951), pp. 149–58, the very construction of lists of repatriates is based upon the model of the ancient amphictyony, a sure sign that those who returned to Zion thought of themselves as the *verus Israel*.

[60] Zerubbabel disappears from the scene, says John Bright, op. cit., p. 167, 'as if he had dropped out of history through a trap door'.

how God was at work in history after the Exile. In Daniel A, consequently, the various parts are presented in 'chronological order'.

(1) Chs. 1—4: The time of Nebuchadnezzar.
(2) Ch. 5: The reign of Belshazzar, his 'son'.
(3) Ch. 6: The time of Darius 'the Mede', which the author makes succeed the autochthonous dynasty at Babylon!

Daniel B follows a similar fictional chronological sequence:

(1) Ch. 7 (first vision): Situated in the first year of Belshazzar.
(2) Ch. 8 (second vision): In the third year of the same sovereign.
(3) Ch. 9 (third vision): The first year of Darius 'the Mede'.
(4) Chs. 10—12 (fourth vision): 'The third year of Cyrus, king of Persia'.[61]

In this way, therefore, the Book of Daniel artificially transports us to Neo-Babylonian and Persian times. The historical errors are numerous and will be taken up in the course of our commentary. We can get an idea of them, however, thanks to the chronological table printed below. It is clear that the Author saw in the period under consideration an excellent model for his own time. In fact, the Persian empire may have been the first empire to make a pretence to being truly universal. All the countries in the Near East with a high culture were gathered under the same sceptre and a common language: the Aramaic called 'of the Empire'. The cults were based upon an enlightened syncretism, thanks to the recognized supremacy of the Babylonian sun god and the adoption of the canvas of Babylonian astral theology.[62]

Chronology

586	The Fall of Jerusalem to the blows of the Neo-Babylonian Nebuchadnezzar (see Dan. 1.1–2).
585–549	Astyages, king of the Medes.
562	Death of Nebuchadnezzar; ascension of Evil-Merodach.
560	Assassination of Merodach; ascension of Neriglissar.
556	Ascension of Nabonidus.
555–549	Cyrus the Persian's revolt against the Median Astyages. He becomes the king of the Medes and the Persians under the name of Cyrus II the Great.

[61] The Greek text, in accordance with 1.21, has 'the first year'.
[62] Herodotus, *The Histories*, I, 131, writes: 'The Persians offer sacrifices to Zeus (Ahoura) on the top of mountains, and they call Zeus the whole circle of the heavens.' He also says, I, 135, 'No race is so ready to adopt foreign ways as the Persian.'

548	In Babylon, Belshazzar removes his father Nabonidus from power. Nabonidus is at Tema (in Arabia) and his son is at least regent of the kingdom (see Dan. 4).
539	Cyrus seizes Babylon. Belshazzar's death (see Dan. 5).
530	Death of Cyrus. Ascension of his son, Cambyses (530–522), (who is not mentioned in Scripture).
525	Cambyses invades Egypt.
522	Cambyses dies. Ascension of Darius I (522–486).
516	Dedication of the Second Temple in Jerusalem.
490	Defeat of the Persian army at Marathon.
486	Darius I dies. Ascension of Xerxes I (486–465).
480	Defeats at Thermopylae and Salamis.
478–477	Xerxes crushes the revolt of Babylon.
465(–4)	He dies of poisoning. Ascension of Artaxerxes I 'Longimanus' (465–424). Nehemiah is governor in Judah.
424(–3)	Xerxes II.
423	Darius II (423–404) 'Nothus' (not mentioned in Scripture).
404	Artaxerxes II 'Mnemon' (not mentioned in Scripture). Governorship of Ezra.
401–400	The Expedition of the 10,000.
359	Artaxerxes III 'Ochus' (359–338).
339	Arses.
336	Darius III 'Codomannus' (336–331). (Perhaps the Darius mentioned in Neh. 12.22.)
	Alexander the Great's victories over Darius III:
334	Battle of the Granicus.
333	Battle of Issus.
331	Battle of Gaugamela near Arbela; founding of Alexandria.
June, 323	Death of Alexander at Babylon. Struggle among his generals for hegemony.
320	Ptolemy I seizes Jerusalem. Ptolemaic domination of the city continues until 198.

The Seleucid period begins in 311 when Seleucus makes himself ruler at Babylon.

1. Seleucus I 'Nicator' (312–281), a Macedonian (see Dan. 11.5).

2. Antiochus I 'Soter', his son (281–261). [In Egypt, Ptolemy II (285–246) founds the Museum and its library at Alexandria.]

3. Antiochus II 'Theos', his son (261–246). He marries the Ptolemaic princess Berenice (see Dan. 11.6).

4. Seleucus II 'Callinicos', his son (246–226). Continual hostilities with Egypt (see Dan. 11.7–9). [In Egypt, Ptolemy III Euergetes (246–221).]

5. Seleucus III 'Soter', his son (226–223). Reprisals against Egypt (see Dan. 11.10).

6. Antiochus III, son of Seleucus II called 'the Great' (223–187). See Dan. 11.11–17: the battle of Raphia (217). His daughter, Cleopatra, marries Ptolemy V (221–203). See Dan. 11.18: Roman opposition. See Dan. 11.14–16: birth of a pro-Hellenic party in Judea. Battle of Magnesia (189)—Antiochus III is defeated by the Romans.

7. Seleucus IV 'Philopator', his son (187–176). See Dan. 11.20; 2 Macc. 3.1—4.7 (the High Priests Onias III and Simon the Just). 176: Heliodorus murders Seleucus IV in an attempt to put his own son on the throne.

8. Antiochus IV 'Epiphanes', son of Antiochus III (175–164). See Dan. 11.21 and *passim*.

Here is the continuation of events as presented in 1 and 2 Maccabees:

1. Ascension of Antiochus IV (175): 1 Macc. 1.11; 2 Macc. 4.7. Onias III is High Priest.

2. The Hellenization of Judea; apostasy of some Jews: 1 Macc. 1.12–16; 2 Macc. 4.17–50. Jason, the brother of Onias III, becomes High Priest due to his support of Hellenization. Shortly after, he is replaced by Menelaus.

3. Persecutions. Profanation of the Temple (168–167): 1 Macc. 1.41–59; 2 Macc. 6.1–9.

4. Martyrdom of the faithful: 1 Macc. 1.60–7; 2 Macc. 6.10—7.43.

5. The Jewish religion is prohibited. The Maccabean Revolt (167–166): 1 Macc. 2.1–31; 2 Macc. 5.27.

6. Victories of Judas the Maccabee (166–160): 1 Macc. 3.1–26; 2 Macc. 8.1–7.

7. Lysias is sent against Judas who wins a decisive victory at Beth-Zur in December 165: 1 Macc. 3.38–9.

8. The Temple is purified and dedicated (164); a royal general amnesty (Winter 164): 1 Macc. 4.36–59; 2 Macc. 10.1–8.

9. Judas in Idumea, Galilee, and Gilead: 1 Macc. 5.1–54; 2 Macc. 10.24–37.

10. Death of Antiochus IV (164): 1 Macc. 6.1–16; 2 Macc. 9.1–28.

Let us recall, once again, that the Book of Daniel was written before the death of Antiochus IV.[63]

---

[63] As it is, this Introduction leaves much in the shadows. The requirements of the publisher of the French edition imposed this relative brevity. Another volume, on *Daniel in his Time* is in production, and will, it is hoped, constitute a companion book to this Commentary.

1 Daniel and his Companions

Text 1. 1–21

(1) In the third year of the reign of Jehoiakim, King of Judah, Nebuchadnezzar, king of Babylon, came to Jerusalem and besieged it. (2) The Lord delivered into his hands Jehoiakim, king of Judah, and some of the vessels from the house of God. He brought them to the land of Shinear, to the house of his gods; and he put the vessels in the treasure-house of his gods. (3) Then the king told Ashpenaz, the chief of his courtiers, to bring in some of the sons of Israel, of royal descent as well as from noble families, (4) boys without blemish and of good looks, instructed in every kind of wisdom, experts in the ways of knowledge, understanding science, and vigorous, so that they would stand in the king's palace, and be taught the literature and language of the Chaldeans. (5) The king assigned to them a daily portion of the king's menu and of the wine he drank, (wanting) to raise them for three years, at the end of which time they would stand before the king. (6) There were among them, from the sons of Judah, Daniel, Hananiah, Mishael, and Azariah. (7) The prince of the courtiers gave them names. Daniel he called Belteshazzar, Hananiah he called Shadrach, Mishael he called Meshach, and Azariah he called Abed-Nego. (8) Daniel resolved not to defile himself with the king's menu or the wine he drank. He requested the prince of courtiers not to make him defile himself. (9) God gave Daniel grace and favour before the prince of courtiers. (10) The prince of courtiers said to Daniel: 'I fear lest my lord the king, who has assigned what you are to eat and drink, should see you with more dejected countenances than those of the other boys of your age for you could risk my head before the king.' (11) Daniel said to the attendant into whose charge the prince of courtiers had assigned Daniel, Hananiah, Mishael, and Azariah: (12) 'Test your servants, then, for ten days; have them give us vegetables to eat and water to drink, (13) then you will observe our appearance and the appearance of the boys who eat the king's menu, and act toward your servants according to what you will have seen.' (14) He heard them on this point and tested them for ten days. (15) At the end of ten days they had the better appearance and were plumper than all the boys who had eaten the king's menu. (16) Henceforth the attendant took away the menu and the wine which they were to drink and gave them vegetables. (17) Now, to these four boys, God gave understanding and he instructed them in every kind of literature and wisdom; while Daniel had the intelligence of every sort of vision and dream. (18) At the end of the days fixed by the king, when they were to be brought in, the prince of courtiers brought them before Nebuchadnezzar. (19) The king talked with them and none among them all was found like Daniel, Hananiah, Mishael, and Azariah. Therefore they stood in the

presence of the king. (20) And whenever the king consulted them on any affair requiring wisdom and intelligence, he found them ten times superior to all the magicians and conjurers that were in his whole kingdom. (21) Such was the existence of Daniel up to the first year of King Cyrus.

Critical Notes 1. 1–21

V.1 Jehoiakim, king of Judah 609–598. Nebuchadnezzar (605–562): in the LXX and Vul.: Nabuchodonosor. Nabu-Kudur-usur or Nabu-Kudurri-usur = 'Nabu guard the frontier' (indicative or imperative). The correct transposition into Hebrew is נבוכדאצר; see Jer. 21.2, 7; Ezek. 26.7. Nebuchadnezzar was the son of Nabopolassar (Nabu-apil-usur) who conquered Assyria (612–609).

Babylon of the Babel of Gen. 11. The pejorative sense of bad omen for Israel is emphasized by the use of Shinear in v.2.

V.2 'To the land of Shinear': *sic* in MT and Θ. LXX: εἰς Βαβυλῶνα— LXX *del*.: 'to the house of his gods.—מקצת: see Neh. 7.70: 'some, a part of. . . .' The Rabbis insisted upon the fact that just a part of the utensils had been carried away to Babylon, see Jer. 27.19— אדני: generally אלהים in the book, but here the contrast with false divinities is intended. Several mss. have יהוה.—בית־האלהים: The article is somewhat unexpected (although not unusual), which is why Saadia Gaon understands the word as designating the judges and refers to Exod. 22.7–8. The expression then signifies 'place of government, court of justice'.—ויביאם: the complement of direct object is difficult. LXX, Θ, Vul. have the neuter plural αὐτά, *ea*. There is an almost perfect parallel in 2 Chron. 36.7 where no confusion exists. The Rabbinic commentators maintain the ambiguity between the masculine and neuter plural. See 2 Chron. 28.5; 36.17–18. . . . It clearly makes more sense to read only a neuter, so as to avoid a nonhistorical exile of Jehoiakim.

V.3 אשפיז: Θ: ’Ασφανέζ; LXX: ’Αβιεσδρι. Same word as Syriac ›ašpazzā or ›ašpizzā, 'inn'. The origin of the word is the Old Persian ašpinja. One can conclude that originally the text had here rab ›ašpinza, the inn-keeper (in the royal palace). The translator into Hebrew thought that it was a proper name and made him rab̄ sarysym. (Communication of E. Lipinski)— סרוס: perhaps originally 'the one at the head of'. Akk. sărēši, š was transcribed as a *samekh* in Western Semitic, where the meaning 'eunuch' became general (cf. Ch.-F. Jean and J. Hoftijzer: *Dictionnaire des Inscriptions Sémitiques de l'Ouest* (Leyden 1965), p. 197. Thus LXX and Θ which translate 'head-eunuchs', but the term has the more general meaning of someone employed at the royal court. Gen. 39.1 and 7 speak of a married 'eunuch' in the person of Potiphar. Cf. Gen. 37.36. According to Josephus (*Ant.* X, X, 1) and Origen (*Hom.* IV *in Ezek.*) the four young men were made eunuchs in the proper sense of the term. Cf. Matt. 19.12—ויאמר להביא: late Hebrew; see 2 Chron. 14.3; 29.21; 31.4; Esth. 1.10.11—ומזדע המלוכה: see 2 Kings 25.25—הפרתמים: Θ transcribes the Hebrew; LXX: 'choose'; Σ: 'Parthians'. The origin of the word is the Old Persian *fratama* with which πρῶτος in Greek is akin. See Esth. 1.3; 6.9.

V.4 ילדים: also applies to adolescents, see Gen. 37.30, etc. According to Ibn Ezra, Daniel was about 15 years old at the time.—כשדים: the Kaldu (Chaldea) of the cuneiform texts.—מַדָע: an unusual vocalization, see 2 Chron. 1.10–12. An Aramaism (Kautzsch, *Die Aramaismen im A.T.* (1902), p. 51).—לעמד: Bentzen, *Daniel*, p. 16, refers to 5.19 and 1 Sam. 16.22 which he translates as 'zum Dienst'. One may also think of texts such as 1 Kings 1.2; 10.8; 12.8; etc.—היכל: habitually designates a temple rather than a palace. The text's emphasis oscillates between the royal and the sacerdotal sides of Daniel's functions. See our commentary.—ספר כשדים: is a construct state=ספר כשדים ולשונם; see Isa. 29.11; 11.2; Ezek. 31.16 (cf. Ges. Kau. par. 128a, Anm. 1).—משכילים: cf. the sense of the word as 'success' in Hebrew Scriptures. Judah J. Slotki paraphrases 'able to make progress in their studies' (*Daniel* (London 1951), p. 2).—ידעי דעת: Ibn Ezra draws attention to the transitive construction of the verb and paraphrases: 'capable of clearly conveying their thoughts'.—כח בהם: for the Rabbis: 'self-control' (J. J. Slotki, loc. cit.).

V.5 וימן: an Aramaism; cf. vv.10, 11; Jonah 2.1; see Kautzsch, *Aramaismen*, p. 108. פתבג is a Persian word, *patibaga*, viands. The separation into two words in Hebrew rests upon a popular etymology which sees in the first syllable the word פת, 'to bite'. In the Bible the word only appears in this book (see Dan. 1.8, 13, 15, 16; 11.26).—דבר יום ביומו: see 1 Chron. 16.37; Jer. 52.34.—משתיו: see Ges. Kau. par. 93ff.—יעמדו לפני המלך: to enter the king's service, see vv.15, 18. ולגדלם: see Isa. 1.2; 2 Kings. 10.6—ומקצתם: see v.2: 'some of them'. This is the opinion of Saadia Gaon. Or: at the end of these three years. (See translation.)

V.6 דניאל: the spelling is a bit different in Ezek. 14.14, 20; 28.3: דנאל.

V.7 שים שמות: Neo-Hebrew; see 2 Kings 17.34; Neh. 9.7; Dan. 5.12.

V.8 וישם: LXX, Θ, Vul., *del.* this second occurrence.—וישם על לבו: see Mal. 2.2; cf. Dan. 6.15 and many of the pseudepigraphic texts given by D. S. Russell, *The Method and Message . . .*, p. 397. The heart is the organ for thinking (whence the terminology of Dan. 6.15) and willing.

V.9 The combination חסד ולרחמים is frequent throughout the Psalter. The construction לחסד ולרחמים לפני is found in 1 Kings 8.50; Neh. 1.11; Ps. 106.46; Test. Jos. 2.3: εἰς οἰκτιρμούς; Judith 10.8: εἰς χάριν (texts cited by A. Bentzen, op. cit., p. 18).

V.10 אשר למה: for this construction see Ezra 7.23; Jonah 1.7–8; Song of Sol. 1.7.—זעפים: the same term is found in Gen. 40.6 (a tormented appearance). In Jonah 1.15, זעף signifies 'anger'. In Samaritan, however, the verb means 'to breathe', whence the Aramaic use of the word as 'to rage against' and the Neo-Hebrew sense 'to be bitter toward'; Prov. 19.3; 2 Chron. 26.19. In Dan. 1.10, Θ translates σκυθρωπά, see Matt. 6.16.—גיל is an *hapax legomenon* in the Bible. It is found in the Talmud. Arabic: *jil.*—וחיבתם את־ראשי: a late Hebrew expression (חיב is an Aramaism). Lit.: 'That you do not make me risk my head.'

V.11 המלצר: the meaning is not certain, but it is not a proper name as in the LXX: 'Αβιεσδρι, Θ: 'Αμελσαδ,' Vul.: 'Malasar'.—Delitzsch and Schrader (cited by A. Bentzen, p. 18) link the word to the Akkadian *massaru*, 'overseer'.

V.12 זרעים = *hapax legomenon*. Lit.: 'what was sown'.

V.13 Lit.: 'Then our looks will appear before you, then the look. . . .'— מראה: see v.4, v.15; 8.15; 10.6, 18.

V.14 וישתע להם לדבר הזה: see 1 Sam. 30.24.

V.15 בשר is rendered by σῶμα in the LXX and more correctly as σάρξ by Θ (see Gen. 41.2–3 and our commentary on Dan. 1.15). The word appears five times in Daniel (10.3 in Hebrew; 2.11; 4.9; and 7.5 in Aramaic). According to D. Lys, *La Chair dans l'Ancien Testament, 'Bâsâr'* (Paris 1967), p. 131, 'Of the 273 uses of *bâsâr* (Aram. *besar*), 104 concern animals and 169 concern man.' See Isa. 17.4; Zech. 11.16; etc.

V.16 ויהי נשא: see Judg. 16.21 (ויהי טחן).

V.17 הבין: the verb בין plays an important role in the Book of Daniel. It appears ten times in the qal and twelve times in the hiphil in the parts in Hebrew. The substantive בינה appears five times (1.20; 2.21; 8.15; 9.22; 10.1). M. A. Beek says, it is what is *seen* today, but what the prophets had already received in the past as revelation, in: 'Zeit, Zeiten und halbe Zeit', *Festsch. Th. Vriezen* (Wageningen 1966), pp. 19–24.—ארבעתם: see Ezek. 1.10; 2 Sam. 21.9 (Qr = שבעתם).

V.20 חכמת בינה: hendiadys. See Isa. 28.14; Dan. 12.2—ידות: see Gen. 43.34.—החרטמים: of Egyptian origin, it normally designates magicians (see Gen. 41.8; Exod. 7.11; etc.). The influence of the Joseph cycle is again apparent.—האשפים: on the basis of LXX and Θ, והאשפים seems indicated. This word appears only in Daniel.

Akk.: *ašipu*, 'exorcist'. This passed into Syriac as a 'snake-charmer'.

V.21 For O. Plöger, op. cit., the use of ויהי is unfortunate. But this is because Plöger has a static conception of the verb היה. For Ehrlich, היה has the same force as חיה. Compare our text with Jer. 1.3; Ruth 1.2; Test. Jos. 11.8; etc. This is also the sense the verb היה has in Neo-Hebrew.

Commentary

The first chapter of Daniel constitutes an introduction to the whole book, and in particular to its first part (chapters 1—6). It transports us to Babylon during the sixth century BCE and Nebuchadnezzar's court (v.1). Since Daniel A takes us up to Cyrus, the founder of the Persian Empire and the author of the edict of 538 permitting the exiled Jews to return to Zion, the historical period explicitly covered by the Book of Daniel is that which runs from the beginning to the end of the Judean exile in Babylon. We saw in our Introduction that this *Sitz im Leben* is artificial.

Verse 1 gives chronological details which are impossible to accept as presented. 'The third year of the reign of Jehoiakim' was 606. But the battle of Carchemish which opened the gates of Judea to Nebuchadnezzar did not take place until 605.[1] According to 2 Kings 24.1–2, in the third year of Jehoiakim, the king of Babylon 'came up' and Juda 'was submissive to him for three years' before revolting against its suzerain (despite the opposition of the prophet Jeremiah).[2]

We might think that the Book of Daniel opens on an historical slip. Does it not subsequently speak of a 'Darius the Mede' (6.1), followed by a 'Cyrus the Persian' (6.29)?[3] It is true that it is not impossible that the author might have confused Jehoiakim and his son Jehoiachin. In that case the date indicated in Dan. 1.1 would be 594, which would agree with the facts. We shall soon discover, however, that the historical information in Daniel is taken almost uniquely from prophetic texts.[4] Verse 1

[1] 605 is also the date of Nebuchadnezzar's ascension to the throne.
[2] Jewish commentators in the Middle Ages already saw the difficulty of maintaining. the text as such. They interpreted it as: 'the third year of Jehoiakim's rebellion against Nebuchadnezzar' (see Rashi, Ibn Ezra, Ps. Saadia, Jephet). This Jewish tradition meant, in effect, that the king of Juda served Nebuchadnezzar for three years, then rebelled against him for another three years. Then he was deposed and his son sent into exile. See *b. Meg.* 11b.
[3] What is more, Nebuchadnezzar did not have a son named Belshazzar (ch. 5). It was Evil Merodach who followed him on the throne, and Nabonidus was the fourth successor. It was during the reign of this latter king that the Babylonian Empire ended. 'Darius the Mede' is unknown. It was Cyrus the Persian who seized Babylon.
[4] With J. A. Montgomery, for example (see op. cit. ad loc.).

combines Jer. 25.1 and 11 (cf. 2 Chron. 36.21) with 2 Chron. 36.6 (a captivity of Jehoiakim unknown from 2 Kings. 24.1). It was during the third year of his reign that this king was deported (2 Chron. 36.9–10) and Jeremiah prophesied an exile of seventy years.[5] At the end of that period, in 538, Cyrus released the Judeans. If there is any confusion between father and son, it stems from 2 Chronicles. It must be said, however, that, by dating the Babylonian siege of Jerusalem to 606 instead of 597, Daniel is able to stretch the exile period to the seventy years foretold by Jeremiah (25.11–14; 29.10; cf. Dan. 9).

Nebuchadnezzar is the leading figure through chapter 4. But already the central heroes of the drama, Daniel and his companions, are on stage. Without a doubt they represent the faithful Israel which, in the midst of the nations, could only expect a brutal hostility. The situation of the young Jews at the Babylonian court recalls—in the very terms used here, see ילדים, vv. 4ff.—the βασιλικοὶ παῖδες, the pages at Hellenistic courts.[6] With this first chapter of Daniel, we are surely in the second century BCE, and the story is an anthological and Midrashic reuse of a popular story from the Daniel cycle, on the one hand, and prophetic texts—especially from Jeremiah—, on the other.[7] If other proof is necessary, the central question of a ritually pure diet (כשרות) in this chapter also orients us in the same direction (see 2 Macc. 6.18–31, where Eleazar undergoes martyrdom rather than eat some pork; we are in the second century BCE). Finally, we will also cite in this context the important association of wisdom and faith or fidelity. This is one trait whose whole polemical point was particularly appreciated in the Hellenistic milieu of the second century. This is amply illustrated in Daniel 1 and, in a corollary form, in chapter 4 where Nebuchadnezzar loses his reason through revolting against God and regains it by submitting to the Most High (see vv. 28 and 31).

The Book of Daniel opens upon a catastrophe, but the salvific divine intervention is being prepared at the same time (vv. 3–7). God, who has abandoned Jerusalem, himself plants the seed of its redemption in the

[5] See Ramir Augé, 'Daniel—Lamentacions—Baruch', in *The Bible of Montserrat* (1954); Review of R. Tournay in *RB*, 62 (1955), p. 289. Jacob M. Myers, The Anchor Bible, *II Chronicles* (New York 1965), *ad* 36.6 note, p. 218: 'The Chronicler's reference is independent and certainly much older than Daniel. Perhaps there is some historical foundation to the story after all.' Similarly, the Chronicle of the Chaldean kings might indicate a Babylonian intervention in Palestine in 605; see D. Wiseman, *Chronicles of the Chaldean Kings (625–556 B.C.) in the British Museum* (London 1956), p. 28, cited by M. Delcor, *Le Livre de Daniel* (Paris 1971), p. 59. We also consider as highly probable O. Plöger's suggestion, op. cit. ad loc., that Daniel meant to indicate that the heroes of his book were part of the first deportation (598/7), hence a part of the élite of the people; a trait emphasized by the Chronicler.

[6] Alexander the Great instituted a corps of royal pages. Polybius mentions six hundred pages during the reign of Antiochus Epiphanes.

[7] See our Introduction.

person of Daniel and his companions. While awaiting the full maturation of salvation, the wise man is sustained by his 'clairvoyance', a sort of prophetic spirit which allows him to see beyond appearances. Liberation implies, after all, a clear vision of what, for the time being, is obscure, an opening on what is, momentarily, closed off (see v.17). This clairvoyance is all the more marvellous in that it has something in common with the science of Babylonian diviners and magicians, although infinitely greater than theirs. Thus the power delegated to Moses and Aaron easily surpassed all Egyptian science. And earlier, the Israelite Joseph had been found to be the wisest man in Egypt and was raised, through his skill in interpreting dreams, to the second place in the governing of the kingdom. This latter hero, above all, inspires all of Daniel A; Daniel is a replica of Joseph in the sixth century BCE.[8] And to make things more dramatic, Daniel finds himself in the very centre of the idolatrous power, par excellence, Babylon. The city is called Shinear (v.2), the ancient name for that region, as in the story of the Tower of Babel (Gen. 11.2). According to A. Richardson, this legend 'contains in story form the essential biblical verdict upon secular civilization represented in the parable by the city and tower of Babel—that Babylon which, throughout the Bible remains the symbol of man's megalomaniacal attempt to achieve world peace and unity by world domination and exploitation.' (*Genesis I–XI* (London 1953), p. 124).[9] Furthermore, it is prophesied in Isa. 11.11 that a remnant of the people exiled in Shinear will return to Zion.[10]

The sacred objects constituted booty *par excellence*. Their character was in no way denied by the enemy who, on the contrary, placed them in his own temples (see 2 Chron. 36.7, 18; Ezra 5.14).[11] This demonstration of power bears not only on the transference of the sacred vessels to Babylon, but also on the employment of young noble Jews, among whom is included Daniel (vv. 3ff.), at the royal court. In this way, the book establishes the relation between the heroes of the stories and the 'supports' of God's presence in the world. **Verse 3** insists upon the young men's nobility. Later Jewish tradition said that Daniel was a descendant of King Zedekiah[12] and already in the Greek version of Bel,[13] it is said that he was a priest. This latter affirmation may have found its point of

---

[8] To the extent that in the description of the young Jews' appearances after their experiment (Dan. 1.15), there is an identity of terms with Gen. 41, when it speaks of the seven fat cows (except that they are יפות תאר where Daniel has simply טוב).

[9] Also cited by E. Heaton, *Daniel* (London 1956), pp. 115–16.

[10] See also Gen. 10.10; 14.1, 9; Zech. 5.11; Josh. 7.21.

[11] King Belshazzar's act in ch. 5 is one of deliberate profanation.

[12] See *b. Sanh.* 93b; Josephus, *Ant.* X.X.1.

[13] One of the five additions in the Alexandrian text as compared with the MT (see our Introduction, p. 13).

departure in the parallel suggested by the text between the educations of Moses and of Daniel at a foreign royal court (see Acts 7.22). This last trait was customary (see 1 Esd. 3.4), and the information provided in Daniel is exact in showing the selected young men as being instructed in various disciplines running from literature (writing, *belles lettres*, and translation) to mathematical and natural science to divination. This is why the term 'Chaldeans' is used here. Everywhere else in the Bible it designates the people of Chaldea, as is the case in Dan. 5.30 and 9.1. In general, however, Daniel designates by כשדים a class of magi, diviners, priests, astrologers, and enchanters (see 2.2). This derived meaning is relatively recent and a supplementary chronological indication for the date of the composition of our book.[14] According to Porteous (*Daniel*, p. 28), it was not until well after the sixth century, when the Chaldean population had been mixed with other peoples, that the word 'Chaldeans' came to designate the descendants of certain priestly milieux.

We are, moreover, in a pronounced priestly context in v.4. The young men must be 'without fault' (or: blemish) like the Israelite priests (see Lev. 21.17–23) or the animals for sacrifice (see Lev. 22.17–25). It is also a prerogative of priests to be 'instructed in all wisdom'.[15] The following chapters will several times oppose the impotence of the 'Chaldeans' occult science to the total knowledge which God imports to his saints (see 2.27–30; 4.4–6; 5.7–12; 9.22–3).

'Good looking' is a royal trait. It recalls the stature of someone like Saul, 'remarkable and handsome' (1 Sam. 9.2; 10.23), or the attractiveness of David (1 Sam. 16.12, 18), or Eliab, a candidate for the kingship (1 Sam. 16.6), etc. These two traits, sacerdotal and royal, united in the persons of Daniel and his companions also evoke a text such as Exod. 19.6 which refers to Israel as a whole as being a 'kingdom of priests'.

Nebuchadnezzar's plan[16] is of cultural order—as was that of Hellenism in the second century. It was to instruct a few elect in ספר and לשון. The first word—lit. 'book(s)'—refers to the cuneiform writing practised up to the Seleucid period in literate circles addicted to the occult.

---

[14] See Herodotus, I, 181, 183; Ktesias, 29, 15; Ed. Meyer, *Geschichte des Altertums*, IV (Stuttgart 1901), p. 124, Anm. 1; H. H. Rowley, *Expository Times*, 38, pp. 423ff.
For the variety of functionaries at Nebuchadnezzar's court, see *ANET*, p. 308.

[15] The overlapping of sacerdotal and sapiential domains is seen in such wisdom Psalms as Ps. 1; 19; 119; 127; 128; etc.; in P in the context of Gen. 1—11; in Ezek. 28; etc. Ezra is a priest, scribe, and sage. After the Exile, Wisdom devoted itself to the study of the Torah as a first-order interest (see R. B. Y. Scott, *Wisdom in the Bible* (New York 1971), p. 77).

[16] Jephet (a Qaraite Jew of the eleventh century, cited by J. A. Montgomery, op. cit., p. 121) writes, 'The king's object was twofold: to gratify his fancy for men of knowledge; and to be able to boast that in his court are the greatest men of the world.'

Daniel 5 assumes that its hero has this type of knowledge. Therefore it is not necessary to follow J. Steinmann,[17] who rejects this meaning in favour of 'books of magic spells'. This idea is contained in the terms used in v. 4, but it does not exhaust their meaning. The second term—lit. 'language'—is not easy to interpret. It is true that in the later linguistic evolution the *lingua chaldaica* or *chaldaicus sermo* referred to Aramaic which was thought to have been the language of the Babylonians. Jerome, for example, understands our passage in this way. But Montgomery and others reject this meaning as too recent and see in this expression the secret language of the Chaldeans. The problem is linked in part to that of 2.4, where one must inquire whether the precision 'in Aramaic' is to be considered as a marginal gloss. If so, the language of the Chaldeans is not identified and the phrase is a purely technical indication to draw the scribe's or the reader's attention to the change in the text from Hebrew to Aramaic. In our Introduction, we have taken a position in favour of the authenticity of the word ארמית, which does not, in our opinion, prevent the word 'language' from having a wider meaning in the present case.

V.5 O. Plöger (op. cit., p. 39) proposes placing v. 5b after v. 4 and v. 5a after v. 8, even though he admits the present order may be intentional, v. 5a indicating the result expected by the king, and v. 8 the actual and superior result attained by Daniel. We will follow the latter possibility, inasmuch as Gen. 42.25 constitutes an interesting precedent as regards the word order (see Ges.-Kau. par. 114 p).

Beginning in the sixth century, the dietary question became of prime importance for Israel in contact with the nations. It was certainly a burning issue in the second century as the books of Maccabees bear witness.[18] In fact, food is one sign of civilization. Daniel and his companions see themselves offered the best of human culture in their day, an honour which they have the boldness to refuse, placing themselves, *mutatis mutandis*, in the situation of Asian immigrants who maintain their national diet when settled in Paris or San Francisco.[19] In any case, Daniel bears witness to the custom in ancient royal courts of introducing important prisoners to the national diet: Jehoiachin also received a portion from the king of Babylon (see 2 Kings 25.29–30). Undoubtedly, Daniel drew his information from 2 Kings or Jer. 52.31ff. and so once again assimilated his heroes into Jerusalem's royal family.

The precision 'for three years', as a time of probation, is, according to Montgomery, who cites the *Avesta*, a Persian rather than a Babylonian

[17] J. Steinmann, op. cit. ad loc.
[18] We have already referred to 2 Macc. 6.18–31 which recounts the martyrdom of Eleazar for having refused to eat pork.
[19] It is worth noting, in this context, that one possible meaning of the word זרעים in verse 12 is 'rice'.

custom. In Babylon, instruction continued from childhood into late adulthood. On the basis of this text, Rabbi Jose, on the contrary, reduced the number of years of study for the Levites from five to three years (*m. Sheq.* 3.26).[20]

V.6 For the first time, the heroes' names are given. 'Daniel already appears in Ezek. 14.14, 20—a text discussed in our Introduction, connected to an ancient Canaanite tradition—Ezek. 28.3; 1 Chron. 3.1; Ezra 8.2; Neh. 10.7. 'Hananiah' is cited as a name in Neh. 8.4 and 10.24; 'Mishael' appears in Neh. 8.4, and 'Azariah' in Neh. 10.3. Daniel probably drew the companions' names from these lists of exiles who returned to Zion. To be complete, let us add that Mishael is the name of a cousin of Moses in Exod. 6.22, that Azariah could be the same name as Azariel in Jer. 36.26 or Eliezer in Exod. 18.4, and that Hananiah is also found in Tobit 5.13 and on Akkadian, Aramaic, and other lists.[21]

One will note the strange absence of any genealogy, all the more striking since it is a question of the royal household. Such people receive an 'enthronement name' when they enter the king's service (v.7). This usage was current in the ancient Near East and is well represented in Scripture, see Gen. 41.45. This latter text is particularly interesting because it indicates a sort of Egyptian naturalization of Joseph.[22] Cf. 2 Kings 23.34; 24.17; etc. Changing names signifies a change of destinies—*nomen est omen*. We know how much the adoption of another name (in this case of Greek origin such as Alcimus or Jason) was a burning question for Jews in contact with Hellenism. Here, the Judean heroes receive their new names by obligation, not by choice. There is no need therefore for surprise as in Porteous that the invocation of foreign gods in their new names did not seem to bother the young men. The question could not arise.[23]

The origins of the four imposed names are complex. Daniel receives a name of Akkadian origin (as does Azariah): *Balatishar-uṣur* = 'protect the king's life!' the divine name Bel being understood. Abed-Nego is an intentional deformation of the Aramaic *Abed-Nabu* = 'servant of Nabu'.[24] Shadrach is probably an Old Persian name *Chithraka* the stem

[20] See Num. 8.24 and 4.31; the calculation is as follows:
30 years—25 years = 5 years of study.
[21] See M. Noth, *Die israelistische Personennamen* (Stuttgart 1928), nos. 378, 508 (cf. 507), 850, 1057.
[22] Ibn Ezra sees this change of Joseph's name as a precedent for our text.
[23] We note with V. Tcherikover, *Hellenistic Civilization and the Jews* (New York 1970), p. 347, that 'Although this phenomenon must inevitably be regarded as a symptom of assimilation, great importance should not be attached to it, nor should every instance of a change of name be interpreted as an act of hostility to Judaism. Jason of Cyrene, Philo and the Hasmonean kings cannot be suspected of deficient national feeling or of estrangement from the elements of Jewish tradition.'
[24] See Isa. 46.1.

of which means 'shining'.[25] The same applies to Meshach which is built on the Old Persian *Mitsaka*, a variant of *Mithra*. The *yod* in MT is a *mater lectionis* (cf. LXX and 1 Q 72.2).[26]

The following verses (vv.8ff.) make up the body of the story. The problem is that of the ritual purity of food, one of the more severe rules for orthodox Jews in the Maccabean period (see Tobit 1.11; Judith 10.5; 12.1–4, 19; Esth. 14.17; 1 Macc. 1.63; 2 Macc. 5.27; 6.18–20).[27] The alimentary prescriptions are presented often and precisely in Scripture, see Deut. 12.23–4; 14.3–21; Lev. 11; cf. Hos. 9.3; Amos 7.17; Ezek. 4.13–14; Isa. 52.11; Zech. 14.21; etc. In pagan countries, it was always possible that wine or meat had been offered to the gods before being served at a meal (see Deut. 32.38; Exod. 34.15; Acts 15.29; cf. 1 Cor. 10.21). Josephus (*Vita*, par. 3) mentions some Jews who, being in Rome, only ate figs and nuts. As Montgomery writes (op. cit., p. 130)—and he also cites the text from Josephus just mentioned—'the extreme of this principle is summed up in Jubilees 22.16:

My son Jacob, remember my words,
Observe the commandments of Abraham, your father:
Separate yourself from the nations,
And do not eat with them;
Do not imitate their works,
Nor become their associate;
For their works are impure,
And their ways are a pollution, an abomination, and an impurity.'[28]

Notice the force of the term used in Dan. 1.8: יתגאל which indicates an almost physical repulsion. The verb belongs to the cultic sphere, see Isa. 59.3; 63.3; Zech. 3.1; Lam. 4.14; Mal. 1.7, 12; Ezra 2.62; Neh. 7.64. One thinks of the profanation of the Temple at Jerusalem by Antiochus IV.

The Author returns to an original trait from his source when he

[25] For Montgomery, however, Shadrach is an intentional transformation of Marduk.
[26] For Montgomery: deformation of Sheshak = Babel, cf. the process called *Atbach* used in the text of Jer. 25.26. For the etymology of those names I am indebted to Professor E. Lipinski. As the *Yod* in Meshach is not a *plene* spelling—a fact confirmed by the Greek transcription Μισακ or Μισαχ—R. Zadok's reading (after H. Hitzig's) in * *Maišaka*- with the sense of sheep, is impossible. (Cf. R. Zadok: 'On Five Iranian Names in the O.T.', *VT* XXVI:2 (April 1976), pp. 246–7.)
[27] In times of persecution, expressions of liberty are reduced to the level of signs. In the context of second century Hellenism, 'collaborators' recognized one another by their lack of scruples about eating at pagans' tables. See V. Tcherikover, op. cit., p. 140. He sees one of the three major themes 'very appropriate to the atmosphere of the period of Antiochus (IV)' in the companions' refusal to eat at the king's table (p. 537, n. 32).
[28] Following R. H. Charles, *Pseudepigrapha* (Oxford 1913), p. 46. The Book of Jubilees may have been written in the second half of the second century BCE.

presents (v.9) the kindness of the 'prince of courtiers'. E. Heaton (op. cit., p. 120) rightly remarks that it is 'a touch characteristic of Hebrew romances, cf. Jer. 40.2–3; Gen. 39.21; 1 Esdras 3.6–7'.

But first the test is long and hard; for ten days the young Jews only have legumes (see our critical notes) and water. A. Bentzen (op. cit., p. 21) remarks that such a delay occurs often in a situation of temptation (see Rev. 2.10; Jub. 19.8; *Pirke Aboth* 5.4; Test. Jos. 2.7).

The number ten is symbolic.[29] H.-A. Brongers[30] has shown that it sometimes designates the largest number (see 1 Sam. 1.8; Gen. 24.22), and sometimes a minimum (see Amos 6.9; 5.3; Gen. 18.32). As hyperbole, it is already found in the letters from Tel el Amarna (fourteenth century BCE).

So, during this period of time of 'ten days', Daniel and his companions only eat זרעים. We should see in this term, along with H. L. Ginsberg,[31] seeds or vegetable pods.[32] Ginsberg writes, 'The great merit of grain (Dan. 1.12) is simply that it does not become unclean by contact with the unclean so long as it is kept dry (Lev. 11.37–8).'[33]

In any case, and without necessarily seeing in v.12 an allusion to ascetic practices, for that is not the point here,[34] it is tempting to establish with J. Steinmann[35] a parallel between the diet chosen by Daniel and that of the Essenes: 'We are near the beginning of the Essenes and the Therapeutae. Daniel and his companions are not necessarily eunuchs. . . . But the young men remain celibate. . . . It appears as though Jeremiah's celibacy set an example. Daniel and his companions almost live like monks.'[36] The Testament of Joseph 3.4 gives an interesting commentary on our text at the same time that it establishes once again the parallel between Daniel and Joseph: '. . . those who fast for the love of God receive a beautiful figure'. What is more, Dan. 1.17 establishes a cause and effect relation between the faithfulness

[29] See B. Pick, *Der Einfluss der Zehnzahl auf das Judentum* (1894); H. Haag, 'Die biblischen Wurzeln des Minjan', in *Festsch. O. Michel* (ed. O. Betz et al. (Leyden 1963), pp. 235–41); Fr. Hauck, 'δέκα', *ThWNT*, II, pp. 35ff.

[30] 'Die Zehnzahl in der Bibel und in ihrer Umwelt', in *Festsch. Th. Vriezen*, pp. 30–45.

[31] H. L. Ginsberg, 'The Composition of the Book of Daniel', *VT*, 4:3, p. 256.

[32] See E. Heaton, op. cit., p. 120.

[33] See G. F. Moore, *Judaism* I, p. 71, n. 4, who refers to *m. Uktsin* 3.1; Maimonides, *Hilkot Tum'at Ikelin*, I, 1.

[34] Our text may be compared to Dan. 9.3 and there are parallels with The Martyrdom of Isaiah S.11, and especially with 4 Esdras 5.20; 6.31, 35; 9.23–5; 14.38–42. D. S. Russell, op. cit., p. 172, concludes that in some cases the visionary's description of his psychic experiences in fact indicates similar experiences of the Apocalypticist himself.

[35] J. Steinmann, *Daniel* (coll. *Témoins de Dieu*, 12 (Paris 1950)), p. 47.

[36] Steinmann's argument is *e silentio* and must therefore be received prudently. That the period of the second century BCE was a time of austerity (involuntarily!), see Josephus, *Vita*, par. 3 (mentioned *supra*); 2 Macc. 5.27; Judith 10.5 (cf. *supra*); Tobit 1.10–11; Rom. 14.1; 1 Cor. 8; 10.23ff.; Col. 2.16, 21.

of the four companions and their knowledge of every science, their wisdom, and their understanding of visions and dreams.[37]

The Book of Daniel gives a large place to premonitory dreams and their interpretation by the man of God. In this, the book is part of a long tradition running back to Akkad[38] by way of Ugarit.[39] In Scripture, prophetic dreams[40] are numerous, see Gen. 37.5–10, 40–1; Num. 12.6; Job 7.14; etc. In the Pentateuch, recourse to dreams as a means of revelation is attributed to the E source (see Gen. 20.3–7; 31.24; etc.). Sometimes there is even a revelation by God of a message to the dreamer (see Gen. 31.11, 13; 28.10–14) and this communication to the visionary is so similar to ecstasy that it is sometimes difficult to distinguish the two (see Gen. 22.1–2; 46.1–3). They are probably purely and simply identified in such later texts as Isa. 29.7; Job 20.8; 33.15.

This new common trait puts Daniel on the same level as the Patriarchs. Joseph and Daniel are both at the court of a pagan king and both, too, do not hesitate in attributing a prophetic dimension to the dreams of their non-Israelite masters.[41] This broad perspective is also reflected in the fact that the science Daniel and his companions learn in the Chaldeans' school is not questioned as to its intrinsic worth. Dreams and sciences are divine means of communicating secrets to those who have wisdom; see 4 Esdras 10.59; 1 Enoch 14.2; 83.7; 85.1; *Shepherd* of Hermas, Vis. II, 4, 1[42]. . . . A dream therefore is a prophetic instrument (Deut. 13.1–5, Jer. 23.25, 32; 1 Sam. 28.6; etc.) and in 1 Kings 9.2, for example, it plays for Solomon[43] the role assumed by the prophet Nathan in the case of King David. Furthermore, it is remarkable that the Pharaoh needs Joseph and Nebuchadnezzar needs Daniel.[44] The corollary is that wisdom leads men like Joseph and Daniel 'to serve among great men, and appear before rulers' (Ecclus. 39.4), for they

[37] This is the relation established by the text, not, as Catholic commentators especially tend to say, one between asceticism and wisdom. Asceticism certainly is not lacking, but the accent is on faithfulness to the Covenant and obedience to the commandments. This is also true for the text cited from Test. Jos. 3.4.

[38] See, for example, A. Guillaume, *Prophecy and Divination* (New York–London 1938), p. 48 and *passim*.

[39] See Baal III, col. 3, beginning; Keret I, col. 1, lines 26–39, 46–51.

[40] Those which S. Freud calls 'typical dreams' and psychologist E. Aeppli calls 'the great dreams', see *Der Traum* (Zurich 1968).

[41] See also Gen. 20.3, 7 (Abimelech); Gen. 31.24 (Laban); 40.5ff. (officers of the Pharaoh); Judg. 7.13–15 (the Midianites); cf. Matt. 2.12 (the wise men); 27.19 (Pilate's wife).

[42] Texts cited by A. Caquot, 'Les Songes et leur interprétation', *Sources orientales*, no. 2 (Paris 1959).

[43] It is important to mention Solomon in this context for the association of the science of dreams with wisdom is also 'Solomonic', see 1 Kings 3.4ff.

[44] See A. Heschel, *Israel, an Echo of Eternity* (New York 1969), p. 48: 'God has a vision. The Bible is an interpretation of the vision. God has a dream. The task of Israel is to interpret the dream.'

stand out among the most sophisticated men (here vv.18–19). In fact, they really have nothing in common with the rest of mankind. They are 'ten times superior' to them (v.20).[45] It is the difference between wisdom of divine origin and wisdom of human origin (see Isa. 47.10ff.; Ps. 58.4–6; etc.); the result of their competition is described in Isa. 44.25:

> I wipe out the augurs' omens,
> I make fools of the diviners;
> I turn back the wise men
> And reduce their knowledge to lunacy.

V.21 adds a chronological 'precision' which contradicts Dan. 10.1. Clearly chapter one once existed separately, making Daniel one of the exiles returning to Zion immediately after the edict of Cyrus in 538, in conformity with the information furnished by the Book of Nehemiah. This chronology counts the 'years of Cyrus' as beginning from his reign in Babylon. It thus agrees with the author's theological and midrashic view—namely, that Daniel came to Babylon with the first wave of deportees (see *supra*) and left again with the first wave of repatriates— but it does not agree with 6.29 and 10.1. There is undoubtedly in this first chapter a reuse of 2 Chron. 26 which also begins with the Exile and ends with the Restoration.

So much for chapter 1. Israel is here represented in the world (the royal court of the greatest empire of the time), no longer by a patriarch (Joseph), or by two giants (Moses and Aaron), but by four companions, that is by a group representing a microcosm of Israel in a world also envisaged in its totality (the 'four empires' of the Book of Daniel).

In this confrontation, the last judgement, the final test, is accomplished. The cause of the Jews is identified with that of God and the ultimate consequences of one's alimentary diet at the Babylonian court are incalculable. It is a matter of God's victory or his defeat, of his life or his death.

---

[45] See the discussion of the number 'ten', *supra*, v. 12.

2 The Dream about the Statue

Text 2. 1–13

(1) In the second year of the reign of Nebuchadnezzar, Nebuchadnezzar had dreams; his spirit was anxious and sleep escaped him. (2) The king ordered that the magicians, astrologers, enchanters, and Chaldeans be called to set forth his dreams to the king. Thus, they came and stood before the king. (3) The king said to them: 'I have had a dream and my spirit is anxious to know this dream.' (4) The Chaldeans spoke to the king in Aramaic: 'Oh king, live for ever! Tell your servants the dream and we will set forth the interpretation.' (5) The king answered the Chaldeans in these words: 'The word is promulgated by me, if you do not make this dream and its interpretation known to me, you will be cut in pieces and your houses will be changed into manure. (6) But if you set forth the dream and its interpretation, you will receive presents, rewards, and great honours from me. Therefore set forth the dream and its interpretation to me.' (7) They answered a second time in these words: 'Let the king tell the dream to his servants and we will set forth the interpretation.' (8) The king answered in these terms: 'I know for certain that you want to gain some time because you see that the word is promulgated by me. (9) If you do not make the dream known to me, your sentence will be uniform. You are prepared to tell me something lying and perverse until the times have changed. Therefore tell me the dream, then I will know whether you have set forth its interpretation.' (10) The Chaldeans answered the king in these terms: 'There is no one in the world who could set forth this to the king, that is why no king, no matter how great or powerful, has asked such a thing of any magician, astrologer, or Chaldean. (11) The question the king poses is exorbitant and no one else could set this forth before the king, except the gods whose dwelling is not with flesh.' (12) Whereupon the king flew into a violent rage and ordered that all the wise men of Babylon be slain. (13) The sentence was published and the wise men were about to be massacred, and Daniel and his companions were sought so that they could be slain.

Critical Notes 2. 1–13

V.1 חלם חלמות: see Joel 3.1. MT = LXX = Θ.—נהיתה עליו: it is useless to emend this to נדרה (cf. 6.19), see 8.27.

V.5 אזדא: several versions say 'to escape' (see LXX, Θ, Vul.: *sermo recessita me*). In the Talmud, אזל = אזד = to go. אזדא, however, is a word with a Persian origin = notice, verdict. See Dan. 6.3 for its meaning. See H. Schaeder, *Iranische Beitraege* 68; E. Schrader, *Keilinschriften und das Alte Testament*, ed. Zimmern and Winckler (1903)[3], p. 617, where we have the dubious translation

34

'certainly'. Rashi also understands 'gone, forgotten', but Ibn Ezra has 'certain'.

V.6 נבזבה: the word comes either from the Persian *ni-baj*=to distribute (?), or the Akkadian *nibzu*=a document and the goods therein enumerated. The sense of a gift is clear (see Dan. 5.17; for the meaning, cf. 2.48).

V.7 פרשה: Θ and Syr. perhaps read פִּשְׁרֵה (his interpretation).

V.8 מן יציב: see 3.24 and 6.13, in both cases without the preposition. There is a parallel at 2.47: מן קשט; Θ says 'in truth'.—עדנא ... זבנין: lit.: 'buy time', see Eph. 5.16; Col. 4.5.

V.9 חדה היא דתכון: the word דת has a Persian origin: *data(m)*= justice. Later Hebrew = 'religion' (see Dan. 6.6). In Daniel the word also covers some other aspects: royal order (2.13, 15); public law (6.9, 13, 16); Torah (7.25). The sentence is absent in Θ. See Esth. 4.11.

V.10 רב ושליט: cf. the Assyrian title 'the great king' *(sărru rabū šarrudannu)*; see 2 Kings 18.28. Cyrus and even Antiochus I Soter donned this title for themselves.

V.11 יקירה: heavy; see LXX, Θ: βάρυς; Vul.: *gravis*. Cf. Ibn Ezra; Ps. 49.9—עם־בשרא: This general use of the word בשר, without any ethical judgement is found in Dan. 4.9 and many of the pseudepigraphic texts (see D. S. Russell, op. cit., p. 399).

V.12 בנס: is a *hapax legomenon*. LXX, Vul. and some Jewish commentators in the Middle Ages break the word into a name (נס) preceded by the preposition (ב). In this case, נס signifies anger; cf. Akk. *nasasu*; cf. Targ. Onk. on Gen. 40.6: *nesisin*. But the Pesh. knows a verb בנס to be angry. It is also used in Targumic Aramaean. Certain Jewish grammarians in the Middle Ages also recognize it. Finally, נסס in Hebrew (see Isa. 10.18) signifies 'to be weak, to faint away'.

V.13 מתקטלין: we may understand the massacre to be under way when Daniel intervenes (vv.14ff.), see v.18b.

Commentary

Chapter 2 presents the first example of Daniel's wisdom. It is made up of four distinct parts: King Nebuchadnezzar has a dream and demands that his wise men and magicians discover and interpret it (vv.1–13). Only Daniel among all the diviners is capable of satisfying the king (vv.14–28). He reveals Nebuchadnezzar's dream and gives its interpretation (vv.29–45). The result is that the king humbles himself before God and Daniel (vv.46–9).

From our discussion of vv.41–3, it will follow that Daniel 2 in its original form is to be dated in the fourth century, although there are secondary interventions from the second century which give it its present form.

The basic motif of this chapter is clear and the story's texture is uniform, the redactional elements having been harmoniously worked into the body of the material. Here, as in the stories in Genesis about the patriarch Joseph,[1] human wisdom, even magic, is judged impotent. God alone because he is Lord of history can reveal its secrets to his seers. He shows them the most powerful empires crumbling into dust. Above all, they 'lack weight'.[2] The schema employed here, and again in chapter 7, deals with those empires which dominated the ancient Near East during the fourth through second centuries: Babylon, Media, Persia, and Macedonia divided into the Seleucids in Syria and the Ptolemies in Egypt (here represented by the iron and ceramic)[3] following the death of Alexander the Great.

Just a little while longer, and an unexpected intervention by God is going to overturn the political scene: the Kingdom of God will replace these pagan empires destined to destruction. The suspense maintained throughout the first part of the chapter—the apex of which is still delayed by the discourse in vv.25–30—corresponds perfectly to the faithful Jews' anxious expectation of divine intervention in the time of Antiochus IV.

The date indicated in v.1 ('The second year of the reign of Nebuchadnezzar') is opposed by the information given in 1.5 and 1.18.[4] The reader constantly runs into these chronological imprecisions in this book, another sign of an independent original existence of the *agadoth* reported and 'dated' by Daniel A.

Everyone agrees that Dan. 2 is a midrash on Gen. 41 (see Gen. 41.8 and Dan. 2.1 where the same expression occurs; cf. Gen. 41.16 and Dan. 2.28; cf. the use of the Egyptian word חרטמים from Gen. 41.24

---

[1] See our commentary on chapter 1.
[2] See chapter 5.
[3] This identification has been made by many authors who are listed in H. H. Rowley, *Darius the Mede and the Four World Empires in the Book of Daniel* (Cardiff 1959). See the Table of Interpretations, col. F, pp. 184–5. They includes: Mss. Peshitta, St Ephrem, Barhebraeus, Eichhorn, de Wette, Bleek, Westcott, Graf, Delitzsch, Künen, Reuss, Vatke, Schürer, Bevan, von Gall, Driver, Marti, Bertholet, Haller, Montgomery, Charles, and Eissfeldt.
[4] O. Plöger, op. cit. ad loc., judiciously comments that the number 2 often appears in Scripture in relation to the length of a reign to emphasize its brevity (see 2 Sam. 2.10; 1 Kings 15.25; 2 Kings 21.19). Also there is an emphasis on the short span of time between the end of Daniel's instruction and his first test before the king.
  For Josephus, *Ant.* X, X, 3, this happened in the second year following the conquest of Jerusalem in 586.
  We might also follow Montgomery, op. cit. ad loc., and see 12 rather than 2 (see Josh. 24.12), or 6, שת for שתים.

in Dan. 2.2 *et al.*; it is true that M. Delcor[5] draws attention to the presence of Egyptian dream interpreters at the courts of Asarhaddon and Assurbanipal: cf. Gen. 41.40ff. and Dan. 2.48; Gen. 41.38 and Dan. 2.47; etc.). The difference in accent in comparison to the Genesis model is especially interesting. Dan. 2 is a piece of Wisdom writing (see above all vv.20–3), for wisdom is that one attribute of God in which especially the saints participate. It is wisdom which allows Daniel to give dimensions of eternity to the king's vision.

We spoke above of the use of dreams as a means of inspiration in the ancient Near East, and in particular in Scripture (see Dan. 1.17). To be noted here is the interesting historical parallel with the Babylonian king, Nabonidus. He was convinced (as was his mother) that the god Sin had ordered him to reconstruct the destroyed temple of Ehulhul at Harran, which had been in ruins since 610. It was also necessary to reinstall the statue of the god Sin there which had been carried off to Babylon. But at the time of Nabonidus' coronation in 556, Harran was in the hands of the Medes. It was only during the third year of his reign that he could realize his desire. The parallel with the structure of Daniel 2 goes so far as to include the following details. Nabonidus wrote, 'I was overcome by the great commandment from the gods, I was seized with fear and my spirit was troubled.'[6] Also, 'During the nocturnal season, one dream was very troubling. . . .'[7] We will also have occasion below (see ch. 4) to note the influence of the history of Nabonidus on Daniel A, but let us immediately note that the statue erected by Nebuchadnezzar in chapter 3 could be a reminiscence of the statue of Sin erected by Nabonidus in Babylon (while waiting to reinstall it at Harran) which so upset the clergy of the god Marduk.

According to conventional oriental thinking, the king was the receptor *par excellence* of oracles.[8] So when Daniel B makes Daniel the beneficiary of prophetic visions, it is not an indifferent matter— independently of the theological suggestion that the Israelite saint is clothed in royal attributes by God—that he is still presented as living at the imperial court. Daniel is the ideal inspired scribe in the monarch's shadow (see Ecclus. 39.1–11). Therefore normally he should have been called with all the other diviners (v.2). Furthermore, it is strange that he should be placed among the magicians whose practices the texts of Scripture are unanimous in condemning,[9] but it is clear that the Author

[5] M. Delcor, *Le Livre de Daniel*, p. 73.
[6] See S. Smith, *Babylonian Historical Texts* (London 1924), p. 44; cf. *ANET* 309f., n. 5; 313; 314b.
[7] See C. J. Gadd, *Anatolian Studies*, VIII (London 1958), p. 63.
[8] See I. Engnell, *Studies in Divine Kingship in the Ancient Near East* (Uppsala 1943), topical index under Divinator; cf. A. Bentzen, op. cit., p. 25.
[9] See Exod. 22.17; Isa. 47.9; etc. Cf. Sib. Or. III, 218–36.

wants 'to play the game' of his own fiction. Hence it would be an error to draw any exegetical–theological conclusions from Daniel's presence among the enchanters. In 2.48; 4.9; and 5.11, he is even their leader.

The ambiguity in v.3 (לדעת את החלום) that the diviners pretend not to understand (v.4) is lifted in v.5. The king has the exorbitant desire (v.10) to hear the exposition of the dream and its interpretation from the mouths of the magicians. This is indubitably the most dramatic and extraordinary element in the story. Oriental parallels of a great king's dream and its interpretation are numerous, but this case of a monarch requiring his magicians to recount the incidents[10] of a royal dream is unique. Moreover, this is what the diviners tell the king (v.10). It would be wrong, however, to dwell exclusively on this characteristic of the popular marvellous tale (the reader expects Daniel's miraculous intervention). A Bentzen[11] reacts against this too narrow a limitation by suggesting that the king had not forgotten his dream, but pretended to do so in order to test his wise men. J. Pedersen[12] points us in the right direction when he writes: 'The unrest is doubly strong, because it comes from his own soul: the dream is fixed in it; the soul has taken a direction which he himself never knows nor controls, because the dream is the manifestation of a context which is strange to him. . . . This must not be understood in the sense that the dream is a kind of allegory, a series of pictures . . . a purely mechanical means of communication from gods to man . . . it does not clash with the psychological process. The dream is a communication from God because it is a direct outcome of reality itself. . . . It is the outcome of the fact that these (seven good and seven bad) years, which Pharaoh shall live to see, already live as a reality in his soul, without his knowing it. He carries these years in his soul, and therefore his soul must create dreams of abundance and hunger.'

Nebuchadnezzar does not 'remember' (*sic*) his dream; in any case he refuses to present its contents because there is a psychological barrier against a revealed truth whose fatal implication he senses.[13] We will return to this point in regard to verse 30. It will suffice for the moment to emphasize the paradoxical, almost exorcistic, meaning of the formula in v.4: 'O king, live for ever!'[14] Certainly, it appears frequently in Akkadian, and we find it used at the Persian court up to the Islamic period;[15] still the present context gives it an unexpected twist.

[10] Whence the plural of the word 'dream' in the Hebrew text.
[11] Op. cit., p. 225.
[12] *Israel, Its Life and Culture* I–II (Copenhagen 1940), pp. 135–6.
[13] 'The secret of redemption lies in remembering' (Baal Shem Tov).
[14] See 3.9; 5.10; 6.7, 22; 1 Kings 1.31; Neh. 2.3.
[15] See J. de Menasce, *Daniel*, p. 26.

The passage from Hebrew to Aramaic in this book[16] is facilitated by the naive comment that the Chaldeans began to speak to the king 'in Aramaic'. Some have taken these words as a marginal indication from a copyist for the use of his colleagues. It then was inserted into the text at some point in error. But several factors oppose this theory: (1) the words in question appear already in the LXX; (2) in the period of the Book of Daniel there was some confusion between 'Chaldean' and 'Aramaic'; (3) Aramaic had been adopted for all purposes as an international language in the Middle East during the seventh century (see 2 Kings 18.26), so it is not anachronistic to put it in the mouths of Nebuchadnezzar's entourage; and (4) J. C. L. Gibson[17] has published the text of the Aramaic papyrus Adon, discovered in 1942 at Saqqara (Memphis) which is a letter sent from Syria or Palestine to the Pharaoh (Necho II) asking his aid against the king of Babylon (Nebuchadnezzar). This letter dates from 603–602 and constitutes one of the oldest Aramaic papyri now known.

In any case, through this naive yet highly practical shift,[18] the Author opens up the possibility of using as such the documents of the Daniel cycle in Aramaic at his disposition (see Introduction).

The punishment decreed by the king, according to v.5, is the cutting in pieces (הדם) of the condemned. This practice is well attested in antiquity; see here 3.29; 2 Macc. 1.16. ... The word occurs frequently in the Talmud and in Syriac. It comes from the Persian *handama*, limb, piece. The second part of the punishment is also habitual, see Ezra 6.11. It is expressed by the word גולי, from the Akkadian for 'to destroy' and it is therefore preferable not to follow Theodotion or the Vulgate which understood 'to confiscate'.[19] Possibly there is an allusion here to the putting to death of the Magus reported in Herodotus III, 77–9.[20] In any case, the royal anger (v.12) has a character of capricious tyranny which led Rinaldi[21] to say that it is almost an attribute of kings (see 1 Sam. 20.20; 2 Sam. 12.5; Esth. 1.12; 7.7). The good sense of the 'Chaldeans'—implicitly admitting their impotence (see Hesiod, frag.

[16] Through chapter 7.
[17] *Textbook of Syrian Semitic Inscriptions*, II, *Aramaic Inscriptions* (Oxford 1975), no. 21, pp. 110–16.
[18] In the first place, the documentation, whether oral or written, underlying Daniel A was certainly in Aramaic which had become the Jews' everyday language. Popular stories in a language which had become a learned language as Hebrew had by the second century BCE are inconceivable. In the second place, as we have shown in our introduction following Ginsberg, the language of the author of Daniel was Aramaic. Those parts of the book which are in Hebrew are translations.
[19] For the meaning of 'manure', see W. Rudolph (HAT) on Ezra 6.11; also see 2 Kings 10.27.
[20] See Montgomery, p. 146; Steinmann, p. 51; and Bentzen, p. 25 ('possible but not certain . . .').
[21] Quoted by M. Delcor, p. 75.

169, quoted by Montgomery, p. 149)—cannot prevail against it. The situation lacks a solution as did that of the readers in the second century. Only a miracle may henceforth solve the crisis. It appears in the person of Daniel (v.13). The Author has artfully earlier characterized the group to which Daniel and his companions belong as 'wise men' (v.12). Hence the scandal indicated above of Daniel's association with diviners and magicians is reduced. In the ambiguous form of Jewish participation in pagan practices, it really is a question of revealing God's plans (see *infra* v.19 and 22), which, in Judaism, is the very function of apocalyptic.

The absence of Daniel and his companions from the confrontation of the wise men and the king has often been noted. However, it is not necessary to draw conclusions on the basis of literary criticism regarding this strange situation when compared with 1.19–20. It is evident that Daniel cannot, even momentarily, be placed in a position of impotence like the others. The reader therefore must imagine meanwhile that he was forgotten by the king or that the triumphal declaration of 1.19–20 anticipated the subsequent unfolding of events.

Text 2. 14–28

(14) Then Daniel made a prudent and measured response to Arioch, the chief of the king's guard who had gone out to slay the wise men of Babylon. (15) He answered Arioch, the king's officer, in these terms: 'Why is the king's sentence so harsh?' Then Arioch made the matter known to Daniel. (16) Therefore Daniel went in and entreated the king to grant him a delay; as for the interpretation, he would set it forth. (17) Then Daniel went home and made known the matter to Hananiah, Mishael, and Azariah, his companions, (18) so that they implored the mercy of the God of the heavens about this mystery and that one would not destroy Daniel and his companions along with the wise men of Babylon. (19) Then the mystery was revealed to Daniel in a nocturnal vision. And Daniel blessed the God of the heavens. (20) Daniel spoke out and said: 'May the name of God be blessed from everlasting unto everlasting, for to him belong wisdom and strength. (21) He is the one who changes the times and the seasons; who overthrows kings and raises up kings; he gives wisdom to the wise men and knowledge to those who have an expert intelligence. (22) He is the one who reveals deep and hidden things, who knows what is in the shadows, and the light dwells with him. (23) To you, God of my fathers, my thanks and praise, for you have given me wisdom and strength and now you have made known to me what we asked of you, since you have made known to us the king's question.' (24) Whereupon Daniel went to Arioch—he whom the king had commanded to destroy the wise men of Babylon—he went and spoke to him in this way: 'Do not destroy the wise men of Babylon, bring me into the presence of the king and

I will set forth the interpretation to the king.' (25) Then Arioch quickly brought Daniel into the king's presence. He said to him: 'I have found among the sons of the deportation from Judah a man who will make known the interpretation to the king.' (26) The king answered Daniel whose name was Belteshazzar in these terms: 'Are you able to make known to me the dream I saw and its interpretation ?' (27) Daniel answered the king in these words: 'The mystery about which the king inquires, no wise man, astrologer, magician, or diviner can set forth before the king. (28) But there is a God in the heavens who reveals mysteries; he has made known to King Nebuchadnezzar what will happen at the end of days. Your dream and the visions (which have struck) your spirit in your bed are as follows.

Critical Notes 2. 14–18

V.14 התיב טעם: a technical term in wisdom. Bentzen, ad loc.: 'in entscheidender Stunde das rechte Wort finden.'—אריוך: concerning this name, see Gen. 14.1; Judith 1.6: it is the Persian name *Ariyauka* (E. Lipinski). But according to R. Zadok (op. cit., p. 246) this name is 'not the same as the much earlier 'rywk in Gen. 14.1,9. Here it comes from the Iranian *Arya-va(h)u-ka* which means 'the good Iranian'.—רב־טבחיא: see 2 Kings 25.8: 'Nebuzaradan, captain of the body guard'. Arab: 'cook', the meaning of the word in 1 Sam. 9.23. But in Gen. 37.36 it is not a question of making Potiphar one of the king's butchers! Ibn Ezra remarks that animals were worshipped in Egypt. LXX and Θ here have 'chief cook', the original sense of the expression.

V.15 מההצפה: in 3.22: מחצפה. In the language of the Targs. and the Talmud, חציף = to be without shame = 'hard (of face)'. Ibn Ezra has 'swift'. Modern translators: 'hard'. The meaning given by Ibn Ezra is that of the Arabic *hasaba* = to get under way, to go quickly. Here the word signifies 'too hasty' (see O. Plöger, p. 46).—Θ omits the beginning of this verse.

V.16 על: from the verb עלל = to enter. In the sense of an audience with the king; see 4.4; 5.8.

V.18 אלה שמיא: see 2.19, 37, 44; cf. מלך שׁ': 4.34; מרא שׁ: 5.23; שׁ = God: 4.23. It is the expression Abraham uses in Gen. 24.7 (a relatively recent text).—רז: this word comes from Persian and is unique to Daniel in the Bible (see Ecclus. 8.18). The μυστήριον of Paul's letters (see 1 Cor. 2.7; etc.).—The LXX adds fasting to Daniel's and his companions' preparations in parallel with 10.3 or Esth. 4; cf. Mark 9.29. This parallel reveals the origin of the Greek addition.

V.19 See Job 4.12–13; Zech. 1.8.

V.20 להוא for יהוה in order to avoid the resemblance to the Tetragrammaton.

41

V.21 יָדְעֵי בִינָה: See Prov. 4.1.

V.22 LXX: 'He knows what is in shadows and what in light, and the solution (of riddles) is found in him.' Probably an allusion to 5.12, 16.

V.23 'Force': LXX has φρόνησις (thought, design).—'Question': Θ has ὅραμα (vision). Re the idea of this verse, see Ecclus. 51.22.

V.24 The preposition עַל gives a dittograph with the verb. It is absent in LXX, Σ, Vul., Syr., and several mss. of Θ.

V.25 בְּהִתְבְּהָלָה: see 3.24; 6.20.

V.26 Kt. הָאִיתַיְ; Qr. הָאִיתָךְ.—בֵּלְטְשַׁאצַר: LXX adds χαλδαϊστί; the mentioning of the Babylonian name clearly is intended to tie this story to chapter 1.

V.27 גָּזְרִין: first appearance in Daniel (lit.: 'those who cut, decide'; perhaps by horoscopes). Misunderstood by Σ, Vul. Akk.: *ashipu* a priest conjurer-exorcist. See E. Dhorme, *Les Religions de Babylonie et d'Assyrie* (Paris 1945), pp. 206–7, 217. This is also the interpretation of A. Dupont-Sommer who refers to the term *gzr* in the Prayer of Nabonidus of Qumran cave IV ('Exorcismes et guérisons dans les écrits de Qoumran'. *Congress Volume* (Oxford 1959, Leyden 1960), pp. 246–61).

V.28 The end of the verse is abridged in the Greek version.—רֵאשָׁךְ: see 4.2, 7, 10; 7.1, 15.—דְּנָא הוּא: A. Bentzen, ad loc., has '*Inkongruenz*', and refers to Cowley, *Aram. Papyri* 22:1, 34:2.

Commentary

The second part of the chapter begins with a note of appreciation for Daniel's natural good sense (v.14). He knows how to be convincing through his level-headedness and tactfulness. Certainly there is something surprising in the facility with which Daniel receives an audience with the king (see *a contrario* Esth. 4.11) and is granted a delay (v.16). But what the story loses here in verisimilitude it regains in terms of rhythm which becomes heart-throbbing. Daniel rushes to Arioch in the palace, then from the palace to his residence (v.17) where he mobilizes his companions to implore divine mercy for the revelation of the mystery (v.18).

Let us note two expressions in this verse which are particularly important in the Book of Daniel. God, on the one hand, is called 'God of heaven' (see our critical notes), and, on the other hand, he is the one who reveals secrets (or mysteries, רָז).[22] Although 'God of heaven' is

[22] The expression certainly also signifies that God is master over astrology, the science of the time (see Num. 24.17; Isa. 45.7).

found already in Gen. 24.7 in the mouth of Abraham, it appears as though we owe Daniel's insistence on this divine title to a Persian influence. With Th. Chary,[23] we think of 'Ahura-Mazda, that supreme divinity whom the reformer Zoroaster (born probably about 660 BCE and perhaps as early as 750) made emerge from the Iranian pantheon in limiting to him alone the quality of God. . . . Cyrus, Cambyses, and Darius I . . . utilized the name of god of heaven for their own sake, which explains why this name occurs fairly frequently in Biblical texts from the Persian period: Neh. 1.4; 2.5, 20; Ezra 1.2; 5.11ff.; 6.9ff.; 7.12, 21, 23; Jonah 1.9; Dan.[24] 2.18; 4.34; 5.23. The sacred writers requisitioned this beautiful name for YHWH.' (We may add to the texts cited, pap. of Aswân [Elephantine, fifth century BCE].) It will be seen that the 'requisition' in question is made all the more easily when the image is not new for Israel, see אלהי מרום in Mic. 6.6 (cf. Isa. 57.5; 58.4; 24.21. Cf. the expression of Canaanite origin אֵל עליון; etc.). In Pseudepigraphic texts, the 'God of heaven' is found in Tobit 10.12; Judith 5.81; 6.19; 11.17.

The constant parallel established by Daniel between the celestial God and the mysterious character of history is remarkable.[25] The manuscripts from Qumran have thrown much light on this conjunction. Their references to 'God's mysteries' (1 QS 3.23; 1 Qp Hab 7.8; 1 QM 3.9; 16.11, 16) concern God's mysterious ways of acting in history to realize his plans, especially for the suppression of evil and iniquity. These mysteries about the divine governing of history were revealed to the prophets and now may be discovered through studying their oracles. See CD 44.10;[26] cf. Dan. 9.

The hymn of praise and blessing which follows (vv.20–3) is not without biblical parallels (see Job 12.1ff.; Ps. 41.14; Neh. 9.5; Esth. 1.13 . . .) but appears as an original composition. It establishes the connection between God's lordship over history and the gift of wisdom to wise men. Porteous (op. cit., ad loc.) notes with H. Kosmala[27] that there is a feature here in common with certain Psalms, Job, and Qumran (see 1 QH and 1 QS).

'May the name of God be blessed from everlasting unto everlasting' is a liturgical expression which became common in the liturgy of the

[23] Th. Chary, *Les Prophètes et le Culte à partir de l'Exil* (Tournai 1955), p. 181.
[24] *Sic!*
[25] See 2.27–30 and 2.28, 37; 3.36, 44, and 45 (in Greek); 4.23 and 24; 4.34 and 33; 5.23 and 24ff. Cf. Wisd. 2.22; 6.22; Ecclus 8.18; 12.11; 11.4 (Syr.: 'marvellous secrets'); Enoch 6.6, see 10.3; 16.3; Book of Mysteries 106.19; 103.1–2; 104.10.
[26] See Annie Jaubert, *La Notion d'Alliance dans le Judaïsme* (Paris 1963), esp. pp. 125–6. Also see 1 Qp Hab 7.5, 8, 14; 'marvellous secrets': 7.8; CD 3.17; 1 QS 4.6, 18; 10.15; 11.5, 19, 20; CD 13.8 (cf. Ps. 119.129, 1 QH 4.27–8). Cf. A. Michel, *Le Maître de Justice* (Avignon 1954), pp. 97–8.
[27] H. Kosmala, *Hebräer, Essener, Christen* (Leyden 1959), p. 222.

synagogue.[28] It is normal that the description of God's deeds follows immediately, for these are what man must recognize and praise (vv.21–3).

'It is God who changes the times and seasons': he changes them for Daniel who, under the menace of death, is going to become the second to the king (v.48) in imitation of Joseph. (There is a new allusion to the story of Joseph in v.25, see Gen. 41.12.) There is a polemic here against Babylonian astrology (see already Jeremiah) and its corollary, the Hellenistic world's concept of 'Fate'. What is profound and hidden (v.22) is revealed to Daniel, since for God shadows are light.[29] Making them visible to men is properly speaking salvific. What Daniel must say to the sovereigns of the nations is never a cause for rejoicing. He announces to them the end of their empire or even of their span of existence. Yet Daniel is invariably repaid with great honours because he makes manifest the light. He makes appear the depths of the soul and will (see v.30), that is, 'the heart's thoughts'!

Now the beginning of this chapter begins to make sense. The king does not force his magicians to undergo a ridiculous test by pretending to make them relate his dream. In reality, the king wants someone else to take his place in order to deliver himself of his own fault.[30] The message of his being is incomprehensible to him. He only knows there is a message because he knows himself to exist. He receives a response to his quest because he seeks it.[31]

Daniel's prayer ends in v.23. It gives us some idea of Jewish liturgies in Aramaic. It seems, everything being taken into account, as if the text was interrupted from v.14 to v.24 without any difficulty. The unity of the language and style with the body of the chapter indicates, however, that it is a question of a later intervention by the same redactor during the second century BCE.[32] We catch his signature in the fact that Daniel is himself a visionary (v. 19) as in Daniel B (chs. 7—12). He is in relation

[28] See also Ps. 41.14; 106.48; 113.2; Neh. 9.5.
[29] See Exod. 24.17; Ezek. 1.27; Hab. 3.4; and above all Isa. 60.19–20 and Wisd. 7.26. In the New Testament, see 1 John 1.5–7; 1 Tim. 6.16; James 1.17. J. de Menasce who cites these texts adds, 'Some ancient Jewish commentators referred to this verse to establish that one of the Messiah's names is "Light" (ad loc.). The Jewish sources in question are *Lam. R.* 36, col. 2 (Vilna edn) and *Psik. R.* on Isa. 60.1 (ed. Friedmann, pp. 161ff.). Also see the beautiful text of Ps. 36.10 (cf. Ps. 56.3; 104.2).
[30] See *Ber.* 55b: 'R. Samuel b. Nahmani said in the name of R. Jonathan, what is shown a man in a dream is something suggested by his own thoughts, as it is said (quotes Dan. 2.29–30). Raba said, this is proved by the fact that no dream has ever shown a man a date palm made of gold or an elephant passing through the eye of a needle!'

56a: 'The emperor (of Rome) said to R. Joshua ben R. Hananyah, You (Jews) pretend to be smart. Tell me what I will dream. He told him you will see the Persians (= the Parthians) reduce you to forced labor, strip you, and force you to impure animals with a gold hook. The emperor thought about this all day long and that night dreamed it.' (Note: Trajan was defeated by the Parthians in 116.)
[31] See Luke 2.35: '. . . that thoughts out of many hearts may be revealed'.
[32] All the more so because it is difficult to reconcile v. 25 with v. 16.

with the One who 'reveals mysteries' (v.28) and who sends 'the visions which appear in one's head' (ibid., cf. 4.2, 7, 18 . . .).[33] It is a question about 'the end of time' (אחרית יומיא). This expression which is common to several books of the Pentateuch and the Prophets[34] comes from Akkadian where it is already eschatological (*ina aḥrât ûmê*), although the term 'eschatological' needs to be nuanced here. It can be used for the first time in its strict sense with regard to Daniel. Previously it would be preferable to speak of teleology.[35] Both terms, however, indicate that God will perfectly communicate his transcendence to men. In this sense, v. 28 is radically opposed to the affirmation of the 'Chaldeans' in v.11, insisting as it does on the non-communication between the divine and the human. Daniel-Israel affirms that God does communicate his transcendence to men, he makes himself immanent for their sake.[36]

Text 2. 29–45

(29) As for you, O king, thoughts came upon you in your bed about what will happen hereafter, and the Revealer of mysteries has made you know what will happen. (30) As for me, it is not that I have some higher wisdom than any other living being if this mystery has been revealed to me, but that the interpretation may be made known to the king and that you should know your heart's thoughts. (31) O king, you have had a vision: Behold a tall statue; that statue was immense and extraordinarily bright. It stood before you and its appearance was terrible. (32) It was a statue whose head was of pure gold, the chest and arms of silver, the belly and thighs of bronze, (33) the legs of iron, and the feet partly iron and partly ceramic. (34) You had this vision until a stone detached itself without the aid of any hand and struck the statue at its feet of iron and ceramic and pulverized them. (35) The iron, ceramic, bronze, silver, and gold were all pulverized and became like chaff arising from the threshing floor in summer which the wind carries away. No trace of it could be found, but the stone which struck the statue became an immense boulder and filled the whole earth. (36) This was your vision and

---

[33] See G. von Rad, *Theology of the Old Testament* I, p. 153, n. 28: the author points out that Daniel is the first biblical book to make the head the site of psychic experiences. See Song of Sol. 4.2; 7.1, 15.

[34] Gen. 49.1; Num. 24.14; Deut. 4.30; 31.29; Isa. 2.2; Jer. 23.20; etc.; Ezek. 38.16; etc. In all fourteen times in Scripture.

[35] Montgomery, ad loc., is correct in pointing out that *before Daniel* the expression is not absolute. But here, it is a question of something more precise than 'the *closing period* of the future so far as it falls within the range of view of the writer using it' (this affirmation—which is erroneous concerning Daniel—is repeated by Heaton, Porteous, etc.). Heaton, however, continues, 'it is similarly the period of the establishment of the Divine Kingdom . . .' and he refers to vv. 34, 35, 44, and 45 (p. 129).

[36] See Norman Snaith, *The Distinctive Ideas of the Old Testament* (London 1944), p. 47.

we will give the interpretation in the king's presence. (37) You, O king, you are the king of kings to whom the God of the heavens has given the reign, power, force, and glory. (38) In whatever place the sons of men, the animals of the fields, and the birds of the air dwell, he has given them into your hands and made you to rule over them all. You are the head of gold. (39) And after you, another kingdom inferior to you will arise. Then another, a third kingdom, the one of bronze which will rule over all the earth. (40) Then will come a fourth kingdom hard as iron, for just as iron pulverizes and hammers everything, as iron crushes everything, it will pulverize and crush. (41) Since you saw the feet and toes as partly of pottery ceramic and partly of iron, this kingdom will be divided. It will have in it the solidity of iron because you saw the iron mixed with ceramic made from clay. (42) As for the toes of the feet partly of iron and partly of ceramic, one part of this kingdom will be strong and one part will be fragile. (43) Since you saw the iron mixed with ceramic made from clay, they will mix through the human seed, but they will not be attached to each other, since iron does not mix with ceramic. (44) During the times of these kings, the God of the heavens will set up a kingdom which will never be destroyed and whose reign will never pass over to another people. It will pulverize and wipe out all these other kingdoms and it will be set up for ever. (45) Just as you saw that from the rock a stone was cut out without the aid of any hand and that it pulverized the iron, bronze, ceramic, silver, and gold, so the great God will make known to the king what will happen, this dream is sure and its interpretation is certain.'

Critical Notes 2. 29–41

V.29 רעיוניך: see רעיון לבו in Eccles. 1.17; 2.22; Dan. 2.30.

V.30 See Gen. 41.16.—לבבך: see Dan. 4.13 (2x); 5.21; 7.4, 28; 10.12 and many pseudepigraphic texts (see D. S. Russell, op. cit., p. 397).

V.31 שניא: del. in Θ. The LXX attaches the word to what follows it, thanks to a different punctuation.—רוה: Canaanite origin, see BLea, par. 1t, 51K'.—ואלו צלם חד: Slotki, ad loc., thinks of the construct: 'The great image of a human being'.

V.32 See Song of Sol. 5.14.

V.33 חסף: cf. LXX, Θ: ὀστράκινον. To be distinguished from טינא = clay. The חסף might therefore be a ceramic decoration on the statue, but it is located in a poor place, where the statue is weakest (Montgomery).

V.34 Here the Greek adds, on the model of v.45: ἐξ ὄρους (=מטורא).

V.35 The reverse order of the materials should be noted.—כעור מן אדרי־קיט: Bentzen refers to Dalman, *Arbeit und Sitte*, III (1933), pp. 67, 76, 138. See Ps. 1.4.

V.36 נאמר: Daniel and God? (cf. v.28). Rather: Daniel and his companions (see vv.17–18). See Rashi: 'me and his Spirit' [cf. Acts 15.28]. He says it is plural of majesty (דרך מוסר) [cf. 1 Cor. 1.6].

V.37 *Casus pendens*, see v.38; 3.22; 4.17–19; Ezra 5.14. See *Papyri of Elephantine* 28.15 ('my sons will pay you that money'); *j. Kilaim* 9.4 (= 32b, line 47).

V.38 LXX: ἐν πάσῃ τῇ οἰκουμένῃ.

V.39 אחרי: omitted by Θ and Vul.

V.40 Bentzen: like the iron which breaks, it will break up all the preceding kingdoms. This reading is correctly rejected by Y. Kaufmann who says that in this case the feet of the statue break up the statue, i.e., the preceding kingdom; then the stone breaks the statue, which is absurd. The LXX, Θ, and Vul. versions yield the text: כלא) כל־קבל די פרזלא מהדק וחשל כלה כלא תקד ותרע instead of (כל אלן): the iron will destroy everything (= the whole earth).— חשל: signifies in late Aramaic: the blacksmith's hammer; in Syriac: to forge metal.

V.41 טינא and די פחד are omitted by Θ. They appear to be part of later glosses.—דאצבעתא: omitted by LXX. Moreover, this trait is not given in the description of the dream. But H. H. Rowley has indicated parallels to this 'snowball style' in the rest of the book (see 4.27 and 33; 7.7 and 19; 8.5 and 21), so we are led to see here a characteristic trait of the Maccabean redactor (see *JTS*, 38 (1937), pp. 426–7; *JBL* (1950), p. 202 'addition of afterthoughts'). This is a further confirmation that the fourth kingdom is Greek. But we must say, with G. von Rad, *Theology*, II, p. 311, that the application to Antiochus IV and his times of an image antedating Daniel is carried out with difficulty.

Commentary

The third part of this chapter begins with v.29. There are several elements in this verse which parallel v.28 and Montgomery, for one, thinks they may reflect very old doublets.

The content of the dream is finally exposed beginning with v.31. The king had seen a huge composite statue, a colossus which makes one think of that at Rhodes or at Thebes. This is what differentiates the statue from the stele in chapter 3. Nabonides, whose importance we have already indicated for the comprehension of certain details in chapter 2, had, as the reader will recall, erected a statue of Sin in Babylon. From another perspective, Herodotus (I, 183) mentions the presence in Babylon of an enormous statue of Bel. Thus the actual models which may have inspired the author are numerous and varied.

Jean Steinmann[37] has written a significant statement concerning Nebuchadnezzar's statue:

Rarely has the synthetic genius of the Bible, which tends to reduce the diversity of different beings to unity, shone forth any better than in the description of this dream. We know that, in Genesis, each people and each race is represented by an eponymous ancestor. And all of humanity is united in Adam. In the time of the apocalypses, the Messiah plays the role of the New Adam. In him, humanity rediscovers its lost unity. Now in Nebuchadnezzar's dream all human empires are brought together in a single symbolic empire which is one in space—because it is deemed to cover the world—and time—because the different dynasties just add up to a single statue. Furthermore, the idea of representing the cosmos in human form was familiar to Egyptian astrologers. Daniel adds to it the course of History which also becomes a man or the image of a man.

We may see a Greek influence in the division of the statue into four parts (vv.32–3). Hesiod (*Works and Days,* 109–201) and Ovid (*Metamorphoses* I, 89–150) speak of a succession of the ages of the world as a process of degeneration: gold-silver-bronze-iron. In the Bible, this idea also appears in Gen. 4, Zech. 1 (the four horses), and Zech. 2 (the four blacksmiths), etc. But we need to emphasize as M. Noth[38] does, that what fundamentally distinguishes Scripture from its environment is the idea that the hand of God is visibly at work in the history of Israel and the nations (v.34). Underlying the empires is an insatiable will to domination; this is why they contain within themselves the seed of their destruction: 'the feet partly of iron and partly of ceramic' (v.33). A small stone is all that is needed to overthrow the edifice of static constructions.

Although it might seem premature to comment here on vv.44–5, it should be noted that the message implied by די לא בידין (v.34) is that God acts independently of human politics, including undoubtedly that of the Maccabees, which moreover is qualified as being 'of little help' in Dan. 11.34.[39] They will not fill the gap produced by the disappearance of the empires, but the stone become a mountain will (v.35).[40] Here, once again, the symbolism is sufficient by itself (see Ps. 103.16; Isa. 11.9). But its richness is not exhausted by the image. The interpretation given in vv. 44–5 emphasizes its meaning.

[37] *Daniel,* p. 49.
[38] M. Noth, 'Das Geschichtverständnis der alttestamentlichen Apokalyptik,' *Gesammelte Studien zum Alten Testament* (Munich 1960)².
[39] 'For history shows that everything begins in mysticism and ends in politics' (Péguy).
[40] Which in no way means that the Kingdom inaugurated by God will be independent of Israel. On the contrary, see v. 44: 'the reign will never pass over to another people'; v. 46: 'then King Nebuchadnezzar fell on his face before Daniel' (as the representative of Israel).

The Canaanites, as is well known, situated the mountain home of their pantheon in the North. Its name was *spn*.[41] For Israel, God (Isa. 14.13) ruled from this mountain which Ps. 48.2–3 audaciously identifies with Zion. Consequently, the symbolism of the Mountain is applied to Israel (see Isa. 2.2–3; Zech. 4.7; 14.10; Ps. 36.7; 50.2; and above all Ezek. 17.23; 20.40; 40.2).

As the place of the theophany, the holy mountain, despite its insignificance in Nebuchadnezzar's eyes, constitutes the centre of history and space: 'It filled the whole earth' (v.35). The meaning of this expression, we believe, is not that the mountain crushes everything beneath itself, but rather that it occupies its proper place on earth, which is to say, everywhere. The whole earth hides Zion, every ארץ conceals הארץ (see Isa. 11.9). The Boulder fills the earth as 'the waters fill the sea basin'. Such an absence of dualism is emphasized by v.37, for example. Before considering its content, however, we need to emphasize the use in v.35 of the word טור (boulder; in Hebrew: צור), which in Scripture is always associated with the divine presence (see Num. 20.8; Deut. 32.4, 15, 18, 30, 31, cf. v.13; Isa. 8.14; 17.10; 44.8; 51.1; etc.). It is also associated with the Exodus from Egypt; so perhaps there is a quiet allusion to the Exodus in Dan. 2.35. In any case, what fills the earth is the Boulder of the theophany; that is, following the explication furnished by vv.44–5, the Kingdom of God. That this kingdom should be associated with Israel (v.44, see *supra*) is all the more striking.

The explanation of the dream which begins in v.36 implies a fourfold division of history. The number four is certainly traditional, for as O. Plöger points out, the author would have been more at ease if he could have apportioned history into five chapters (op. cit., p. 53). We possess literary sources from the second century[42] where the division into periods follows the same fourfold scheme: Assyria-Media-Persia[43]-Greece.[44] It became classic during this period, says Martin Noth (op. cit., pp. 194–214), who refers to Polybius (*History* XXXVIII, 22).

[41] See the texts from Ugarit 51: IV:19; V:117; 49: I:28, 34 (Anat I, 21.22). Cf. O. Eissfeldt, *Baal Zaphon, Zeus Kasios und der Durchzug der Israeliten durchs Meer* (Halle 1932), pp. 20ff.

[42] See here Dan. 7.

[43] The number 'four' plays an important role in Zoroastrianism.

[44] See the Greek Ctesias, the doctor of Artaxerxes II, who, while studying Persian history, first occupied himself with the Assyrian Empire, then with the Median Empire and only then with the Persian Empire. It has been demonstrated, says H. L. Ginsberg, *Studies*, p. 5, that the initial source of this theory of the four monarchies is to be found in the trimonarchic doctrine of the Achaemenids (Darius I–Xerxes–Artaxerxes = 521–424), which held that the great Assyrian Empire had become the inheritance of the Medes and then of the Persians. To these three empires, Alexander the Great added a fourth, the Macedonian. 'However, the disgruntled non-Hellenic peoples of western Asia cherished a hope that the fourth would be followed by yet a fifth native Oriental, monarchy.'

Daniel, however, replaces the Assyrians by the Babylonians. It looks as though this substitution is due to the perspective of a Judean whose country had been conquered by Babylon and not by Assyria. According to Ginsberg, this explains 'the absurd sequence Chaldean kingdom—Median kingdom . . . upon which the chronology of the whole book is predicated'.[45]

King Nebuchadnezzar is identified with the gold head (v.37, cf. v.38).[46] He is called 'king of kings' in imitation of the Persian kings (see Ezra 7.12). But we also find this title applied in a gloss to Nebuchadnezzar in Ezek. 26.7 and it is equivalent to the Akkadian title *šar šarrani*. It is not here necessarily anachronistic therefore,[47] although rather reflecting a situation typical of the Achaemenids. More impressive is the mention in v.38 of the royal domination over 'the animals of the fields and the birds of the air'. There is no doubt that we here have a reference to the myth of the primitive man. The Babylonian kings generally pretended that they ruled over the savage beasts and the wild birds. They kept animals captured while hunting in menageries, probably as symbols of their universal domination.[48] At the base of this practice is certainly the repetition of the myth of the primitive man as dominant over the animals. This feature belonged to the New Year liturgy at Babylon, of which we will speak again in chapter seven. In dependence upon Mesopotamian tradition, Genesis too makes Adam dominant over the whole of creation (see 1.28; 2.19–20). The LXX even adds to our verse in Daniel a mention of the 'fish of the sea', which is further proof that the relation between our text and creation was established very early. It is also present in Ps. 8.7–9; 1 Baruch 3.16; and above all in Jer. 27.6 and 28.14 upon which Dan. 2.38 is based.

Clearly nothing could be more flattering to Nebuchadnezzar than to hear himself compared to the primordial king, the perfect man from the time of origins. Yet v.38 is aimed at another goal, to show that, in speaking about the Babylonian Empire, the Author is really speaking about the dawn of time. Daniel combines the motif of the first Adam, the first king, with that of the three empires plus one. Like his master Jeremiah, he identifies Nebuchadnezzar with the 'first man' on the basis of a functional analogy: universal domination. In chapter seven, we find the same procedure applied to the 'son of man'. In the end he will be the cosmic dominator and will be so absolutely.[49] Between this beginning (here Nebuchadnezzar) and end (here the 'stone', in chapter

---

[45] Ibid., p. 5.
[46] On the basis of Jer. 27.6ff; cf. 51.7.
[47] It should be noted, however, that the successors to Alexander bore the title κύριος βασιλέων.
[48] See Slotki, op. cit. ad loc.
[49] For example, 7.14 and 7.27 reproduce more or less faithfully the terms of 2.37–8.

seven, the 'son of man'), all the kingdoms of history are just a single undertaking doomed to destruction. There is no place here for speculation[50] on the fact that the four empires did not really succeed one another since they are all rolled up into one. There is really just one long idolatrous kingdom and 'four' reigns, as emphasized by Y. Kaufmann.[51] This unity of the idolatrous empire indicates, from another point of view, that the Kingdom of God is contemporaneous with the events described even though it is spoken of as a future reality.

The second reign (v.39), in the historical scheme adopted by the Author, is the Median Empire.[52] It is distinguished from the Persian Empire (the third reign) whose scope had exceeded everything the ancient Near East had previously known.

The fourth empire is Greek. Alexander the Great founded it in a splendid achievement, but its unity was ephemeral (see the following verses). Perhaps the 'toes of the feet' in v.42 refer to the Greek kings who succeeded Alexander. However that may be, we find interesting parallels to our text in chapters 7 (see v.7, 23–4), 8 (vv.5ff.; 21ff.), and 11 (vv.3ff.). Begun as an iron mass, this empire ends up as an impossible mixture with mud. They are the Seleucids (the iron?) and the Ptolemies (the clay?) who directly affected Jewish history.

A. Jepsen has devoted several important 'remarks' to the problem of the sources of Dan. 2.[53] He sees in vv.41–3 a fragment of a gloss which, as such, overloads the context.[54]

Reconstructing the text without the later glosses gives:

(41b):   the kingdom will be divided, part of it will be as strong as iron, and as you saw the feet, part will be iron and part clay.

(42b):   Part of the kingdom will be strong and part fragile, as you saw the iron mixed with the clay.

(43aβ):   And they will mix through the seed of man and not hold together as iron does not mix with clay.

---

[50] For example, as in H. L. Ginsberg, op. cit., pp. 6ff.

[51] The word means power, kingdom, supremacy (empire), but also *reign* (see G. Dalman, *Worte Jesu*, pp. 75ff.). We may also refer to the very nature of the image used by the author, as does McNamara. The statue is not destroyed piece by piece, but as a single entity: 'This final kingdom is said to destroy all the preceding ones, as if the four still existed at its inauguration. This is a detail required by the nature of the image and not by its meaning. In 39ff. the kingdoms are said to arise successively.' *A New Catholic Commentary on Holy Scripture* (London 1969), p. 656.

[52] According to 6.1, 'Darius the Mede' took power after the last Babylonian king. Daniel sometimes speaks conjointly of Medes and Persians (5.28; 6.9, 13, 16; 8.20), but he also sometimes distinguishes them (6.1; 9.1 in relation to 1.21).

[53] A. Jepsen, 'Bemerkungen zum Danielbuch,' *VT*, XI (1961), pp. 386–91.

[54] Jepsen's proposed solution is an elegant reply to H. H. Rowley's criticism that the suppression of the expression 'and the toes' in 2.41a, as well as in verses 41b–43, is an 'emasculation' ('The Unity . . .', p. 252).

Jepsen continues: the image of the feet is explained in the present form of the text in three different ways. Only the first is original and it probably dates from the time following the division of Alexander's empire (fourth-third centuries). The fourth empire is divided, yet something of the strength of iron remains in it. The Kingdom of God is close, but its coming is delayed, so the second explanation (v.42b) puts the day of reckoning off a bit longer: the accent is now placed on the weakness of the alloy of iron and clay. This may reflect a judgement on the Ptolemaic kingdom.[55] The third putting off of the coming of the Kingdom into the future, v.43a, shows that the ties between two entities so different from each other cannot last. There is a reference here to the rupture between Syria and Egypt (second century) despite the inter-marriages between Ptolemies and Seleucids mentioned in v.43 and recalled again in ch. 11 (252 and 193 BCE). J. A. Montgomery (p. 190) recalls that Alexander the Great had inaugurated a political programme for fusing the races without any parallel in ancient history. We may also follow H. H. Rowley here and think of the number of mixed marriages among Hellenized Jews in the second century. For the Author, these are not a divinely inspired means of unification.[56] It is this contrast between comparable terms with opposing values which v.44 emphasizes. Between the statue and the stone there is the conflict between kingdoms made by human hands and the Kingdom of God. Yet this latter kingdom is not an extraterrestrial kingdom, for its reign will not pass over to another *people*.[57]

It is striking that in a book so decidedly oriented toward perspectives on the end, its eschatology should be so little marked by Messianic features. They are not completely absent, however. The stone, mentioned in vv.34–5 and interpreted in v.44 as the Kingdom of God, belongs to the Messianic sphere. This follows from Gen. 28.10–22,[58] and above all from one text so abundantly reused by Daniel, Gen. 49.24. God, as the 'rock of Israel', supports Joseph.[59]

Verse 45 is in parallel with several texts in Daniel (see 8.26; 11.2;

[55] Jepsen here follows Rowley's reading. If v. 43 refers to the marriage between Cleopatra, the daughter of Antiochus III, and Ptolemy V, v. 42 places us in the immediately preceding period, that is, at the time of the superiority of Antiochus III who imposed this marriage on Ptolemy V. The plan behind this union failed—see Dan. 11.17—when Cleopatra the Seleucid chose to support her adopted country, Ptolemaic Egypt. This fact is deliberately overlooked by H. L. Ginsberg. See 'The Composition . . .', p. 251.

[56] All the more so because they are opposed to the prophetic promise as, for example, in Jer. 31.27–8.

[57] See Dan. 7.13, 18, 27.

[58] The stone Jacob set up as a *maṣebah* to commemorate the opening up of the gate of heaven.

[59] See Isa. 28.16; Zech. 3.9; Ps. 118.22; etc.

12.7) and with Scripture in general (see Job 34.19–20). The title 'the Great God' is somewhat unexpected but perfectly in order in a dialogue between a Jew and a pagan. It is also found in the letter of the satraps of Darius concerning the reconstruction of the Temple, called 'the house of the great God' in Ezra 5.8.

Text 2. 46–49

(46) Then King Nebuchadnezzar fell on his face and worshipped Daniel. He commanded that an oblation and perfumes be offered to him. (47) The king spoke to Daniel in these words: 'It is the truth that your God is the God of gods and the Master of kings, he reveals mysteries, since you could reveal this mystery.' (48) Then the king elevated Daniel and gave him many rich presents, he put him in charge of the whole province of Babylon and (made him) the chief prefect of all the wise men in Babylon. (49) Daniel made a request to the king, and he commanded that the administration of the province of Babylon be given to Shadrach, Meshach, and Abed-Nego. As for Daniel, he remained at the king's Door.

Critical Notes 2. 46–49

V.46 מנחה: avoided by *A* and *Σ* which translate δῶρα.—סגד: is used for the worship of the statue in 3.5, 6.

V.47 אלה אלהין: see 11.36: אל אלים; see Deut. 10.17; Ps. 136.2; 50.1; Josh. 22.22; cf. Qumran, 'Sayings of Moses' II:1–2, frag. 18. See Carmignac in *RQ*, vol. 4, pp. 91–2. In I Q Gen Ap (in Aramaic; 1st century CE), God is frequently called 'Lord and master of the universe and of all the kings of the earth' (20.12–13; see 22.16, 21–2; 20. 14–15). Nabonidus calls the moon-god Sin 'king of the gods', 'Lord of lords' (Gadd, op. cit., p. 59, etc.; *ANET*, pp. 311ff.). According to Ezek. 26.7; 7.12 (cf. Deut. 10.17), 'lord of kings' was a title given to sovereigns. On the universality of the divine reign, see 2 Chron. 20.6; 2 Kings 19.15; Zech. 14.9; Ps. 46.11; 47.3, 8; 67.5; 95.3; 99.1; Esth. (Vul.) 14.12; 2 Macc. 3.24; 7.9; 12.15; etc.— מן יציב = מן קשט of 2.8.

V.49 'At the Door': LXX: ἐν αὐλῇ (at court) is a good translation, as in Esth. 2.19, for example. On the Door, see Esth. 2.21; 3.2, 3; 4.2; 5.9, 13; 6.10; Wisdom of Aḥikar, III, 32–48. To stand at the Door is the position of court counsellor.

Commentary

The last part of chapter 2 begins in v.46 with a surprising feature: the

53

Author makes Nebuchadnezzar prostrate himself before Daniel.[60] The terms used are those of the sacerdotal vocabulary as, for example, in Lev. 1—7. The verb נסך properly signifies the pouring out of libations. The 'perfumes' here designate incense (in contrast to Ezra 6.10). It is clear that, for the Author, Daniel represents his people; before it, according to the prophets, the pagan powers must fall down and lick the dust.[61] It is not advisable to oppose v.46 and Acts 14.11ff.

It is really necessary to replace this verse in its *Sitz im Leben*. Alexander the Great and his enlightened successors practised a liberal religious policy; YHWH was recognized as a god as were others. The 'Nebuchadnezzar' of Dan. 2 reflects this situation. But, in a parallel development, the evolution of this policy also went in the direction of a divinization of the Hellenistic kings. More and more they had themselves worshipped as divine epiphanies. Dan. 2.46 'demythologizes' this practice: a 'god' (the king) worships a man (Daniel). Perhaps, within the perspective of the pogrom led by Antiochus IV, we might also risk the suggestion that for the Author of Daniel there can be no 'neutral' attitude toward Israel. Either one persecutes Israel and seeks its life (the beginning of ch. 2), or one honours it as God's special representative (the end of ch. 2).

The literary parallels to the elevation of Daniel and his companions described in vv.48–9 are numerous and varied. One thinks of Joseph (Gen. 41.37–44) or of Mordecai (Esth. 8.1–2). On this point, wisdom literature is formal. 'For the maxim-writers, the content of reward is "life", to which is attached that which invests life with worth, namely wealth, honour, the good name, and the continuance of a man's "name" or life, in his posterity . . . "Righteousness saves from death" (Prov. 11.4). With this simple and less particularized picture drawn by the proverb-writers, the Book of Deuteronomy has a close connection.'[62]

Verse 49 is not a literary success. It indicates that Daniel stands ready to counsel the king (see our critical notes regarding 'the Door'), but that, at his request, the administration properly speaking of the

---

[60] This scandalous element is taken at face value by the Rabbis (see *Sanh.* 93a) who use it to explain Daniel's absence in chapter 3—the same king could not have thrown him into the fiery furnace.

[61] See Isa. 45.11–24 (especially v. 14; cf. 4.23: to prostrate oneself before Israel is to prostrate oneself before God); Isa. 49.23; 60.14; cf. 43.3–4; Zech. 8.23; etc. See also Josephus, *Ant.* XI, VIII, 5: Alexander the Great prostrated himself before Simon the High Priest. It is of further interest that he explained his action to Parmenion by saying, 'It is not him (Simon) I was worshipping, but the God who honoured him with the office of High Priest.' As regards Dan. 2.46, this is also what Jerome understood: '*Non tam Danielem quam in Daniele adorat Deum*' (quoted by Montgomery, ad loc.).

[62] See O. S. Rankin, *Israel's Wisdom Literature* (Edinburgh 1964), p. 78.

province of Babylon was assigned to his three companions. This explains Daniel's absence in the next chapter. Daniel is not personally concerned because he renounced his political charges for the profit of Shadrach, Meshach, and Abed-Nego.[63]

[63] Hence he may have been somewhere far from the province of Babylon where the events of chapter 3 took place. The Talmud, to indicate that the slave always stands in relation to his master and that he represents him everywhere, quotes that 'Daniel was at the King's Door' (wherever he actually was), see *Erubin* 73a.

3 The Crematory Oven

Text 3. 1–7

(1) King Nebuchadnezzar made a gold statue. It was sixty cubits tall and six cubits wide. He set it up in the valley of Dura in the province of Babylon. (2) King Nebuchadnezzar sent to gather the satraps, prefects, governors, counsellors, treasurers, magistrates and police commissioners, and all the province chiefs so that they would come for the dedication of the statue which King Nebuchadnezzar had set up. (3) Then all the satraps, prefects, governors, counsellors, treasurers, magistrates and police commissioners, and all the province chiefs gathered for the dedication of the statue which King Nebuchadnezzar had set up. They stood before the statue which Nebuchadnezzar had set up. (4) The herald cried loudly: 'To you, of every people, nation, and language, it is said: (5) At the time you hear the sound of the horn, the flute, the lyre, the sambuca, the psalterium, the bag pipe, and of every sort of musical instrument, you will prostrate yourselves and worship the gold statue which King Nebuchadnezzar has set up. (6) Whoever does not prostrate himself and does not worship will immediately be thrown into a crematory oven.' (7) Whereupon, the moment that all the peoples heard the sound of the horn, the flute, the lyre, the sambuca, the psalterium, and of every sort of musical instrument, of every people, nation, and language, they all prostrated themselves and worshipped the gold statue which King Nebuchadnezzar had set up.

Critical Notes 3. 1–7

V.1 LXX: 'The eighteenth year'. Borrowed from Jer. 52.29. Consequently the erection of the statue is a commemoration of the destruction of Jerusalem and of the Temple (see 2 Kings 25.8; Jer. 52.12). This trait is further emphasized by the addition 'having subdued towns, provinces, and all the inhabitants of the earth, from India to Ethiopia' (see Esth. 1.1; 8.9; 3 Esdras 3.2).— 'Sixty cubits . . . six cubits': 30 metres by 3 metres!—'Dura': Θ: Deira; probably a region near Babylon. In any case, not Dura-Europos on the Euphrates.—'a gold statue': a stele covered with bas-reliefs.—'King Nebuchadnezzar': is here the literary type of the persecuting, divinized tyrant (see Judith 3.8; 6.2). He symbolizes the conflict of authority between God and Caesar (see Acts 5.29).

V.2 אחשדרפניא: cf. 'satarpanu' on the lists from Sargon II speaking of Median chiefs. It became a technical term during the Persian period (O. Plöger refers to Ed. Meyer, *Geschichte des Altertums*, IV/1, p. 45, n. 2). It is identical with the old Persian '*kshathrapân*' = 'protector of the kingdom'. The word appears three times in chapter 3 and six times in chapter 6 (vv.2, 3, 4, 5, 7, 8) in Aramaic. —סגניא: see 2.48; Aramaic form of the Assyrian *sǎknu*.—פחותא: see R. H. Charles, op. cit., p. 61: from the Assyrian *(bel) pahati* = 'a chief of a district'; cf. the Hebrew פחה (Neh. 5.14; etc.).— אדרגזריא: Persian: *andarzaghar*. Cf. v.3—גדבריא: Persian *ganzabara* = גזבר in Ezra 1.8; 7.21. See Schäder, *Iran. Beit.* I, 47f.— דתבריא: Persian: *databar*; cf. v.3—תפתיא: Persian *tipati*: police commissioner? Cf. Elephantine *typty*'. (Communication E. Lipinski.)

V.4 See Esth. 1.22; 3.12; 8.9; cf. Rev. 5.9; 7.9; 10.11; 11.9; 13.7; 14.6; 17.15; see Isa. 66.18; Judith 3.8; etc.—כרוזא: is according to Marti, e.g., an Aramaic word on a root כרז one finds in the haphel form in Dan. 5.29. However, only the haphel is utilized in Talmudic Hebrew as well, an invitation to see here a denominative verb formed on the noun *karoza*', from the Greek κῆρυξ. (Communication E. Lipinski.)

V.5 קרן = קרנא = κέρας, an instrument made from horn, wood, or metal. It is already mentioned in the letters from El Amarna (14th century BCE). See Josh. 6.5; 1 Chron. 25.5; Dan. 3.5, 7, 10, 15.— משרוקיתא = συρισμός = flute (of a shepherd, used to call his flock; see Judg. 5.16: שרקות). It could be made from reeds, wood, or bone, and had a sharp tone.—קיתרס = κιθάρα. Only in this chapter. Strictly non-religious. An Asiatic variant of the zither (כינור, the most noble of instruments). It had a minimum of three strings and a maximum of twelve. An aristocratic instrument, it was often made of precious metal or ivory.—סבכא = σαμβύκη. Only in Dan. 3. A Syrian instrument with a bad reputation among the Greeks: poor musicians and prostitutes played it (Macrobius, *Satires*, III, 14, 7). Plato forbad it (*Rep.* III, 399f.). No sure picture of it is known.—פסנתרין = ψαλτήριον = in Persian and Arabic: *santir*. Only in Dan. 3. This instrument is found throughout the eastern Mediterranean world from the first millennium BCE. It consists of ten strings stretched across a resonating drum which are plucked with a small pick.—סומפוניא = συμφωνία. With the sense of a musical instrument the word first appears in Polybius about 200. See Polybius XXVI:10; XXXI:4 (Antiochus IV brought shame on himself by dancing to the sound of this instrument). Probably a bagpipe—זני: plural construct of *zn*, Persian, *zana* = sort; it was taken up into Aramaic very early. See 2 Chron. 16.14.

V.7 The list of musical instruments as in vv.5, 10, 15, except for the absence here of the סומפוניא, which is usually inserted in the text on the basis of 'mlt. MSS Θ var. Vul.' (see B.H., ad loc.).

CHAPTER 3

Commentary

In this chapter where Daniel does not appear,[1] the agadic part of the book continues. Dating it depends above all, at least as regards its final redaction, upon the presence of terms which have a Greek origin. It is true that the LXX adds in verse 1 the words 'the eighteenth year of Nabuchodonosor', that is 587. For the LXX, the erection of the royal statue is an act commemorating the ruin of Jerusalem. However, if there is here a possible indication that the story originated in the sixth century, it is clear that the musical instruments mentioned several times in this chapter point toward a much later date. In fact, it is within the context of the persecution of the Jews by Antiochus IV and the installation in the Temple of the 'abomination of desolation' (1 Macc. 1.54; Dan. 9.27, 11.31) that our chapter gets all its meaning. It is an exhortation to martyrdom (cf. 1 Macc. 1.57, 60–3; 2 Macc. 6.9–11, 18, 31; 7). Perhaps the miraculous salvation of the young men who emerge from the furnace unharmed is not unrelated to the announcement of the resurrection as we find it in Daniel B (see 12.1–3; cf. the use of Dan. 3 in primitive Christian art).

As regards the unity of this chapter, its impressive structure adds to this possibility. In fact, we are reminded of a liturgical text with its deliberate and balanced repetitions, its key words which call up other key terms, and its step by step progression. In this chapter the Author demonstrates a true mastery of this domain which recalls to us the ties which later existed between the apocalyptic milieu and the rebellious sacerdotal community at Qumran.[2] The 'concatenating' style is all the more successful here because it is a question of the cultic inauguration of an idol by King Nebuchadnezzar.

Due to the fact of its independent existence in oral tradition, it is not surprising that Daniel 3 presents a Nebuchadnezzar whose state of mind is quite different from that presented at the end of chapter 2. The redactor responsible for the joining together of these two stories may have realized that the contrast thus established between the two kinds of royal attitudes could only help his overall purpose.

The statue (or rather, the stele; see our critical notes) may not represent the king, but perhaps, to cite one example, the god Marduk;[3]

[1] Chapter 6 offers a parallel story where Daniel is the hero. His absence here is one indication that the legend reported by this chapter originally existed independently.
[2] See our Introduction: 'The Formative Milieu of the Apocalypses'.
[3] Hippolytus of Rome (quoted by M. Delcor, op. cit., p. 91) offers the seductive idea that the king wanted to construct the statue he had seen in his dream (chapter 2). He had become intoxicated by the interpretation of the gold head as representing him. Jerome also thought of a statue representing the king (Migne, *PL*, vol. 25, col. 505).

yet, even in this case, we must remember that the Babylonian king was the god's right hand man.[4] The absence of any formal identification is not necessarily a weakness for this chapter. In the words of Y. Kaufmann,[5] 'two stories illustrate Israel's struggle against idolatry in an especially striking manner: the golden calf—stigmatizing Israel's idolatry (Exod. 32)—and the later one about the statue set up by Nebuchadnezzar (Dan. 3), describing pagan cults . . . (In both cases), idolatry is just the cultus rendered to a nameless idol, which represents no god, and which is worshipped for itself. Even in an epoch as late as the Persian and Syro-Greek period, the Jews' behaviour with regard to idolatry was still determined by the belief that pagans worshipped idol-fetishes.'[6] In any case, the stele represents the empire and is the manifestation of a grotesque hubris.[7]

The administrative functions described in v.2 are difficult to identify. They are almost all Persian in origin and therefore represent a tradition going back to Persian rule over the territory of Israel. Yet among the musical instruments enumerated in v.5, the absence of percussion instruments—a feature of Greek, not oriental orchestras—and the division into string and wind instruments should be noted.[8] Some critics have thought that a blasphemous parody of the sounding of the horn on Jewish New Year's day is intended.[9]

The first literary reference to $\psi\alpha\lambda\tau\acute{\eta}\rho\iota\upsilon$ is found in Aristotle; and to the $\sigma\upsilon\mu\phi\omega\nu\acute{\iota}\alpha$ in Plato, but in the sense of harmony. As a musical instrument, it is attested to by Polybius (c. 200–118) who even says that Antiochus IV shocked public opinion by dancing to the wild sounds of the $\sigma\upsilon\mu\phi\omega\nu\acute{\iota}\alpha$. Thus the Maccabean period constitutes the *terminus a quo* for Dan. 3.[10]

Against this interpretation, see Dan. 3.12, 14, 18 (but cf. LXX at v.12; for the Alexandrian translator, who was influenced by the self-divinization practised by some Hellenistic kings, the statue represented Nebuchadnezzar).

[4] In particular, during the New Year festival.

[5] Y. Kaufmann, *Connaître la Bible* (transl. from the Hebrew) (Paris 1970), p. 23.

[6] See N. Porteous, op. cit., p. 56: 'The polemic . . . meets the challenge of paganism with the weapons of ridicule and satire. . . .' See such texts as Deut. 4.28; 28.36, 64; 29.16; Jer. 10.5; Dan. 5.23. . . .

[7] See J. Steinmann, op. cit., p. 30: 'Never in any other inspired writing do we find any witness to such a profound consideration of the nature of arrogance, the essential characteristic of all tyranny.'

[8] See the discussion on 'Musical Instruments of Israel' by Ovid R. Sellers, in *The Biblical Archaeologist Reader*, ed. G. E. Wright and D. N. Freedman (New York 1961), p. 93. For other, more classically Israelite lists, see Ps. 150 or 2 Chron. 13.8; 15.19.

[9] See N. Porteous, op. cit., p. 58.

[10] See A. Bentzen, op. cit., p. 38. The alluvial deposits continued beyond this date, as the two Greek versions (and the secondary versions based upon them) bear witness. There is, for example, a prayer by the three companions in the furnace (vv. 24–90 in the enlarged text) whose original version was probably Semitic.

Not only does the orchestra seem Greek, but the order given to 'every people, nation, and language' to prostrate themselves at the signal given throughout the empire is manifestly Hellenistic in character. In the words of 1 Macc. 1.41–2: 'The king then issued a decree throughout his empire: his subjects were all to become one people and abandon their own laws and religion. The nations everywhere complied with the royal command.'[11] I shall discuss in my commentary on Dan. 11.37ff. the hypothesis that King Antiochus attempted to establish 'a common religion to all nations of his empire'.[12] It is not indifferent that in the immediate context of 1 Macc. 1.41–2 cited above, we find in v.50: 'anyone who does not obey the king's order will be punished by death' (cf. Dan. 3.6) and, in v.54, 'the king had built the abomination of desolation upon the altar' (cf. all of Dan. 3).

Regarding v.6, O. Plöger (op. cit., p. 64) recalls that fire accompanies theophanies in the Bible.[13] The furnace belongs to this same ideational complex.[14] Thus, according to Deut. 4.20, the exodus from Egypt was salvation from the furnace, and the conjunction of Dan. 3 with this text was certainly recognized by the Author and his Israelite readers.[15] Another sure scriptural source is Jer. 1.13ff. and 29.21–2. Such a richness of biblical references naturally lent itself to an abundant agadic development.[16]

Text 3. 8–12

(8) Whereupon, at that very moment, the men of Chaldea came together and

[11] The authenticity of this text is disputed, although F.-M. Abel does not discuss this, *Les Livres des Macchabées* (Paris 1949), ad loc.

[12] See L. Cerfaux and J. Tondriau, *Le Culte des Souverains dans la Civilisation Gréco-romaine* (Tournai 1957). We will quote the following passages. Hellenism created 'a peculiar kind of divinization: the comparison or identification of the reigning sovereign, or of a member of his family, with one member of the Pantheon or another.' Since this phenomenon occurred from the end of the fourth century BCE through the fall of the Roman Empire, it cannot be explained away by invoking paranoic reactions of those kings (see p. 76). In fact, 'the cult of the sovereigns was one of the more symptomatic manifestations of the Hellenistic period. A monarchical rather than a religious institution, it "surely constituted one of the more curious innovations of the period" (Aymard, *Orient et Grèce antique*, p. 414)' (p. 262).

[13] See Deut. 29.22; Isa. 13.19; Amos 4.11; etc.

[14] See Isa. 48.10; Mal. 3.2, 19; Prov. 17.3.

[15] See O. Plöger, p. 64. Furthermore, the vocabulary of Dan. 3.6 is that of the Decalogue concerning idolatry (Exod. 20.3–5).

[16] On this subject, Montgomery refers to Wace, *Apocrypha* II, pp. 305ff. See *Tanh.* 6: The High Priest Joshua left the fire uninjured. See L. Ginzberg, *The Legends of the Jews* I, pp. 198ff.: Abraham also emerged from the same torture uninjured (*Ur-Kasdim* interpreted as signifying 'the Chaldeans' fire'); cf. 1 Kings 19; Isa. 30.33; 2 Macc. 7 (with Antiochus Epiphanes on stage). . . . Tradition added another direction to this symbol, the furnace becoming the place of the great last judgement— evil men are thrown into it by God (see Dan. 3.22, 29; 6.25; 1 Enoch 10.6; 18.11; 21.7–10; 54.6; 90.24–5).

brought accusation against the Jews. (9) They spoke up and said to King Nebuchadnezzar: 'O king, live for ever! (10) You, O king, have given the order that anyone who hears the sound of the horn, the flute, the lyre, the sambuca, the psalterium, the pipe, and every sort of musical instrument must prostrate himself and worship the gold statue. (11) Whoever does not prostrate himself and does not worship will be thrown into a crematory oven. (12) There are men of Judea whom you have charged with the administration of the province of Babylon, Shadrach, Meshach, and Abed-Nego. Now these men have not obeyed your order, O king. They do not serve your gods or worship the gold statue which you have set up.'

Critical Notes 3. 8–12

V.8 Θ is shorter.—אכלו קרציהון: an ancient Akkadian expression which became common in every Semitic language, according to Montgomery, ad loc. (see Targ. Ps. 15.3). In Syriac, אכלקרצא = ὁ διάβολος; see Luke 16.1: διαβάλλειν. The expression already appears in the letters from El Amarna (fourteenth century BCE), see 44.25. Montgomery draws attention to the popular French expression: 'manger le morceau', i.e., to turn someone in, see V. Hugo, *Les Misérables*, Part IV, bk. 7, ch. 2.—כל־קבל דנא: according to Plöger, a gloss on the model of v.7.

V.9 'O king, live for ever': protocol, see 2.4; 5.10; 6.7.

V.10 טעם: does not have the same sense here or in v.12 as in Dan. 2.14 and 3.12. See Θ: δόγμα.

V.12 Θ reads, not the Qere (your God), but the Ketib (your gods). LXX: καὶ τῷ εἰ δώλῳ σου οὐκ ἐλάτρευσαν καὶ τῇ εἰκόνι σου τῇ χρυσῇ .... Also in v.18—פלחן: religious service or royal service.

Commentary

The second part of ch. 3 opens in v.8 with a denunciation of the Jews by the 'Chaldeans' (in the sense of the people or class of wise men in Babylon). The Aramaic speaks of calumny, when in reality the accusation is based on facts. What is slanderous is presenting the Jews as poor administrators of the affairs of the kingdom (see v.12).[17] Antisemitism readily embraces economic, social, political, and racial accusations.

It is gripping to see that only the Jews refused to participate in a religious parody become an affair of state. His faith—even when it is not aggressive as in the case of Daniel and his companions—leads the Jew to death. But it is not a death for nothing, it is fecund as the grain in the

[17] On the theme of a king fooled by his courtiers, see Dan. 6.5–10, 25; Supplements to Esther, Addition E, 1 (XVI).2–12 (in Charles, *Apocrypha*, pp. 680f.).

earth (v.26), while that of the executioners is totally absurd (v.22) for it is always a form of suicide.[18]

Text 3. 13–18

(13) Then Nebuchadnezzar, irritated and furious, commanded that Shadrach, Meshach, and Abed-Nego be brought to him. Then these men were brought into the king's presence. (14) Nebuchadnezzar spoke up and said to them: 'Is it deliberately, Shadrach, Meshach, and Abed-Nego, that you do not serve my gods and that you do not worship the gold statue which I set up? (15) Are you now ready, at the moment you hear the sound of the horn, the flute, the lyre, the sambuca, the psalterium, the bagpipe, and of every sort of musical instrument, to prostrate yourselves and to worship the statue I made? If you do not worship it, you will immediately be thrown into a crematory oven, and what god will deliver you from my hands?' (16) Shadrach, Meshach, and Abed-Nego answered the king in these terms: 'Nebuchadnezzar, we do not need to answer you in this matter. (17) If our God, whom we serve, can deliver us, he will deliver us from the crematory oven and from your hands, O king! (18) If not, be it known unto you, O king, that we do not serve your gods and we will not worship the gold statue which you have set up.'

Critical Notes 3. 13–17

V.13 Θ has simply at the end of this verse: 'and they were brought...'.

V.14 הצדה = אזדא 'deliberate' (see the critical notes on *azda* 2.5, 8). A semantic evolution led to a confusion with the root *yaṣad*, hence, a deliberate intention, cf. Arabic *waṣada* = to be firm.— Θ: $\epsilon i\ \dot{\alpha}\lambda\eta\theta\hat{\omega}s$. But LXX: $\delta\iota\dot{\alpha}\ \tau\iota$; ('What is that?'). The ־הֲ is interrogative and gives the hybrid form. It is already represented on an ostracon in Aramaic (see M. Lidzbarski, *Altaramäische Urkunden aus Assur* (1921), cited by Montgomery, p. 207).

V.15 שיזב: Aramaic form of the Akkadian verb *šezib*.—ידי: Θ, hand, in the singular (LXX: plural = MT).

V.16 No caesura between 'king' and 'Nebuchadnezzar' in Θ, LXX, Syr., and Vul.—פתגם: Persian origin: *paiti-gama*, message, order, word; see Ezra 4.17 and above all 5.11 (with the verb תו'ב). See Dan. 4.14; Ps. of Solomon 24.7, where the word פתגמא has the same sense of a juridical defence.

V.17 הן = if. Torrey, cited by Montgomery, understands 'if it be so',

---

[18] Think of the deaths of the first born of Egypt or the social and cultural decline of Spain and Portugal after the expulsion of the Jews in 1492.

in parallel with יֵשׁ וישׁ in 2 Kings 10.15. The disjunctive accent of the MT may contribute to this interpretation. The different versions are bothered by this dubitative 'if', which they render by 'for'; Vul. *ecce enim*; also the Jewish commentators of the Middle Ages, whose philological science is here caught in an error.—A. Bentzen follows Torrey. Plöger, Porteous, and others take it in the sense of leaving it up to God to save them or not (see our commentary).

Commentary

The king's anger (v.13) is part of the popular and caricature-like character of the tale. Porteous establishes a parallel with 'the arrogant and blasphemous claim' of Rabshakeh when he tried to intimidate King Hezekiah (Isa. 36.13ff. and 2 Kings 18.33–5).

The proud reply of the three accused men (v.16) responds to the requirements of the literary genre. It also allows us to accept the caesura in the MT between the words 'king' and 'Nebuchadnezzar', even though this makes the companions become discourteous.[19]

In v.17, the two words איתי + participle are inseparable.[20] We must read therefore: 'If he is capable, the God whom we serve, of saving us . . .'. It is unexpected, some have said, to find God's power called into question in a popular tale,[21] but this argument is the result of a misunderstanding for we are not in the realm of idealism in the Book of Daniel. What is said here about the test of strength between the weakness of God and the power of Caesar in no way surpasses the capacities of a *Jewish* 'popular' tale.[22] The negation in v.18 certainly has to do with the power of God. It may be that God will be unable to save them, but this is not sufficient to undermine the three martyrs' fidelity. Their attachment to God is wholly without expectation of a reward.[23]

In his great book, *L'Exil de la Parole, Du Silence biblique au Silence d'Auschwitz* (Paris 1970), pp. 224ff., André Neher recalls the Midrash of *Song of Songs R.* 7.8, where Hananiah, Mishael and Azariah ask the prophet Ezekiel whether they will be saved from the hand of Nebuchadnezzar. The divine answer is negative, God shall not save them! The three Jews, however, decide: 'Whether or not he rescues us, we are

---

[19] The words 'King Nebuchadnezzar' moreover appear nine times in this chapter. The Masoretic editors would have certainly been sensitive to the unexpected change in construction.

[20] See R. H. Charles, p. 69.

[21] See Charles, Heaton, etc.

[22] See 1 Cor. 1.25; 2 Cor. 12.9, 10; 13.9. These are not popular tales, but they are addressed to the people.

[23] See Job 1.9; 13.15 (*qere*); etc. Cf. Gen. 22. The three companions in Daniel 3 make us think of the three Patriarchs, the fathers of the faith.

ready for martyrdom.' They then say to Nebuchadnezzar: '. . . If not, if this our God whom we revere does not save us, NOTWITHSTANDING be it known unto you, O king, that we do not serve your gods and we will not worship the gold statue which you have set up!'

Text 3. 19–25

(19) Then Nebuchadnezzar was filled with fury and the expression on his face was changed concerning Shadrach, Meshach, and Abed-Nego. He spoke up and said to heat up the oven seven times more than it was usually heated. (20) Then he ordered some men who were heroes in his army to bind Shadrach, Meshach, and Abed-Nego and throw them into the crematory oven. (21) Then these men were bound, dressed in their coats, tunics, hats, and other garments, and thrown into the middle of the crematory oven. (22) Whereupon, since the king's order was strict and the oven was extraordinarily hot, the men who had hoisted up Shadrach, Meshach, and Abed-Nego were themselves killed by the fire's flames. (23) And as for these three men, Shadrach, Meshach, and Abed-Nego, they fell into the middle of the crematory oven, all bound up. (24) Then King Nebuchadnezzar was astonished and suddenly stood up. He spoke up and said to his counsellors: 'Did we not throw three men bound into the midst of the fire?' They answered the king in these words: 'Certainly, O king.' (25) He spoke again, saying: 'Well I see four free men moving about in the midst of the fire and they are not hurt. The appearance of the fourth one resembles that of a son of the gods.'

Critical Notes 3. 19–25

V.19 צלם: LXX: ἡ μορφή; Θ: ἡ ὄψις. Generally the LXX has εἰκών, as for example in Gen. 1.26.—למזא: from the root אזא, used in the Targums and Talmuds for 'to heat a bath'.—חזה: Θ probably understood the word as also coming from the same root אזא to reinforce the idea, so he translates it adverbially as εἰς τέλος, 'extremely'.

V.21 סרבל: the meaning is not certain. Θ: σαράβαρα (a piece of clothing mentioned by the comic poet Antiphanes: breeches); see Vul.: braccis. Also, in Arabic, sirbal = trousers. Talmudic Aramaic, on the contrary, prefers the meaning 'mantles' and this is also the translation chosen by Ibn Ezra. LXX: ὑποδήματα (but in 3.27, σαράβαρα). According to Charles, op. cit., p. 71, the word in Persian originally signified: mantle and trousers.—פטישיהון: the meaning is not certain: trousers or tunics (in the Talmud's Hebrew: trousers). LXX has incorrectly read: ἐπὶ τῶν κεράων =

בראשיהון. The word order in Θ must be inverted (currently we find καὶ τιάραις καὶ περικνημίσι tiaras and leggings).—כרבלתא: hat. Akkadian: *karballatu* = helmet or hat. The Greek versions are therefore correct: κυρβασία. We may think of the pointed cap worn by the Scythians and Greeks. Talmud: helmet, cock's comb. See S. A. Cook, 'The Articles of Dress in Dan. 3.21', *Journ. of Phil.* (1899), pp. 306–13.

V.22 *Casus pendens.*—Θ has a shorter text. He does not mention the deaths of the executioners.—שביבא די נורא: cf. Job 18.5: שביב אשו; Talmud: שיבא spark, fragment. Akkadian: *šababu*: to burn.

V.23 Perhaps a later addition by a redactor who wanted to introduce the Prayer of Azariah and the Song of the Three Young Men. See the destructive analysis of this verse by Charles, op. cit., pp. 72–3. The Greek and Latin versions introduce the literary fragments mentioned above following v.23. They consist of 66 verses (vv.24–90), where v.91 corresponds to v.24 of the Aramaic text.

V.24 להדברוהי: only appears in this book: 3.24, 27; 4.33; 6.8. Of Persian origin, the term designates a high royal officer. LXX: φίλοι. On this subject, see O. Plöger, op. cit. ad loc., who asks whether the LXX has not read the Aramaic text as חבר. He cites Xenophon, *Cyropaedia* VIII, 3.13, where he indicates that he counted relatives of the king among his close acquaintances. See also Ezra 7.14–15, where it is a question of seven counsellors (another word) of the Persian king.

V.25 בר אלהין: בר indicates belonging or participation. The expression designates an angel (so the Jewish commentators; Ibn Ezra thinks of the appearances of the Angel of YHWH). See Gen. 6.2; Job 1.6; 38.7; 1 Kings 22.19; Ps. 148.2. . . . LXX: ἄγγελος Θεοῦ; also see v.28. *A*, *Σ*, *Θ*: 'a son of God'. The expression is used in the inscriptions at Karatepe and Ugarit where it designates the members of the divine court.

Commentary

V.19 introduces the fourth part of the chapter; it takes us beyond the threat to its execution. The king's anger is a common theme in popular tales. It makes the reader participate more fully in the action described by the story. Nebuchadnezzar's face changes and the oven is heated up seven times hotter than usual. These two features correspond—the furnace is a prolongation of the royal furor.

The number seven plays an important role in the Book of Daniel (see 4.13, 20, 22, 29; 9.25). This also may be said of its multiple seventy

65

(9.2, 24), and its fraction, three and a half (7.25; 9.27).[24] It is the rival of the number ten as indicating the maximum, totality, or excellence. Dan. 3.19, therefore, is deliberately hyperbolic.

To insure that the operation succeeds, the Jews are tied up (vv.20, 21), which at the same time establishes a new parallel between this episode and the patriarchal tradition. Isaac, too, had been bound (Gen. 22.9).[25] And whereas Isaac had been substituted for by a ram, here the executioners die and their victims survive (v.22).

As is characteristic of Daniel A, here again only the king sees the miracle (vv.24–5); for the miracle is never seen except by the one whom it concerns (see Acts 9.7; cf. here 10.7).

King Nebuchadnezzar is the witness to the presence in the furnace of a fourth personage who is a divine epiphany. God is with his children in the middle of the fire. In Babylon as in Egypt, he 'is with them *in* distress' (Ps. 91.15), in the burning bush (Exod. 3.4), and in the crematorium flames. The executioner-king has a vision of the 'Lord whom he persecutes' (Acts 9.5).

Thus the absent Daniel is replaced by a mysterious fourth personage. In the final analysis, Daniel is perhaps not so far from chapter 3 as we might have believed. The one who substitutes for the absent Daniel is 'like a son of God/the gods'. This expression recalls several other familiar elements in the Book of Daniel. First, what is said about its hero, see 4.5, 6, 15; 5.12; 6.3. Next, if the angel in chapter 3 is 'like a son of the gods' to the eyes of the pagan king, he is 'like a son of man' to the eyes of the Israelites (see 8.15; 10.5; 12.5). The people of the saints as a whole is 'like a son of man' (7.13), and Daniel himself is a 'son of man' (8.17). This direct relation between the faithful Israelites, the 'saints' of chapter 7, and the angelic beings is further emphasized by the fact that these latter ones too are 'saints' (cf. 8.7 and 8.24). We will return to this subject with regard to chapter 7 below. In Dan. 7.13 it is a question of the faithful Jewish community undergoing the test of its fidelity, here the three companions are Israel in Exile saved through divine intervention. In chapter 7 a 'man' is opposed to the animals, here

[24] In the Bible the number 7 may:
  be an indication of time: Gen. 8.10; 31.23; 50.10; Judg. 14.12, 17;
  be a hyperbole: Gen. 33.3;
  or have a cultural meaning: Exod. 12.15, 19; 13.6; 23.15; Lev. 8.33; 12.2.
 It is found in the letters from El Amarna (137; 147; 234; 250; etc.), and it has the same significance throughout the Semitic world, and even among the Greeks, Romans, and Germans. This identity of thinking should probably be attributed to a common observing of the phases of the moon. See H. A. Brongers, in *Festsch. Vriezen.*
[25] The text of Gen. 22 does not say if Isaac was first undressed. It is possible that Dan. 3 is making an argument *e silentio.* Normally the condemned were nude (see Ps. 22.19).

it is an angel who is opposed to men—the passage from one level of comparison to another does not entail any essential change.

As regards the angelology of this chapter, it will suffice to cite two brief, yet profound comments. Y. Kaufmann[26] says that the angels reveal at the same time that they conceal. They constitute a barrier and a bridge between God and men. And Fleming James, audaciously reversing the relation of the terrestrial and celestial personages in Daniel 3, writes, 'The saint is not alone; he is in the midst of celestial friends.'[27]

Text 3. 26–30

(26) Then Nebuchadnezzar approached the opening of the crematory oven. He spoke out and said: 'Shadrach, Meshach, and Abed-Nego, servants of the Most High God, come out and hither.' Then Shadrach, Meshach, and Abed-Nego came out of the midst of the fire. (27) The satraps, prefects, governors, and counsellors of the king gathered. They saw that the fire had no power over the bodies of these men, that the hair on their heads was not singed, that their coats were not changed, and that the odour of the fire had not passed upon them. (28) Nebuchadnezzar spoke out and said: 'Blessed be the God of Shadrach, Meshach, and Abed-Nego who has sent his angel and delivered his servants. They trusted in him and have changed the king's order. They gave up their bodies rather than serve or worship any other god than their god! (29) I order that any man of any people, nation, and language who speaks against the god of Shadrach, Meshach, and Abed-Nego will be torn in pieces and his house turned into manure; for there is no other god who can deliver in this way.' (30) Then the king promoted Shadrach, Meshach, and Abed-Nego in the province of Babylon.

Critical Notes 3. 27–30

V.27 גשם (Ar.) or בשר (Heb.), (see 3.27, 28; 4.30; 5.21) designates the living human body. However, in 7.11 גשם means the dead body of the beast.—ריח: see Judg. 16.9. Except for this verse, this word is used to refer to the appeasing odour of sacrifices: 43 passages, above all in Leviticus (38 times in P). See D. Lys, *Ruach* (op. cit.), pp. 23, n. 1; 168.

V.28 שׁזיב: Shaphel, borrowed from the Assyrian *šuzub(u)*.—ויהבו גשמיהון: LXX and Θ complete 'of the fire'. The Greek versions are perhaps the origin of the vocabulary found in 1 Cor. 13.3—שׁניו: haphel as in Ezra 6.11. The verb also has a secondary sense, 'to

---

[26] *History of the Israelite Faith* (in Hebrew), vol. II (Tel Aviv 1952), pp. 422–32.
[27] *Personalities of the Old Testament* (New York 1939), p. 571.

disobey'. In Syriac, שׁנא מן = to disobey. Consequently $\varSigma$ here translates: ἠθέτησαν.

V.29 Kt. שׁלה: Qr. שָׁלוּ as in 6.5. Possibly we should read as Kt.: שָׁלָה = שׁאלה = 'word, thing', as in 1 Sam. 1.17 and Dan. 4.14. Rashi and Ibn Ezra connect שׁלוּ and שׁגו, שׁנה = 'inadvertent error'. The Targ. correctly translates these verbs with שׁלא (see Job 6.24; 12.16). See Montgomery, ad loc.—כדנה: cf. Ezra 5.7. But A. Bentzen, p. 30, and others translate, 'no other god but this one'.

V.30 $\varTheta$ adds: 'and he judged them worthy to govern all the Jews who were in his kingdom'. Plöger, ad loc., asks whether this interpretation by $\varTheta$ is correct (an elevation of the three companions) or whether it is a question in this verse of a *restitutio in integrum*. Cf. 1 Macc. 2.51–61.

Commentary

Verses 26–30 constitute a fifth part of this chapter. In v.26, the most noteworthy expression is the appellation 'Most High' applied to God by Nebuchadnezzar. We find diverse designations for the God of Israel in the Book of Daniel. We have already encountered 'the God of Heaven' in 2.18, and 'the God of gods and the Lord of kings' in 2.47. Daniel 6.20 speaks of 'the living God', 7.9 of 'He-Who-Endures', and 8.11 of 'The Prince of the Army'. We also find one rather unusual title in the plural (with the same root and a meaning similar to our 'Most High') in 7.8, 22, 25, 27. אלהא עליא is found in 3.32; 5.18, 21; (א) עלי without אלהא in 4.14, 21, 22, 29, 31; and 7.25. It corresponds to the Hebrew אל עליון and the Greek Θεὸς ὕψιστος. We should understand, says G. F. Moore,[28] not 'the most high of the gods', but 'the elevated God' (the God of the heavens). N. W. Porteous[29] refers to a Phoenician deity 'Ελιουν καλούμενος ''Υψιστος, mentioned by Philo of Byblos (see Eusebius, *Praep. Evang.* I, 10, 12f.). This rapprochement is all the more interesting in that, the Psalms excepted, the expression is usually placed in the mouth of pagans.[30] Montgomery notes, 'This monotheistic term became current in circles more or less influenced by Judaism' (p. 216), which agrees well with Nebuchadnezzar's confession.

Despite himself, the king is forced to confess to the enduring character of Israel (v.28). The Author once again establishes the cause and effect

[28] Op. cit., I, p. 430, n. 1.
[29] Op. cit., p. 61.
[30] See Gen. 14.18, 19, 20; Num. 24.16; Deut. 32.8, Moses is speaking, but in connection with the nations; Isa. 14.14; see also 2 Macc. 3.31; 1 Esdras 2.3; 6.31 . . . as well as numerous texts in 1 Enoch; Test. of the XII Patriarchs; Jub.; As. of Moses; Psalms of Solomon; 2 Bar.; 4 Esdras; Philo and Josephus. In the New Testament, see Mark 5.7; Acts 16.17.

relation between the power and majesty of God and the survival of the people of Israel. Nebuchadnezzar sees the proof for the existence of the living God in the Jews who emerge from the furnace.[31] The God of Israel is attached to historical individuals, to a particular people, and thus becomes 'their god' in a sense without any parallel elsewhere.[32]

Following the internal logic of the agadah, the pagan by blessing Israel condemns himself and throws into his own oven his possessions which previously he had not allowed anyone to touch (v.29); cf. Dan. 6.24–5.[33]

Text 3. 31–33

(31) Nebuchadnezzar, the king, to everyone of all peoples, nations, and languages, that dwell in all the earth, peace be multiplied unto you. (32) The signs and wonders that the Most High God has wrought toward me, it seems good to me to set them forth:

> (33) How great are his signs,
> how mighty his wonders!
> his kingdom is an everlasting kingdom,
> and his dominion is from generation to generation.

Critical Notes 3. 31–33

V.31 Verses 31–3 (or 4.1–3 in Θ) are missing in the LXX, which immediately begins at v.1 (= v.4) with the date, 'the eighteenth year', as in 3.1.—שלמכון ישׂגא: a common salutation; see 6.26 (cf. I Pet. 1.2; 2 Pet. 1.2; etc).

V.32 Θ abbreviates '. . . to make known how great and powerful they are'. Greek: σημεῖα καὶ τέρατα (cf. Mk. 13.22; Rom. 15.19).

V.33 Cf. 2.44; 4.31; Ps. 145.13.

Commentary

We may consider vv.31–3 as ending this chapter as did the tradition, but it is more exact to see these verses as the opening of chapter 4, as does

---

[31] One day, in another time, before the Great Crematorium of the Third Reich, the confession 'Sire, the Jews who emerged from the furnace', had to find its ultimate complement: 'Sire, the Jews who did not escape'.

[32] A. Alt, in his famous study 'Der Gott der Väter', was not justified, we believe, in setting aside this text (as well as 2 Kings 2.14) to establish a thesis we find more alluring than substantial.

[33] Re the king's repentance, see Dan. 6.27–8; LXX Esth. 8.12ff. (Ahasuerus' letter); 3 Macc. 7 (the conversion of Philopator); Qumran 'The Prayer of Nabonidus'.

Theodotion. On v.31, Raymond Hammer (*The Book of Daniel* (Cambridge 1976), p. 49) writes: 'The formula used at the beginning is similar to that used in ancient letters and decrees (cf. the letter in Ezra 5.8 and the proclamation of Cyrus as recorded in Ezra 1.2f.; it also occurs in Aramaic papyri from Elephantine in Egypt and elsewhere).' The poetry in v.33 is beautiful as *b. Sanh.* 92b recognizes: 'He (the king) has tried to purloin (for his own use) all the songs and praises pronounced by David!'

It is perhaps not an exaggeration to see in chapter 3 a parallel to chapter 12,[34] for even if the original composition of this chapter goes back to an epoch before the Maccabees, it was only at a very small cost that it was 'modernized' so as to be readable by the persecuted under Antiochus Epiphanes. In this sense, to announce that there was a salvation in the 'oven' signifies nothing other than a resurrection of the dead.

[34] See A. von Gall, *Einheitlichkeit* . . . (Giessen 1895), p. 115; J. Steinmann, op. cit., pp. 70–1; etc.

4 The Dream about the Cosmic Tree

Text 4. 1–15

(1) I, Nebuchadnezzar, was living quietly in my house, prospering in my palace. (2) I had a dream which made me afraid; the phantasies upon my bed and the vision of my spirit frightened me. (3) I gave the order to have all the wise men of Babylon brought to me so that they could make known the interpretation of my dream. (4) Then the magicians, exorcists, Chaldeans, and conjurers came in; I told the dream in their presence, but they could not make its interpretation known to me. (5) After them, Daniel, who was named Belteshazzar, after the name of my god, and who had the spirit of the holy gods in him, came in. I told him the dream: (6) 'Belteshazzar, chief of the magicians, who have, I know, the spirit of the holy gods in you, and to whom no mystery is difficult, tell me the visions of my dream and its explication. (7) (Here are) my spirit's visions upon my bed. I had a vision: Behold, a tree in the middle of the earth, of great size. (8) The tree became large and strong and its height reached up to the heavens and it could be seen from the ends of the whole earth. (9) Its leaves were beautiful and its fruit abundant; it had enough food for everyone; in its bower the beasts of the fields had shadow, the birds of the sky dwelt in its branches, and all flesh was fed from it. (10) In my spirit's visions upon my bed, I had this vision, and behold, a Watcher, a Saint, descended from the heavens. (11) He cried out loudly and spoke as follows: Cut down the tree and cut off its branches, pull off its leaves and scatter its fruits; let the beasts flee its bower and the birds its boughs. (12) But leave the stump of its roots in the earth, bound with iron and bronze, in the grass of the field. He will be watered by the dew from the sky and share the forage of the earth with the beasts. (13) His heart will no longer be human, a bestial heart will be given to him. Then seven periods will pass over him. (14) This sentence is a decree from the Watchers, this speech is an order from the Saints, so that living beings know that the Most High rules over the kingship of men and gives it to whom he pleases, he raises up the most humble of men. (15) Such is the dream I saw, I, King Nebuchadnezzar. You Belteshazzar, tell the interpretation, for all the Wise Men in my kingdom were unable to make known to me its interpretation. But you, you can do it, for the spirit of the holy gods is in you.'

Critical Notes 4. 1–15

Despite omissions, this chapter in the LXX is considerably longer than in the MT.

V.1 LXX adds: 'in the eighteenth year of the reign of Nabouchodonosor'.—בהיכלי: *del.* in Θ.—שלה: cf. Jer. 49.31; Ps. 73.12; 122.6.—רענן: for a tree (cf. the king's dream here), cf. Ps. 92.13ff.; 37.35; 52.10.

V.2 דחל: see 2.31: נורא=דחיל. Here the form is the masculine pael imperfect, with the first person suffix, as in the form (in the plural) יבהלני. For this idea, see 7.15.—הרהר: (impure) phantasy; mirage (Syr.) illusion (Mand.). This is the only occurrence of this word in the Bible. Perhaps (see Montgomery) it should be connected with the Hebrew הרה: to conceive (bad thoughts). Cf. Ibn Ezra: 'mental "harhor" without an ejaculation'.—וחזוי ראשי: see Montgomery; it breaks the metrical equilibrium; an explicative gloss (*del.* in LXX).

V.3 Vv.3–6 are missing in the LXX. ומני שים טעם: cf. 3.10, 29; 6.27.—לכל חכימי בבל: see 2.12, 48; cf. 5.7, 8.—די פשר וכו: see 2.30.

V.4 The four classes of wise men are found again only in 5.11.—חרטמיא: see 2.4 and note.—אשפיא: see 2.27 and note.—כשדיא: see 1.4 and note; 2.2.—גזריא: Θ: γαζαρηνόι! Σ: θύται; Pesh.: 'magi'; Vul.: *haruspices.* גזר = to decree; M. Delcor; op. cit., p. 110, cites G. Furlarni who he says has shown that the meaning of the word is 'conjurer' (in *Atti della Accademia Nazionale dei Lincei, Classe di Scienze morali, storiche e filologiche,* Ser. 8, 4 (1948), pp. 177–96). The word also appears in 4 Q or Nab where it designates the Jewish exorcist calling Nabonidus to repentance.

V.5 ועד אחרין: Kt.: 'to the end'; Qr.: ועד אחרן = 'and until another' (cf. Θ: ἕως), or 'and yet another'. See Luc.: ἕτερος = Vul.: *donec collega* (ἑταῖρος for ἕτερος); see Ibn Ezra: אחרון; but Rashi: עד אשר אחרונה הרבא, which is correct, since the plural form of אחרין indicates that it is a question of an adverb. בלטשאצר כשם אלהי a popular etymology on the basis of the first syllable, בל. See 1.7 and note. The interpretation would be correct if it were a question of the king's name in Dan. 5.1: בלשאצר, but we must not confuse them.—רוח אלהין קדישין בה: Θ: πνεῦμα θεοῦ ἁγίου, see 4.6, 15; 5.11, 14; cf. 6.4.

V.6 אנס: Only found here and in Esth. 1.8 in the Bible. In post-biblical Hebrew: to commit an outrage, to force. Behrmann, cited by Charles, pp. 88–9, remarks that the words כל רז לא אנס לך are a quasi-Aramaic version of Ezek. 28.3, where the Targ. has this text: כל רז לא יתכסא מנך.—חזוי חלמי: uniquely in Daniel. Charles sees here a supplementary confirmation that verses 3–7a were added by a redactor.

V.7 וחזוי ראשי: concludes the secondary intervention of the redactor begun in v.2 (see Charles, p. 89). Moreover, they are absent in Θ.

V.8 וחזותה: Θ: 'its trunk' (also in v.17). Cf. Heb.: חזות in 8.5. LXX: ἡ ὅρασις, which is correct.

V.10 עיר: cf. v.14, 20. LXX: ἄγγελος; Θ: 'Iρ; ΑΣ: ἐγρήγορος; Vul.: *vigil*. Bentzen notes that one rapidly associated Θ's Iρ and 'Iris', rainbow; see Hippol., p. 123.—קדיש: angel; cf. Dan. 8.13; Job 5.1; 15.15; Ps. 89.6, 8; Zech. 14.5; etc.

V.11 קרא בחיל = 3.4.

V.13 שבעה עדנין: LXX: seven years; cf. 7.25; 12.7. There are two senses of the word עדן in Daniel. We have already met the first one, 'time': 2.8–9, 12; 3.5, 15; see also 7.12. It corresponds to מועד in Hebrew. The second sense, 'year', is peculiar to Daniel: see 4.13, 20, 22, 29; 7.25; and 12.7; (12.29?). H. L. Ginsberg, op. cit., pp. 1–2, sees a direct influence here of the Greek χρόνος which is also used in the sense of a year. Cf. Rashi; Ibn Ezra.

V.14 ומאמר: Mss.: ובמאמר; similarly in citations of this verse in the Talmud (see *Sanh.* 38b). But Θ = MT. The preposition demanded by the parallelism is understood (Hebrew examples in G.K. par. 119, hh).—שאלתא: see Montgomery, p. 237; cf. Eccles. 8.11: decree. The Rabbis translated etymologically: 'request' (cf. Rashi: God first consults the Saints), cf. Θ; Vul. In Arabic, *mas'alat* = 'thing'; here the thing in question, hence the 'decision'. See Targ. on Jer. 12.1: שאילת דינין for the Hebrew משפטים.— עד: read על (see B.H.). See 2.30. But cf. LXX and Vul.!—אנשם: read: אנשא *(laps. calam.).*

V.15 דנא: is in evidence, see 2.36; Ezra 5.4.—פשרא: Mss. Qr.: פִּשְׁרֵהּ.— אלהין קדישין: Montgomery: in fact, a singular; cf. Θ. For the Rabbis, Nebuchadnezzar was a prophet of the pagans (and consequently a mixture of good and bad). For Calvin and other ancient Christian commentators, the plural indicates that Nebuchadnezzar did not really repent (see Hengstenberg, Pusey, Keil).

Commentary

Chapter 4 presents a new *agadah*. Nebuchadnezzar has a vision of a cosmic tree, a theme common to many ancient forms of literature.[1] Ezekiel had already utilized this element from the international folklore treasury to describe the glorification and subsequent fall of the Pharaoh.[2] In relation to the preceding tale (ch. 3: the stele), the religious colouration is less apparent, but it is far from absent. The cosmic tree is one form of union between the gods and men, a bridge between the two worlds.

---

[1] See Mircea Eliade, *Images and Symbols* (New York 1961), ch. 1: 'Symbolism of the "Centre"'; *Patterns in Comparative Religion* (Cleveland and New York 1963), ch. 10: 'Sacred Places: Temple, Palace, "Centre of the World".' Perhaps Nebuchadnezzar's vision was of the cosmic tree.

[2] Ezek. 31. For trees as metaphors of powerful kings, see Ezek. 17; Zech. 11.2; etc.

Of course the gods may ascend and descend this ladder at will, but for men it is the means by which they may approach the divine in so far as it is possible for them to do so.[3] The punishment of Nebuchadnezzar's arrogance therefore is not so general that we cannot find some trace of the mad political and religious ambition of Antiochus IV in chapter 4. It is true that there is no trace here of any active persecution on the part of a paranoid king. His relations with Daniel are for the most part friendly and there is a great distance between the polemic in 3.16–18 and Daniel's wish as expressed in 4.16. It is evident, however, that a reader in the second century BCE would have no difficulty in distinguishing, beneath the features of Nebuchadnezzar, Epiphanes whom his adversaries called Antiochus Epimanes, the mad man.

It is possible that the literary source for Dan. 4 has been found in the manuscripts from the wilderness of Judea.[4] This is a text entitled 'The Prayer of Nabonidus' (4 Q or Nab) in which we read that the king of Babylon, Nabunai, was struck by a grave illness: col. I, line 2: 'by an evil inflammation by order of the M(ost High go)d in Teim(an) . . .'; line 3: 'I was afflicted for seven years.'[5] Following this, a Jewish exorcist exhorted him to repent and promised he would be healed. The king thanks the true God and denounces the incapacity of the false gods to whom he had previously prayed to heal him.

The parallel to Dan. 4 is manifest, although there are some striking differences. They have been enumerated by Dupont-Sommer:[6]

(a) The description of the sickness: in 4 Q or Nab it is a question of an 'evil inflammation'; in Daniel, of lycanthropy.

(b) The place of confinement: it is not specified in Daniel, but in the Qumran document it is named: Teiman.

(c) The name of the king: Nebuchadnezzar in Daniel; Nabonidus in 4 Q or Nab.

(d) The king's prayer: in Daniel, to the true God; in 4 Q, first of all to pagan gods.

(e) The intervention: of Daniel; in 4 Q or Nab of an anonymous Jewish exorcist.

Comparing the similarities in the two texts is no less instructive. They have provided a new perspective on the inscriptions by Nabonidus in

---

[3] 'Religion' means tying together earth and heaven.
[4] See J. T. Milik, *Ten Years of Discovery in the Wilderness of Judaea* (London 1959), p. 37. Cf. *RB* (1956), pp. 411–15 ('Prière de Nabonide et autres écrits d'un cycle de Daniel'); D. N. Freedman, 'The Prayer of Nabonidus', *BASOR*, 145 (1957), pp. 31–2; Rudolf Meyer, *Das Gebet des Nabonid* (Berlin 1962); J. Carmignac, E. Cathenet, H. Lignée, *Les Textes de Qumrân*, vol. 2, pp. 289ff.
[5] Translated into French by J. Carmignac, etc.; see note 4 above.
[6] A Dupont-Sommer, *Ecrits Esséniens* . . ., p. 339.

the temple at Harran,[7] as well as for the Babylonian Chronicle which records concerning Nabonidus, 'the king is mad'.[8] As for the inscriptions, the king there recounts (again in the first person as in 4 Q or Nab) that he received in a dream an order from the god Sin to quit his capital (I.22–3). So he travelled the routes linking Teiman and various points in Arabia (I.26–7) for ten years. Another premonitory dream from Sin made him return to Babylon where he was warmly received. He attributes his survival and restoration to his throne to god (I.27–31; II.11–42, 12–35) for whom he rebuilds the temple at Harran (III.17–35).

The change from 'Nabonidus' to 'Nebuchadnezzar' is easily accounted for. Nabonidus is never cited in the Scriptures. Nebuchadnezzar, on the contrary, is the pagan king *par excellence* who destroyed Jerusalem and the Temple. Even the abrupt passage from the first to the third person[9] has here its parallel.[10] According to information provided by the hostile priests of Marduk (Pamphl. II.17ff.),[11] Nabonidus left the regency to his son Bel-shar-usur during his absence from Babylon. This is the Belshazzar of Daniel 5 who thereby is given a sort of historical 'confirmation'.

To finish this review of the historical, literary, and folkloric sources of Daniel 4, gravitating around Nabonidus, we will also cite the strange tradition reported by Eusebius of Caesarea (*Praep. Evang. = PG* XXI, 762A) which says that Nabonidus prophesied the invasion of his country by the Medes and the Persians and pronounced oaths against the 'Persian Mule' (Cyrus),[12] whom he cursed to wander in the desert amid the savage beasts.[13] These literary sources plus the present form of this chapter in Daniel authorize us to draw the critical conclusion that Dan. 4 was worked out before the second century. Its message, for example, reflects the meaning of Isa. 2.9ff. It invites the reader to recognize that the kingship, power, and glory all belong to God, and to humble oneself before him (see Dan. 4.14, 22, 29, 31, 32).

In the first division of the chapter—which consists of three parts— vv.1–15; vv.16–25, and vv.26–34[14]—King Nebuchadnezzar speaks in

[7] Published by C. J. Gadd, *Harran Inscriptions of Nabonidus*, in *Anatolian Studies*, 8 (1958), pp. 35–92.
[8] See *ANET*, p. 314 (IV), (Pamphl. IV.5).
[9] In Daniel 4, vv. 1–15 are in the first person, vv. 16–30 in the third person, and vv. 31–3 are again in the first person.
[10] See Gadd, pp. 91ff. The same thing occurs in Tobit: 1.3—3.6 in the first person, 3.7ff. in the third person.
[11] Published by S. Smith, *Babylonian Historical Texts*, ch. 3.
[12] There are many doubts regarding the legitimacy of the birth of Cyrus (see Xenophon, *Cyropaedia*, etc.).
[13] A final source of information is furnished by Josephus, *c. Apion* I, 146 (Nebuchadnezzar fell sick and died after reigning for 43 years), but it does not contribute much to our understanding.
[14] Or four, if we divide vv. 26–34 into 26–30 and 31–4.

the first person. The atmosphere is completely different from that of chapter 3. Here the king is much more human and his relations with Daniel are almost affectionate. Points of contact with the preceding chapters are not lacking, if only the king's name, the analogy of a pre-monitory dream, the reduction of God's and Daniel's enemies into manure (3.29), and into a savage beast of a king who would be god (chapter 4 *passim*). More important, here as in chapter 2 the king knows the purport of his dream and where it comes from (4.6). There is even a rough outline in 4.6 of a perfect parallel to chapter 2: 'Tell me what I saw in my dream and its explanation.'

Once again the non-Jewish hero of the story is a king. E. Heaton (op. cit., p. 146) puts it nicely: 'Rulers, by reason of their opportunities for exercising power, are more exposed than other men to the temptation of forgetting their status as creatures.' Numerous texts of the Scriptures undertake to remind them of it (see Deut. 17.14–20; Ezek. 31.10; 28.2; etc.). In parallel with the themes already encountered above, the king's dream draws on the story reported in Gen. 41 (cf. Dan. 2), and the impotence of the magicians (see Gen. 41.38) gives a contrast to Daniel's freedom of movement (see 2.11; 5.11; cf. Ezek. 28.3). We would there-fore ask the reader to consider again our commentary on chapter 2 and our remarks on the 'psychological barrier' set up by the king. Here, again, he first calls upon his diviners before turning as a last resort to Daniel, who he knows (v.6) is the only one who can save him. Freedom then is never easy; still less, according to Saadya Gaon,[15] after having looked with vanity upon his own power and wisdom. To complete the irony, the king has seen himself in his dream as a fool and a madman.

In v.5, the king, in polytheistic language normal to Babylon, recog-nizes in Daniel the presence of a 'spirit of the holy gods'. As a purist, Theodotion translated this as 'the spirit of the holy God'. But the expression is inspired by Gen. 41.38 and appears regularly in the mouths of pagans speaking of God. The formula 'the holy gods' is also found in the Phoenician inscription by Eshmunazar II, the king of the Sidonians, in the fifth century BCE (lines 9 and 22).[16] Whereas for M. Delcor the use of רוח here is normal (he refers his reader to Num. 11.29; 2 Sam. 32.2),[17] for D. Lys,[18] there is not only confusion regarding the identity of God here, but also regarding the 'spirit' which is of a wholly different type than elsewhere in the Scriptures.

---

[15] Quoted by Slotki, op. cit., ad loc.

[16] See G. Cooke, *A Text-Book of North Semitic Inscriptions* (Oxford 1903), pp. 30–1. This inscription is important in more ways than one for Daniel 4. It too begins, for example, with a description of the peace the king found in his tomb having been 'taken before (his) time [by death]' after having built 'the houses of the gods' and conquered new territories in Palestine.

[17] P. 112.   [18] *Ruach*, op. cit., p. 44, n. 1.

The Masoretic Text indicates in v.5 that the king recounted his dream to Daniel in conformity with the remainder of the chapter (vv.7ff.). Theodotion, on the contrary, omits the word 'dream', so we have a text ('I said in his presence') which announces v.6[19] and establishes a striking parallel with Dan. 2, even though this theme here is not pursued further. Charles (op. cit.) sees the intervention here of a redactor. And to avoid any disaccord in chapter 4, Montgomery proposes that in v.6 we read, not חזוי 'the visions of', but חזו 'behold': 'Behold the dream, interpret it.' Theodotion has the text: 'Listen to the dream I have had and tell its interpretation'.

The image of the tree, whose description begins in v.7, is for the most part borrowed from Ezekiel 31.2–18. The Pharaoh of Egypt is there compared to an immense cedar sheltering all the birds of the air, the most beautiful tree in the garden of God (vv.8–9) or in Eden (vv.9, 16, 18a, 18b). But Pharaoh is delivered over to the power of Nebuchadnezzar (v.11), and the tree is cut down (v.12). He descends into Hell (v.18) and the Abyss closes over him (v.15). We may also think of Ezek. 17.2–24 where Nebuchadnezzar is once more on stage, this time in the form of a royal eagle (v.2). Here the cedar represents the royal house of Judah and its crown, Jehoiachin, is deported to Babylon (v.4). The tree of Israel is cut (v.9), but YHWH will replant one of its branches 'on a high and lofty mountain' (v.22) and it will become a cosmic tree sheltering all the birds of the air (v.23), for YHWH is the God who 'cuts down the high tree and raises up the low tree' (v.24).

Geo Widengren[20] notes that in these texts the Tree of Life is identified with the Cosmic Tree, although these two are usually distinguished. It is certain, he says, that this type of language comes from Mesopotamia by way of Canaan (pp. 57–8). We may consider, for example, a dream of the Median King Astyages who, according to Herodotus (I, 108), saw a vine growing out of the abdomen of his daughter, Mandane, which spread over all of Asia. This vine was Cyrus. Another comparable episode given by Herodotus (VII, 19) is Xerxes' dream where he saw himself crowned with an olive branch whose shoots spread over all the earth.

The symbolism of this Tree in the history of religions is well known.[21] It is the *axis mundi* which crosses through all the cosmic zones. As concerns Israel, the myth was adopted at least in terms of its language. G. Widengren[22] and the Uppsala School believe that we may conclude

[19] In the MT; Θ has another text, see *infra*.
[20] *The Tree of Life in Ancient Near Eastern Religion* (Uppsala 1951), p. 57.
[21] See G. van der Leeuw, *Phänomenologie der Religion* (Tübingen 1933), p. 39, or Mircea Eliade, *Patterns in Comparative Religion* (New York 1958), pp. 106–8; 265ff.; 298ff.; 380; see Subject Index under '*axis mundi*', p. 474.
[22] Op. cit., p. 58.

that Israel shared in the very ancient notion of the king as a powerful tree planted in paradise, in the Garden of God, 'in the middle of the earth'. The human heart attributed to the tree in Dan. 4.13 seems to go in this direction, as do vv.8–9.[23] However, it should be noted that when this image is applied to foreign kings by Scripture it implies their destruction. Plöger concludes from this that the arrogant all want to be represented as righteous by the cosmic tree, but this cannot last for, in the end, the tree is cut down (Ps. 37.35–6). It is not the same, clearly for the righteous man (Ps. 1.3; 92.13–15; Isa. 61.3; Jer. 17.8). In some ways occupying an intermediate situation, Nebuchadnezzar's tree is cut down but not eliminated. It serves as a witness to God's universal domination. It remains a stump (v.12), 'bound with iron and bronze'. A. Bentzen emphasizes that it is not so much a question of guaranteeing the perpetuity of the tottering tree as to promise the prolongation of Nebuchadnezzar's kingship.

E. Heaton (p. 149) asks rhetorically whether we should not see a reminiscence of the 'tree of knowledge of good and evil' from Gen. 2.9 in the royal tree. Here, too, the abuse of its fruit leads to humiliation, but not to destruction.

In v.10 an angel (here called 'a Watcher, a Saint', see *infra*) intervenes whose role is to take part in the action represented in the vision. Further in the book, the angel goes so far as to interpret the vision. There is a novelty here.[24] In Zechariah, we certainly find repeated in different instances the expression, 'the angel who talked to me' (1.9; 2.2; 4.1; 5.5; etc.). He explains everything and uses prophetic terms such as 'thus says YHWH' (1.14; 2.12; 3.7; etc.). He has become a necessary intermediary between God and men. But in Daniel 4.10 for the first time he gives commands and is called 'the Watcher'. This term is best explained by the intellectual parallel furnished by Isa. 62.6: 'Upon your walls, O Jerusalem, I have set watchmen (שמרים); all the day and all the night they shall never be silent. You who put the Lord in remembrance, take no rest' (RSV). 1 Enoch 39.12 says of the angels, 'they do not sleep' (and we think of Ps. 121 speaking of God 'who neither slumbers nor sleeps'. The same idea is also found in Ezek. 1.18 and Zech. 4.10.) The title 'Watchers' came to appear frequently in the Apocrypha (see 1 Enoch 1.5; 20.1; 2 Enoch 7; 18; Jub. 4.15; Test. of Reuben 5.7; Test. of Napht. 3.5; etc. In the literature from Qumran, see C D 2.18; 1 Q Gen

---

[23] See Lam. 4.20; Isa. 10.33—11.1; Jer. 46.22–23; cf. *Ant. Bibl.* 12.8 (ed. Kish, p. 148): Israel is a vine whose roots reach into the depths and whose shoots reach up to the Throne of God; 1 QH 6.15ff.; the holy community is the Cosmic Tree; similarly 1 QH 8.8–9; cf. H. Ringgren, *The Faith of Qumran* . . .(Philadelphia 1963), p. 195; Matt. 13.32 and parallels on the Kingdom of God.

[24] In Ezekiel, the angels act more than they talk; in chapters 1—18, they do not say one word to the prophet.

78

Ap 2.1. In this latter text, as in many others, we find the Watchers assimilated with the Saints, as here in Dan. 4.10, 14, 20). But here, as is common to so many other developments in Scripture, the origin of this notion and the vocabulary which transmits it are incontestably pagan. Traditional Jewish literature, moreover, conserved the memory that 'the names of the angels were brought by the Jews from Babylon' (see *Gen. R.* 48 and *j. R. h. Sh.* 1.2). Some have sought to identify these heavenly beings with pagan gods, transformed here, for good reasons, into YHWH's court. They refer above all to the Amesha Spentas from Persian religion, a sort of guardian angel (so considered by Philo, the Mandeans, and Syriac Christians).

In parallel with the mysterious 'son of the gods' in chapter 3, L'Empereur (1633), followed by d'Envieu,[25] thought they recognized the Angel of YHWH, the Son of Man, the Messiah, the second person of the Trinity. This interpretation is surely tendentious and would not merit being mentioned here if it did not judiciously bring together comparable elements in the Book of Daniel. We saw in chapter 3 the relation between the 'son of god/the gods', the son of man in chapter 7, the angels, and Daniel himself. We pass, indeed, following our Author from the 'guardian angels' to those who are guarded. There is a fundamental unity between the two groups[26] and a similar insistence on the angelic (hence divine) dimension of man. If it cannot be a question here of 'the second person of the Trinity', we do find underlying the whole Book of Daniel the notion of continuity between God and the righteous ones of Israel. This will be of decisive importance for our reading of chapter 7. Here, in a fresco presenting an Eden-like Tree representing man's empire, there is a restatement of what is really important by the Watcher, the Saint:[27] man's ultimate dimension does not lie in a demonstration of his will to power, but is angelic, divine. Man stands against the over-man.

In v.11 we do not know to whom the Watcher's order is directed. Montgomery says: 'to the celestial executors' and he refers to Isa. 40.1. This textual comparison does not appear required to us. It seems rather that the meaning here is impersonal: 'let the tree be cut down', etc. As Bevan (ad loc., p. 91) writes: 'Possibly this vagueness is intentional, indicating that the judgment upon the king is to be brought about by wholly inscrutable means.'

In any case, the tree is cut down, but not uprooted. In imitation of Ezek. 31.10–14 and Isa. 6.13 (applied to Judah) it remains as a promise

---

[25] *Le Livre du Prophète Daniel*, 2 vols., 1888–91, p. 388.
[26] The idea goes back to Ezekiel who often calls an angelic being simply שׁיא, man.
[27] In the same way that the Israelites in Dan. 7 are the people of the Saints and are collectively Man.

of regeneration (v.12). We mentioned above the importance, in this respect, of the circle of iron or of the bronze chains around the amputated trunk. Nebuchadnezzar's throne is maintained. There is, however, an ambiguity inherent in the image. For Bevan (p. 91), it is 'a figure of speech for the stern and crushing sentence under which the king is to lie'. Similarly for Jerome it is a sort of strait jacket, while for Rashi it is what assures the stability of the throne (see v.23).

V.12 suddenly moves from 'the metaphor of the tree to the actuality figured', as Montgomery puts it.[28] It becomes clear that the king will be struck by lycanthropy, a disease sadly illustrated by King George III of England and by Otto of Bavaria. Here the superstition about werewolves finds its material basis. Nebuchadnezzar, to boot, is here reduced to a bovine state. In one agada about Adam we find his pathetic prayer that he be not obliged to graze on grass like an animal.[29] Thus, in the myth of the Garden of Eden, as it is reused in this chapter (see *supra*), Nebuchadnezzar who thought himself capable of becoming an over-man is reduced to the status of an animal. The conjunction of 'grass' and 'dew' in this verse recalls Gen. 2. Nebuchadnezzar experiences the return to the state of potentiality described in the first chapters of Genesis. This is the radical alternative concerning which the Bible sees man debating with himself: either become Israel, or become bestial. Everything happens as though humanity were divided into prisoners and guards in a concentration camp. For Daniel and his companions this is the only historical dialectic. Sometimes it crops out of everyday phenomena with so much convincing force that it might be asked how the pagans can remain so blind and deaf to it?[30] It really takes the substitution of a bestial for a human heart (v.13). Nebuchadnezzar's 'heart'—that is, his understanding, his will, his character[31]—loses every human quality to such an extent that in his confrontation with the Living God the king loses his memory. This would mean extinction if there were not a temporal limit to his chastisement: 'seven times'—an expression whose meaning is probably 'seven years'.[32]

That the king's madness is for a fixed period of time affirms that there is one possible escape. It is not true that 'the chips are down'; the game

[28] Page 233. Similarly in Ezek. 31.11; Matt. 22.13; Luke 12.46; Isa. 5.1ff.
[29] See *ARN* 1.14: 'When Adam heard the Holy One, blessed be he, he said to him, "You will eat the grass of the fields"—his limbs began to tremble and he said, "Master of the World, will I and the livestock eat from the same manger?" The Holy One, blessed be he, replied, "Because your limbs trembled, I will bless you. You will get your bread from the sweat of your brow."'
[30] See Luke 16.31.
[31] See Jer. 5.21; Hos. 7.11.
[32] This is what was understood by the LXX, the Rabbis, Josephus, *Ant.* X, X, 6, etc. See our critical notes for this verse.

remains open to the end. With these verses, it is true, we have the most extreme expression of the Book of Daniel's so-called 'determinism'. Montgomery (p. 83) speaks of 'the most un-Biblical expression', adding moreover that we should remember that this is the only language Nebuchadnezzar could understand. But, from another point of view, this determinism is corrected by the call to repentance (v.24). Yes, the 'sentence is a decree from the Watchers' (v.14), but it is no more irrevocable than the pre-exilic prophets' announcement of the destruction of Nineveh.[33] The decree is not significant *in et per se*, but in service of a lesson which 1 Sam. 2.5–8 has already made explicit.[34]

Freedom, in Scripture, is not a static notion. Man *becomes* free. Maimonides says that Israel received the commandment to be free. For here, freedom is liberation: the free man frees the world he lives in. The 'alienated' man enslaves himself and his environment. The alternative is to transcend one's milieu or to become absorbed into it. Consequently, man is the field for a tension between two poles: determinism (or alienation) and freedom (or project). Nebuchadnezzar is trapped by 'Babylon, the great city' (v.27) until he frees himself by recognizing God's liberating transcendence over the world, Babylon, and Nebuchadnezzar himself.

'The sentence', 'the decision', 'the decree', the 'seven times', etc. belong to the vocabulary of the negative pole. Israel does not deny, in effect, determinism as such. She does affirm, however, that it stands in contradiction to freedom, a freedom which enacts itself and which transcends determinism. Thus on another plane, close to this one, cyclical time[35] is not unknown to Israel, but it is transcended by a 'linear' time which opens the cycles to an always unexpected future. The 'eschaton' is the last 'future'. Until then time may have been fixed as 'seventy weeks' (9.24–7), for example. It is the time of the divine forbearance which is not unlimited, but which, through grace, limits the scope of man's revolt and gives him a thousand occasions to repent and to live.[36]

---

[33] Montgomery refers to such texts as 1 Kings 22.19ff.; Isa. 44.26; Job 1—2; Ps.89.6–8. Cf. *Sanh.* 38b: 'The Holy One never does anything without having first consulted the Family (פמליא) on high; as it is said . . . (Dan. 4.14).' To Charles (p. 93), this kind of Talmudic text is 'extravagant, even blasphemous'; we do not see why.

[34] See as well, Ezek. 17.24; Ps. 113.7–8; Job 5.11; Luke 1.52; 1 Cor. 1.26ff.; Wisd. 6.3; Esth. (Vul.) 14.11. Re Daniel 4.14b, Montgomery writes: 'one of the immortal sentences of the Hebrew Scriptures!' (p. 236).

[35] The seasons, the succeeding generations, the astral and human cycles, etc.

[36] The Rabbis draw attention to the fact, that, in condemning Adam to death, the last word pronounced by God which will always echo in his ears in תשוב: you will return (Gen. 3.19). Similarly R. Meir read טוב מאד in Gen. 1.31 as *tov moth*: death is good. In 2 Chron. 36.21, the delay of 70 years is a delay of grace for the Land.

CHAPTER 4

Text 4. 16–25

(16)Then Daniel, whose name was Belteshazzar, was appalled for a moment and his thoughts frightened him. The king spoke up and said: 'Belteshazzar, do not let the dream or the interpretation frighten you!' Belteshazzar spoke up and said: 'My Lord, may the dream be for your enemies and its interpretation for your adversaries! (17) The tree you saw, which became large and strong, whose height reached up to the heavens and which could be seen from all over the earth, (18) this tree, whose leaves were beautiful and whose fruits were abundant, which had enough food for everyone, in the bower of which the beasts of the fields found shelter, and in whose branches dwelled the birds of the air, (19) is you, O king, who have become great and strong, whose greatness has increased and reached up to the heavens, and whose dominion extends to the ends of the earth. (20) Next the king saw a Watcher, a Saint, descend from the heavens and say: cut down the tree and destroy it—but leave the stump of its roots in the earth bound with iron and bronze, in the grass of the field. Let him be watered with the dew from the sky and let him have his share with the beasts of the fields, until seven ages have passed over him. (21) Here is the interpretation, O king, here is the decree of the Most High which has reached out to my Lord the king: (22) You will be driven from men and will dwell among the animals of the fields. You will be given forage to eat like cattle and you will be watered by the dew from the sky. Seven ages will pass over you until you know that the Most High rules over the kingship of men, which he gives to whomever he pleases. (23) Whereas it was said that the tree's stump of roots should be left, your kingship will be secure for you as soon as you recognize that the heavens rule. (24) Wherefore, O king, may my counsel be pleasing to you! Break off your sins through almsgiving and your faults through compassion for the unfortunate; perhaps your tranquillity will continue.' (25) (All this happened to King Nebuchadnezzar.)

Critical Notes 4. 16–24

V.16 עשה: cf. 3.6.—אל־יבהלך . . . ענה: missing in LXX and Θ, probably by homoioteleuton.—אשתומם: Jerome translates as *intra semetipsum tacitus* (cf. Rashi: שתק). See 8.13: embarrassment, perplexity, etc.

V.20 *del.* in LXX.

V.22 טרדין מן: to drive out, expel; cf. v.29. In the passive: 4.30; 5.21.

V.23 Θ: 'Leave. . . .'—Θ: 'as soon as you have recognized the power of the heavens.'—שמיא: the only instance in the Hebrew Scriptures where 'the heavens' is a substitute for God. But it is used frequently in Jewish and Christian literature; see 1 Macc. 3.19; 4.10, 40; etc., *P.A.* 1.3; etc.; Luke 15.18, 21; etc.

V.24 Θ: 'Perhaps God will be patient with your faults.'—צִדְקָה: alms-giving, see commentary. In Dan. 9.16, another meaning.—אַרְכָה: prolongation of tranquillity (cf. v.26a). But Ibn Ezra has read ארכה as in Hebrew = healing, and שְׁלוּתָךְ as 'error' (= Verss.): 'a healing of your error'. See Θ: παραπτώμασις; Vul.: *delictis*. Cf. Prov. 10.2; Ecclus. 3.30; Tobit 4.11; 12.9.

Commentary

In v.16 the second part of the chapter begins. What is immediately striking is the passage to the third person for speaking of the king. This phenomenon—which is also found in the Book of Ṭobit, for example, as we indicated above—is due to the dramatic character of the story. Montgomery writes (p. 223): 'The dramatic propriety involved appears from the fact that probably most readers do not stumble over the incongruity.' In fact, the style of the account ingeniously suggests that Nebuchadnezzar has completely lost control of the situation: he will soon be spoken of (vv.25ff.) as one speaks of a tree.[37]

The repetition of the earlier elements from vv.17ff.—sometimes in an abbreviated form—gives the presentation a certain rhetorical effect similar to the repetition of a theme in a song. It culminates in an un-expected feature: 'It is you, O king' (v.19). We find the same construction in 2.37–8. This already announces the eventual repentance since Israel found it difficult to conceive that anyone could stupidly resist divine chastisement. This is so true that the author of 2 Maccabees could not imagine that even Antiochus IV would not confess once he was come before his judge. He offers us an excellent parallel to the text of Daniel (see here v.22) in chapter 9 (vv.11–12): 'Then it was that, broken in spirit, he (Antiochus IV) began to lose much of his arrogance and to come to his senses under the scourge of God, for he was tortured with pain every moment. And when he could not endure his own stench, he uttered these words: "It is right to be subject to God, and no mortal should think he is equal to God"' (RSV). His repentance, though, comes too late and the parallel to Daniel 4 ends at this point.

Another allusion to the time of Antiochus IV is found in v.23 in the use of 'the heavens' to designate God.[38] G.F. Moore[39] nicely brings together this use of the general Hellenistic religious atmosphere: 'That the heavens were the seat of the highest god was the universal belief of the age, and various Syrian gods of heaven were seeking their fortunes in the Roman world under the name of the sky-god Jupiter—Jupiter

[37] Note that the king returns to speaking in the first person in the fourth part, in v.31, just when he recovers his human stature.
[38] See our critical notes ad loc.
[39] G. F. Moore, *Judaism* (Harvard 1932), vol. 1, p. 367.

Heliopolitanus of Baalbek, Jupiter Dolichenus of Commagene, and the rest; while conversely the Zeus whom Antiochus IV installed in the Temple in Jerusalem was in Syrian speech a "Lord of heaven" (2 Macc. 6.2 *bis*).'

However, what in the 'universal belief' implies an uncrossable distance between the gods and men—the former being in the heavens and the latter on earth—entails for Israel, on the contrary, that God is sovereign over men and not indifferent to the movements of their hearts. Nebuchadnezzar (v.24) is invited to 'break off' his sins.[40] This verb gave rise to a substantive in Aramaic (*purkana*) signifying 'salvation' or 'redemption'.[41] Sin, in effect, is seen as a yoke which must be broken and thrown off. The lordship of the heavens is not the enslavement of the earth, but its liberation.

Sin is broken by צדקה. It is well known that in classical Hebrew this word is used in many senses, meaning 'justice, innocence, faithfulness to the Covenant . . .'. In the time of early Judaism, however, the word designated 'good works', especially alms-giving (cf. Matt. 4.1–14). This is how v.24 is understood in the versions and the *parallelismus membrorum* in this verse proves that they were correct. We are not in a context of 'salvation through faith or through works'[42] with this motif, but rather in the context of the Noachic covenant: alms-giving expresses the minimum required of a pagan. It is the sign of repentance which alone is capable of saving a man or a community from death (cf. Jonah). It alone overturns destiny: a delay of twelve months is allowed to permit Nebuchadnezzar to conform to Daniel's advice (v.26).[43] The virtues of alms-giving are, in effect, placed high in the hierarchy of values. It means meeting God himself (see Prov. 14.31; 19.17; Tobit 12.9; 14.11; Ps. 112.4; *P.A.* 5.13 (19); etc.). We have shown elsewhere[44] the organic ties established by the Law and the Prophets between the poor and oppressed, on the one hand, and the community of Israel, on the other: they share a common destiny. There is no essential difference between the king prostrating himself before Daniel (2.46) and his 'compassion toward the unfortunate' (here).

With v.25, which closes this part of chapter 4, two points of style are

---

[40] LXX: λυτρῶσαι; Vul.: *redime*.

[41] See Ps. 136.24; Lam. 5.8 (both texts in Hebrew).

[42] N. W. Porteous, op. cit., p. 72, feels obliged to say here that 'Good works are not to be despised. What Christianity supplies is a new motive for performing them.'

[43] L. S. Rankin's judgement concerning Wisd. 11.24 is just as applicable to our text of Daniel which precedes Wisd. by about a century: 'The thought that the goodness and mercy of God are calls to sinners to repentance appears apparently for the first time [here] in Judaism in the pre-Christian era.' *Israel's Wisdom Literature* (Edinburgh 1936), p. 42.

[44] In *Migration Today*, no. 15 (Autumn 1970), pp. 54ff.: 'The Stranger in the Old Testament'.

to be noted. First, as A. Bentzen notes, vv.25–32 are composed in the style of oriental royal inscriptions. Next, the story, which was in the second person, moves into the third person through v.30 (see our commentary *supra* on v.16).

Text 4. 26–30

(26) Twelve months later, while he was walking in the royal palace at Babylon, (27) the king spoke and said: 'Is this not great Babylon which I built as a royal residence through my mighty power, to the glory of my majesty!' (28) The words were still in the king's mouth when a voice fell from heaven: 'It is said to you, King Nebuchadnezzar. Your kingship is taken from you. (29) You will be driven from men and you will dwell with the animals of the fields. Like the cattle, you will be given forage to eat and seven ages will pass over you; until you recognize that the Most High has dominion over the kingship of men and gives it to whom he pleases.' (30) Immediately these words were accomplished on Nebuchadnezzar and he was driven from men and he ate forage as cattle do. His body was watered with the dew from the sky so that his hair grew like (the feathers) of eagles and his nails like birds' (claws).

Critical Notes 4. 26–30

V.26 על־היכל: the roof of the palace or its hanging gardens; see 2 Sam. 11.2.

V.27 'great Babylon': see Rev. 14.8; 16.19; 18.2; Jonah 1.2; 3.2.—'royal residence': see Amos 7.13.

V.28 'A voice came from heaven': the בת קול of Judaism, see T. Levi 18.6; T. Jud. 24.2; 2 Bar. 13.1; 22.1; Matt. 3.17; 17.5; John 12.28; 2 Pet. 1.17; etc. See G. F. Moore, *Judaism* I, p. 422.—נפל: cf. Isa. 9.7.—עדת: see 2.21; Job 28.8; Prov. 25.20.

V.29 Almost a word for word repetition of v.22.

V.30 LXX: Daniel's discourse ends here and the king takes up the end of the story in the first person.—Θ: instead of 'eagles', lions; which gives a more satisfactory meaning. LXX: the feathers of an eagle and the claws of a lion. Cf. Dan. 7.4.

Commentary

As v.26 clearly indicates, twelve months pass between the second part of the story and the third part which begins here.[45] The king is now a

---

[45] Rabbinic literature blames Daniel for the twelve month delay. In *B.B.* 4a, Daniel is punished for his dilatory intervention. He is identified with Hatach (from Esth. 4.5) whose name means 'cut off' (from his grandeur). Or too, it is due to his advice to the king that Daniel was thrown into the lion pit.

simple *persona dramatis*. At the moment he believes himself to be at the peak of his power, he is really already only a plaything in the hands of the destiny he has forged for himself. We can well imagine the implications of such a testimony for the persecuted under Antiochus IV.

The king's declaration (v.27) recalls v.1. It should not be considered as simple boasting. History knows Nebuchadnezzar as a great builder.[46] With Plöger (ad loc.), we should think that the king acts as though nothing had happened earlier. The comparison to v.1 is significant. It is, furthermore, a warning to Israel who too often did not listen to the prophets.

It is truly the king himself who unleashes his own condemnation. The chips were not down. The continuation of the story shows, moreover, that chastisement is only worthwhile in that it leads the sinner to repentance, to amend his ways.[47]

As Saul lost the kingship through arrogance (1 Sam. 13.13–14; 1 Chron. 10.13–14) and as David fell ill for the same reason (1 Chron. 21.1–27), Nebuchadnezzar learns at his own expense that 'God has dominion over the kingship of men' (v.29). V.30 describes him as struck by lycanthropy. On this subject—beyond the examples already mentioned from modern history—parallels have been noted with the 'Babylonian Job'[48] and the 'Story of Aḥikar'.[49] Bevan, Montgomery, Jeffery, and Porteous all draw attention to the resemblance to the Bacchant queen in Euripides (*Bacchae*, 1265ff.). They note that the Bacchants are assimilated to animals, clothed with the skins of beasts and suckling young fawns and wolves.[50]

There is a sort of visceral fear of animality in the Book of Daniel. Beasts play a considerable role, always to the detriment of man's integrity. Finally, in chapter 7, the 'son of man' puts an end to the reign of the Beasts and inaugurates the human empire of the Saints. Moreover, this important motif in this book is linked to a reuse by Daniel of the myth of creation. We have indicated this in several places—and again here as concerns the equation of the king and the first Adam, the tree at the centre of Eden and Nebuchadnezzar's vision, the condemnation to graze upon grass and Adam's horror at the thought that he could be

---

[46] Rather than being a great conqueror as were his predecessors, says R. H. Charles, p. 98, who quotes Schrader, *KB* III, 2, p. 39: 'Then built I my palace, the seat of my royalty'; and VII, 34, p. 35: 'In Babylon, my dear city which I love'. See also Josephus *C. Apion.* I, 138.

[47] See 2 Macc. 6.12–17; Wisd. 11.22–6; 12.20–2.

[48] 'Like one of the *nâkim* or a demon-*suku* he made my nails grow' (see Montgomery, ad loc.).

[49] 21.1: 'I prostrated myself on the ground; my hair fell over my shoulders, my beard reached my chest, my body was covered with dust, and my nails were as long as an eagle's talons.'

[50] The queen, too, recovers her reason by lifting her eyes toward heaven (cf. here v.31).

placed at the rank of a bovine, etc.—and we will have to return to it again in the following chapters. For as Scripture clearly indicates, man's natural inclination is to 'turn' towards animality.[51] Between 'zero and infinity', the whole range of possibilities is open to man. 'What is man that you are mindful of him, and the son of man that you care for him? Yet you have made him little less than God, and crown him with glory and honour' (Ps. 8.4–5). The serpent in Genesis, the representative *par excellence* of the animals of the fields, introduces itself into the dialogue between God and man and pulls man down towards the ground where itself is henceforth condemned to crawl and grovel.

It is not without interest that, in the symbolism of the dreams, 'the eagle symbolizes sudden astonishment, a consuming passion of the spirit'. Hair is 'brute nature' in relation to civilization, to virility. E. Aeppli—from whom we are borrowing these analyses—speaks on this subject of 'extremely primitive forces', of 'natural man' and 'wild man'; it is 'our animal nature' which surfaces here.[52]

Text 4. 31–34

(31) At the end of these days, I Nebuchadnezzar, lifted my eyes to heaven and my reason returned. I blessed the Most High and I praised and magnified the eternally Living, for his dominion is an eternal dominion and his rule lasts from generation to generation. (32) All the inhabitants of earth are (for him) reputed as nothing. He acts as he pleases with the army of the heavens and the inhabitants of the earth. No one can stay his hand or say to him: What are you doing? (33) At that moment, my reason returned to me; the glory of my royalty, my majesty, and my appearance returned to me. My counsellors and my lords reclaimed me and I was re-established in my kingship, and still more power was added to me. (34) Now, I, Nebuchadnezzar, praise, exalt, and magnify the king of the heavens, whose every work is true and his ways just and who can abase those who walk in pride.

Critical Notes 4. 31–34

V.31 'The eternally Living': see 12.7; Rev. 1.18; 4.9; 5.13; 15.7; Ecclus. 18.1; 1 Enoch 5.1.—'His dominion . . . generation': see 4.3; a doxology based on Ps. 145.13 which had already been used as a model in Dan. 3.33.—In the LXX—which has totally different text—the healing of the king is due to his repentance and an angel announces to him his re-establishment on the throne of

[51] Albert Cohen: 'We stand opposed to nature.'
[52] Op cit., pp. 279, 159, 162.

Babylon.—יתוב: 'Metsudath David' (seventeenth century) insists on the sense of the unaccomplished and sees here a prayer of Nebuchadnezzar which is not completed until v.33.

V.32 See 2 Chron. 20.6; Isa. 40.17; 43.13; 45.9; Job. 9.12. We are also reminded of Nabonidus' praises to the moon god: 'Sin, lord of gods . . . in your hands you hold every function of the sky, king of kings, lord of lords . . . with fear of your great divinity, earth and sky are filled . . . without you, who could do anything?' (see Gadd, 61).—כלה=כלא: cf. Isa. 40.17; 59.10; (51.6). Targ. on Isa. 63.3: חיל שמיא.—לא חשיבין: cf. Luke 2.13: στρατιὰ οὐράνιος. Cf. Isa. 24.21.—ימחא בידה: a technical expression in Targ. and Talm.: 'reprove, oppose oneself to'. Cf. 2.34–5 where the verb is in the qal (= to strike). The last part of v.32 appears almost textually in the Targ. Eccles 8.4.

V.33 Θ: 'I returned to the glory of my royalty and my majesty came back to me.' = Vul.; Syr. omits all this part of the sentence.—הדרי: the ancient Vss. understand this as a verb (Θ: ἦλθον; Vul.: perveni). Rashi explains that 'return' is in Aramaic, הדר, later spelled הדר. But Saadia sees a parallel to זיו (re this word, see 2.31) in הדרי.

V.34 'The king of the heavens': this expression is unique, but see Jer. 10.7, 10; Ps. 48.3; 93.1; etc.

Commentary

The period of the king's madness and humiliation is considered here as purifying: chastisement leads him to repentance and to confessing that only the God of Israel is the master of kings and empires (v.31). Now, Nebuchadnezzar's avowal leads him well beyond the limits of the Noachic covenant. His experience of the depth of the abyss leads him to a peak of faith. O. Plöger here gives a minimizing commentary. But the Rabbinic literature, on the contrary, insists on the extraordinary character of this phenomenon. It even sees a retroactive effect here. Thus the commentator from the Middle Ages, Rashi, sees the growth of the king's hair as a sign that he was a Nazirite![53]

[53] See *Psikta Rabbati* 36.2, which establishes a parallel between the dew from the sky watering Nebuchadnezzar and Song of Sol. 5.2 where it is a question of God himself: 'my head is wet with dew'. For God, according to this Rabbinic text, cannot sit on his throne since Nebuchadnezzar took the Temple. He suffers the same woes as are inflicted upon Nebuchadnezzar in Dan. 4 which, thus, are no doubt to be understood as a revelation to the sinner of what he is making God endure. Similarly, the death of the first-born Egyptians was a response to the Pharaoh's murdering the Hebrew male infants and to his policy of exterminating the *bekhor YHWH*, Israel. *Psikta Rabbati* continues by speaking of the 'true messiah, Ephraim', whose sufferings are expiatory. At the news of God's sufferings, Ephraim says, 'The servant is satisfied to be like his master.'

Note the intimate relation between the confession of faith and reason (vv.31, 33), a representative point of view of wisdom literature for which (חכמה) ראשית דצת ה׳ יראת (see Ps. 111.10; Job 28.8; Prov. 1.7). Fear of God and reason are linked because it is only by means of the former that man recovers the real meaning of things. What was absurd becomes significant. This is what Nebuchadnezzar recognizes in v.31b: God's universal kingship gives everything a meaning.

This admission, moreover, leads the king to affirm—by means of a terminology proper to a tyrant such as he was—that men and history are only toys in God's hand (v.32; Ps. 104.26).[54] True kingship lies in the stewardship of God's goods, just as freedom is in the overcoming of alienation from oneself and wisdom is in the fear of the heavens.[55]

In the words of Bentzen, Dan. 4 stands against the *Königsideologie* of the Orient. With the Anglo-Scandinavian School, we may see here the repetition of the 'pattern' of a king humiliated then exalted peculiar to the ancient Near East.[56] Yet it is probably no more than a question of a formal canvas for, in point of fact, Nebuchadnezzar is only re-established to his glory by recognizing the eternal and unfailing dominion of the Most High.

[54] Although here it is not a question of men, but of the monster Leviathan.
[55] Recall that the 'Prayer of Nabonidus' (1 Q or Nab) also ends with a similar doxology.
[56] They also draw attention to the parallel between the 'seven times' in Dan. 4 and the full restoration of Baal's power after seven years.

5 The Inscription on the Wall

Text 5. 1–7

(1) King Belshazzar gave a great feast for a thousand of his lords, and in the presence of these thousand men, drank wine. (2) While tasting the wine, Belshazzar commanded that the vessels of gold and silver which Nebuchadnezzar, his father, had taken from the Temple of Jerusalem, be brought so that the king could drink from them, as well as his lords, concubines, and courtesans. (3) Then they brought the vessels of gold which they had taken from the Temple—the House of God—of Jerusalem, and the king, his lords, his concubines, and his courtesans, drank from them. (4) They drank wine and they praised the gods of gold and silver, of bronze, iron, wood, and stone. (5) Immediately the fingers of a man's hand came forth which wrote on the plaster of the wall of the royal palace opposite the candle holder, and the king saw a detached hand writing. (6) Then the king changed colour and his thoughts frightened him. The joints of his loins were loosed, and his knees began to knock. (7) The king cried aloud that the exorcists, Chaldeans, and conjurers should be brought in. He spoke and said to the wise men of Babylon: 'Whoever reads that inscription and makes plain its interpretation will be clothed in purple and, with a gold collar around his neck, will be in the governing triumvirate of the kingdom.'

Critical Notes 5. 1–7

V.1 בלשאצר: Akk.: Bel-shar-uṣur: 'Bel, protect the king'. Cf. Jer. 39.3, 13; Nergal shar-uṣur: 'Nergal, protect the king'.—עבד לחם: cf. Heb., Eccles. 10.19 (עשה לחם); cf. Esth. 1.2; Ecclus. 34.23.— רברבן: cf. 4.33.

V.2 בטעם חמרא: Rashi, Ibn Ezra, Jerome: 'in the wine's humour (counsel)' (cf. טעם in 2.14). Similarly, Prince, Driver *et alii*. See our commentary.—מאניא: = Heb. כלים; cf. Isa. 52.11; Ezra 1.7f.; Baruch 1.1, 8.—שגלתה: Heb. גבירה, but the term means the king's mother (see Jer. 13.18) or grandmother (see 1 Kings 15.13 ‖2 Chron. 15.16), not his wife. In Ps. 45.10, we also find שגל (the titular queen); cf. Neh. 2.6 (= queen of Persia). See R. de Vaux, *Ancient Israel* (New York 1961), Part II, ch. 6, pp. 117–19.—לחנה: in the Aramaic papyri from Elephantine this term designates a member of the Jewish temple personnel in the region (a singer?) and his wife. In the Targs. the word means concubines. The term שגל comes from the Assyrian *ša ekalli*, 'queen', lit. 'the one of the palace'. לחנה is the Akk. *laḥḥanatu/laḥḥinatu*, a female miller at the service of a shrine. The term may have evolved toward the meaning of sacred prostitute (communication of E. Lipinski). Some biblical texts speak of two classes of women in the royal harem: see 1 Kings 11.3; Song of Sol. 6.8—אבוהי: that Nebuchadnezzar was the father of Belshazzar is mentioned seven times in this chapter (vv.2, 11b, 11c, 11d, 12, 18, 22). We are not inclined therefore to see a 'reviser's work' in one of the three occurrences in v.11.

V.3 Θ and Vul. add: 'and silver' (cf. v.1).—Θ: 'the Temple of God which is in Jerusalem'.

V.5 נברשתא: of unknown origin (Persian?). Montgomery (ad loc.) cites Halévy who proposes the following semantic evolution of the word: mabrart < nabrart < nabralt < nabrašt, from בר״ר 'to be clear'. A: λαμπάς; this translation is cited in Yoma 41a. J. Yoma (Schwab, III, p. 198) says that it is not the candle holder with seven branches (but see J. Steinmann, op. cit., p. 90).—גירא: Heb. גיר; cf. Isa. 27.9.—פס: Jastrow, Dict., ad loc.: 'the hand from the palm to the finger tips'. Ibn Ezra: 'a detached hand', cf. Θ: ἀστραγάλους = Vul.: articulos. In Gen. 37.3, both hands and feet; Isa. 47.3 מֵי אֲפָסַיִם: water as high as one's ankles (see Montgomery, citing Maurer). Cf. Josephus, Ant., X, XI, 2: 'a hand detached itself from the wall'.

V.6 An anacoluthon construction: 'then the king, his colours changed (on) him', cf. vv.9, 10.—זיוהי: cf. 2.31 (plural as פנים). LXX: ὅρασις (reading: ריוהי), whence the Vul.: facies.—קטרי חרצה: the same expression is found in Targ. Jon. on Gen. 50.11. Heb.: חלצים. Charles, op. cit., p. 119, judiciously refers to the Homeric sentence: αὐτοῦ λύτο γούνατα (Od. IV, 703; Il. XXI, 114).—ארכבתה: cf. 6.11: ברכוהי. A sign of intense fright, cf. Nah. 2.11; Isa. 21.3; Ezek. 21.11; Ps. 69.24.

V.7 להעלה לאשפיא: see 2.2 for the idea here. For the vocabulary, see 4.3, 4.—פשר: cf. 2.5; etc. Cf. 1 Q p Hab. 2.6–9: an interpretation of prophetic terms thanks to divine inspiration (so H. Ringgren, The Faith of Qumran, p. 9).—ארגונא: cf. Esth. 8.15; 1 Esdras 3.6; Xenophon, Anabasis I, 5, 8; Cyropaedia I, 3, 2 (where it is stipulated that ornaments such as purple, collars, and bracelets are Median and not Persian. The Persians maintained a grand simplicity); II, 4, 6 (the same idea in reference to Cyrus); cf. 1 Macc. 10.20; 14.43.—והמנוכא: Qr.: והמניכא. A collar (see Gen. 41.42) was a sign of distinction among the Persians, where the word is hamyanaka, whose Aramaic transcription should be hmymk' (cf. edn of Ginsburg) (communication E. Lipinski). See Anab. I, 5, 8; 8, 29; I, 2, 27; Cyrop. XIII, 5, 18; Herodotus, III, 20; IX, 80; 1 Esdras 3.6. The Targ. on Gen. 41.42 uses the term מניכא in the story of Joseph.—תלתי: Θ: τρίτος; but LXX (and Josephus, Ant. X, XI, 2–3): a third (of the kingdom). We may see here a reminiscence of *šalšu* in Babylonian (which in Heb. gives שָׁלִישׁ = captain, see Exod. 14.7): high official. Or again, in the light of 6.3, we may see one of the members of a triumvirate (whence our translation). In Test. of Jos. 13.5, Potiphar is called 'third after Pharaoh'.

Commentary

In our Introduction we briefly indicated the 'friendly' atmosphere which develops between the king and Daniel in this chapter. H. L. Ginsberg draws the legitimate conclusion from this that its redaction preceded the second century and the persecution under Antiochus IV Epiphanes. Yet it is also possible to see Antiochus behind the Belshazzar of this chapter. Epiphanes, indeed, had plundered the Temple in Jerusalem in 169, before profaning it with idolatrous objects and practices (see 1 Macc. 1.20–8, 54, 59; 2 Macc. 6.2–4). In short, we agree with Ginsberg that chapter 5 of Daniel had an older origin than the second century, but it was read and interpreted in a modernizing sense by the Redactor in light of the events of 169.[1] From this, the death of Belshazzar at the end of the chapter becomes a liberating announcement of the death of the Syrian tyrant and the message of this chapter is put on the same plane as that of Daniel B (see 7.24–6; 8.23–5; 9.26–7; 11.36–45).

The historical fiction proffered by Dan. 5 does not stand up under historical criticism; yet it testifies to some interesting reminiscences concerning the end of the Babylonian Empire. To do them justice, we must remember that with Nabonidus absent from his capital—the event underlying chapter 4—his son, Belshazzar, assumed the regency at Babylon.[2] On this subject, two contrary pieces of information must be taken into consideration: on the cuneiform tablets we find the names of Nabonidus and his son Belshazzar associated, an unusual fact which seems to militate in favour of a *reign* of Belshazzar.[3] But, from another side, the 'Chronicle of Nabonidus' insists that the New Year festival could not take place at Babylon given the king's absence. In either case, the 'great history', to assume the expression O. Plöger uses here, is not far off base since it knows a *Bel-shar-uṣur*, the son of Nabonidus. Perhaps it is not really in any fundamental disaccord with a reign or a

---

[1] We may accept M. Delcor's affirmation, op. cit., p. 132: 'This story, it seems, appeared and circulated independently during the Persian period or at the beginning of the Greek period between 400 and 300.'

[2] Belshazzar was the son of Nabonidus, not the son or grandson of Nebuchadnezzar. We have explained above the reasons for this substitution. We find the same confusion in Baruch 1.11–12.

[3] Even more clear is the following text published in 1924, London, by Sidney Smith, *Babylonian Historical Texts*, p. 88: Chronicle col. II, lines 20–1: 'He struck his hands, he entrusted the kingship to him, while he himself set out on a far journey.'

'regency' of Belshazzar at Babylon at the time Cyrus took the city. Certainly Nabonidus had returned from Teiman, but the 'Chronicle of Nabonidus', after having indicated the long absence of the king and spoken of the 'royal prince', tells us that Nabonidus fled the Persian troops when Babylon was captured by Cyrus. 'The sixteenth day, Gobryas the governor of Gutium and the army of Cyrus entered Babylon without battle.'[4] It is not impossible therefore that Belshazzar might have regained the reins of power in the interval.

What is more, chapter 5 of Daniel places the fall of the Babylonian Empire[5] in the paradoxical setting of an orgy in the royal palace. Now, here too, the ancient historians of the capture of Babylon confirm this fact in their own ways. Herodotus (I, 191) recounts that the inhabitants of the centre of the city did not know that the outskirts had been captured by Cyrus until long after the fact, for 'there was a festival going on, and they continued to dance and enjoy themselves until the hard facts told them the news (that the city had been captured)'. Xenophon, in turn writes:[6] 'However the trenches had been excavated.[7] Cyrus learned that this was the time of a great festival at Babylon, during which the citizens drank and enjoyed themselves all night long.'

Chapter 5 opens without any indication as to the date. It is implicit in the information supplied by vv.30–1: the last night of the Babylonian dynasty, 11 October (15 Tishri), 539. The king—or perhaps the regent (see *supra*)—gives a banquet and, on this occasion, seems to confirm the ancient historians who held that Babylonians were addicted to wine. Thus, Quintus Curcus (V, I) writes: 'Babylonii maxime in vinum et quae ebrietatem sequuntur effusi sunt.' We note also that according to Herodotus (V, 18), the Persians admitted women to such festivities: 'At important dinners like this . . . it is our custom in Persia to get our wives and concubines to come and sit with us in the dining-room.' For Plutarch (*Symp.* I, 1) and Macrobius (VII, i), just the concubines were at the feast.[8] A large crowd of guests seemed to have taken part in such affairs (see Esth. 1.5, etc.).

[4] See *ANET*, p. 306. Nabonidus was taken prisoner when he returned to the city.
[5] Y. Kaufmann and others insist too much on the absence of war or the rumbling of war in Dan. 5, we believe. Kaufmann speaks of a palace revolt preceded by a peaceful period. In fact, Dan. 5 is, unexpectedly, more interested in the individual punishment of the royal blasphemer than in the sensational fall of a worldwide empire. We must remember, however, that for the Redactor in the second century and his readers everything centred upon Antiochus IV Epiphanes. Twenty two hundred years later, in the forties of our own century, the hope was for 'the fall of Hitler'.
[6] *Cyropaedia* VII, 5, 15–16.
[7] To turn aside the flow of the Euphrates. Josephus attempts to reconcile Daniel and other more correct historical data (see *Ant.* X, XI). For example, he makes Cyrus (reigned 539–530) and Darius (reigned 521–486) contemporaries!
[8] See also 1 Esdras 4.29–31.

In the course of what had become an orgy, perhaps under the influence of alcohol,[9] the king orders that the sacred vases from the Temple at Jerusalem be brought to him (v.2). If the feast was not originally a religious one, which is not established,[10] it plainly becomes one. Furthermore, it was a custom to offer libations to the gods after feasts, as A. Bentzen points out.[11]

Vv.1–4 could serve as an illustration of the Augustinian definition of evil as *privatio boni* or *amissio boni*. An impious man can never do anything but profane the sacred vessels. In so doing, he acts within a pre-established framework which he must respect, since he is congenitally incapable of creating another one. Evil is not his creation, for evil is only an absence (*privatio, amissio*). The only thing left to the impious man is to attempt to empty the 'vases' of all content, to render impure what had been pure, to violate their innocence, and to debase their nobility. Man can only strike the Creator by means of the creation.

The king tries to reassure himself by degrading what frightens him. At the same time he tries to raise himself as a man to the rank of a joyous crony untouched by metaphysical problems. In fact, his search for security is a mad dash toward the abyss; he brings his own punishment down on himself; he 'makes' the hand which writes on the wall. This is why he is the only one to have the vision (vv.5, 6). It is also why, when everything is over and done, he covers Daniel with gifts (see *infra*).

It is always upsetting for Holy Scripture to see what poor substitutes men exchange the Living God for (v.4).[12] The materials enumerated here recall those of the statue in chapter 2,[13] as well as the Prayer of Nabonidus (4 Q or Nab, end of col. 1): 'For seven years I prayed to [the gods of] silver and gold, [bronze and iron], wood and stone and clay, because [I believ]ed that th[ey] [were] gods[. . .].'[14] Finally, it will be recalled that in the second century Menelaus gained the good graces of Andronicus, the representative of Antiochus IV, by giving him several gold vases which he took from the Temple treasure. 'The Temple treasury had now become the private treasury of the powerful men and the rulers of Jerusalem.'[15]

The Author, as we have seen, is a master story-teller. The story takes

[9] As for the Talmud, it insists several times on the fact that the king was not drunk on wine, but rather that he had 'lost his wits along with his wine' (see *Meg.* 12b). On wine and its effects, see Ecclus. 11.25–31.

[10] See J. Steinmann (p. 90), A. Bentzen (p. 47).

[11] On the contrary, it seems an exaggeration to say that Dan. 5 is a midrash on Isa. 21.5 or Jer. 51.39–57.

[12] See Ps. 115.4–8; Jer. 10.3ff.; Rev. 9.20.

[13] Except for the wood instead of ceramic and also the fact that in chapter 2 the stone comes from without. See J. Steinmann ad loc.

[14] *Les Textes de Qumrân traduits et annotés* (op. cit.), p. 294.

[15] V. Tcherikover, op. cit., p. 172.

on a visual character: the orgiastic feast is suddenly interrupted by a detached hand silently writing on one of the palace walls (v.5). A popular motif in ancient folk-tales,[16] this is still an effective image today.

We emphasized above the fact that the king is the only one to view the miracle. Through his profanatory act, the king has 'desired' the writing on the wall. He has challenged God and his challenge has been accepted. It is solely an affair between God and Belshazzar, to everyone else the palace wall stays blank, there is no message.[17] For the thousand people surrounding the king (v.1), we ought to eat and drink for there is nothing else to man's lot. The crowd is 'neutral', it is lost in negativity. To probe the absurdity of an existence without the Word, it places nonsense into the very heart of what is reputed to be significant (vv.2–3). What happens when the Spirit is dislodged from the vases where it was hiding? Daniel answers: it then openly reveals itself on the whitewashed wall from whence it can never again be erased.[18]

Teilhard de Chardin expresses this in his own way: evil is that 'plaster' which fills the cracks in creation. For the king truly was the instrument of his own confusion as well as of the revelation given to him. It is indeed at the level of human choice and historical events that the Word is pronounced and written. In retrospect, once the sign[19] has been given and once the precise circumstances of its apparition are taken into consideration, a new problem arises. It is the act of iniquity which called forth the divine intervention. In this sense, we may well understand St Augustine's exclamation: 'Felix culpa!' 'According to Jacob Boehme, there is a supreme law which governs the divine as well as the human; it is that every revelation requires a contrast: Just as light is only visible when reflected by some dark body, so anything whatever only appears in opposition to its contrary. What never meets any obstacle always outruns itself and never returns to itself. It never really exists either for itself or for others. If the divine Spirit must reveal itself, it does not remain within itself, but calls forth its contrary. This is not all; in then acting on this contrary it assimilates it to itself and spiritualizes it.'[20] A theophany—in the words of the Talmud concerning the Messiah— is 'for an entirely righteous generation or for an entirely wicked

[16] See H. Gunkel, *Märchen* (1917), p. 142; W. Baumgartner, *Das Buch Daniel* (1926), p. 9.

[17] Vision and visionary are always one (see Dan. 9.24), for the vision always arises from the *élan vital*.

[18] See O. Plöger, ad loc.: to the praise of gods lacking life responds a living hand, a concealed theophany.

[19] A sign, not a marvel, for the natural laws are not violated. After all, the king had been drinking and his 'vision' may be explained by his drunkenness or his having become delirious.

[20] Emile Boutroux, 'Le Philosophe allemand Jacob Boehme', in *Etudes d'Histoire de la Philosophie* (Paris 1897).

generation'. In the first case, the 'hand' or 'finger' writes the tables of the Torah (Exod. 31.18); in the second case, 'the finger of God' manifests itself through the plagues directed against the Egyptians (Exod. 8.15)[21] or through the inscription on the wall of Belshazzar's palace.

Text 5. 8–12

(8) Then all the king's wise men came in, but they could not read the inscription or make known to the king the interpretation. (9) Then King Belshazzar was greatly frightened; he changed colour and his lords were dismayed. (10) The queen, due to the king's and his lords' words, entered the festival hall. The queen spoke out in these words: 'O king, live for ever! Let not your thoughts frighten you or (your face) change colour. (11) There is one man in your kingdom who has the spirit of the holy gods in him and in whom, in the days of your father, they found light, understanding, and a wisdom like unto the wisdom of the gods. And King Nebuchadnezzar, your father, made him chief of the magicians, exorcists, Chaldeans, and conjurers; (so acted) the king, your father. (12) Whereas they found in him, in Daniel, to whom the king had given the name Belteshazzar, an extraordinary spirit, knowledge, and understanding, the faculty to interpret dreams, to explain riddles, and to loosen enigmas, let Daniel be called and he will make plain the interpretation.'

Critical Notes 5. 8–12

Vv.8–10 Several terms from these verses are missing in Θ. Similarly in vv. 11–12.—לבית משתיא: cf. Jer. 16.8; Eccles. 7.2.

V.11 Cf. Prov. 1.1ff.; Ecclus. 39.1ff.; Test. of Levi, ch. 18.—רוח אלהין קדישין: Θ: 'a spirit of God' (cf. 4.5, 6, 15; 5.14). Cf. Gen. 41.38.—אבוך מלכא: del. in Θ probably a marginal gloss which was later inserted in the text.

V.12 The last three expressions are in post-stasis in relation to v.12a: whereas ... therefore. Θ makes them participles: 'he was interpreting dreams, etc.'—קטרין: lit.: 'knots'. It is a question of difficulties (Yebam. 61a; 107b; cf. Pesh.), or conjunctions of stars, or magic charms. Cf. Enoch 8.3. Θ here has λύων συνδέσμους.—אחידן: a technical term from Aramaic wisdom which early entered into Hebrew (e.g., Judg. 14.12): חידה; cf. 1 Kings 10.1; Prov. 1.4–5; Ecclus. 39.1ff.—די־מלכא ... בלטשאצר: del. in LXX (but present in Θ; Syr.; Vul.).

Commentary

V.8 onwards constitutes the second part of this chapter. It opens on a

---

[21] See O. Plöger, ad loc.

failure. The Babylonian wise men can neither read nor, for that reason, interpret the inscription. Regarding this subject, we may recall the mysterious character attributed to the cuneiform writing still in use during the Seleucid period in those Mesopotamian circles addicted to divination. We even know of one magic text worded in Aramaic where the writing is cuneiform.[22]

However valuable this comparison may be, it must be completed by other considerations. There is a deliberate parallelism between the deciphering and interpretation of the writing here and the narration of Nebuchadnezzar's dream and its interpretation in chapter 2. There Nebuchadnezzar threw up a psychological barrier so as not to remember his dream;[23] in chapter 5, the inscription 'desired' by the king (see *supra*) provokes similar characteristics of a 'mental block' in him.

The מלכותא in v.10 is not the king's wife, but the widow of Nebuchadnezzar (v.11), who, in this fictional account, is the father of the reigning king.[24] Josephus (*Ant.* X, XI, 2) prefers seeing her as his grandmother. In either case, her situation as queen-mother (the powerful גבירה in the ancient Near East) no doubt authorizes her to take the initiative and enter the feast hall.[25] What is more, Nitocris, the wife of Nebuchadnezzar, enjoyed a solid reputation of being wise. According to Herodotus (I, 185–7), she was the one who fortified Babylon against the Medes and the Persians. In this story in chapter 5, she plays a role parallel to that of Arioch in chapter 2 (see vv.14, 16, 24–5). As for the 'ignorance' of Daniel's existence professed by Belshazzar, it is part of his psychological 'block' and is in parallel with Exod. 1.8: 'Now there arose over Egypt a new king who did not (want to) know Joseph' (so in Targs; *Sotah* 11a; Rashi; etc.).

Daniel is described (v.11) in a manner which recalls 4.5–8. Moreover, 'his light' is a divine attribute according to 2.22. It recalls texts such as 2 Sam. 14.20 concerning David or 16.23 about Ahithophel. According to v.12, Daniel had 'an extraordinary spirit' in him (cf. 6.4). To be sure, the LXX sees here a πνεῦμα ἅγιον and Susanna 45 (Θ) says: 'God aroused (ἐξήγειρεν) the holy spirit of a young man called Daniel.' But the passage from 5.11 to 5.12 is more likely—following D. Lys[26]—the passing from theology to anthropology, 'without our being able to

---

[22] Personal communication from Fr Pierre Grelot.

[23] See *supra* ad loc.

[24] In the midrashic use of this text in the New Testament, the 'queen' becomes Pilate's wife.

[25] Which his wife could not have done (see Esth. 4.11). The LXX would rather avoid any logical objection by replying in advance: τότε ὁ βασιλεὺς ἐκάλεσε τὴν βασίλισσαν περὶ τοῦ σημείου. On the power of the queen-mother in Scripture, see 1 Kings 15.13; 2 Kings 10.13; 24.12.

[26] See op. cit., pp. 254–5.

strictly delimit the domain of man's *ruach* and that of God's *ruach* (Ezek. 36—7!); not that there is any confusion or transition between the two, but that it is a matter . . . less of entities than of a dynamism.' Once more one does not see how a man of such a broad intelligence, and but recently the head of the diviners (see 2.48), could have been unnoticed in the king's court. If the story is to have any internal unity and an elementary character of credibility, we must imagine that it implies more than it says.

Text 5. 13–16

(13) Then Daniel was brought into the king's presence. The king spoke and said to Daniel: 'Are you that Daniel from among the exiles from Judah whom the king, my father, brought from Judah? (14) I have heard about you that you have the spirit of the gods and that one finds in you light, understanding, and an extraordinary wisdom. (15) Now they have brought into my presence wise exorcists to read that inscription and to make known to me its interpretation, but they could not show the interpretation of those words. (16) I have heard about you that you can give interpretations and loosen difficult problems. Now, if you can read that inscription and make known to me its interpretation, you will be clothed in purple and, wearing a gold collar, you will be in the governing triumvirate of the kingdom.'

Critical Notes 5. 14

V.14 Cf. 4.5; 5.11.—אלהין: in the Kennicott and de Rossi variants, the word קדישין is added; also in the Codex Marchalianus Lucianus of Θ. Without this addition, the expression corresponds to Gen. 41.38.

Commentary

V.13, in turn, closely recalls chapter 2 (see v.25), which allows Daniel (vv.18ff.) to reproach Belshazzar for having ignored the lessons of his 'father's' reign. Moreover, a supplementary confirmation of our interpretation of chapter 5 is found in the fact, pointed out by O. Plöger (ad loc.), that the king repeats his mother's words, but carefully omits the reference to the Jew's high position under his father, Nebuchadnezzar. We cannot follow E. Heaton therefore when he marvels at Daniel's poor reception (v.17) of 'Belshazzar's friendly welcome and proposal' (p. 160).[27] Similarly, we do not draw the critical conclusion drawn by

[27] It is clearly not a question of what Porteous (ad loc.) sees here, namely a rhetorical refusal (since Daniel accepts the reward in the end) or a simple didactic lesson intended for Jewish sages.

Plöger, Delcor, *et al.* from the 'interrogation about his identity' (Delcor, p. 129), that chronologically chapter 5 preceded chapter 2. In this case, Daniel's reproaches (vv. 18ff.) would lose much of their meaning.[28]

Text 5. 17–30

(17) Then Daniel spoke and said in the king's presence: 'Let your gifts be for yourself; and give your presents to others! However, I will read this incription, O king, and I will make known the interpretation. (18) O you who are king, the Most High God gave to Nebuchadnezzar, your father, kingship, greatness, glory, and majesty. (19) Because of the greatness he gave him, men of every people, nation, and language trembled in fear before him. He killed those whom he would and he let live those whom he would; he elevated those whom he would and put down those whom he would. (20) But when his heart was lifted up and his spirit hardened to the point of arrogance, he was deposed from his royal throne and deprived of his glory. (21) He was cast out from among the sons of men, his heart became like that of the beasts, and he dwelt with the wild asses. He was fed with forage like the cattle and his body was watered with the dew from the sky until he recognized that the Most High God has dominion over the kingship of men and he sets up over it whom he pleases. (22) Now you, Belshazzar, his son, you have not humbled your heart even though you knew all this. (23) You have lifted yourself up against the Lord of heaven, and you have had the vessels of his house brought before you, and you drank wine from them, you and your lords, your concubines and your courtesans. You praised the gods of silver, gold, bronze, iron, wood, and stone, who do not see or hear, and who know nothing, and you have not glorified the God who holds your breath and all your ways in his hand. (24) So, on his behalf, this detached hand has been sent and this inscription has been written. (25) Here is the inscription which has been written: "Mene, mene, tekel u-pharsin". (26) Behold the interpretation of these words: "Mene" (numbered): God has numbered your reign and ended it. (27) "Tekel" (weighed): you have been weighed in the balance and you have been found wanting. (28) "Peres" (divided): your kingdom has been divided and given to the Medes and Persians.' (29) Then Belshazzar commanded that Daniel be clothed in purple, that he be wearing a gold collar, and that it be proclaimed that he was in the governing triumvirate of the kingdom. (30) That very night, Belshazzar, king of the Chaldeans, was killed.

---

[28] It is possible that we have an interesting parallel for v. 13 in 4 Q or Nab I.4, at least if we follow the reconstruction of Dupont-Sommer in *Les Ecrits esséniens* . . ., p. 337: 'it was a Jewish (man), one of t(he deportees . . .).' Cf. J. T. Milik, 'Prière de Nabonide et autres . . .', *RB*, no. 3 (1956), p. 408. (This restitution is not found in *Les Textes de Qumrân*, p. 294.)

Critical Notes 5. 17–28

V.17 See 2.6 in general, as well as for the word נבזבה which is explained there.—עגה: *del.* in Θ.

V.18 Lit.: 'You, O king . . .'; the rest is in anacoluthon.—אלהא עליא: see 3.26.

V.19 מחא: aphel part. of חיה, but some Vss. have understood מְחָא = to strike (see Θ, Vul.); cf. the parallelism with קטל (not so in Syr.; Saadia; Rashi; etc.).

V.20 רם לבבה: cf. Deut. 8.14, etc. (רם לבבך). רם is a pe'il participle: cf. Dan. 5.22; 8.25; 11.12, 27, 28.—ורוחה: the *ruach* of man in its negative reality. Cf. Deut. 2.30; God hardened the heart of King Sihon so that he would not make a wise decision. Cf. Zech. 7.12.

V.21 See 4.22, 29, 30.—מן־בני אנשא: in chapter 4, we find מן אנשא three times; Θ always gives ἀπὸ τῶν ἀνθρώπων.—שוי: Kt.; שויו: Qr. The Qr. is in the third person plural perfect of the pael. שוא עם = Heb. משל עם (Ps. 28.1).—ערדיא: certain mss. have עדריא, flock, a facilitating reading. ערדיא, wild asses, cf. Job 39.5ff.; Gen. 16.12.—ולמן די . . . יהקים עליה: Θ: 'which he gives to whom he wants to'.

V.22 כל קבל די: atypical sense of 'even though' (cf. 2.8).

V.23 מרא־שמיא: see 2.18 (אלה שמיא).—מאניא: see 5.2.

V.25 מנא מנא: a repetition which does not appear in LXX, Θ, Vul., Josephus, or in vv.26–8, which seem to require three, not four, terms. It is evident that the *lectio difficilior* is represented by the MT as opposed to the Vss.—ופרסין: is again an anomaly with respect to vv.26–8 which use the term in the singular: *'peres'*. Furthermore, what is here a series of four names is interpreted there as verbs. In fact, vv.26–8 play on the assonances. It is not necessary to correct them as in the Vss.

V.26 מְנָא: may be effectively a passive participle: numbered. But for the other words to be of the same nature, תקיל and פריס would have been necessary (see Charles, p. 135). As small change, see Ezek. 45.2; Ezra 2.69. In Ps. 90.12, we find the same form in Heb.: מני. In Isa. 65.11, we must think of the Arabic *maniye* = destiny.

V.27 תקל: 'weighed', cf. Ps. 62.9; Job 31.6; Prov. 16.2; 21.2; 24.12; Enoch 41.1 (constructed from our passage).—במאזניא: influenced by the Heb. See 1 Q Isa. 40.12: מוזנים; 40.15: מזנים; in the Non-Jewish dialects of Aramaic, as well as at Elephantine, the word lacks the א: מוזנא (personal communication from Y. Kutscher ז"ל).

V.28 In the Talmud, פרס designates a half-mina.

Commentary

The fourth and final part of the story begins with Daniel's refusal to accept payment for his good offices (v.17). According to the interpretation which we have proposed, the king's promise is one more attempt to bribe the 'divine' and to change a 'fate' which he intuits as being fatal for him. We are reminded of Balak's pathetic and vain efforts to reorient Balaam's prophecy in a favourable direction (Num. 23—4).[29]

Not as a concession to the king's power, Daniel adds (v.17b): 'However, I will read this inscription, etc.' When the Word is spoken, it requires an interpreter and an interpretation.[30] The Word calls forth prophecy.[31] In chapter 2, a stone overturns the statue of the Babylonian Empire; in chapter 5, a hand writes on the palace wall that the empire's days are numbered. Between these two occurrences, sadly, there 'is nothing new under the sun'. The son has learned nothing from his father. Daniel could still show pity for the latter, but not for Belshazzar. There is nothing more to be expected from him, neither presents nor honours. Whether a Jew serves the government or not, history has a sense and it moves toward its omega, even though men untiringly repeat their choice for nonsense.

V.19 is certainly unexpected. Everywhere else in the canonical and noncanonical documents, such expressions are reserved for God alone (see Deut. 32.39; 1 Sam 2.7; Ps. 75.8; Job 5.11–16; Ecclus. 7.11; Tobit 4.19). In fact, few of the other Israelite writings go as far as the Book of Daniel in the dialectic of power. Every reign, all grandeur, all glory, and all majesty (v.18) can only be the echo of the lordship of God. There is no human power without the One who is Power and who founds every sovereignty.[32] This conception is fundamental for understanding the whole Book of Daniel; it is the cornerstone of chapter 7.

So Belshazzar is not excusable (v.22). He would be no doubt if it were a question of a theory which he had badly assimilated. But he had a demonstration of the truth in the life of his 'father'. The only conclusion possible is that the king is obstinately hostile to God. For Montgomery (ad loc., p. 261), 'there is no finer example of the preacher's diction in the Bible than this stern and inexorable condemnation'. We are reminded of the prophet Nathan's condemnation of David (1 Sam. 12). What is more, Belshazzar's blindness also recalls that of Rehoboam the stupid, the son of wise Solomon (1 Kings 12.1–20).

---

[29] See also 2 Kings 5.16; Amos 7.10ff.; Num. 22.18; Mic. 3.5, 11; cf. Acts 8.18ff.
[30] This is the gist of Rom. 10.14ff.; 1 Cor. 12.10; etc.
[31] See Amos 3.7–8.
[32] See 1 Sam. 8.1–7. All 'value' is founded in God who guarantees its worth; cf. Hag. 2.7–8.

The king is stupid. As does v.4, but with more force, v.23 once again expresses the Jew's astonishment at the incomprehension of the 'nations'.[33] The point of culmination is reached when what belongs to the true God is attributed or consecrated to other divinities. 'God holds your breath and all your ways in his hand.'[34]

Finally, after a long period of suspense, the inscription on the wall is read by Daniel (v.25). It consists of four words, one of which is a repetition of the first word.[35] It seems evident that the number four is a deliberate parallel to the four empires in chapters 2 and 7. But in the explanation which follows (vv.26–8), the cryptograms are reduced to three, for their interpretation is based on their assonance. The text thereby gives up one metaphor to adopt another.

In v.25 the words are to be understood as substantives. Clermont-Ganneau[36] has presented the attractive theory that it is a question of pieces of money of decreasing value: 'a mina, a mina, a shekel, and two half-minas'.[37] In fact, in this series, the shekel has the least value, the proportions represented being 60, 60, 1, and 30. R. H. Charles (op. cit., p. 136) suggests considering ופרסין as an explicative gloss on an original פרס (to draw attention to the assonance with 'the Persians') which entered the text as a replacement for its model. As, with Haupt and Prince, he reads the first מנא as a verb ('it has been counted'), the original enumeration in v.25 for him was 'a mina, a shekel, a half-mina'—that is, successively: Nebuchadnezzar, Belshazzar, the Medo-Persians.

We do not follow Charles into this terrain. ופרסין has a plural form which corresponds too well to the Median-Persian duality to be rejected. In this sense, ופרסין is to be understood as a dual. In returning over the series, the shekel—whose weight is ridiculously light by way of comparison—is Belshazzar. He is, in the fiction maintained by Daniel, the last king of Babylon and it is to him that the disastrous interpretation is addressed. The 'mina' is his 'father', Nebuchadnezzar—which corresponds well with what is said about him in vv.18–19. Only the first mina is left, which no one generally knows what to do with. Haupt, Prince,

---

[33] See Deut. 4.28; Ps. 115.4ff.; 135.15ff.; Rev. 9.20.
[34] Ibn Ezra refers to Eccles. 12.7: 'The spirit returns to God who gave it.' Re the 'ways', see Jer. 10.23; Num. 16.22; Enoch 47.4. Re the 'breath', see Gen. 2.7 and Job 12.10.
[35] See our critical notes. In the Jewish tradition we find the opinion that the inscription was in Hebrew. Certainly the Chaldeans were capable of reading it, but not of understanding it, for it appeared as an anagram laid out in three lines of equal length for a five letter word which had to be read from top to bottom:

ממתוס

נוקפי

אאלרן (see Slotki, op. cit. ad loc.).
[36] *Recueil d'archéologie*, I (1886), pp. 136–59.
[37] See Taanith 21b about a man who was better than his father: 'a mina son of a half-mina' (= peras).

Charles, *et al.* adopted the solution proposed by Hans Bauer[38] in his day (see *supra*), that is they understood the term מנא in the first place as a verbal form. For us, on the contrary, it is a question of a deliberate dittography of the substantive מנא. There were originally three terms: מנא תקל ופרסין. They designated Nebuchadnezzar, Belshazzar,[39] and the Medo-Persians. A later Redactor added 'a mina' to the beginning of the nomenclature to arrive at the sum of four terms and so establish a parallel with the four empires in chapters 2 and 7. He therefore saw the following succession: Babylon (a mina), Media (a mina), Persia (a shekel), Alexander's divided empire (*some* half-minas and not, in this context, two half-minas unless only the Ptolemies and the Seleucids are intended).

Two possible objections against this reconstitution are easily resolved. The first is that Belshazzar seems to be lost along the way. But this is a false impression. Belshazzar represents the decline of the Babylonian Empire immediately replaced by the Median Empire (the second mina). What is more, the Redactor in the Maccabean period was more interested in a 'prophecy' concerning the Ptolemies and the Seleucids of his day than in the fate of the Babylonian King Belshazzar in the sixth century.

The second objection appears to be more serious. In the chronological succession and the judgement of qualitative value, one would not expect that the Persians would be estimated as a shekel while the Medes weighed sixty times as much. Historically the proportion ought to be inverted. But, for Daniel, it must be remembered that the Medes far surpassed the Persians. This is so because of Scripture (whence the Author draws most of his information about history). Thus, for Isa. 13.17 and 21.2, the *Medes* are going to destroy Babylon; for 2 Kings 17.6, the inhabitants of the Kingdom of Israel were deported to Median cities; finally, and above all, Jer. 51.11 announces: 'The Lord has stirred up the kings of Media because he wants to destroy Babylon.' It is easy to imagine the probable chain of thought: the prophet Isaiah, in the eighth century, prophesied the destruction of Babylon;[40] for the Deuterono-

---

[38] Hans Bauer, 'Menetekel', in *Vierter deutscher Munzforschertag zu Halle/S.* (1925), pp. 27–30, cited by A. Bentzen.

[39] We do not see how one could follow H. L. Ginsberg (*Studies . . .*, pp. 24–6) who sees Evil Merodach in the shekel. It is true that he is mentioned in the Bible (2 Kings 25.27–30 and Jer. 52.31–4), but he is completely absent from the Book of Daniel. It would have been nearly impossible for an 'average' reader to grasp this allusion.

The meaning of the 'half-mina' is confirmed by a bilingual Assyro-Aramaic inscription (*CIS* II, no. 10), another bilingual Aramaic-Babylonian one from the Persian era (*RES*, no. 1784), and by the Talmudic understanding of the term *prs*. (Communication of E. Lipinski.)

[40] Isa. 21.1–10 dates from the time of Sargon (721–705). E. Dhorme has shown that the title 'the oracle of the wilderness of the sea' in verse 1 alludes to the Babylonian low country in the time of Sargon (*mat tamti*), see *RB* (1922), pp. 403–6. It cannot be

mist of the seventh century, the exiles from the North were 'in Median cities'[41] which only makes sense in regard to the prophecy in Isaiah; Jeremiah takes up as his own the announcement made by his illustrious predecessor (51.11). Now, historically, the Persian Cyrus conquered Babylon, but he is 'king of the Medes and Persians'. The prophets Isaiah and Jeremiah were therefore almost right. Yet the 'almost' is bothersome. Daniel, in the second century, comes to the aid of prophecy (see, for example, 9.2 and 24) and gives chronological and qualitative precedence to the Medes: 'Darius the Mede' seizes Babylon (6.1; 9.1). He precedes 'Cyrus, king of Persia' (10.1). The same fiction was adopted by the final Redactor of Daniel 5.25.[42]

In the interpretation which follows next (vv.26–8), the metaphor changes. The cryptograms פרס, תקל, מנא become verbal forms and Belshazzar is involved in each instance. 'Mene' now signifies 'counted', 'numbered', 'tekel' is 'weighed', and 'peres' is 'divided'.[43] This is—as M. Delcor says (p. 131)—an exegetical method which 'strongly resembles (that) of the peshers or commentaries found at Qumran'. We note, moreover, that the term used to designate the interpretation of mysterious writing is פשר as at Qumran. S. B. Frost[44] writes: 'That a kingdom should be weighed in a balance[45] and found wanting is the very stuff of prophecy; that it should be divided is a pronouncement of divine judgement in the very manner of an Isaiah; but that it should be *numbered* is the thought of an apocalyptic alone. The whole school is impregnated with the conception of periods predetermined by divine decree.'

Jewish interpretation in the Middle Ages saw in the root פרס the correspondent of שבר: to break (Saadia, Rashi, Ibn Ezra). Von Lengerke (1835) and Hitzig (1850) followed this reading. More recently, J. Steinmann (p. 96) gives this paraphrase: counted (his bad deeds); too

a case of a prophecy *post eventum* as in Isa. 13.2–22 (written after the victory of Cyrus) for the fall as described is grim or painful and the visionary is overcome by it. Kissane has even put forth the unsupportable hypothesis that it originally concerned Jerusalem laid siege to by the Assyrians.

[41] Or the 'mountains of Media', see J. Gray, *I–II Kings, A Commentary* (Philadelphia 1963), ad loc.

[42] Charles (p. 137) notes that the Greeks spoke of their conflicts with Darius and his successors as τὰ Περσικὰ or, indifferently, τὰ Μηδικά.

[43] H. L. Ginsberg (*Enc. Bibl.* col. 692, 'Daniel' in Hebrew), shows that this passing from one nature of a word to another is attested to in Rabbinic literature. He gives the example of the word קנה to buy (or) a reed. 'Whoever sees a reed (קנה) in a dream can hope for wisdom' (*Ber.* 56b on the basis of Prov. 4.5: קנה חכמה: to acquire wisdom). Ginsberg also refers to *j. Maaser Sh.* 55c.

[44] *Old Testament Apocalyptic* (London 1952), p. 186.

[45] The idea probably originated in Egypt. The Book of Daniel, however, speaks rather of the *person* of Nebuchadnezzar being weighed (*contra* Frost). Such an idea is not prophetic, but sapiential, cf. Job 6.2; Prov. 24.12; cf. Ps. 68.10; Wisd. 11.22.

light (his character); broken (his kingdom): 'counted, weighed, cracked'. We will also quote P. Oschwald's fine translation—though his commentary lacks 'weight'—'the *accounting* is done: you have been *weighed* and given over to the *destroyers*'.

The condemnatory judgement seems to fall from the sky, 'by divine decree'. But, in fact, it is the concrete Kingdom of Babylon which is 'found light'. It is a question of intrinsic worth, of what it merits from its history. The empire is spatially immense. Its political 'weight' is incomparable. But its being is light, it lacks weight. Such is the reversal of values brought about by God according to Israel. The importance of a kingdom is not measured by its size or the weight of centuries, but by its reason for being. Here is the whole argument of the Book of Daniel: history is the bearer of God's judgement. History is both theophany and verdict.[46]

As 'Mount Sinai was wrapped in smoke because the Lord descended upon it in fire' (Exod. 19.18), so the theophany consumes Belshazzar (Dan. 5.30), but first it transfigures him (v.29). In the encounter between Daniel/God and the king, we pass from 'I-it' to 'I-thou'. Belshazzar is revealed to himself. What is proper to revelation is that it is convincing because it is liberating, triumphant because it is creative. The king, become a 'thou' for Daniel, and, through him, for God, ceases to exist in darkness, in absurdity. He is paradoxically freed from his alienation by the announcement of his condemnation.[47] For Belshazzar judged is at last the authentic Belshazzar. He is no longer vainly and absurdly seeking himself where he knows in advance he will not find himself. Sisyphus is freed from his destiny. Even the blasphemy of drinking intoxicating beverages from the sacred chalices was only an act of despair, a leap into the abyss because all the props of existence were revealed to be false. Belshazzar is at last face to face with himself, having discovered—as in Jacob Boehme's vision, *supra*—the obstacle which prevents him 'from always outrunning himself without ever returning to himself, from never really existing for himself or for others'.

'That very night, Belshazzar, king of the Chaldeans, was killed' (v.30). There could be no other sequel to the king's liberation. The last word was pronounced not only *about* him, but *by* him. He accepted (v.29) his death as the ultimate way to self-realization. This is evidently why Daniel accepts after all the honours he had previously rejected

[46] See Deut. 18.15–22; Acts 5.38–9.
[47] See Josephus, *Ant.* X, X, 4: '(The king) did not refuse what he had promised Daniel, although he was become a foreteller of misfortunes to him.' To us, Josephus seems better inspired than is A. Bentzen (p. 47) for whom the king attempts to avoid the bad tidings by in any case giving Daniel the presents he had earlier refused. Nor do we see how O. Plöger arrives at the conclusion for v.29 that the king resembles a condemned man who has just received his sentence: he has no reaction.

(v.17). For Nebuchadnezzar, accepting the truth had the consequence of returning his reason to him (4.34); for Belshazzar, it allows him to die. In every way, it is the passage from one era to another, the eruption of the new at last.

There exists no historical confirmation of the murder of Belshazzar worthy of acceptance. We already know how little this embarrasses our Author: his next story opens with an enormous historical error (6.1). But chapter 5 is a paraenesis. In its present form it probably has in mind the succession of Antiochus IV after Antiochus III in 175 (see Dan. 11.10–19, 21–45).[48] As for its original form, A. Bentzen suggests characterizing it as a *jüdische Missionpredigt* in imitation of Jonah (but, according to Bentzen, without any possibility of repentance). In this case, we should date it about 300 BCE.

[48] See O. Plöger, p. 91.

6 The Lion Pit

Chapter 6 constitutes the last agadah in the Book of Daniel. It is constructed on the same model as chapter 3 and the parallel between the two tales goes so far as to include a common vocabulary (6.5 ‖ 3.29; 6.8 ‖ 3.2; 6.14 ‖ 3.12; 6.22 ‖ 3.22; 6.26 ‖ 3.29, 31; 6.27 ‖ 3.29; 6.28 ‖ 3.28, 29, 32, 33; 6.26–9 ‖ 3.21, 33). Furthermore, the general plan of the two stories is similar:

6.2–9 ‖ 3.1–7:	Introduction
6.10–19 ‖ 3.8–23:	First part
6.20–5 ‖ 3.24–7:	Second part
6.26–9 ‖ 3.28–30:	Conclusion

As for the structure, we indicated in chapter 3 the repetitions clearly in a liturgical fashion of the principal motifs. The same phenomenon—in a less grandiose form, it is true—is reproduced in chapter 6. Earlier about the three young men, here about Daniel, the story progresses in a dramatic manner all the while untiringly repeating itself. We will cite just a few of the principal expressions in chapter 6: 'The king' appears 31 times; 'Daniel' 21 times; 'the kingdom' 10 times; 'to pray, to address one's prayers, to desire, etc.' (בע״ה) 7 times; 'throw into a lion pit' 4 times; 'the pit' (alone) 6 times; 'the lions' 9 times; etc.

The goal of the *agadah* is clear in both chapters 3 and 6: the faithful of Israel are miraculously saved while their persecutors are devoured by their evil undertakings. Even though this theme was current in Jewish literature (see Judith, Tobit, Susanna, Bel and the Dragon, Wisdom of Aḥikar), it admirably suits the situation of the Judeans in the second century BCE. Yet this is not the origin of chapter 6. First, Antiochus IV would not allow himself to be so cunningly manipulated by his counsellors;[1] second, we may accept H. L. Ginsberg's comment that Daniel 6 makes no allusion to Hellenized Jews. We are therefore once more in the presence of a reuse, for a second century audience, of an older oral or written tradition.

Indeed, the story gets all its meaning from the fact that in 169, Antiochus IV wanted to force the Jews to worship the dynastic god Baal

---

[1] It is true that there was nothing of a marionette in Darius I either. But the Author can have a historical figure from the forgotten past assume features which could not be attributed to a contemporary figure.

Shamem (identified with the Olympian Zeus) whose epiphany he considered himself to be. The epiphany of the living God (see vv.21, 27) in the lion pit is the response to this monstrous pretension,[2] according to our *agadah*. King Darius withdraws into his palace-temple (היכל v.19). But the God of Daniel is always there where we least expect him to be: in a stone, a crematory oven, on a whitewashed wall, or in a pit of ferocious beasts.

Primitive Christian art saw an announcement of Christ's resurrection in Dan. 6. And there is a correct intuition at the basis of this apologetic interpretation. Here, as in chapter 3, we find the essence of the resurrection, that is, less a phenomenon of a life after death as the triumph of life over death, of hope over despair, of significance over nonsense.

Before moving on to our commentary on chapter 6 in the proper sense of the word, we need to point out one proposition of A. Bentzen[3] in order to reject it. He suggests that Daniel's sojourn in the lion pit is an echo of the myth of the descent of a hero, particularly a king, to hell. This ritual death, parallel to that of the king of Babylon, or that of Orpheus, etc., belongs to a *cycle*. After life comes death, after death comes a new life, also doomed to die, etc. The Scandinavian School seems incapable of accepting the fact that Israel breaks the circle. It is false to consider 'Jewish religion' as a constitutive element of the history of religions. Israel destroys the religious, it does not contribute to it.

Text 6. 1–6

(1) And Darius, the Mede, received the kingship, being sixty two years old. (2) Darius thought it good to set over the kingdom one hundred and twenty satraps, so that they would be throughout the kingdom; (3) and over them, three ministers, one of whom was Daniel, to whom the satraps would give account so the king would suffer no harm. (4) Now this Daniel surpassed the ministers and satraps because he had an extraordinary spirit in him; and the king planned to set him over the whole kingdom. (5) Then the ministers and satraps desired to find some grievance against Daniel regarding (the governance) of the kingdom, but they could find no grievance or corruptness, for he was faithful, and no negligence or corruptness could be found against him. (6) Then these men said: 'We will not find any grievance against that Daniel unless we find something in the Law of his God.'

---

[2] However, the primary material in the traditional story could hardly have underscored this monstrosity. Instead the crime was thrown back upon the ministers and counsellors, which would place the date of this original form near the Persian period or at the beginning of the Hellenistic period.

[3] *Daniel*, pp. 55–6; *Bertholet Festsch.* (1950), pp. 58–64; *Eissfeldt Festsch.* (1947), pp. 57–60.

Critical Notes 6. 1–6

V.1 LXX (= 5.31): substitutes 'Artaxerxes, king of the Medes', for Darius the Mede. Then in 6.1, Darius' age is changed to 'and Darius was full of days and renowned in his old age'.—קבל מלכותא: Charles, p. 140: 'He received the kingdom in accordance with the will of God, the Ruler of all.' Cf. in Greek: 6.29 (28); Bel and the Dragon 1; 2 Macc. 4.7; 10.1; Josephus, *Ant.* X, XI.2.

V.2 אחשדרפניא: see 3.2, 3, 27; 6.5, 7.—שפר קדם: see 3.22.—120: LXX: 127 (cf. Esth. 1.1; 8.9; 1 Esdras 3.2).—There is a hendiadys in this verse which accents the two successive acts of envisaging a possibility and then carrying it out.

V.3 סרכין: from the Median term *saraka* (minister): 6.4, 5, 7, 8, 16.— טעמא: for the meaning of this word, see Ezra 5.5. In the Targ. on Prov. 26.16, one also finds יהבי טעמא.—נזק: cf. Ezra 4.13f. Θ translates poorly as 'upset'.—LXX: Daniel 'had power, in the kingdom, over everyone', etc.

V.4 מתנצח: originally, נצ״ח in Aramaic signified 'to shine'.—עשית: in the ethpael, this verb signifies 'to think, to have a care for', see Jon. 1.6. Cf. Ps. 146.4: עשתנות, thoughts. Θ has simply 'set him over'.

V.5 Θ omits the end of the verse beginning from 'and no negligence . . .'—עלה: Θ: πρόφασις, which corresponds to the use of this word in the Peshitta (legal accusation, see Matt. 27.37; or, pretext, see Mark 12.40); see Montgomery, ad loc.—שחיתא: see 2.9; cf. Ecclus. 30.11.—שלו: see 3.29.—מהימן: see 2.45.

V.6 דנה: *del.* in Θ, which has a short text: '. . . no grievance, except in the Law of his God'.

Commentary

As we said, v.1 of chapter 6 represents an insurmountable historical problem. There is, at best, some confusion between 'Darius the Mede' and Cyrus who seized Babylon in 539. The Author may have confounded two seizures of Babylon, the one by Cyrus and the other by Darius in 529. We indicated above the determinative role of certain prophecies (Isa. 13.17; Jer. 51.11, 28) in the attribution of the destruction of the Babylonian Empire to the Medes. Yet that there is a direct reminiscence of Darius I Hystaspis (522–486) in Daniel 6.1 seems proved by the fact that the organization of the empire into satrapies is attributed to the king in v.2. Now, Hystaspis, according to the ancient historians, was a great organizer. According to Herodotus (III, 89), 'he set up twenty . . . satrapies'. This number varies according to the text cited: 120 in Dan. 6.2; 23 in the inscription from Behistun (col. 1, par. 6); 29 in the inscription on the tomb of Nakh-i-Ruchtan (1.7–19); Esth. 1.1

mentions 127 under the reign of Xerxes (486–465), cf. 1 Esdras 3.2; Josephus, *Ant.* X, XI, 4 speaks of 360 provinces in the empire.

On the basis of contractual tablets dating from the first year of the reign of Cyrus upon which the names of Cyrus and his son Cambyses are associated, some have attempted to identify 'Darius the Mede' with Cambyses.[4] Other hypothetical identifications with historical personages have also been advanced. They are discussed and rejected in turn by Rowley who concludes in favour of a confluence of traditions all confounded with one another. Even the age attributed to Darius in v. 1 (62 years old) is difficult to accept for he reigned for another 36 years (see tablets, Syncellus, Eusebius). Cyrus, on the contrary, would have been about that old in 538 (see Cicero, *De Divin.* I, XXIII, 46). Moreover even the Greek authors constantly confused Persian and Median names and events.

If we are to take **verse 2** seriously in its historical pretensions, we need to think, with Plöger, of centrifugal tendencies in Darius' Persian Empire. These could have been counterbalanced by a stronger attachment to the king by certain persons. The envy of Darius' courtiers in regard to Daniel would be explained by a rivalry of the 'centrists' against an official of the decentralization, and all the more so, since Daniel is a foreigner promoted to the highest functions. He is one of the 'three plenipotentiary ministers' (v. 3)[5] and the king is even thinking about making him his appointed representative (v. 4) for he has 'an extraordinary spirit' (see 5.12) in him. We have already noted the parallel with Joseph on this topic. Daniel, too, is on his way to becoming grand vizir. His 'spirit' is appreciated by the king who evidently places it on a political plane. But there is clearly some ambivalence in the term.[6] Faith gives understanding about everything. It makes one apt for the conducting of the *res publica* (see the demonstration in chapter 4). Note also, here again, the post-Exilic use of רוח as characteristic of man as the image of God. It is given to everyone—like the light in John 1.9. Everyone has the possibility of being a 'Daniel', although just one person really is for his peers in his generation. Dialogue is possible between the Jew and Darius.[7] This does not prevent the רוח יתירא of Daniel from arousing envy since he does not follow the beaten path consecrated by the use of mediocre men; indeed one may be His Majesty's Chancellor even though one only has a very ordinary spirit. As in the parallel stories of Joseph and Esther, his enemies resort to devious methods (v. 5), and,

---

[4] See Winckler, Riessler, Boutflower. H. H. Rowley, *Darius the Mede and the Four World Empires in the Book of Daniel* (Cardiff 1959), rejects this solution.

[5] See 1 Esdras 3.9.   [6] The LXX, for example, understands: 'Holy Spirit'.

[7] We find the same perspective in the Talmud when, concerning this verse, it draws the general conclusion: 'Whoever knows that his neighbour is greater than he, even in just a single way, ought to honour him' (*Pes.* 113b).

since hatred of the Jew[8] is always religiously inspired, it likes to clothe itself in a sacred character. Pogroms are organized in the name of the Fatherland, Justice, Race, Blood, the doctrinal purity of the Party. In Dan. 6, the sacred cause is to prevent an alien from assisting in the dismemberment of the empire. Two דתות oppose each other, the one as imperative as the other: there is Daniel's Law (v.6) and there is the 'immutable, irrevocable, and unchangeable' law of the Medes and Persians (vv.9, 16). Joshua (24.15) concludes from this situation: 'choose this day whom you will serve'.

Text 6. 7–11

(7) So these ministers and satraps rushed to the king and spoke to him as follows: 'King Darius, live for ever! (8) All the kingdom's ministers, prefects, satraps, counsellors and governors, are of the opinion that a royal edict should be published and that an interdict should be put into force that anyone who, during thirty days, addresses prayers to any god or man except you, O king, will be thrown into the lion pit. (9) Now, O king, establish the interdict and sign the decree, so that it may be immutable following the irrevocable law of the Medes and the Persians. (10) Whereupon King Darius signed the decree and the interdict. (11) When he learned that the decree had been signed, Daniel returned to his house whose windows in the upper chamber were open toward Jerusalem; three times each day he kneeled upon his knees, praying and thanking God, as he had done previously.

Critical Notes 6. 7–11

V.7 אלין: del. in Θ.—הרגשו: Θ: 'presented themselves'. In biblical Hebrew (see Ps. 2.1) the root signifies 'to be in a throng' or 'to make tumult'. The Rabbis conserved the sense of a throng; see Ibn Ezra: 'assembly'. Whence Montgomery (p. 273): 'they acted in concert, harmony'. Saadia here translates 'came before'; in v.12: 'quarrelled with'; and in v.16: 'rushed against'. Montgomery remarks that in Ps. 55.15, ברגש is in parallel with סוד, whence LXX: ὁμονοίᾳ and Syr. + Vul.: cum consensu (idem, Ps. 64.3). In v.7, Rashi understands 'to go surreptitiously', and in v.12, he adds the explicative note: וחפשו (and they searched, spied), a use of the root רגש attested to by Targ. Jer. on Exod. 2.3; Niddah 13a; Shab. 129a, 13b; Meg. 15b; Ned. 13a (cf. Charles, p. 153).

V.8 סגניא: see 2.48; 3.2, 3, 27.—הדבריא: see 3.24, 27; 4.33.—פחותא: see 3.2, 3, 27. Cf. Ezra 5.3, 6; 6.6, 13; 5.14; 6.7.—קים :לקימה קים מלתא קים:

[8] H. L. Ginsberg is wrong in trying to exonerate Daniel's enemies of any antisemitism (see Studies, p. 128, which is accepted by A. Bentzen, p. 53).

Dan. 6.18 Targs: an established thing, law, statute, alliance, oath. The term appears in the literature from Qumran, see 1 QH 13.11–12.

Rashi understands מלתא as a complement of direct object and translates: 'to uphold the king's law by force' (because Darius being a new king and foreigner needed the help of his partisans). —לתקפה אסר: cf. Num. 30.3–4. Talmud: אסור = interdiction. תקף, see Job 14.20; 15.24; Eccles. 4.12.—גב: Heb.: בור.

V.9 די לא תעדא: Heb: ולא יעבור: Esth. 1.19; 8.8.

V.11 וכוין פתיחן: see Prov. 7.6; 2 Kings 1.2.—עליתה: see Acts 10.9; Tobit 3.12; Judith 8.5.—מצלא: Θ: προσευχόμενος, rare in the sense of 'to pray'. In the inscription of Commagene (North Syria, first century BCE; *Ditt. Or.* I.383), Antiochus uses it in the sense of an intercession (li. 227 and 233).

Commentary

The second part of the story (vv.7–11) opens with the conspiracy of all the wheels of State against the Jew (v.8). We rediscover here the official titles mentioned in Daniel 3.2 with others added. Several are Persian in origin, which is not unexpected since the Persian administrative structure was maintained under Alexander, then under the Seleucids, and finally in the Parthian Empire.

One person is intended by the supposedly general order. *Senso strictu*, the royal pretension to divinization[9] is anachronistic in the time of Darius. It does have its place under Antiochus Epiphanes. Nothing prevents such a motif having been developed in the pre-Maccabean version of the story, however. No monarch, especially in the ancient Near East, was safe from the temptations of power. When the idea that the king is (half-) divine emanates from his courtiers, the temptation to believe it is all the greater for the prince. It is clear, of course, that the wise men's devotion to the king is not sincere. The 'divinized' king is only a means to attain a quite different goal than to provide the foundation of his power. He is so little his subjects' god that he becomes a puppet in their hands; although it is not certain that the king is duped for it is possible that he sees in his courtiers' initiative a divinization of the Reasons of State and therefore a well tested means against 'free men'.[10] The proclamation of new or old 'religions' does not always fool

[9] See Judith 3.8; 6.2. It is stigmatized in 2 Macc. 9.10, 12; Dan. 11.36–9.
[10] See Jean-Paul Sartre, *The Flies*, trans. by Stuart Gilbert (New York 1946):
    AEGISTHUS: A free man in a city acts like a plague-spot. He will infect my whole kingdom and bring my work to nothing (p. 104).
    ZEUS: Once freedom lights its beacon in a man's heart, the gods are powerless against him. (Ibid.)

their prophets or their followers. One just chooses to 'go along' and let come what may. 'The clown does not laugh.' The best game, the one that most allows one to let go, is to hate others, especially if these others are Jewish. Therefore it seems to us that it is risky to see, with M. Delcor *et al.*, a 'weak-willed and immature personage' (p. 135)[11] in the description of the king. Whoever does not go along with the illusion and who, consequently, unmasks the mystification, must die 'in the lion pit'. In effect, one conclusion follows from two possibilities: either 'religion' is a vital necessity or it is useless. If someone can live (and even prosper as Daniel does) outside of it, it is not indispensable and it collapses. This is why the Jew is always an alien body in the illusory constructions of the nations. In Tillichian terms, the royal decree puts a 'preliminary concern' before man's 'ultimate concern'. It was already so in the preceding chapters (3 and 5), but now the field of persecution moves from the plane of public observances to that of private observances.[12] Note that Antiochus IV also included such practices in his interdict (see 1 Macc. 1.42; 2 Macc. 6.6).

The use of lions as punishment is an allusion to Ezek. 19.2–9, perhaps also to 1 Kings 13.23–6. These animals represent the powers of chaos as is evident from Ps. 91.13, for example, or from 1 QH 5.6–7. Bentzen is thus correct when he sees a representation of the nether world in the pit where Daniel will be thrown (op. cit., pp. 55–6; see *supra*).

According to our text (v.9), the law of the Medes and Persians is unchangeable. It is not impossible that this feature is correct (see Esth. 1.19 and 8.8). Diodorus of Sicily (XVII, 30), in fact, reports the case of a man put to death under Darius III (336–330) even though he was known to be perfectly innocent. '(Darius III) immediately repented and blamed himself for having committed such a great error, but it was impossible to have undone what had been done by royal authority.' There are clearly two דתות (laws, 'religions') which confront each other in this chapter, that of the Medo-Persians and that of Daniel. Two ways of thinking, two contradictory choices. Darius' 'immutable law' is monstrous, it leads to the condemning of an innocent man to death for reasons of State. As for the divine character of the king, it leads him to cry the whole night long in his bed and, in the early morning, over a tomb excavated at his order (vv.19–21).

The following scene stands in contrast to the preceding one because of its calmness. Daniel does not 'rush about' in his room, as do the ministers and satraps; he simply perseveres in the exercise of his faith in the Living God. Daniel's resistance lies in his constancy and faithfulness. There is no bravado or provocation on his part. He demonstrates

[11] See J. Steinmann, op. cit., p. 79: 'Daniel stands for the Jewish people.'
[12] In this, the parallel is with chapter 1.

that the authentic movement is not agitation, but conformity in the faithfulness one has chosen. The royal counsellors' sudden fits and spurts echo an atomistic conception of time. Israel's dynamic, on the contrary, is not made up of leaps or of fluttering about, it does not wipe out the past. Time is *one* and history has a meaning. Jerusalem is always the goal to be attained. This is why, in the post-Exilic period, prayer was directed toward The City.[13] Jerusalem is always present yet always still to come, always given yet always to be won, always calming yet always disquieting, always lived yet always hoped for. Daniel turns toward it to pray three times each day,[14] on his knees.[15] What the Babylonian wise men—representing the nations caught up in their static world view—hold against Daniel-Israel is his hope.

Text 6. 12–18

(12) Then these men rushed over and found Daniel who was addressing prayers and supplications before his God. (13) Then they went to the king and spoke to him about the royal interdict: 'Did you not sign an interdict (stating) that anyone who, during thirty days, addresses prayers to any god or man except you, O king, would be thrown into the lion pit?' The king answered: 'The matter is certain following the irrevocable law of the Medes and the Persians.' (14) Then they spoke in these terms in the king's presence: 'Daniel, who is one of the sons of the deportation from Judah, has no respect for you, O king, or for the interdict you have signed. Three times a day he says his prayer.' (15) When he heard this report, the king was greatly dis-

---

[13] The first mention of this practice is in 1 Kings 8.44 where many see a Maccabean addition to the Prayer of Dedication (J. Gray, *I and II Kings, A Commentary* (London 1963), p. 210, sees an intervention of the Redactor, 'the second Deuteronomist'); cf. vv.38, 48. It is also found in 2 Chron. 6.34; Tobit 3.11 (in Greek); Judith 9.1 (LXX); 3 Esdras 4.58; *m. Ber.* 4.4, 5, 6; cf. Acts 3.1.

[14] See Ps. 55.17–18 (the text of which perhaps should be emended according to B.H., but then it loses its precise parallelism with Dan. 6.11). See also Josephus, *Ant.*, IV, VIII, 13 (twice a day); cf. Strack-Bill., *Kommentar* II, 696; Acts 3.1; 10.9; indirectly Matt. 6.5. The morning and evening times coincide with the two sacrifices in the Temple: Exod. 29.39; 1 Chron. 23.30. It should be noted that at Qumran we find a ternary prayer punctuating the day (to which there seems to correspond a ternary prayer dividing up the night into vigils; see H. Ringgren, *The Faith of Qumran*, p. 223). For the Rabbinic writing *Tanḥuma* (section 'Kitabo', par. 1 beginning, ed. Buber), the ordinance was promulgated by Moses, see Deut. 26.1ff.; even the Patriarchs conformed to it. Abraham instituted the *šaḥarith*, Isaac the *minḥah*, and Jacob the *ma'arib* (see *Ber.* 26b; *j. Ber.* 7a; *Tanḥ.* 'Mikkeṣ' par. 11). Since the *minḥah* has no cultural correspondence, R. Josuah b. Hananyah maintained that it was not obligatory (see Moore, *Judaism* II, pp. 219–20). On the basis of Dan. 6.11, the Rabbis ordained that one should (a) not pray in a house without windows, (b) pray three times a day, and (c) pray turned toward Jerusalem (see, e.g., *Ber.* 31a).

[15] On one's knees: see 1 Kings 8.54 (where some see a post-exilic addition, see, e.g., J. Gray, op. cit., p. 214); Ezra 9.5; Ps. 95.6; Luke 22.41; Acts 7.60. It is once more a question of a post-exilic practice.

pleased. He set his heart on Daniel to save him and he strove until the sun went down to deliver him. (16) Then these men rushed to the king and said to the king: 'Know, O king, the law of the Medes and the Persians is that every interdict and decree that the king establishes is unchangeable.' (17) Then the king ordered Daniel to be brought in so that he could be thrown into the lion pit. The king spoke to Daniel in these terms: 'May your God himself, whom you serve with perseverance, save you!' (18) A stone was brought and placed over the opening to the pit; the king sealed it with his ring and with the rings of his lords so that nothing would be changed with respect to Daniel.

Critical Notes 6. 12–18

V.12 הרגשו: see the discussion of v.7; Θ: 'spied upon'.

V.13 Θ del.: 'about the interdict'.—Θ connects the phrase 'O king' to the following sentence.

V.14 שׂם טעם: see 3.12.—Θ del. 'O king.'

V.15 בל = לב only here in biblical Aramaic, but the word has this sense in Arabic and Syriac. Cf. Heb.: שׂים לב (1 Sam. 9.20).

V.16 Θ del. 'hurried to the king'.—v.16b: see 4.9.

V.17 For the symbolism of lions as a type of mortal peril, see Ps. 22.14–29; 91.13. Cf. the mosaic iconography at Noarah, near Jericho; also a favourite subject in Persian art.
　　Cf. from Qumran, 1 QH 5.5ff.: '... You have helped my life (to escape) from the pit and You have given (...) in the midst of lions destined for the sons of guilt, the lions who break the bones of the powerful and drink the blood of the brave ... You have closed the young lions' mouths ... they did not open their mouths against me ... You have succoured the soul of the destitute in the lions' lair, who have sharpened their tongues like a sword. You, my God, you have muzzled their teeth, etc.' Cf. li. 15ff.: 'You have acted wondrously toward the poor man ... You placed him in the fur(nace like gol)d worked in the fire. ...'

V.18 רברבן: see 4.33; 5.1–3, 9, 10, 23.—צבו ... לא: 'not a thing', cf. Syriac, Palmyr. Aramaic. In Heb.: חפץ, see Eccles. 3.1; 5.7.— The LXX adds the explanation: so that Daniel could not be helped to escape by them or the king. See the parallel in Matt. 27.62–6.—בעזקתה: royal seal; cf. 1 Kings 21.8; Esth. 3.12; 8.8, 10.

Commentary

The third part of this chapter (vv.12–18) takes up again, in v.12, the theme of the agitation of Daniel's enemies in contrast to his calm. They arrange between themselves (v.13) not to mention to the king that the affair began with them: 'Did you not sign . . . ?' The king is caught in his own trap. In attempting to rid himself of 'free men' (see *supra*), he has put himself in chains. An 'irrevocable law' gives a legislator a comfortable sense of power—the unforeseen is put outside the law. But 'the chips are down' only for the dead. In the name of his dynamic דת, Daniel is thrown into the pit; yet after all he is the living one. From the point of view of real freedom, the king's licence, his autocracy, his arbitrariness, is a form of alienation. Daniel's obedience to the 'Law' is deliverance. For the one, the Idea crushes man; for the other, 'the Sabbath was made for man'.

The Reasons of State consume the king (v.15). A pogrom is suicide (in both its intention and its end; see 3.22). It deliberately sets wheels into motion (v.9) which become ruthless. There is probably an allusion to the Jewish aristocracy in Jerusalem in the second century in the fact that Daniel's eminent position does not spare him from being ground up by the machine of State. Even the personal friendship of the king is not sufficient to save the condemned man. Misfortune comes to the Jew who counts on the assurances of his 'friends'. They are quickly revealed as a broken reed which pierces the hand of whoever leans on it (see Isa. 36.6).

The king's attitude is ambiguous; he now appears to wish that his cowardice should not have any effect. A captive to himself, he dreams of freedom and peaceful relations with the Jew. But the king's troubled conscience is a luxury which his subjects-tyrants will not permit him. Note the absence of any courtly formula in v.16. Not only is the rapidity of the action thereby indicated—the king must not be left any time to reassert himself—but there is clearly a discourteous note in the fact that the preposition למלכא is used instead of קדם מלכא.

In testing Daniel, the king knows, according to our tale, that he is testing God (see v.20). 'May your God save you!' (v.17), this wish by the king is in contrast with 3.15 and in parallel with 3.17–18 (but there it is the young men who raise the possibility of being saved from death by God). If the rescue of Daniel implies the triumph of God (vv.27–8), his death then would imply the death of God. Now the king knows in his heart of hearts that that would mean the end of everything, whence his profound inquietude (vv.15, 19–21).

Text 6. 19–25

(19) Then the king went into his palace and spent the night fasting. No concubines were brought to him and sleep fled from him. (20) Then, in the early morning, at the break of day, the king arose and went quickly to the lion pit. (21) While approaching the den, he moaned in a sad voice Daniel's name.

Speaking up, the king said to Daniel: 'Daniel, servant of the Living God, has your God whom you serve with perseverance been able to save you from the lions?' (22) Then Daniel began to speak with the king: 'O king, live for ever! (23) My God sent his angel and shut the mouths of the lions who have not hurt me, for I was found innocent before him; and before you too, O king, I have done no hurtful act.' (24) Then the king was overjoyed about him and he ordered that Daniel be hoisted up out of the pit. Daniel was hoisted out of the pit and they could find no hurt on him for he had had faith in his God. (25) The king ordered that the men who had slandered Daniel be brought and thrown into the lion pit, they, their children, and their wives. They had not reached the bottom of the pit when the lions seized them and broke their bones.

Critical Notes 6. 19–25

V.19 דחון: the meaning is uncertain ('concubines?'), and interpreted in various ways: 'tables, musical instruments, perfumes, food-stuffs, etc'. LXX does not have the word; Θ: ἐδέσματα = food-stuffs = Syr. = Vul.; Rashi: tables; Ibn Ezra: musicians = Pseudo-Saadia = Calvin; Saadia Gaon: female dancers; Bertholet refers to the Arabic *daḥâ: subiecit feminam*; Montgomery adopts ultimately the neutral meaning proposed by the Jewish Version (1917): diversions.—the LXX has a longer text.

V.20 בשפרפרא: an anomaly: there are 'capital' and 'small letters' in the word: בשׁפרפרא. This difference does not appear in the Babylonian punctuation where the word is divided into בשפר פרא. The root שפר appears in Targ. Ar. and in Syr. in the form צפרא. Arabic *safara* = to light (by the sunrise). Manipulating the letters allows two readings: *Ketaltal* or *Ketal*.—נגהא: see Prov. 4.18.—בהתבהלה: see 2.25. We may also understand 'troubled, fearful'.

V.21 The LXX adds: 'God, having taken care of Daniel, closed the lions' mouths and they did not torment Daniel.'—ענה: *del.* in Θ.—אלהא חיא: see Deut. 5.26; Josh. 3.10; 1 Sam. 17.26; Jer. 10.10; 23.36; Ps. 42.2.

V.22 Instead of 'O king, live for ever!', the LXX has, 'O king, I am alive.'

V.23 זכו: is the term used in the Targ. as corresponding to the Heb.: צדקה, legal innocence.—Regarding this verse, cf. Ps. 91.10–13.

V.25 אכלו קרצוהי: see 3.8.—שלטו בהון: also signifies in Aramaic 'to fall upon, attack', see Targ. Judg. 8.21; 15.12; 2 Sam. 1.15. . . .—הדקו: || Jer. 50.17 and Isa. 38.13: break the bones, tear out the bones.

Commentary

Perhaps we should see the king's hasty return early the next morning (v.20) in the perspective of the ancient Babylonian custom that the victim would be pardoned if he were tortured and had not died by the following day. In the same vein, two other details in the text can be given a welcome historical illustration. We know, for one thing, that the Assyrians, then the Persians, captured lions alive and put them in cages. It is also historically exact that the Persians inflicted upon the wives and children of condemned men the same penalty given them (see v.25).[16]

The text's willingness to mitigate the king's culpability becomes manifest in this part of the chapter (vv. 19–25). In **verse 21**, Darius uses the theologically richly significant title 'Living God' (see our critical notes, ad loc.). Repentance has been at work in his heart since the preceding night. Its salutary evolution advances through the acknowledgement that the God of Daniel is Living; and it continues by the punishment of the guilty. Finally it reaches its apex in the edict which ends the chapter.

In v.21, the king recognizes that, when man has chosen death, only God can change death into life. This is the whole message of Jewish apocalyptic. Its antecedents are evidently prophetic, especially from the exilic period (see Ezek. 37; Isa. 53; cf. Isa. 26.14–15). Darius, too, pronounces a prophetic utterance. Israelite popular tales loved to imagine pagans, unknowingly, gripped by the Spirit. From Balaam in the Book of Numbers (or even his ass!) to Titus or some Roman emperor in Rabbinic literature, by way of Pilate in the Gospels, God in a way plays with these powerful figures of this world as he plays with Leviathan in Ps. 104.

As for v.23, Heaton recalls that it inspired Heb. 11.33ff. This latter text is interesting from more than one point of view. It combines the motif of the lions' den with that of the furnace (see Dan. 3).[17] Moreover, it 'significantly associates Daniel and his companions with the Maccabean martyrs, thus unconsciously anticipating the conclusions of modern scholarship'.[18] We should read Dan. 6 in the light of the historical perspective of martyrdom for the faith. We must not be short-changed by the 'mythological' appearances of the text. The angel present in the pit is not a *deus ex machina*. It is nothing other than the very presence of God, as the LXX has well understood. The miracle occurred, according to our

---

[16] See Herodotus, III, 119.
[17] See our quotation from 1 QH 5.6ff., in our critical notes on Dan. 6.17.
[18] E. Heaton, op. cit., pp. 167–8.

tale, on the plane of history, by God's engagement in history. Here again, the 'stone' of chapter 2 is interpreted existentially: God *is* in the pit, just as he was in the furnace (chapter 3).

Above, we recalled Balaam and his ass. Like the ass who was more clairvoyant than its master the 'prophet', the lions had more sense than the king. They did not want to burden themselves with the blood of a righteous man despite the natural law which itself is not irrevocable. Even animal instincts bend before justice (צדקה or זכו). Man's voluntary blindness, on the contrary, takes him to a lower rank than an animal, lower than the apocalyptic beast which allegorically represents the chaotic monster.[19]

But Darius has by now his eyes opened. He is 'overjoyed about (Daniel)' (v.24). In seeing that God is not dead along with Daniel in the abyss of shapelessness, the king is himself liberated. He is cured of his inhibitions and of his psychic traumas and existential alienation. Note that here again, as in chapters 2, 3, 4, and 5, only the king sees the miracle.

However, as in the preceding chapters, the royal 'conversion' is ambiguous, a feature which coheres with the general conception of history in this book. We must, indeed, see in the punishment of the slanderers of Daniel (v.25) the putting into play of one principle of wisdom as is expressed by the Deuteronomist:[20] 'life for life, eye for eye, tooth for tooth, hand for hand, foot for foot' (Deut. 19.21; cf. Exod. 21.23–5; Lev. 24.18–21). This is not only an order to be followed, it is the order of things that God alone conserves. Daniel's message to a persecuted people is that their innocence will save them from the 'lions' pit' where they have been thrown by Antiochus Epiphanes.[21] As for him, he will suffer what he had tried to inflict upon others. 'The righteous man is delivered from disaster and the evil man takes his place' (Prov. 11.8).

It remains that 'Darius the Mede' does not end up any more exalted in the reader's eyes. It seems that, even when touched by grace, the pagan continues his dangerous foolishness, like the lions who are pacified for a while but whose nature has not really changed (v.25b).

[19] See J. Steinmann, op. cit., p. 81: 'These lions are apocalyptic beasts similar to the monsters which Daniel sees in the dream reported in the following chapter.'

[20] The influence of Wisdom on the Deuteronomist is coming to be more and more recognized as such by modern exegesis. See, e.g., D. J. McCarthy, *Treaty and Covenant: A Study in Form in the Ancient Oriental Documents and the O.T.* (Analecta Biblica 21 (Rome 1963)), ch. 9: 'Deuteronomy, the Central Discourse', especially pp. 114ff.; cf. H. Duesberg, *Les Scribes Inspirés* (Paris 1938–9), vol. 1, pp. 109, 371, 385.

[21] O. Plöger opines (concerning v.25) that the collective punishment of the guilty is best understood under Antiochus IV when there were among the people denunciations to the authorities.

Darius clearly makes others pay for his own cowardice, feigning that his weakness was their fault. Thus he is even 'smaller' than before.[22]

So ends the next to the last part of chapter 6. It constitutes a sort of midrashic comment on Gen. 45.5–8 which is part of the Joseph epic.

Text 6. 26–29

(26) Then King Darius wrote to the men of every people, nation, and language that dwell on all the earth: 'May your peace increase! (27) I give the order that, in every domain of my kingdom, men fear and tremble in the presence of the God of Daniel.

for he is the Living God and he endures for ever!
His rule is indestructible and his dominion will last to the end.
(28) He saves and delivers, he works signs and wonders
in the heavens and on earth,
for he has saved Daniel from the power of the lions.'

(29) As for this Daniel, he prospered under the reign of Darius and under the reign of Cyrus the Persian.

Critical Notes 6. 27–29

V.27 שׂים טעם: see 3.29.—זאעים ודחלים: see 5.19.—קים: see Targs.; Samar.; the Rabbinic literature for the Heb. חי, living; cf. 3.10; Judg. 8.19.

V.28 See 3.28, 29, 32, 33.—מיד אריותא: see I Sam. 17.37.—The LXX has a different text for this verse: 'I Darius, I will worship him and serve him during all my days for the idols made by human hands cannot save, because the God of Daniel did save Daniel.'

V.29 LXX: the chapter ends with the death of Darius and the ascent of Cyrus the Persian: ... καὶ Κῦρος ὁ Πέρσης παρέλαβε τὴν βασιλείαν αὐτοῦ (Darius).

Commentary

The edict of Darius which ends chapter 6 (vv.26–9) is parallel to Dan. 3.29–30. We find expressions in it similar to those of 3.29 and 3.31. The

---

[22] Above all in the light of texts well known to Daniel—at least in substance—such as Deut. 24.16; Jer. 31.29–30; Ezek. 18. We cannot follow E. Heaton for whom Dan. 6.25 shows that 'moral idealism' was the least of Daniel's concerns. This reading is partly corrected by F. James, *Personalities of the O.T.*, p. 571: '(The Book of Daniel) is singularly free from vindictiveness. . . . Only once does the spirit of revenge flare up (6.24) and that but for a moment.'

formula 'he endures for ever', which appears frequently in the Targums, is inspired by texts such as Exod. 15.18; Jer. 10.10; and Ps. 10.16; 29.10; 66.7; 102.13.

A new name is introduced in the closing note of this chapter and, at the same time, in Daniel A: כורש פרסיא, 'Cyrus the Persian'.[23] The chronological telescoping which occurs in v.29 is a subtle indication that we are now leaving the popular tale for the apocalypse. Before that, however, we are told, in a surprisingly neutral and almost off-hand tone, of the definitive realization of Darius' initial project concerning Daniel which had been presented in 6.4. All the energy, rage, and violence of the evil men therefore was spent in vain. God's plan is accomplished by means of Darius' project. The forces of evil may retard the evolution of history, but they cannot prevent it from reaching its goal, the God of Israel's Project.

[23] The vision in chapter 10 in Daniel B dates from after the reign of this monarch.

7 The Four Animals and the Son of Man

In our general Introduction we indicated the division of the Book of Daniel into two parts. Daniel B begins with chapter 7. Its language is still Aramaic even though we have passed from one literary genre to another, that of Daniel's apocalyptic visions. We said that the kinship between chapters 7 and 2 indicates why they were both written in Aramaic, despite the fact that chapter 7 is so intimately linked also with chapter 8 (and 9—12) written, or rather translated, in Hebrew.

That chapter 7 starts a second part of the book of Daniel is clear not only from its content, but, as John J. Collins has shown, from its structure in common with the one of the following chapters (cf. *JBL* 93, no. 1 (March 1974), pp. 50–66, esp. p. 55). Be it in Dan. 7.1–14, 17–18; 7.19–22, 23–7; 8.1–12, 20–5; or 10.20—12.3, one finds throughout a tripartite pattern A, B, C,

A—Events prior to the Career of Antiochus
B—Career of Antiochus
C—Eschatological Outcome

Daniel B is, strictly speaking, the apocalyptic part of the book of Daniel. From the outset of this new development of his work, the Author takes us to the summit of the mountain. For the vision reported in chapter 7 is the most important one; it constitutes the veritable centre of the book. With it, Holy Scripture reaches one of its highest summits. In this way, even from a purely literary point of view, the 'open-ended' conception of the Scriptures towards the future, characteristic of Jewish apocalyptic, is confirmed, for everything was not said in the past; events of decisive importance, defying all description, are yet to come. The *Endzeit* responds to the *Urzeit*, it assumes the same characteristics so that one vocabulary serves to describe them both. As in the ancient cosmologies common to the whole Near East, the wind from the four cardinal directions stirs up the waters of the Primordial Sea to extract, in a fashion, potentially terrestrial creatures from it.[1] Between sea (v.2) and sky (v.13), there is a dialogue called earth. But, faithful to its genius, Israel 'demythologizes' this cosmology. The creatures born of primordial chaos are historical empires which may be identified—following the canvas already encountered in chapter 2—as Babylonia, Media,

---

[1] In contrast to chapter 2 note that here Daniel's evocation of universal history goes all the way back to its origins all the while maintaining the fourfold division familiar to him. There is thus introduced a tension between a process of re-mythologization and the customary Israelite de-mythologization of the borrowed material.

Persia, and Macedonia. Furthermore, these empires, which at first glance reflect human greatness, are here only monsters more and more contrary to every human dimension (cf. v.4 and vv.6–7).

The parallels between chapter 7 and chapter 2 indicate that it is a question in both instances of the same kingdoms.[2] The first is the Neo-Babylonian Empire (cf. 2.38: 'you are the gold head'; Dan. 7.4 could be a reference to Nebuchadnezzar's madness, cf. 4.13 and 31).[3] The fourth empire is the one founded by Alexander the Great (see the Syriac version).[4] The ten horns are ten kings (difficult to identify precisely) and the eleventh horn is without a doubt Antiochus IV Epiphanes, the supreme expression of savagery and inhumanity according to the Author (see Dan. 11.21, 25; Sib. III, 397; 4 Esdras 12.10–12).[5] Within this framework, the second and third kingdoms are those of the Medes (v.5) and the Persians (v.6). This was already understood by the Syriac version[6] and by St Ephrem. We have indicated several times above that the scriptural sources of this historical reconstruction are to be found in Isa. 13.17; 21.2; and Jer. 51.11, 28.

Two comments are necessary: Certainly the Author does not see an absolute beginning in the Neo-Babylonian Empire. But he does consider the last instalment of history which begins with the Babylonian Kingdom to be its quintessence.[7] A four-fold schema is imposed upon this *pars pro toto* for the number 4 was considered as 'the ultimate number leading to the consummation of history'.[8] The particular place

---

[2] See however the dissent by H. Gressmann in *Der Messias* (Göttingen 1921), pp. 344–5, 367; the four monsters are the four kingdoms, avatars of Alexander's empire. They do not succeed one another therefore as do those in ch. 2. J. Bright, *The Kingdom of God* (Nashville 1953), pp. 156ff., 'Holy Commonwealth and Apocalyptic Kingdom', seconds this thesis.

[3] According to Jerome, Hippolytus, Aphraat, Nicholas of Lyra, and, among the moderns, Wright, Bertholet, Montgomery, etc. This comparison is contested by Charles, op. cit., pp. 176f. (cf. H. H. Rowley, *Darius the Mede*, pp. 61ff.).

[4] Pesh. Dan. 7.7: 'king of Greece'. The *terminus ad quem* of the Peshitta is AD 200–50.

[5] Even though 4 Esdras 11.1 and 12.10ff. identity the beast with Rome. This is confirmed by Rev. 13; Apoc. of Baruch 39; Josephus *Ant.* X, XI, 7; Ep. of Barnabas 4. In the Talmud and Midrash, see *Lev. R.* 13.5; *Gen. R.* 44.20; *A.Z.* 1b; *Mid. Tanh.* p. 91; Targ. Hab. 3.17. Ibn Ezra reconciles these two theories by seeing both the Greeks and Romans in the fourth animal, for Rome was born from Greece. It is perfectly clear that his identification of Rome with Greece was made at a time when Alexander's empire and the Diadochies had been overshadowed by the power of Rome.

[6] The Polyglot of London text.

[7] One expects to see Assyria in the first place, yet with Elias Bickerman we must say: 'For a Jew ... not Assyria, but Babylon of Nebuchadnetsar the conqueror of Jerusalem, must have been the first world's lordship. Thus in the Jewish schema the four empires were Babylon, Media, Persia, and Macedonia.' (*Four Strange Books of the Bible* (New York 1967), pp. 67–8).

[8] Martin Noth, 'Das Geschichtsverständnis der alttestamentlichen Apokalyptik', *Gesammelte Studien zum Alten Testament* (Munich 1960).

accorded the fourth animal indicates a new concentration of history in its development. 'The totality of universal history must be included in the expectation of the imminent arrival of the Kingdom of God.'[9] This procedure arises from the conception of a 'corporate personality'[10] which is at the very heart of Dan. 7. According to this conception, on a horizontal plane, the community is a corporate personality beyond the simple sum of its members. However, it is totally *present* and perfectly *represented* in each individual member of the group. On a vertical plane, the solidarity among generations of the same community is such that the whole history of the clan is telescoped into and experienced by each one of them. This inner relationship between 'the one and the many' is everywhere and always deemed true, but especially at the beginning[11] and end of history, the *Urzeit* and *Endzeit*. The resemblance between the first and last animal described in Dan. 7 reflects this.

Dan. 7 evokes a renewed creation. 'Here too', says G. von Rad,[12] 'what is obviously older material[13] has been made—though not without some difficulty—to refer to the persecution of Israel for her faith by Antiochus IV. Like the four rivers in Gen. 2.10ff. or the four horns in Zech. 2.1, the four beasts represent the world in general. In Dan. 7.3 an idea that the four beasts came up contemporaneously out of the sea is still clearly visible. This would completely correspond to Zechariah's picture of the four horns.'

We may go even further. The parallel with Dan. 2 is so clear that several scholars think that the two chapters are glosses from the Maccabean period in an otherwise older work.[14] Not only is it a question here and there of four kingdoms or reigns, but in chapter 2, the 'stone not cut by human hands' (v.34) represents Mount Zion, the Temple not built by human hands.[15] So the vision in chapter 7 has the Temple as its

[9] Ibid.

[10] In our opinion Dan. 7 is proof that the idea of a 'corporate personality' was still alive such a long time after Ezekiel. The Saints benefit from the privileges of the 'son of man' by communal participation in him.

[11] The first word of Genesis בראשית signifies much more than a simple 'in the beginning'. It speaks of excellence and ultimacy, because all the force and dynamism of the evolution which follows is found in its premisses.

[12] *Old Testament Theology*, vol. 2, p. 312 and n. 25.

[13] Let us add that this older material is diverse. It seems, for example, that the 'Demotic Papyrus' with its commentaries offers an Egyptian parallel from the second century. It makes allusion to events since the Egyptian King Tachos (360) up to the end of the third century BCE, and announces the end of the Greeks and the liberation of Egypt. This assurance was not realized.

[14] See Hölscher, *T.S.K.* 92, pp. 120–3; Sellin, *Einl.A.T.*⁶, pp. 153f.; Haller, *Das Judentum*², pp. 279f.; M. Noth, *T.S.K.* 98–9, p. 155; Montgomery, op. cit., pp. 176f.; etc. See esp. A. Lenglet, 'La structure littéraire de Dan. 2—7', *Biblica* 53 (1972), pp. 169–90; ('symétrie concentrique', 2 ‖ 7; 3 ‖ 6; 4 ‖ 5).

[15] See our commentary ad loc.

framework. It is true that the text does not expressly say this anywhere, but the reason for this silence is that the Temple had been profaned by Antiochus IV and was temporarily unfit for a theophany. Yet the imagery is Ezekiel's, in particular that of Ezek. 8—11 which describes God's presence in the Temple (which, by the way, there too is profaned by 'the idol of jealousy who provokes jealousy', 8.3). Ezek. 1 should also be read from the same perspective. The Author draws a large part of his materials from Ezekiel, especially for the description of 'The-One-Who-Endures' and 'someone like a son of man'.

In its present form, therefore, Dan. 7 seems to have been written about 168, that is at the time of the religious persecution and the profanation of the Temple.[16] The High Priest Onias III had been ousted and Jason named in his place. The 'enthronement' of the latter was a new stain which could only be erased by the coming of the ultimate High Priest with 'an eternal and irrevocable dominion' and 'an indestructible kingdom' over 'the men of every people, nation, and language'.[17]

Recall that the Maccabean High Priests were also civil and military leaders (see Test. of Reub. 6.11–12; Test. of Sim. 5.5; cf. Dan. 7.11–12, 22, 26). They were the first to bear the title 'priests of the Most High God':[18] see *Rosh-ha-Shanah* 18b: '. . . in the year such and such of Johanan, High Priest of God Most High.'[19] Ps. 110, where Bickell has demonstrated an acrostic on the name of the High Priest Simon (142–134), links the title to Melchizedek (v.4; cf. Gen. 14.18), which is an allusion to the mysterious origin of the priesthood, but also— according to a suggestion of Mannati's[20]—a manner 'of emphasizing the poetic nature of this priesthood, which does not need a special consecration' and which combines within itself the royal dimension.

We must not allow ourselves therefore to be carried away by the heavenly decor of Dan. 7.13ff. The enthronement of the 'son of man' as High Priest has its place entirely within its normal framework of the

---

[16] See 1 Macc. 1.41–59; 2 Macc. 6.1–9. Cf. the chronological table appended to our General Introduction.

[17] Dan. 7.14. Cf. Ass. Mos. 10.2, where an angel is ordained priest.

[18] See Melchizedek, Gen. 14.; Jub. 32.1: 'Levi dreamed that he had been commanded to be the priest of the Most High God, he and his sons, forever . . .': Ass. Mos. 6.1: 'Then kings elevated themselves above him, exercising the power, they called themselves priests of the Most High God' (date: 7–30 CE); Josephus *Ant.* XVI, VI, 2: 'Hyrcanus, the High Priest of the Most High God . . .' See below our development on the 'son of man' as Melchizedek.

[19] יוחנן כהן גדול לאל עליון, the complete text is interesting: '. . . the Greek government (= Syrian) had forbidden the Israelites from mentioning the name of God. When the Hasmonean government became powerful and victorious, it ordered that people refer to the name of God, even on bindings. They wrote in this way: "in the year such and such (etc.)".'

[20] M. Mannati, *Les Psaumes* (Paris 1968), vol. 4, pp. 36ff.

Temple which is even considered in its transcendent and ultimate form. It is the Temple in Jerusalem 'such that eternity finally changes it into itself'. It is evident that the political circumstances strongly contributed to the transfer from the 'signified' to the 'signifier'. The Temple is there where God is, and the High Priest sits at his side.

The influence of this exegesis is large for the critical examination of the structure of chapter 7. The association of a personage 'like a son of man' with 'the people of the Saints' (see v.27) has often been found suspect. But we believe it is essential. If we take into account other developments in the subsequent chapters of Daniel (9.24, for example), it is clear that the spiritual Temple is also the community of the Saints.[21] In the terms of A. Feuillet:[22] 'The three oracles in 7.13–14; 8.14; and 9.24 mutually complete one another and contribute to the expression of the same reality. The wholly spiritual sanctuary which God anointed (9.24) is assured of the divine presence thanks to the coming of the Son of Man on the clouds (7.13–14) and it is in this manner that God avenges (8.14) the material Temple profaned by Antiochus . . . Daniel opposes to the Temple trampled under foot and even destroyed (8.13; 9.26–7) a spiritual sanctuary made up of believers over whom reigns the Son of Man.'

However, O. Procksch, followed by M. Noth,[23] interprets the word 'saints' by 'angels' or heavenly court. It is only by following the gloss in vv.21–2, say these scholars, that the term may be attributed to Israel. For L. Dequeker,[24] Dan. 7 originally consisted of a pre-Maccabean text already combining two versions that were once distinct, centring about vv. 9–10, on the one hand (the monstrous animals), and 13–14, on the other (the son of man).[25] Two successive redactors reworked the text in the Maccabean period. One added vv.8, 11a, 20, and 24–5a (which intend Antiochus Epiphanes), and the other added vv.21 and 22b (the war against the Saints).[26] For Dequeker, the Saints within the Bible always designate supernatural beings (see Gen. 12.1; Ps. 16.3; 89.6; Job 15.14–15; Zech. 14.5; Dan. 4.14; Wisd. 5.5; etc.). Similarly at

[21] As a bit later at Qumran.
[22] A. Feuillet, 'Le Fils de l'Homme de Daniel et la Tradition Biblique', *RB*, 1953, (pp. 170–202; 321–46), pp. 197–8.
[23] *Ges. St. z. A.T.* (Munich 1957), pp. 274–90; O. Procksch, *Theologie des A.T.*, p. 537.
[24] L. Dequeker, 'Daniel 7 et les Saints du Très Haut', *ETL*, 36 (1960), pp. 353–92; 'Les Qedošim du Ps. 89 à la lumière des croyances sémitiques', *ETL*, 39 (1963), pp. 469–83; cf. J. Coppens, 'Le fils de l'homme daniélique et les relectures de Daniel 7.13', *ETL*, 37 (1961), pp. 5–51; 'Les saints du Très-Haut sont-ils à identifier avec les milices célestes?', *ETL* 39 (1963), pp. 94–100; 'Les saints dans le psautier', *ETL*, 39 (1963), pp. 485–500.
[25] See M. Noth, 'Zur Komposition des Buches Daniel', *T.S.K.* 98–9, 1926.
[26] For H. L. Ginsberg, *Studies . . .*, ad loc., vv.8, 11a, 20, 21, 22, 24b, and 25 are also late.

Qumran, in the Books of Jubilees, Enoch, etc. At Ugarit, the high god El was surrounded by his court of 'Saints'.

We do not believe that L. Dequeker's thesis can stand up under examination. In Ps. 34 (v.10), for example, the term 'saints' designates Israel. And in several of the verses cited the meaning is uncertain.[27] Also, Dan. 7 is a late text and it would seem appropriate to undertake a deeper inquiry into the literature of that epoch. The results obtained from such an examination of apocrypha, pseudepigrapha, and the texts from Qumran indicate a balanced use of the expression to designate angels or men.[28] In this regard, texts such as 1 Enoch 39.4–5 and 47.2 are typical. We can, moreover, subscribe to Dequeker's judgement that 'this usage (the application of the term 'saints' to men) was born under the control of a theology which tended to conceive of the faithful of YHWH as the companions of angels and which ended up by assimilating them to these most faithful servants of God.'[29] Let us add that in Dan. 7 the dominion and the royalty are given to the Saints while we nowhere find any mention of an angelic kingdom.[30] On the contrary, there is abundant material on the eschatological kingdom of the redeemed people.[31] Finally, the term *'am* (people) in no way applies to the angels.[32]

One conclusion follows: in the time when the Author (or authors) of Dan. 7 wrote, the accent was placed on the correspondence between the holy community of Israel and the community of the Holy Angels.[33] In

[27] One cannot help but become suspicious when C. Colpe (*TWNT*, VIII, p. 407), à propos Ps. 80 where the people of Israel is a 'man', even a 'son of man' at God's hand, represented by a king sitting side by side with God (v.17, as in Ps. 110), draws the conclusion that the collective dimension here as in Dan. 7 is the working of 'the glossator'.

[28] In this last sense, see 3 Macc. 6.9; T. of Levi 18.11, 14; T. of Isaac 5.4; Test. of Dan 5.11, 12; 1 Enoch 38.4, 5; 39.4; 41.2; 43.4; 45.1; 48.1, 4, 7, 9; 50.1; 51.2; 58.3, 5; 62.8; 65.12; 93.6; 99.16; 110.5. All these texts are pre-Christian in origin. For Qumran, see J. Carmignac, *La Règle de la Guerre* (Paris 1958), on 1 QM 1.16; 9.7–8; 10.12; 12.14; 18.2. 1 QM 10.10 speaks of the 'people of the saints of the Covenant'.

[29] 'Les Qedošim du Ps. 89.'

[30] Except for 1 QM 17.6–8 which mentions the domination exercised by the Archangel Michael. On this point, see *infra*. V. S. Poythress seems to be right when he says: '... an eschatological angelic kingdom is unknown to the Old Testament and intertestamental literature.' Moreover, says he, 'The language about the oppression of the "holy ones" is inconsistent with the angelic view.' ('The Holy Ones of the Most High in Dan. VII', *VT* XXVI.2 (April 1976), p. 209.)

[31] See CDC 20.33, 34; 1 Q 28 P 5.21; Wisd. 3.8; 5.6; 6.20, 21; 1 Enoch 38.5; 48.9; 91.12; 95.7; and above all 92.4; 96.1; 108.12.

[32] As was seen by M. Noth who translates it by *Schar* instead of *Volk*! Per contra, cf. C. H. W. Brekelmans, OTS 14 (1965), pp. 305ff.; R. Hanhart, VTS 16 (1967), pp. 90ff.; A. Lenglet, op. cit.

[33] Qumran followed up on this, see 1 QH 3.21–2: the army of the Saints [and the people: *'am*; at least if we must not read *'im* = with] the congregation of the sons of heaven. Cf. 1 QS 11.7–8. Cf. 1 QM 15.14 where is found an expression in striking parallel with the Danielic 'the Most Haughty Saints', [*gi*]*borei elīm*, which

Dan. 7, the *verus Israel* identifies itself with the eschatological community already existing in the heavens.[34] Each nation, moreover, according to the Book of Daniel, has its special angel who represents it.[35] By this, we believe, we should understand that each people has a transcendent dimension, the ultimate meaning of its historical destiny.[36] Israel sees its own transcendence seated at the side of 'The-One-Who-Endures' judging all nations. This 'son of man' is surely the first-born of God, the ראשית of the nations, because he is the first of the righteous.[37] 'He is as he ought to be (that is the fundamental meaning of the Hebrew word for "righteous"); and he is the one who will one day cause all things in the new aeon to become what they ought to be. . . . (He is) the one who in himself fulfils, and enables men to fulfil, the goal for which God created them, to be to the honour and praise of the Almighty. . . . The Son of Man is the primordial sage, the primordial righteous man . . .

J. Carmignac translates 'les vaillants des (êtres) divins' in whom he sees celestial beings including 'souls' of deceased Jews. A little further on the same line 14, the 'qedošīm' refer to earthly beings (*La Règle de la Guerre* (Paris 1958), p. 223).

[34] See S. Mowinckel, *He that Cometh*, p. 380: '. . . the eschatological community already exists in heaven. . . . Because their souls (cf. 2 Bar. 30.2ff.) now belong to the heavenly community, they, too, are called "the holy ones" (1 En. 38.4; 39.4; 47.2, 4; 48.1; etc.) a name which is used in the O.T. only of supernatural divine beings.' Cf. Annie Jaubert, op. cit., p. 198: 'In entering into the covenant of the community, which was by definition God's Covenant, the new member enrolled himself in an immense *ecclesia*, including both angels and men, about which we may perhaps say without paradox that it was more heavenly than earthly. It was the communion of the sons of light, the sons of truth, the "Saints", be they of heaven or earth.'
Although at one point of his demonstration, John J. Collins writes: 'the people [of Israel] can no longer be distinguished from its [angelic] patrons' ('The Son of Man and the Saints of the Most High in the Book of Daniel', *JBL* 93, p. 62), the whole of his article is based on such a distinction. Between the ones and the others, he rather speaks of 'fellowship' (p. 63) but is careful to maintain a gap in between. Such a cautious treatment would be right for the ancient Israelite and Near Eastern conceptions reused here in Daniel. But some apocalypses and Qumran are at least one step further (cf., e.g., 1 QM 7.4–6; 1 QH 3.19–23; 11.13f.; 1 QSa 2.3–11). They *identify* the two former components (heavenly and earthly) in a single community (same thing possibly in 1 En. 91.12–17; 93). Thus J. J. Collins is on a firmer ground than he himself thought when he speaks of 'Apocalyptic Eschatology as the Transcendence of Death' (*CBQ* xxxvi: 1 (Jan. 1974), pp. 21–43).

[35] See 10.20–1, for example.

[36] For Judaism, everything determinative is pre-existing: the Torah, Wisdom, Israel, its Land, the name of the Messiah. . . . This is one reason to be mistrustful of the division between a national eschatological current and a transcendental and universalist current. 'Heaven' is not forgotten, nor is the universal in the expectation of a son of David, no more than is the 'Land' in Dan. 7. Cf. 2 Baruch 29.3–4.

[37] See S. Mowinckel, op. cit., p. 378.
Israel is the (sacerdotal) ecumenical and cosmic intercessor. With regard to Ps. 96, R. Martin-Achard writes: 'Israel substitutes itself in its liturgical service, for the world' (*Verbum Caro*, 71/72 [1964], p. 27). It offers its songs of praise to the nations and the whole cosmos. In so doing, it 'assumes Adam's vocation, that of being the world's respondent before God' and 'of representing God before the world, of being the image of God in the face of creation' (ibid., p. 27 and n. 22).

the pattern man, the prototype of humanity',[38] in the same way that Epiphanes is the quintessence of evil.[39] Antiochus is the 'last enemy who must be conquered', which can only be accomplished by a messianic act of judgement, that is to say, by war.[40]

The question of origins of the imagery in Daniel 7 has received in the last decades a conclusive response. The Ugaritic literature, as a matter of fact, provides the missing source of the mythopoetic scenes so widespread in the Apocalypses. J. A. Emerton, e.g., has written an interesting article on that topic.[41] The grey hair of God here recalls closely what is said about the great god El of the Canaanite pantheon (cf. Baal II.5.4; V. 5.2, 24f.). More importantly, the description of the son of man in Daniel recalls closely the god Baal, vanquisher of the dragon and of Yam, and himself enthroned as king.

In Canaan, these were cosmogonic myths celebrating, in conformity with the whole of the ancient Near Eastern world-view, the victory of fertility over barrenness and death. But, Israel, in reusing that mythic material, has from the beginning (the oldest written attestations are from the twelfth century BCE) shifted its meaning from 'Götterkampfmythus' to 'Völkerkampfmythus', i.e., from the cosmic to the historical. In doing so, however, Israel maintained a mythopoetic framework, viz. the Holy War ideology. There belongs to that particular context, e.g., the Divine Council of thousands and myriads which in Dan. 7.10 stand before The-One-Who-Endures. Indeed in the original myths all the great gods have a celestial court around them. The courtiers have the particular duty and role of helping their suzerain in his warring

---

[38] S. Mowinckel, op. cit., pp. 373 and 385.

[39] At Qumran, in the same way, the Master of Justice was opposed to the Wicked Priest. Recall also that for Ferd. Kattenbusch ('Der Quellort der Kirchenidee', Harnack-Festgabe (1921), pp. 143ff.), the communal character of the son of man in Dan. 7 was the basis for the New Testament idea of the Church.

[40] As is well known, Israel's wars were considered as YHWH's (see 1 Sam. 18.17; 25.28). He stands in the midst of his people (Josh. 3.10) whose enemies are his own (Judg. 5.31; 1 Sam. 30.26; especially 1 Sam. 17). God fights on behalf and instead of Israel (Josh. 23.3; 1 Sam. 7.10). In fact the victory is won even before the intervention of the army (2 Chron. 20.20–5). The rites of preparation for the Holy War are definitely liturgical: sacrifices (1 Sam. 7.9; 13.9), fasting (1 Sam. 14.24), sexual abstinence (1 Sam. 21.6; 2 Sam. 11.11), and of course the consultation of God's will (Judg. 1.1; 20.18; 1 Sam. 14.37; Jer. 21.2). Other rites such as the brandishment of flags, the waving of the hand and, above all, the teruah (cry of war and of acclamation of YHWH) are attested to in Deut. 23.10–15; 1 Sam. 21.6; Jer. 22.7; 51.28; etc. The soldiers are called 'the consecrated ones' (Isa. 13.3; cf. Jer. 51.27; Joel 4.9). The 'intertestamental' literature takes advantage of such an ancestral conception for its description of the advent of the messianic era. See Sib. III, 653; 1 Enoch 46; 51–53; 4 Esdras 11.46; 12.34; 13.5, 37–8, 49; 2 Baruch 35ff.; 70.9; T. of Jos. 19; and above all, Ps. of Sol. 17. Cf. CD 9.10ff.

[41] J. A. Emerton: 'Origin of the Son of Man Imagery', JTS, n.s. IX, Pt. 2 (Oct. 1958), pp. 225ff.

endeavours.[42] The One-Who-Endures is therefore not an old weakling. On the contrary, Daniel 7 describes a total war against the four beasts and among them the *Ur-End*-dragon. The victory of the 'Saints' is only obtained through a gracious participation in the Holy War waged by God and his heavenly court. As P. D. Miller puts it: 'At the center of Israel's warfare was the unyielding conviction that victory was the result of a fusion of divine and human activity . . . it was . . . possible for the people to see themselves as going to the aid of YHWH in battle (Judg. 5.23). The emphasis, however, lay on the activity of the divine, the involvement of YHWH as warrior and commander of the heavenly armies . . . YHWH fought for Israel even as Israel fought for YHWH (Josh. 10:14; Judg. 7.20–2; and so on) . . .'.[43]

Daniel takes over again this very old motif (cf. Exod. 15, twelfth century; Judg. 5, end of twelfth century; Deut. 33; 2 Sam. 22 = Ps. 18; Hab. 3; all of eleventh–tenth centuries; Ps. 68: late tenth century),[44] whose origins are clearly pre-Israelite (Mesopotamian, Canaanite)—Paul Hanson, among others but with an unparalleled vigour, has shown that a characteristic trait of Apocalypticism is precisely the revivification of the mythopoetic language and categories, resuming a fashion which preceded the prophetic process of demythologization.[45] Here, the terrible events of the Apocalypticist's time are definalized as God is the one who precedes the ages and outlives them, and whose judgements spell out utter destruction for the forces of chaos and ultimate salvation for the 'Saints'. As F. M. Cross has written: 'The old songs of the wars of YHWH were transformed into eschatological songs of imminent war in which YHWH's universal rule would be established. . . . [The language used for that is the one] of the battle with Yam or Leviathan, dragon of chaos. The myths of creation, in short, were given an eschatological function.'[46]

We must, however, at this point strike a note of caution. True, Daniel and in general the Apocalypticists describe the ultimate victory as eschatological and cosmic. But, in contradistinction to myth—for which such 'a theme would remain beyond its preoccupations—here the triumph of God is on behalf of his *people* (cf. also Ps. 24; Hab. 3; 2 Sam. 22 = Ps. 18; Josh. 10.12–13; etc.). The apocalyptic use of a mythopoetic

---

[42] Cf. Patrick D. Miller: *The Divine Warrior in Early Israel* (Cambridge, Mass. 1973) (cf. pp. 66ff.); Frank M. Cross: *Canaanite Myth and Hebrew Epic. Essays in the History of the Religion of Israel* (Cambridge, Mass. 1973).

[43] P. D. Miller, op. cit., p. 156.

[44] Cf. David Robertson: *Linguistic Evidence in Dating Early Hebrew Poetry* (Yale 1966).

[45] Paul Hanson: *The Dawn of Apocalyptic. The Historical and Sociological Roots of Jewish Apocalyptic Eschatology* (Philadelphia 1975).

[46] F. M. Cross, op. cit., p. 345.

language must not blind us into exaggerating its bearing. As P. D. Miller realizes: 'The false dichotomy that results from separating the cosmic from the historical . . . is clearly revealed when the theophanies of Judg. 5; Deut. 33; and Ps. 68 are looked at in their contexts.'[47] This, which is true for ancient pre-prophetic Hebrew texts, is also true for late post-prophetic Apocalypses. The merger of the cosmic and the historical has to be fully acknowledged if one wishes to appreciate the total association of the divine and the human we came across when dealing with the Divine Assembly (cf. Ps. 68.12–13, 18; etc.).

This latter thematic element in particular will help us to understand against what background the Author of Daniel 7 has coined the expression 'the Saints of the Most High' or, more correctly, 'the most haughty Saints'. As we indicated earlier, it is here a question of men *before* it is a question of angels. The proof texts from Qumran cited by the defenders of the angelic theory do not say what they wish to read in them (e.g., 1 QH 3.21–2, cf. M. Noth: *Laws*, op. cit., p. 223).[48] On the contrary a text like 1 QM 12.8–9 leaves no doubt as to the conjunction of the heavenly and the earthly in the community of the elect: '. . . the congregation of Thy Holy Ones is among us for everlasting succour . . . the King of Glory is with us, people of the Holy Ones. Pow[ers] of the angelic host are among our numbered men, and the Hero of wa[r] is in our congregation; the host of His spirits (is) with our foot-soldiers and horsemen, [like] clouds . . .'[49] In other words, at least in Qumran, the Divine Assembly is made up with angels and men, together 'numbered . . . with our foot-soldiers and horsemen'.

The Israelite origin of such a conception can be found in the prophetic claim that they stood in the 'Council of YHWH' where they received their inspiration and commission as messengers (cf. Jer. 23.18, 22; Amos 3.7; Isa. 6 . . .).[50] Be that as it may, it is clear that Daniel and, later, Qumran have radicalized that conception because they saw in their own communities (of Hassidim, of Essenes) congregations of prophets (as well as priests, and sages, and kings, and angels)! Already in Daniel 7, the people of the Holy Ones are, in the image of their head, the son of man, celestial as much as earthly.

The bearing of this on the eschatological vision is of course crucial. Daniel, like Qumran and some layers of 1 Enoch (cf. 38.5, e.g.) share a conception of 'realized eschatology'), a fact which does not in the least prevent those apocalypses from looking forward towards the coming of

[47] P. D. Miller, op. cit., pp. 106–7.
[48] Cf. V. S. Poythress, op. cit.
[49] French translation J. Carmignac: *Guerre*, op. cit., pp. 178, 180.
[50] Cf. F. M. Cross: 'The Council of YHWH in Second Isaiah', *JNES* 12 (1953), pp. 274–8.

the *eschaton* in an imminent future. J. J. Collins writes: 'Even at Qumran, where the emphasis is very heavily on present experience there remains a promise of future consummation,' for 'the hope of final vindication confirms and even makes possible the present experience of righteousness and divine approval.'[51]

Far from a mere borrowing of the Canaanite mythological imagery, therefore, Daniel (followed by other apocalypses) has transformed the material in a decisive way. There are not any more two levels/stories, one above the other. The two have become one, *thus revealing the truth of their unity from the beginning.*[52] The beautiful text of 1 QS 4:18–19 spells it out this way: '. . . at the season of visitation He will destroy (the period of wrong-doing) for ever; and thus the truth of the world will appear forever.' As for the book of Daniel, it uses daring expressions to show that Antiochus' onslaught against Israel hits a mixed community of heavenly and earthly beings (cf. 7.25; 8.10; 11.36).[53] And what is more, it is from such a perspective that Daniel winds up his message by speaking of an everlasting life for the righteous. For the doctrine of resurrection of the martyrs (12.2–3) follows naturally on the steps of the merger of heavens and earth. The resurrection is no consolation prize for the losers in this life. It is not granted by God as a supererogatory dessert. It in fact realizes and manifests what has been historically true always and ever, even though not seen by Antiochus IV and his clique. In another apocalyptic text, written some 40 years later, 2 Macc. 7.19, the martyr reveals to Antiochus IV that, in the persons of the Israelites, he is in fact warring against God, for, as the A text of v.34 puts it, the Jews are 'heavenly children'!

One more step must be made. After considering the holy community and its double rootage in heaven and on the earth, we can approach the figure of the 'one like a son of man' (7.13). He is presented as the epitome of the Saints, for he more than anybody else bridges heaven and earth. Not that he would be half-god and half-man, or 'entirely god and entirely man', but he is the *telos* of righteous humanity. This theme, by the way, is not as novel as might seem at first glance. A. Bentzen, for instance, has shown that the Davidic King was regarded as the Primal Man, the latter being the very source of the kingship ideology in the

---

[51] J. J. Collins: 'Apocalyptic Eschatology as the Transcendence of Death', op. cit., pp. 42, 41.
[52] Prognostic rejoinder of Apocalypticism to so many modern scholars who use and abuse the expression 'apocalyptic dualism'!
[53] Similarly, in Dan. 10.20f., Michael and the Prince of Persia are not necessarily fighting each other in single combat. Rev. 12.7–8 anyway understood that it is a question of entire armies. The archangels are patrons of nations and involve with themselves the peoples they represent. The same applies to the son of man.

ancient Near East.[54] More on this will be found below in our commentary on Dan. 7.13. At this point, however, we need to ask ourselves through which instrumentality the second century author of Daniel 7—12 conveyed his highly sophisticated, yea philosophical, conception of the achieved teleological humanity.

First, he relinquished the king title or the Messiah title for his hero. In fact, he refrained from using any title at all, for 'son of man' is no title.[55] He preferred to call him simply 'Man', exhibiting thus the root of all kingly or messianic '*ṣemaḥ*' (shoot) in Israel. Second, the Author identified him, not only with the heavenly–earthly community of 'the Most Haughty Saints', but also, implicitly in chapter 7, explicitly in several passages of chapters 8—12, with the angel Michael. This fact has been already recognized, in 1900, by N. Schmidt in an article of the *Journal of Biblical Literature*.[56] N. Schmidt was basing his demonstration on the fact that in the following chapters of Daniel B, the angels are described as having a human appearance.[57] As the origin of this 'humanization' of an angel, Schmidt thought of Marduk from Babylonian mythology. Whatever the case may be on this latter point (which, personally, we would not press too far), we think that Schmidt's fundamental thesis is correct. Again here the Qumran literature is very à propos. 1 QM 17.6–8 promises: 'He (God) will send eternal succour to the company of His redeemed by the might of the princely Angel of the kingdom of Michael . . . He will raise up the kingdom of Michael in the midst of all flesh.'[58] In another text from Qumran, Michael is identified with Melchizedek and assumes various roles, military (11 Q Melch. 13–15), juridical (v.9), priestly (v.8 and the significant choice of the name Melchizedek). Hence, Michael is a 'son of man' in Daniel 7; he is 'Melchizedek' in a text of Qumran; he is also intimately associated with the Messiah in the Book of Revelation chapter 12. There, Michael and

---

[54] Cf. A. Bentzen: *Messias, Moses Redivivus, Menschensohn* (Zurich 1948); in ET, *King and Messiah* (London 1954). Recall that, in Gen. 1, Adam is kingly; cf. also Ps. 8 (cf. Ps. 80.17); Mic. 5.1ff.; Job 15.7f.; Ezek. 28.11ff. F. M. Borsch, op. cit., follows Bentzen on that ground.

[55] Cf. N. Perrin: *Rediscovering the Teaching of Jesus* (New York 1967); Géza Vermès: Appendix E on the Son of Man to Matthew Black's *An Aramaic Approach to the Gospels and Acts* (Oxford 1968)³.

[56] 'The Son of Man in the Book of Daniel', *JBL*, 19 (1900), pp. 22–8. N. Schmidt was followed by T. H. Cheyne in 1914 and G. H. Box in 1932. More recently, it is also the opinion of J. Coppens ('Le Fils d'Homme daniélique . . .'; 'La Vision daniélique . . .'); U. Müller: *Messias und Menschensohn in jüdischen Apokalypsen und in der Offenbarung Johannes* (Gütersloh 1972); J. A. Emerton: 'The Origin of the Son of Man Imagery', *JTS* n.s. IX, Pt. 2 (Oct. 1953), pp. 225ff.; J. J. Collins: 'The Son of Man and the Saints of the Most High in the Book of Daniel', *JBL* 93 no. 1 (March 1974), pp. 50–66; etc.

[57] See Dan. 8.15; 10.16, 18.

[58] Translation G. Vermès: *The Dead Sea Scrolls in English* (Harmondsworth 1962), pp. 145, 146.

his angels overcome the Dragon ... so that the Kingdom is given to Christ (v.10). Besides, as J. J. Collins writes: 'The identification of Christ with the archangel Michael was explicitly made in the *Shepherd of Hermas*[59] (cf. Hermas, Vision 3; Similitudes 8.3, 3; 9.12, 7–8)'.

Other intertestamental texts uphold this flexibility of the Michael figure.[60] We therefore feel on a firm ground when we see in the personage of Daniel 7.13ff. the transcendent dimension of the people of Israel. We recall once more that according to this book every nation has its special angel who represents it in 'heaven'. It is within this perspective that we equally understand the equation of the son of man in Daniel with the angel Michael.

> Then thou, O Israel, shalt be happy,
> And thou shalt mount upon the necks and wings of the eagle.
> And they shall be ended.
> And God will exalt thee,
> And He will cause thee to approach to the heaven of the stars,
> In the place of their habitation.
> And thou shalt look from on high and shalt see thy enemies in Ge(henna),
> And thou shalt recognize them and rejoice,
> And thou shalt give thanks and confess thy Creator.
>
> (Assumpt. of Moses 10.8–10, tr. R. H. Charles)

Text 7. 1–14

(1) In the first year of Belshazzar, king of Babylon, Daniel saw dreams and visions of his head (while) in bed. Then he wrote down his dream, telling its substance. (2) Daniel spoke in these words: I saw this vision during my visions (which come) with the night: Behold the four winds of heavens were stirring up the Great Sea. (3) Four enormous animals rose out of the sea, each different from the others. (4) The first was like a lion and had an eagle's wings. I saw this vision until its wings were pulled off. It was lifted from the earth and put upright on two feet like a man, and a human heart was offered to it. (5) Behold another animal, the second, resembled a bear. It was put upright on one side. It had three ribs in its mouth, between its teeth; and it was told: arise, eat much meat! (6) After this, I saw a vision of another one. It was like a leopard. It had four wings of a bird on its back and this animal had four heads. Dominion was offered to it. (7) After this, I saw this vision during my nocturnal visions and behold a fourth animal, terrible, dreadful,

---

[59] J. J. Collins: 'The Son of Man and the Saints ...', p. 66. He refers to J. Daniélou: *Theology of Jewish Christianity* (London 1964), vol. I, pp. 121–7.

[60] 3 Baruch 11.2 describes Michael as in charge of the keys to the kingdom of the heavens; Ass. of Mos. 10.2 says he leads Israel in combat; etc.

and of extraordinary strength, which had enormous iron teeth. It ate (things) and broke them in pieces and trampled upon what was left. It was different from all the preceding animals and had ten horns. (8) I looked at the horns and behold among them another little horn arose before which three of the first horns were uprooted. And behold there were eyes similar to the eyes of a man on this horn and a mouth which uttered enormities.

(9) I saw the vision

> that thrones were erected and The-One-Who-Endures sat down,
> his raiment was white as snow and the hair on his head (was) like clean wool,
> his throne was (made) of fiery flames and its wheels were burning fire.
> (10) A stream of fire was poured out and came out from before him
> a thousand thousand served him and a myriad of myriads stood before him
> The tribunal sat down and books were opened.

(11) I saw this vision: then, due to the din of the enormities the horn was uttering, I saw the vision that the animal was killed and its body was destroyed and given to the burning fire. (12) As for the rest of the animals, their dominion was taken away from them and a prolongation of life was offered them for one moment, for one period.

(13) I saw this vision during my nocturnal visions
> and behold with the clouds of heaven came one like a son of man
> he reached up to the One-Who-Endures, and was brought before him.
> (14) He was offered dominion, glory, and kingship
> and the men of every people, nation, and language served him.
> His dominion is eternal and will not be taken away,
> and his kingdom is indestructible.

Critical Notes 7. 1–14

V.1 Most of the mss. of Theodotion read 'the third year'. Some Greek mss. insert: 'first vision'.—אמר: gives a doublet with the beginning of v.2.—ראש מלין אמר: *del.* in Θ, probably a marginal gloss which was added to the text. However, cf. Ps. 119.160.—'I saw a vision . . . and behold': see 2.31; 4.7, 10.—On this verse, cf. Isa. 30.8; Hab. 2.2; Rev. 1.19; Enoch 33.3, 4; 4 Esdras 14.42.

V.2 ענה דניאל ואמר: *del.* in LXX and Θ—רוחי־: see 8.8; 11.4; Zech. 2.10; 6.5; 4 Esdras 13.5—ימא רבא: for תהום רבה, see Isa. 51.10; Ps. 74.13; Job 3.8; 7.12; Ps. 18.17; Hab. 3.14; Add. Esth. 1.9.—מגיחן: see Mic. 4.10; Ezek. 32.2; Job 38.8.—עם ליליא: A. Bentzen judiciously recalls the temporal use of עם in 3.33 and 4.31. Charles is bothered by the preposition, but cites Talmudic texts where עם has the same temporal sense: *m. Shab.* II.7; *Yoma* 87b.

V.3 חיון: see Ps. 68.31; 4 Esdras 6.49–50; 2 Baruch 29.4; 1 Enoch 60.7.—

סלקן: see 2 Baruch 29.4; cf. 4 Esdras 11.1; 13.3 (in the Syriac version).

V.4 הקימת: a hybrid form combining the active and passive factive.— גף: wing; see v.6. Cf. Exod. 21.3–4.—חזה הוית עד די: always announces an ultimate catastrophe (Ginsberg, op. cit., p. 65, n. 7).

V.5 LXX: 'another beast'. Θ: 'a second beast'. MT combines these two precisions.—בשר is translated by both LXX and Θ as κρέας = animal meat; as in Dan. 10.3.

V.6 LXX: καὶ μετὰ ταῦτα ἐθεώρουν . . .; Θ: ὀπίσω τούτου ἐθεώρουν καὶ ἰδοὺ . . .—LXX: θηρίον ἄλλο, whence the 'restoration' of חיות before אחרי by some critics (see in particular, Charles, op. cit., p. 178).

V.7 LXX: corruption of the Aramaic text.—רברבן: = LXX; del. in Θ.—משניה: Θ adds 'much'.—'ate': see Ps. 79.7; Jer. 10.25; Zech. 12.6.—'broke': see Exod. 32.20; Mic. 4.13; Isa. 28.28; 41.15—'trampled': see Job 39.15; Isa. 25.10; Hos. 10.11; Hab. 3.12; Ezek. 32.2; Ps. 68.31.

V.8 מִשְׂתַּכַּל הֲוֵית instead of the usual חזה הוית (cf. vv.4b, 6, 9, 11a, 11b, 21). Probably because there is here no change of scene. (Cf. Z. Zevit: 'The Structure . . .' ZAW 80, p. 388, n. 16).—אתעקרו: read אתעקרי (the Qr.: אתעקרה is Targumic Aramaic). Similarly in 7.20, נפלי should be read instead of נפלו or נפלה. See the note to Dan. 5.5.—The LXX adds: 'it made war upon the saints'. Charles accepts this text as authentic, referring to the parallels in 7.21 and 25; cf. Rev. 11.7; 12.17; 19.19.

V.9 Θ: '. . . like clean wool'.—LXX: 'having a mantle like snow and the hair on his head was pure like white wool' (see Rev. 1.14; Enoch 46.1).—רמיו: to lay the foundations (cf. Rashi, Ibn Ezra: 'to pull down').—עתיק יומין: Rashi: God; Jephet: an angel; Ibn Ezra: the archangel Michael.

V.10 מן קדמוהי: understood as designating the throne in 1 Enoch 14.19; cf. Rev. 4.5; 11.1; but in fact it is about God.—נגד ונפק: LXX omits the first verb, Θ the second one. Vul. and Pesh. = MT. —רבון: Aramaic form for the Heb.: רבו, see Jonah 4.11.—ישמשונה: ἐλειτούργουν (Θ); ἐθεράπευον (LXX).—פתיחו: ἠνεῴχθησαν (Θ); ἠνοίχθησαν (LXX).

V.11 חזה הוית: del. in LXX and Θ; Vul. and Pesh. = MT.—באדין: Charles, op. cit., p. 185, notes that this word appears 51 other times in Daniel and always at the beginning of a sentence. However, LXX and Θ support the abnormal word order here; see also 1 Enoch 90.26.—גשם: see the note to 3.27. But, in opposition to 3.27, 28; 4.30; 5.21, the term here designates the dead body of an animal.—ליקדת אשא: see Isa. 64.10 in Hebrew.

V.12 שאר חיותא: LXX τοὺς κύκλῳ αὐτοῦ which G. Jahn, Das Buch Daniel

nach der Septuaginta hergestellt, übersetzt und kritisch erklärt,
1904, p. 70, takes as the original text. But the same phenomenon
occurs in 7.7 (κύκλῳ) and 7.12 (κυκλόθεν).

V.13 עם ענן: in the peshers from Qumran, the movement is from
heaven to earth. For the contrary, see 4 Esdras 13. Here the LXX
has ἐπί (vehicle of the 'son of man'); Mark 13.26 has ἐν (on the
basis of the theophanies in Exod. 16.10; 19.9; Lev. 16.2; Num.
11.25). See 2 Sam. 22.10: descent of God on a thick cloud. Taking
texts about theophanies as its authority, *Sanh.* 98a also understands the movement as going from heaven toward the earth.
The coming of the Messiah depends on the merits of Israel: he
comes on clouds according to Dan. 7 or on an ass according to
Zech. 9.7. The same movement: *Tanh.* B 70b; *Num. R.* 13.14;
etc. (see Str.-Bill., *Kommentar* I, p. 957). On the contrary, for
movement from earth toward the heavens: *Mid.* on Ps. 2.9 and
21.5 (see N. Perrin, *Rediscovering the Teaching of Jesus* (New
York 1967), pp. 171ff.). The latter meaning is to be preferred, see
'he reached up to the One-etc.'; cf. T. W. Manson, 'The Son of
Man . . .', *BJRL*, no. 32 (1950), p. 174. N. Perrin dissents, op. cit.,
p. 171: 'It should be understood as introductory to the whole
scene, the clouds forming the background or frame to the
celestial scene, and not a description of the approach of the Son
of Man figure to the throne.' J. A. Emerton (op. cit.) also rejects
our understanding for the scene is a theophany and this sup-
poses a movement from heaven to earth. We confess that we are
not convinced. The clouds, which so closely recall the theophanies, are now the vehicle of a 'man'. The outcome of his
'trip' is that 'he reached up to The-One-Who-Endures' and is
enthroned. The imagery is the one of the coronation of the
Canaanite god Baal, but Dan. 7 democratizes the figure into the
representative of '*verus Israel*', i.e., a human community
which will be vindicated. Moreover, despite the (weak) arguments thereagainst of Emerton, the translation to heaven of
Enoch, and the rising to heaven from the sea of the Man in
4 Esdras 13, must be invoked as witnesses to the early understanding of the earth-to-heaven fare of the Danielic 'son of
man'.—הקרבוהי: in the texts B 130 of Θ, the verb is προσήχθη αὐτῷ
or προσηνέχθη, with the sacrificial sense found, e.g., in Ezra 6.10,
17 (see Montgomery, p. 304).—LXX: 'those who were there
approached him' (so Tertullian and Cyprian; see Charles,
p. 187).

V.14 יהיב: 'This defectively written passive participle is found in
Biblical Aramaic in Dan. 7.14 and frequently in Palestinian
Syriac, Matt. 19.11 (A, B, C); Luke 7.25 (B, C); John 6.66 (B);
7.39 (B, C); 19.11 (B, C)' (M. Black, *An Aramaic Approach to the
Gospels and Acts* (Oxford 1967)³, p. 285).

CHAPTER 7

Commentary

According to Martin Noth,[61] chapter 7 is a late addition to Daniel A. This, plus the fact of the clear parallelism with chapter 2, explains why Dan. 7 should also be written in Aramaic.[62] From the point of view of its ideas, however, the chapter belongs instead to Daniel B: chapter 8 follows it in a logical fashion, and beginning in 7.2 through to the end of the book, Daniel speaks of himself in the first person.[63] Notice that Daniel 7—12 offers four visions which chronologically parallel the episodes of chapters 5 and 6.[64] Another tie to Daniel A, moreover, is that from time to time we find the expression 'vision of his head' (see 2.28; 4.2; 7.1). The word 'dream' which we also find here in parallel with its use in Daniel A serves as a transition, for Daniel speaks instead of *visions* in talking about what concerns him (see 7.2, 9, etc.). It is a question in chapter 7 of a symbolic dream first recounted (vv.2–14), then explained, no longer, however, by Daniel as in the first part of the book, but rather by an angel (vv. 15–18).[65] The revelation presented here is so important in the eyes of the narrator that it cannot be imagined as having been given to a pagan king, even Daniel does not understand it.

The vision is supposed to have come to Daniel during the reign of Belshazzar. From chapter 5 we already know how hard-hearted this monarch was and how he died. The vision of monsters representing historical empires could not have a better political setting.

The nations proceed from chaos (v.2) and are the works of chaos.[66] The sea is the symbol of the unformed, the potential, the undetermined.[67] The imagery used in the first part of this chapter draws its materials from the ancient cosmologies. The four winds, for example, are instruments in the hand of Marduk which prevent Tiamat (the Primordial Ocean) from escaping.[68] We might also think of the Canaanite version of the myth of the god Yam ('sea').[69] Thus A. Bentzen sees an instance of

[61] M. Noth, 'The Understanding of History in O.T. Apocalyptic', in *The Laws in the Pentateuch and Other Essays* (Philadelphia 1967).
[62] Also sharing this opinion are E. Bickerman, *Four Strange Books . . .*, p. 102, and O. Plöger, op. cit., p. 119.
[63] Except in 10.1. See the Introduction to chapter 7 and the discussion of its structure, common to Daniel B as a whole.
[64] First and second visions: first and third year of Belshazzar (7.1 and 8.1); third vision: first year of Darius the Mede (9.1); fourth vision: third year of Cyrus (10.1).
[65] On the intervention of an angel interpreter, see Ezek. 40.42 and Zech. 1—6.
[66] See Isa. 17.12, 13; Jer. 46.7, 8; Rev. 17.15.
[67] See M. Eliade, *Patterns in Comparative Religion*, p. 188.
[68] See *Enuma Elish* IV, 42–3.
[69] See Baal III, C, B, A, in G. R. Driver, *Canaanite Myths and Legends* (Edinburgh 1956), pp. 76ff. Furthermore, Thomas Fawcett (*The Symbolic Language of Religion* (Minneapolis 1971), pp. 110ff.) comments that the symbolic features of water or the primordial ocean are practically universal (Hinduism: Shesha; Egypt: Apep; Phoenicians: Yam; Babylonia: Tiamat); cf. M. Eliade, op. cit.

remythologization here (of Ps. 2, for example). He explains this phenomenon by the fact that mythological language no longer presented any
danger in Daniel's day.[70]

The animal symbolism found in v.3 occurs frequently, especially in
post-exilic texts (see in particular Ezek. 29.3ff.; Isa. 27.1; Ps. of Sol.
2.29; I Enoch 85–90). Wisdom of Solomon places animal monsters in
parallel with the plagues which struck Egypt.[71] The first monster here is
a lion with an eagle's wings (v.4). H. L. Ginsberg's reorganization of this
text is well-known (vv. 4a, 5aγ–b, 4da–β, 5aa–β, 4bγ–δ). It makes no
difference as regards the attribution of wings to a lion for it is a fact that
in Babylonian mythology the primitive waters engendered winged
monsters.[72] According to E. Bickerman,[73] 'In Babylonian astral geography, lion, bear, and leopard respectively symbolized the south
(Babylonia), the north (Media), and the east (Persia).' The description
of the 'humanized' lion has also been linked to the evolution of the
Babylonian Nebuchadnezzar described in chapter 4 (see vv.13, 31). We
may be surprised by this feature, but Rashi suggests a parallel between
being human and weakness. Montgomery goes even further: 'The
humanization involves the elimination of heaven-vaulting ambition.'[74]

The parallel with the Babylonian cosmogonic myth ends here. In the
poem *Enuma Elish* which transmits it, Tiamat (= ocean) does give birth
to a lion, but the other monsters which emerge from its depths have
nothing to do with the incredible animals in Daniel. The question as to
their origin[75] has not received any convincing solution. We believe they
are an original creation of the Author.[76]

[70] See *King and Messiah* (London 1954), pp. 74–5.
[71] See 2 Macc. 4.25; 5.11ff.: a description of the High Priest Menelaus and of Antiochus
IV in terms of the features of a ferocious beast. 'In reference to the beasts, the world
of apocalyptic subsumed the anthropological and the "historical" under nature and
the cosmic. Its dramatis personae included not only animals but also stones, stars,
clouds, waters, weather, cedar trees and gardens. Man was related to nature much
as a modern space fiction, ecological concern, and the thought of Teilhard de Chardin.
So far as polarization took place, there was the recognition that our warfare is not
with flesh and blood. . . .' (Amos N. Wilder, letter to the editor, *The Christian
Century*, July 28, 1971).
[72] Nebuchadnezzar is compared to a lion in Jeremiah (4.7; 49.19; 50.17) and his
troops act with the speed of an eagle: Jer. 49.22; Hab. 1.8; Ezek. 17.3.
[73] E. Bickerman, *Four Strange Books* . . ., p. 102.
[74] Op. cit., p. 287. Jerome had already seen the fall of Babylon's arrogance implied in
this human feature of the first animal.
[75] See A. Caquot, 'Sur les Quatre Bêtes de Daniel', *Semitica*, 5 (1955), pp. 6ff.;
M. Delcor, op. cit., pp. 144–7. Caquot believes that the four animals represent 4
zodiacal signs for south (lion), north (bear), east (panther) and west (a monster
instead of the 'conventional sign')!
[76] Proof of this is the blurred description of the fourth animal. The Author has run out
of hyperbole after the first three animals and his inspiration seems to have dried up.
All the more so if he drew part of his inspiration from Hos. 13.7–8 (lion; panther;
she-bear; lioness); here also with Hosea we remain short of a different fourth
animal.

CHAPTER 7

The second animal (v.5) represents Media. Well known for its cruelty (see Isa. 13.17–18; 21.2ff.), its emblem is the bear who is second only to the lion in strength and ferocity (see Hos. 13.8; Amos 5.19).[77] If therefore we are to accept the text as given and not change it following H. L. Ginsberg's suggestions (see *supra*), Media is characterized as having an insatiable appetite for destruction. The 'three ribs', scraps from some bloody feast (see Amos 3.13), thus represent either the Babylonian kings known to Jewish tradition: Nebuchadnezzar, Evil-Merodach, and Belshazzar;[78] or, following a suggestion from R. M. Frank,[79] the Aramaic term rendered by 'ribs' in fact signifies, on the basis of Arabic: 'fangs'. In this case, the three fangs amidst the bear's teeth indicate its brutality.[80] Its position 'put upright on one side' shows it crouched down ready to spring[81] or standing up on its back legs in an aggressive position.[82]

The leopard or panther represents Persia (v.6).[83] For H. L. Ginsberg[84] the four wings in v.6a are a secondary motif in relation to the four heads in v.6b. The Author's goal was to show that the third animal (Persia) comes right after the first (Babylon with an eagle's wings) on the plane of cruelty. Whatever the validity of this argument, it would seem necessary to see the same motif in both the heads and the wings of the monster. It is a question either of the four corners of the world,[85] or, as in Dan. 11.2, of the four Persian kings known to Scripture: Cyrus, Artaxerxes, Xerxes, Darius III Codomannus (who was defeated by Alexander the Great).[86] It is Alexander's kingdom, 'terrible, dreadful, and of extraordinary strength', which is at issue in the following verse (v.7).[87] It differs from the preceding ones in several points. First, it comes from the west and brings a wholly different civilization. Next, Alexander's con-

---

[77] On the basis of the term דבא in the Targums, Ibn Ezra renders this word as 'wolf'. In the Talmud, the bear or the wolf symbolize the Persian Empire, for the Persians 'eat and drink like a bear, are fat like a bear, have long hair like a bear, and are agitated like a bear' (*Kidd* 72a). *Yoma* 77a calls the guardian angel of Persia 'God's bear'; cf. *A.Z.* 2a. For the Peshitta, on the contrary, it is rather a question of Media.

[78] See *Song of Sol. R.* 3.3; *Est. R.* 3. Ibn Ezra: three Assyrian cities conquered by the Medes. Ewald: Babylon, Assyria, Syria.

[79] R. M. Frank, *CBQ*, 21 (1959), pp. 505–7: 'The Description of the Bear in Daniel 7.5'.

[80] See Vulgate: *tres ordines erant in ore ejus.* Many of the older commentators followed this reading; see H. H. Rowley, *Darius the Mede*, p. 151, n. 1.

[81] Driver, op. cit., p. 82; Montgomery, op. cit., p. 288.

[82] H. Junker, *Untersuchungen . . . des Buches Daniel* (1932), p. 41.

[83] See Hos. 13.7; Jer. 5.6.

[84] *Studies*, p. 12.

[85] See the Babylonian title 'king of the four regions.' See also the impression of a wave breaking over the whole universe made by the Persian conquests in Isa. 41.3.

[86] So Montgomery, followed, for example, by H. H. Rowley and H. L. Ginsberg.

[87] See 2.40; 8.5; 11.3.

quests were without parallel in ancient history. They really did break up the Asiatic cultures, replacing them with Greek culture.

The image of this fourth monster is unclear, as though the Author's imagination had failed him. A. Bentzen believes he recognizes the Leviathan from the Ugaritic literature, but this parallel is not obvious. The ten horns are manifestly a royal attribute (see Dan. 7.24; 8.5ff.; 1 Enoch 90.9). Their number is hardly explained except by a historical allusion. The vitriolic description of Alexander's kingdom found in the Sibylline Oracles III.381–400 also speaks of 'ten horns' (line 397) and it is a question of Alexander's successors, although here again they cannot be identified with any satisfactory precision.[88] Line 400 adds, in parallel with the 'eleventh horn' in Dan. 7.8: 'and then a parasitic horn will have power'.

In the little arrogant horn, we must see Antiochus IV, the personage in view of whom everything which precedes and which follows was written by the Author; cf. 8.9, 23.[89] Antiochus, in fact, had to overthrow several other claimants to the throne in his ascension to power. Who these three evicted horns are remains a debated point. A *status quaestionis* is presented in H. H. Rowley, *Darius the Mede* . . ., pp. 98–120.[90]

The symbolic description of Antiochus IV reuses material found elsewhere in Daniel and other texts. On arrogant eyes, see 8.23; cf. Isa. 2.11; for the immodest mouth, see 7.25; 11.36; Ps. 12.3; 1 Macc. 1.24–5; 2 Macc. 5.17; Rev. 13.5. It is well known that the king indicated that he was divine by giving himself the name Epiphanes. In his old age he had himself represented on coins with the features of Zeus Olympios. For D. S. Russell,[91] we have here and in Dan. 11.36, 40–1, 45, the oldest reference in apocalyptic writings to an Antichrist.[92] Antiochus is certainly Evil's ultimate assault against the people of God. Hence the

---

[88] Is it exclusively a question of the Seleucid line? (see H. L. Ginsberg: two Alexanders, four Seleuci, and four Antiochi, the last of whom is Epiphanes, *Studies*, pp. 18–23). For A. Lods, it is a question of Alexander, the seven Seleucids coming before Antiochus, then the two kings overthrown by him, Heliodorus (who poisoned Seleucus IV Philopator and assumed the crown for himself) and Demetrius (the son of Seleucus IV and legitimate heir to his throne). *Histoire de la Littérature* . . ., p. 843.

For other authors, the number ten only indicates infinity, see Zöckler, *The Book of Daniel* (1876), pp. 153, 165; Montgomery, op. cit., p. 293, n. 1; B. Rigaux, *L'Antéchrist* . . . (Gembloux-Paris 1932), p. 165.

[89] Already identified as such by Porphyry. Antiochus IV usurped the Seleucid power on 3 September, 175 BCE.

[90] For Porphyry, the three horns are Ptolemy VI, Ptolemy VII, and Artaxias of Armenia. It would have been preferable, says E. Bickerman, *Four Strange Books* . . ., p. 105, to stay in Egypt and to see Cleopatra II in the third horn, the sister and wife of the Ptolemies in question, who was subdued by Antiochus IV in 170.

[91] *The Method and Message* . . ., p. 277.

[92] See Ass. of Mos. 8.1ff.: Antiochus IV or a combination of him and Herod the Great; Ps. of Sol. 2.29: Pompey; etc.

war takes on mythic overtones so that it is even possible to see in the blasphemy of the 'little horn' an echo of the same motif in what H. Ginkel calls the *Chaosmythus*.[93]

The text, which has been in prose up to this point, changes over to poetry in vv.9–10. The same thing also happens in vv.13–14 and 23–7. Montgomery nicely calls these passages 'poetic rhapsodies'. It is fitting to turn to poetic language to describe the royal court of The-One-Who Endures (see 1 Kings 22; Ps. 9; 50; 82; 93; 96; 98; Job 1). The scene especially calls to mind Isa. 6 or Ezek. 1. See also 1 Enoch 14.15ff.[94] and *Sanh.* 38b.

Without any transition, the narration transports us to heavenly places. They are, so to speak, on the same level with the scenes of human history. Thrones are brought forth, one of which is first occupied by God. He sits as a judge.[95] There is at least one other throne where the 'son of man' will sit,[96] and perhaps others for the angelic assistant judges and the 'Saints' associated with the 'son of man'.[97]

The title given to God is עתיק יומין, a unique expression, although corresponding titles can be found in 1 Enoch 46.1–2; 47.3; and 98.2: 'Head of Days'.[98] The parallels within canonical Scripture are more ideological than linguistic (see Isa. 44.6; Ps. 55.19). Charles cites Wisd. (Syriac text) 2.10: 'old man rich in days', which he compares to Gen. 24.1. But in both cases it is a question of men and not of God. 1 Baruch 4.10, 14, and 20 call God 'the Eternal'. The origin of this notion should probably be sought in the literature from Ugarit where the high god El is *mlk ab shnm* (king, father of years).[99] Not only is the idea the same

---

[93] *Schöpfung . . .*, p. 329. He refers to Ps. 74.18; Ps. of Sol. 2.32f.; Ezek. 29.3; Ps. 68.31; Ps. of Sol. 2. In the end, God brings an end to chaos: Ps. 89.2, 3, 15; 74.14; Isa. 51.9; Job 26.12; Ps. 89.10; Job 9.13.

[94] Where God in an unusual way is called 'The Great Glory'.

[95] See Ps. 122.5.

[96] For *Sanh.* 38b, one of the thrones is for David. The same opinion is expressed by R. Akiba in *Hag* 14a. But R. Jose the Galilean successfully reproaches him for this exegesis. It is rather a question of 'a throne for justice and one for grace'. Rashi understands: one throne for judgement and another for justice.

[97] See Dan. 7.18ff.; cf. Matt. 19.28; Luke 22.30; 1 Cor. 6.2; 1 Enoch 45.3; 90.20.

[98] See also 55.1; 60.2; 71.10–14. In these texts the title is perhaps a later interpolation. See A. Michel: *Le Maître de Justice* (Avignon 1954), p. 98.

[99] See I AB 1.7. It is true that at Ugarit *šnm* instead of *šnt* is a little surprising. But F. M. Cross (*Canaanite Myth . . .*, p. 16) calls attention to newly published texts in *Ugaritica V*. There, El receives the epithet *mélek 'ôlām*, 'eternal king'. Cross finds nothing irregular in the plural *šnm* side by side with *šnt*, for both 'were available in Old Canaanite, and the Ugaritic materials reflect more than one level of dialect' (p. 16, n. 24).

Another possibility, of course, would be to take *'attiq* in its etymological sense. In Akkadian, *etequ* means 'move, proceed' [in Ugaritic, *'tq* = go, pass] (cf. K.-Baum, *Lexicon*, p. 748b). One finds this sense also in Hebrew, e.g., in Prov. 25.1. God in Dan. 7 would then be described as the One who forwards time, i.e., the One who rules over time.

in both instances as regards the eternity of the divinity, but at Ugarit as here, this perduration of God is linked to his enthronement as king and judge.[100]

It is from this perspective of judgement that we need to examine the motif of the whiteness of God's vestments and hair. Whiteness represents innocence (see Isa. 1.18; Ps. 51.9), while the white hair also clearly indicates experience. The goddess Anat, in demanding a palace for Baal from El, threatens to stain the white hair of the father of gods with blood.[101]

The description of the throne which follows is heavily dependent upon the vision of the *Merkaba* in Ezek. 1 and 10. Fire is the dominant motif, a sign of a theophany (Exod. 24.17; Ps. 50; 97; Ezek. 1; Deut. 4.24; 9.3) and of divine judgement (Ps. 50.3; 56.9; Mal. 3.16; Ezek. 13.9; Rev. 3.5; 20.12; Ps. of Sol. 15, 6–7; Apoc. of Ab. 31).

The throne has wheels like all royal and divine thrones in the Ancient Orient (see Ezek. 1.15–28). A river of fire springs out from it (v.10). 'In Persian eschatology', says Carl H. Kraeling,[102] 'the mountains which are made of metal melt at the end of the world, and the molten metal pours over the earth like a river. All men pass into this river of molten metal and in so doing are either purified or destroyed.' He believes that this is the origin of 'all those realistic interpretations of the function of fire in the final judgement, and thus also the source of Daniel's river of fire and its variant, the fiery breath of the Messiah.' In fact, it is rather a question here as elsewhere of how Iranian influence reinvigorated certain elements of Israelite tradition. The same theme is also found in 1 Enoch 14.18.

The scene of the adoration by a multitude is in parallel with several other texts (see Deut. 33.2; 1 Kings 22.19; Isa. 6.1; Ps. 68.18; etc. *Sanh.* 38b speaks of the 'Tribunal on high'. See also 1 Enoch 1.9; 71.8, 13; 91.15; Sib. Oracles III, 689–92.[103] The angels are lined up in military fashion (cf. Jubilees 2.2), the divisions being grouped according to the decimal system.[104] Charles refers us to 1 Enoch 14.22, written he believes before 170 BCE.

There are several categories of 'books' in Jewish literature. Their

---

[100] At Ugarit, too, judgement is a royal and divine attribute: Yam (= Sea) is 'Judge River' (*tpt nhr*).

[101] See II AB IV–V, 65–7 (the god El). *Hag.* 14a speculates that God's hair is black (cf. Song of Songs, 5.11) when he goes to war as a young man. His hair is white when he sits in session in the tribunal as an old man.

[102] *John the Baptist* (New York 1951), p. 117.

[103] S. Mowinckel, *He that Cometh*, p. 273, n. 4, refers to numerous texts from the Pseudepigrapha. See also Norman H. Snaith, *The Jews from Cyrus to Herod* (New York 1956).

[104] On the number 10, the powers of ten, and its hyperboles, see H. A. Brongers, op. cit., pp. 30–45.

origin lies in ancient Egyptian and Babylonian religion.[105] In one book are written all of man's acts, both good and bad (see Isa. 65.6; Mal. 3.16; Ps. 56.8–9; Luke 10.20; Rev. 20.12; Jubilees 30.22; *P. Aboth* 2.1). There is also the book of life (see Exod. 32.32–3; Ps. 69.28; 1 Enoch 90.20; Test. of Levi 5.5: 'the heavenly tables' [which remind one of the Tablets of Fate seized by Marduk]). This book 'contains the secret of the future of the world. It is essentially a question not of reading this book, but of opening it. Once the seals are broken the events begin to occur before the seer's eyes.'[106]

Vv.11–12 return to prose to reveal to us the sentence written in the book. This passage from 'poetic rhapsody' to prose explains the dittography, 'I saw a vision'. Perhaps we should suppress the first part of the verse,[107] but as such it has a solemn cast which fits well with its message: the fourth empire is condemned to be destroyed because of the arrogance of its last representative, Antiochus Epiphanes. He is thrown into the fire which was mentioned in the preceding verses. Charles is perhaps correct in seeing hell ablaze here.[108] He refers to texts he considers older than Dan. 7.11 such as 1 Enoch 10.6; 18.11; 21.7–10. See also 1 Enoch 91.24–7 which is of Maccabean origin. Maybe we have here the 'eschatologization' of the theme of executing criminals by fire from Josh. 7.25 (cf. Isa. 30.33; Ezek. 39.6). There is, in any case, a deliberate contrast between this mode of destruction and the aquatic origin of the monsters. God's victory over chaos is total and definitive (see Ps. 74.13ff.; 89.9ff.; Job 9.8, 13; 26.12; Isa. 51.9ff.; 27.1; Jer. 51.34–7; Ezek. 29.3–4).

However, a prolongation of life is accorded the other kingdoms—no doubt to indicate that a similar judgement is not indifferently applied to the four monsters, the arrogance, nature, and destiny of the fourth one being beyond comparison. As in chapter 2, where annihilation was the fate of all the world's empires, it is evident that the survival of three of them is just a respite or deferment. H. H. Rowley explains this by the fact that the Author 'might look for Media and Persia and Babylonia to become independent states for a time . . . until the Messianic Kingdom which was to be established in Palestine should spread to include them and fill the earth.'[109] Similarly, E. Heaton recalls the tradition that one day all the nations will serve the People of God.[110]

---

[105] See Montgomery, op. cit., ad loc.
[106] Note to Rev. 5.1 in *Le Nouveau Testament, Traduction nouvelle* by M. Goguel and H. Monnier (Paris 1929), p. 422.
[107] With A. Bentzen, through the second 'I see' (op. cit., p. 50). See H. L. Ginsberg, *Studies . . .*, p. 16: Every allusion to an eleventh horn is secondary, so that in v. 11, we should read: '. . . Then . . . the beast was slain and its body destroyed, etc.'.
[108] Op. cit., p. 185. Despite the opposition of E. Heaton, p. 181; M. Delcor, p. 153; etc.
[109] See *Darius the Mede*, p. 123.
[110] P. 181. He cites Tobit 13.11; Isa. 14.1–2; 49.22–3; 60.12; Zech. 8.22; Ps. 89.9. Cf. here vv.14, 27.

By returning to a poetic style the Author now introduces a personage 'like a son of man' (v.13). The statement raises a problem. We may, with J. B. Frey,[111] see an approximation in it: 'The seer[112] . . . does not undertake to say anything about the intimate nature of the extraordinary things which he has contemplated. . . . These ways of speaking have the advantage of giving the stories an air of mystery, of the inexplicable, which must have increased one's curiosity at the same time as it inspired an even greater respect for such high revelations.' Or we may see a *Kaph veritatis* as does P. Joüon.[113] This is also the opinion of A. Bentzen who thinks of the Akkadian *Kime* with the sense of resemblance or identity. Along the same lines, N. Porteous sees the man-like character of the kingdom symbolizing its divine character.[114] With W. Baumgartner,[115] we would say that 'This comparative and allusive manner of expression is, from Ezekiel onward, one noteworthy feature of the apocalyptic style. It characterizes the domain of the "visionary".' We believe that the meaning of 'like (a son of man)' is to be located somewhere between the two definitions given above. We indicated in our introduction to this chapter that the 'son of man' participates in the divine stature by his enthronement side by side with God and by the exercise of the divine judgement.[116] This clearly does not mean that he takes God's place. The 'like' indicates both distance and proximity in relation to The-One-Who-Endures. This is not a new notion. We find it constantly affirmed in the liturgy of the royal enthronement festival.

---

[111] Op. cit., col. 337.
[112] In Dan. 7.13; Ezek. 1; 1 Enoch 14.10–13; etc.
[113] *Grammaire* . . . (Rome 1947), p. 407, par. 133g.
[114] Op. cit., p. 110.
[115] Baumgartner, 'Ein Vierteljahrhundert Danielforschung', *ThR*, 11 (1939), pp. 216–17, quoted by A. Bentzen, p. 50.
[116] It has been definitively established that the expression 'son of man' is no title but simply means 'a man, someone'. To the material adduced by G. Vermès, N. Perrin, and others, it is also highly interesting to add Canaanite witnesses. W. Albright refers to the Ugaritic text 12 (= *CTA* pp. 25ff.) li. 33: *bnš* = bin-('e)naš = man, somebody. (*BASOR* 150 (1958), pp. 36–8, 'Specimens of late Ugaritic Prose'; cf. C. H. Gordon: *Ugaritic Textbook*, Glossary *ad* no. 468.) In the Scfire inscription as well, the expression means 'a man' (cf. *K.A.I.* text 224, li. 16).
  As far as Israel is concerned, however, 'human form is no reduction to mere humanness' (L. Köhler: *Theologie des A.T.* (1949)², p. 6). In a polemical move, Daniel 7 shows that not the god Baal, not the megalomaniac and bestial Epiphanes, but *man* is enthroned as king of the universe and to him is granted the judgement over all.
  See S. Mowinckel, op. cit., p. 393: 'Thereby he acquires a status similar to that of God Himself.' That judgement belongs to God and ought to belong to him is indicated by the texts assembled by this same author on p. 393, n. 4. Cf. Isa. 60.19, 20; Zeph. 3. The Jewish tradition does not hesitate before the paradox of 'man' designating God. With regard to Zech. 1.8, 'a man riding on a red horse', *Sanh.* 93a says: '"man" designates nothing other than the Holy One blessed be he—for it is written: " the Lord is a man of war; the Lord is his name" (Exod. 15.3).'

Thus Harald Riesenfeld can say: 'YHWH and the Israelite king form one and the same entity.'[117] With the Exile this festival 'disintegrated' into several ritual elements—it was 'democratized' in the sense that what had previously been applied to the pre-exilic king was now seen as applied to the People. Thus the royal title 'Son of God'[118] was transferred to Israel *qua* elect people and to the individual righteous man.[119] It is this phenomenon which occurs in Dan. 7. The 'son of man' is the personification of the righteous People, the perfect image of the righteous individual.[120]

In the introduction to this chapter we spoke of the importance of clouds as one accompaniment of a theophany. Out of a total of about a hundred occurrences in Scripture, in 70% of the cases, clouds refer to Sinai, or to the Temple (see 1 Kings 8.10–11; 2 Chron. 5.13–14; 2 Macc. 2.8; cf. the vision of the *Merkaba* in Ezek. 1.4 and 10.3–4), or to eschatological theophanies (Isa. 4.5; Ps. 97.2; Nahum 1.3). It is a supplementary tie with Messianism as well. McNamara, therefore, is perfectly correct in emphasizing the messianic character of the kingdom promised to believers in this chapter.[121] Even before him, Aage Bentzen

---

[117] *Jésus transfiguré* (Copenhagen 1947), p. 50. Cf. also C. Colpe (*TWNT* VIII, p. 416): 'Another possibility is that Dan. 7 reflects ideas of the harvest-feast in which prior to the exile the victory over the chaos dragon and the enthronement of the victor as king were celebrated, and which played a decisive role in the rise of eschatology.'

[118] See Ps. 2.7; 89.27; 25.7, 14; 1 Chron. 17.13.

[119] Re all of this, see Riesenfeld, op. cit., especially pp. 68–9. On a deeper level as well, the 'one like a son of man' is the result of a democratization process. F. M. Cross writes that the personage 'is evidently young Ba'l reinterpreted and democratized by the apocalyptist as the Jewish nation.' (*Canaanite Myth . . .*, p. 17).

[120] Here again the book of Daniel is a pioneering work. Apocalyptic and pseudepigraphic literature pursued the theme inaugurated here. The New Testament was the direct heir of this notion, which in the meantime had been radicalized. This does not mean that on the level of Dan. 7, one may say as Norman Perrin does: 'That the figure is "one like unto a Son of man" is probably pure accident' (*Rediscovering the Teaching of Jesus*, p. 167).

[121] McNamara, *A New Catholic Commentary . . .*, par. 534d: 'Since the Kingdom promised to the faithful of Israel in Dan. 7 is, *de facto*, Messianic, it is but natural that the chapter came to be interpreted later in the light of those other texts [Gen. 49.10; Isa. 9.5–6; 11.1–5; Ps. 2; 110; etc.] and that "one like a son of man" in 13f. was considered as the Messiah, all the more so as the Messianic prerogatives of many earlier texts (e.g., Gen. 49.10; Isa. 9.6) correspond to those granted to the "Son of Man" in Dan. 7.13f. . . .' Cf. H. Riesenfeld, *Jesus . . .*, p. 78: The person of the Messiah is inseparable from his Kingdom. On the other hand, 'the idea of the Kingdom implies that of the people' (p. 79).
The history of the origins of the clouds motif goes in the same direction. F. M. Cross (*Canaanite Myth . . .*, p. 17) sees the clouds as 'belong[ing] to the traditional entourage of Ba'l, the (deified) storm clouds (or cloud chariot) accompanying him or on which he rides'. (Cross refers to *C.T.A.* 2.1.18, 35; 4.8.14; 1.3.17; 3.4.76; and esp. to 4.4.58–60.) As for P. D. Miller (*The Div. Warrior . . .*, p. 30), he thinks that the clouds belong to the retinue of Baal, a 'host of divine beings;' cf. Ugaritic text

had written that 1 Enoch, 4 Esdras 13, the Gospels, Acts, and Revelation, which see a messianic individual in the 'son of man' in Daniel 7, could not have been purely and simply the victims of a misunderstanding (p. 63). The origin of such an equation goes back to the ancient notion of a man-king or *Urmensch* as found in Iran, India, Mesopotamia, and, through syncretism, in Judaism (see Gen. 1; 2; Ps. 8; Wisd. 10.2; etc.). 3 Esdras (= additions to Ezra), for example, eulogizes the king as being 'the most powerful thing' for 'do not *men* excel in strength, that bear rule over the sea and land, and all things in them? But yet is the king stronger . . .' (3 Esdras 4.2). This is only one example. Gnosticism (in all its forms) speculated about Man and even though we must be prudent in using this literature to clarify older texts, it is still true that from the point of view that interests us here, the Gnostics developed a theme solidly anchored in the older Israelite mentality. Poimandres 10.25 says: 'Man on earth is a mortal god; God in the heavens is an immortal Man.' The powerful Sethian sect identified the 'son of man' with Seth 'the son of Adam' on the basis of Gen. 4.25–6; 5.3ff. According to the Manicheans, 'the Primal Man dwells in the world, macrocosmically as the "world soul" and microcosmically as the "individual soul". To think of the Primal Man as dwelling simultaneously in heaven and on earth did not involve a contradiction for Mani.'[122]

Finally, for the Mandeans, the First Man Anush or Anush-uthra (uthra = angel!) was both microcosm and macrocosm. Every Mandean, at the time of his baptism—which was an authentic royal enthronement —became like Anush. He was the archetype of spiritual humanity and of *the priesthood*.

In the next verse (v.14) we note a new feature of the promotion of the 'son of man' to divine stature. The terms here are 'used elsewhere of the sovereignty of God; see 3.33; 6.27', says Charles.[123] This is why he is *served* by all peoples. The term פלחן used here always refers to divine

---

51 (= *C.T.A.* 4) li. 18, 34–5. On p. 195, n. 77, Miller recalls that 'the phrase *rwḥy ʿnn* appears in the angelology of Qumran (4 Q Ber) and the pseudepigraphical literature'.

In his article mentioned above, J. A. Emerton ('Origin . . .') emphasizes that a man cannot come on clouds, it would be 'the only exception out of about 70 passages in the O.T.' (p. 232). He agrees with the Harvard school that the son of man is indeed on the model of the god Baal, vanquisher of the dragon and of Yam. With Dan. 7, however, the evolution is the following: Baal is converted into YHWH enthroned by the great god El (cf. 4 Esdras 13: the Man has divine features: in Sib. Or. V.413–33, the Man comes from heaven). Practically, as the Jewish conception could not tolerate polytheism, the transference of the Baal attributes has been made onto the angel Michael. Emerton adds: 'This would help to explain the attribution of an exalted status to such beings as Michael and Metatron in later Judaism' (p. 242).

[122] See C. H. Kraeling, *Anthropos and Son of Man* (New York 1927), p. 22.
[123] Op. cit., p. 187.

service (see 3.12, 14, 17, 18, 28; 6.17, 21;[124] Ezra 7.24). A. Feuillet rightly says: 'In Daniel 7.14, 21, we have the same phenomenon as the use of שרת in Isa. 60.7, 10; 61.6; the Israelites serve YHWH and the foreigners serve the Israelites, which is indirectly to serve YHWH as well.'[125] See our commentary on 2.46.

Text 7. 15–28

(15) I, Daniel, my spirit was distressed in its sheath, the visions of my head frightened me. (16) I approached one of those who stood there and asked him what was sure in all that. He told me, he made known to me the interpretation of all these things. (17) These enormous animals, which were four in number, are four kings who will arise out of the earth; (18) but the Most Haughty Saints will receive the kingdom and retain the kingship for ever, from eternity to eternity. (19) Next I wanted (to know) for certain about the fourth animal, who was different from all the others, extremely terrible, with iron teeth and brass claws, who ate (things) and broke them, and trampled upon what remained; (20) and about the ten horns on its head and the one which arose and before whom three fell away; that horn had eyes, a mouth uttering enormities, and a more imposing appearance than did its companions. (21) I saw a vision that this horn undertook to fight against the Saints and was prevailing against them, (22) until He-Who-Endures came and rendered justice to the Most Haughty Saints and the moment arrived when the Saints retained the kingship.

(23) He spoke as follows:

the fourth animal
is a fourth kingdom which will exist on earth, different from every other
  kingdom;
it will devour all the earth, crushing it and breaking it into pieces.
(24) As for the ten horns,
they are ten kings which will arise from this kingdom and another will arise
  after them
different from its predecessors, it will put down three kings.
(25) It will speak out against the Most High and wear out the Most Haughty
  Saints,
it will think about changing the times and the Law,

---

[124] M. Delcor was rightly struck by the coincidence between the use of פלח in Dan. 3; 6; and 7. He believes the import of this verb ought to be minimized, referring to 7.27 and Targ. Jer. 27.6, 7, 8. These references, however, are not convincing. Instead Dan. 7.27 proves that we must maximize the sense of this verb. Recall that Targ. Jer. 27 translates the Heb. עבד; for, precisely in the light of Dan. 3, nothing prevents the Targ. from dramatizing the MT in a cultic sense.

[125] A. Feuillet, op. cit., p. 189.

(the Saints) will be delivered into its hands for one period, two periods, and a half period.

(26) Then the tribunal will be seated and take away its dominion and it will be ruined and totally destroyed.

(27) The kingship, dominion, and grandeur of all the kingdoms under heavens will be

offered to the people of the Most Haughty Saints.

His reign is an eternal reign and every ruler will serve and obey him.

(28) Here is the end of the story. As for me, Daniel, my thoughts frightened me greatly and my face changed colour; I kept this matter in my heart.

Critical Notes 7. 15–28

V.15 בגוא נדנה: Vss. read 'due to this' (= בגוא דנה); see LXX: ἐν τούτοις. Nidâna is Persian. It is found in Heb. in 1 Chron. 21.27. Levy, *Chaldäisches Wörterbuch über die Targumim*, gives the spellings לדנה and נדנה. The latter form is only found in *Sanh.* 108a and *Ber. R.* par. 26. The word signifies 'sheath'. The correction to בגין is only supported by the Jerus. Targs. (see Weiss, *Zeits. der Deutschen Morgenl. Gesel.*, 32, p. 754). It would then be preferable to read בגודנה with בגו in the sense of a preposition. But this ingenious reading is weakened by the discoveries made at Qumran. *The Genesis Apocryphon* contains the expression: 'inside his sheath', אתכרית רוחי.—נדנה: see 2.3 in Heb.

V.16 חד מן־קאמיא: 'Especially idiomatic in Hebrew and Aramaic is a usage of this pronoun with a following genitive or partitive *min* where the compound expression means nothing more than "a certain so-and-so" . . . see Gen. 37.20; 21.15; Lev. 14.30; 1 Macc. 4.38' (M. Black, op. cit., p. 105).—יציבא: see 2.8, 45; 3.24; 6.13; 7.19. Θ: 'the truth' (see 11.2: אמת).

V.17 אנין: some mss. have the less good lection אנון.—מלכין: LXX and Θ: βασιλεῖαι (= מלכן) but it is a free translation (see 8.21).— 'which were four': del. in LXX.—יקומון מן ארעא: LXX: 'which will be destroyed from the earth' (ἀπολοῦνται); this version is more satisfying logically for it does not contradict the aquatic origin of the monster according to v.3, as does the MT. Vul.=MT; Pesh.: 'on the earth' (= Θ). See our commentary.

V.18 קדישי עליונין: LXX and Θ: ἅγιοι ὑψίστου. עליון is in Heb. In Aramaic it would be עליא, עלאה (4.14, 21).—ו . . . עד עלמא: del. in LXX and Θ. Pesh. and Vul. = MT.

V.19 וטפריה די־נחש: missing in the description in v.7, of which this verse is a quasi-imitation. Hippolytus had already inserted this missing phrase in v.7; H. L. Ginsberg also proposes that it should be done. But there are other new details in the explanatory section (vv.9–22): notably, the horn with the eyes and mouth of a man.

V.20 ונפלו: Qr. ונפלה: see 5.5 where we find the same situation.

V.22 ודינא יהיב: LXX: τὴν κρίσιν ἔδωκε. Θ: τὸ κρῖμα ἔδωκεν. Both therefore read יְהַב. Ewald has conjectured a haplography: ודינא יתב ושלטנא יהיב. But cf. 1 Cor. 6.2.

Vv.23–4 Following the Masoretic punctuation, we have: 'The fourth animal: there will be a fourth kingdom, etc. . . . As for the ten horns: from this kingdom, etc. . . .'—כל ארעא: see 2.39 (where it is a question of the Persian Empire). Re Alexander the Great, see 1 Macc. 1.3. Re the accumulation of verbs, see Isa. 9.11; Jer. 10.25; Isa. 41.15; Mic. 4.13; Dan. 2.40.—In v.24, Θ adds: '. . . who will surpass all the others in evils.'

V.25 מלין . . . ימלל: a semitism often taken over as such in texts written in Koine Greek: see LXX and Θ on this text or on Job. 2.9. See Luke 12.10 = Matt. 12.32; Acts 6.13, 11, where the meaning is clearly like Dan. 7.25: to blaspheme (see M. Black, op. cit., p. 195).—לצד: the meaning is clear and the versions have correctly seen that it is adversative, but the use of the preposition is somewhat unexpected. In 11.36, a parallel text, we find על.—בלא: Heb.: בלה; LXX: καταρρίψει; Θ: παλαιώσει: to use, to wear out. M. Noth remarks: 'BL', here in the intensive mode, derives from a root represented in all the Semitic languages. It signifies "to be consumed", "to be used up, exhausted", etc. It is principally used with regard to clothing.' The complement of the personal object causes some difficulty, unless the verb is understood in a figurative sense. M. Noth suggests another Arabic root bala: 'to put to the test, treat harshly, torment, offend against'. It will be seen that this suggestion serves the interpretation of 'the Saints' as designating celestial beings, but the same word is used in 1 Chron. 17.9 in place of the verb 'to subjugate' used in 2 Sam. 7.10.

V.26 דינא יתב: see 7.10, 11, 22. The use of משפט in the same sense of 'tribunal' is found in 1 Qp Hab 10.4.—עד סופא: = 6.27, but the meaning here is 'totally'.

V.27 Θ: 'and his kingdom' (God's); similarly for the service and obedience of the nations which are addressed to God.—תחות כל שמיא: see Deut. 2.25; 4.19; Dan. 9.12.—עם . . .: Hexapl. Θ 62–147: τῷ λαῷ ἁγίοις ὑψίστου (apposition); LXX = Pesh.: 'the holy people of the Most High' (hendiadys).

V.28 רזיוי: (plural); see 5.6, 9, 10.—עד כה: as in Heb., see Exod. 7.16;

Josh. 17.14.—רעיוני: see 4.16; 5.6, 10.—מלתא בלבי נטרת: see LXX 4.25; Gen. 37.11; T. Levi 6.2; 8.19; Luke 2.19 (texts suggested by Charles, ad loc.), Montgomery adds: 4 Esdras 14.40.

Commentary

The second part of this chapter begins with v.15: the explanation of the vision by an angel-interpreter.[126] There is a discussion in our critical notes of the unusual expression 'the spirit in its envelop (sheath)'. There is no place here for a Platonic formulation. The chest is the 'coffer', the case for man's breath (spirit). Think of the expression 'to cut off one's breath'. The verb אתכרית, moreover, signifies 'to be pinched for space' in Syriac.

Daniel has no other resource remaining except to question one of the angels in the divine court (cf. v.13).[127] The angels, says J. A. T. Robinson, 'stand for the belief . . . that there's always an inside to events, a personal as well as an impersonal aspect, a spiritual as well as a material, that the entire universe is shot through with God and his living activity.'[128]

According to the angel's explanation (vv.17ff.), the four animals are four kings. J. de Fraine comments that the Author uses 'king' or 'kingdom' indifferently.[129] They 'will arise out of the earth', says the Masoretic Text. Charles prefers the reading in the LXX ('they will be destroyed', but see our critical notes), but it is evident that the *lectio difficilior* is on the side of the Aramaic version. E. Heaton succinctly, yet rightly, says that there is no contradiction with v.3 for the Hebraic mentality. We should add: on the contrary, the insistence on the terrestrial origin of these four kings opposes them to the heavenly aspect of the 'son of man'. The empires in Dan. 7 are telluric in origin, they have the static character of nature abandoned to itself. In flagrant contrast, the 'Saints' receive a kingdom in which nature has been transfigured (v.18).

We have already discussed what meaning should be given to the word 'Saints' in this chapter,[130] but there is still one oddity in the vocabulary to consider. The Saints are called קדישי עליונין and the plural form of 'Most High' is a problem. From the third century BCE on, Jews have commonly called God 'Most High'. The expression (in the singular)

---

[126] The angel interpreter was introduced, before Daniel, in Ezek. 40—42; Zech. 1—6.
[127] In the later literature this motif came into its own, see 1 Enoch; Test. XII Pat.; Jub.; 2 Baruch; 4 Esdras.
[128] John A. T. Robinson, *But that I can't Believe!* (New York 1967), p. 125.
[129] *Adam et son Lignage* (Tournai 1959), p. 173; cf. v.23: the fourth beast is a 'kingdom'; as for Dan. 8.20–1, it speaks of kings while 8.22 speaks of 'four kingdoms'.
[130] See our introduction to Dan. 7.

occurs again 48 times in Ecclus. (between 135 and 105).[131] The Maccabean High Priests, as we said, adopted it to designate the God of Zion.
The plural עליונין is interpreted by Montgomery (ad loc.) as a plural of
majesty. The same phenomenon may be found in קדושים in Hos. 12.1
(cf. Josh. 24.19: אלהים קדשים; also perhaps Prov. 9.10; 30.3). But E.
Heaton seems to us closer to the truth when he draws from the unusual
form of the expression the conclusion that the Author wanted to
emphasize that 'the Jews symbolized by the figure were no ordinary
members of Israel, but a special group nearer to the ideal of "a kingdom
of priests, a holy nation" (Exod. 19.6), than the rank and file of
Judaism.'[132] Some commentators translate: 'the Saints among the
heavenly beings'. We, too, think that the Author is making an audacious
allusion to the 'divinized' status of the Saints. They are the 'Saints of the
Most High' and *participate* in him, the community exalted as high as
heaven.[133] This is why we translate 'the most Haughty Saints'.

Vv. 19–20 strongly resemble vv.7–8, and if we adopt the position of
H. L. Ginsberg,[134] the resemblance is even closer still since all mention
of an eleventh horn is secondary, so there are just the words 'and about
the ten horns on his head' left in v.20. Thus the addition of the extraordinary growth of the last horn, in relation to the vision in vv.7–8 falls
away of itself. In the same vein, Elias Bickerman sees in vv.20–2 an
addition made in December 167 (following the persecutions of Antiochus) to a text written between Autumn 169 and the end of 167.[135] M.
Noth, too, sees in vv.21–2 an interruption 'taking us back to the style of
the vision'. These verses are responsible for the humanized conception
of the 'Most Haughty Saints' and this is probably the ultimate goal of
their being expressed by a phrase which, as shown by other references
to the Saints in Scripture, was originally referring to angels.[136]
O. Plöger thinks that vv.21–2 can be maintained as such, for they
bring a definite amelioration in relation to vv. 19–20. With him, let
us note the simplified formula, 'the Saints', rather than 'Saints of the
Most High' (or 'Most Haughty Saints') for here, they are defeated. 'The

---

[131] This is all the more remarkable in that it is a Greek expression, at least in appearance
($\theta\epsilon\grave{o}s$ $\H{v}\psi\iota\sigma\tau os$) and Ecclus. is anti-Greek (see E. Bickerman, *From Ezra* . . . (1947),
p. 67).

[132] Op. cit., p. 187.

[133] See our introduction to this chapter; see also Wisd. 3.8; 5.16; Test. of Levi 19.1–3;
Test. of Napht. 8.4–6; Jub. 14.18–20.

[134] Op. cit., p. 17.

[135] *Four Strange Books*, pp. 107–8. This is not a new position, see the general introduction. H. L. Ginsberg, more prudently, places the additions to chapters 7 and 8, as
well as all of chapter 9, between the end of 167 and the winter of 164 (the time of the
royal amnesty).

[136] For M. Noth's discussion of this position (along with L. Dequeker; J. Coppens;
etc.), see our introduction to chapter 7.

same situation seems to also explain v.22a and 22b.' O. Plöger is not far, it seems to us, from sharing our opinion on the worth of the expression 'Most Haughty Saints'.[137]

The text of v.22 is difficult. We may understand that justice is rendered to the Saints or that they are associated with God's judging the nations.[138] Ibn Ezra translates 'they will get their revenge' (= the judgement was made in their favour; see Deut. 10.18; Ps. 140.13).[139]

Regarding vv.23-4, we will refer the reader to our introduction to this chapter. McNamara, we believe, gives a succinct résumé of the most satisfactory solution: 'The three kings whom he laid low were very probably the two sons of Seleucus IV, the legitimate heirs to the throne, and his own son Antiochus who was co-regent with his father from 175 to 170 BC (cf. *Bib.* 36 [1955], 262; J. Starsky, *Les Livres des Maccabées. B.J.*, p. 248, n. *a* to 2 Macc. 4:38). The ten kings of 24a may include the three of 24b; Antiochus IV was the eighth Seleucid king.'[140]

It is certainly Antiochus who is in question. He is the great blasphemer, the enemy of God and his People, the deicide seeking to strike His victim where He is most vulnerable: in his children. According to the biblical image, God's 'Achilles' tendon' is 'the apple of his eye' (Deut. 32.10). He is named anew 'the Most High' in v.25, but this time the term is purely Aramaic עליא (Qr. עלאה), no longer in Hebrew עליון, or in the plural עליונין. This shows once more, we believe, that the קדישי עליונין in the preceding verses and in v.25b has a special meaning (see *supra*).

It is well known how in following his political programme of Hellenization with a fanaticism without parallel, Antiochus IV forbade the Jews to practice their religion, notably with respect to the Sabbath and other festivals. In this calendar context, R. Hammer (op. cit., p. 81) writes that Antiochus IV not only 'combin[ed] the worship of Ba'al Shamem (identified with Zeus Olympios) and Melcarth (identified with Hercules), but he also laid emphasis on the winter solstice in place of the equinoctial days, introducing a feast which coincided with the Roman Saturnalia'. This first religious persecution in the history of Israel lasted for just over three years between 168 and 165. The expression 'one period,

---

[137] Dan. 8.24 could also be included in this judgement.
[138] See in particular Θ (see our critical notes).
[139] In the Rabbinic literature we find the idea that the Messiah will come when the distress is at its culmination; see *Sanh.* 98a; *j. Taan.* 64a with reference to Exod. 16.25 combined with Isa. 30.15. S. Mowinckel thinks that this concept has its origin in the liturgy for the royal enthronement of God. God's new victorious creation, he thinks, was celebrated at the moment when the distress was at its highest point, see Ps. 46 and 48 (*He that Cometh*, p. 297).
[140] Op. cit., par. 533 K (p. 664).

two periods, and a half period' should be understood from this perspective as 'one year, two years,[141] and a half year'. We find confirmation of this reading in 'the half week of years' in Dan. 9.27, as well as in the successive attempts at a more precise approximation of time in 8.14[142] and 12.11.[143] We have understood the word 'periods' in 4.13 in the same manner and this interpretation also holds for 12.7. In the Book of Revelation (11.2, 3; 12.6, 14; 13.5) the same lapse of time is expressed in months (42 months) or in days (1,260 days), or with the help of the apocalyptic expression 'one time, two times, and a half time', with the same fundamental sense of a period of calamities allowed to happen by God, but whose term is fixed to comfort the afflicted. In Rabbinic literature, 'three and a half years' came to mean 'a long time'. In Luke 4.25 and James 5.17, it has become stereotyped.

The calamity of three and a half years, for our Author, is specifically expressed in the debasement of the Law[144] and the liturgical periods of the festivals. The Temple calendar was rejected and all correspondence between heavenly and earthly time broke down. This question continued to preoccupy orthodox Jews for long.[145] 'To change the times' is God's exclusive privilege (see Dan. 2.21; cf. *Siddur: tephilat' aravit le ḥol*, the first response of the congregation is 'God is the one who in his understanding changes the periods, he transforms the times'). Symmachus (in Jerome) has for this v.25: *sermones quasi deus loquitur* (cf. 2 Thess. 2.4).

Vv.26–7 describe the judging of the beast in terms similar to those in vv.11–14, 18. The passage from the 'son of man' to his collective dimension, that is, to those who, like him, receive 'the kingship, dominion, and grandeur of all the kingdoms under heaven' is the dominant theme in this chapter in its present form. The assimilation of this people of Israelite Saints to divine stature is clearly expressed in the eternity of their reign, and in the cultic reverence and obedience of a religious order

---

[141] To our understanding, this is one of the earliest origins of the Rabbinic principle that an indefinite plural in Scripture is to be understood as a dual (*contra* Gunkel, *Schöpfung* . . ., p. 201). In Ezek. 47.13, however, the plural of the last word ('portions') is understood by Targ., Vul., the Rabbis, and modern translators as coming in place of a dual.

[142] '2300 evenings and mornings' = 1,150 days.

[143] '1290 days.' See our commentary on 12.11 for a discussion of these computations.

[144] For the general meaning of the word *dath* in this period, see 2 Macc. 2.20–1, 27. . . .

[145] See 1 Macc. 1.41ff.; 1 Enoch 72–82; Jub. 6; 15.1; 16.2–31, 50; 1 QS. . . . The Book of Jubilees is a treatise on the immutability of the festival calendar. At the basis of this concern is the concept of an authentically human (and divine) rhythm which the persecuting king was trying to upset. For this whole question, see A. Jaubert, *La Date de la Cène. Calendrier biblique et Liturgie chrétienne* (Paris 1957).

which is rendered to them by the nations (see Deut. 2.25; Job 28.24).[146] Among these nations, however, the 'fourth kingdom' does not play a part because it will be totally destroyed (not just its representative *par excellence*, the 'little horn').

According to E. Heaton, v.28 concluded not only the chapter 7 but the whole book (see Eccles. 12.13; Jer. 51.64). Jeffery is on the contrary of the opinion that v.28 introduces the following chapters.[147]

---

[146] See 1 Qp Hab 10.13; 5.4; 1 QH 4.26; cf. Rev. 7.15–16 and the commentary by Dom Thierry Maertens: 'The sumptuous tent reserved for the messiah will shelter all the just who will eternally share with him his messianic gifts: "He who sits upon the throne will dwell with them" [Rev. 7.15]'. (*A Feast in Honor of Yahweh* (Notre Dame, Ind., 1965), p. 93.)

[147] Op. cit., p. 468; Porteous, op. cit., p. 117, agrees.

8 The Vision of the Ram and the He-Goat

Our study of chapter 7 allows us to discern in chapter 8 the same secondary hand responsible for the touching up of the presentation of the four animals and the 'son of man'. In fact, chapter 8, too, speaks of a little horn arising out of another one and growing in an extraordinary manner. The glossist's intervention dates from 166–164 (after the profanation of the Temple, but before the general amnesty). This second hand is especially recognizable in vv.9–14 and 23–5. Maybe, with H. L. Ginsberg, it is also permissible to see an even later addition in v.16 to prepare for chapter 9 (see 9.21).

Everyone agrees that there are numerous specific parallels with chapter 7 in chapter 8. It is once again partly a question of the same empires, here too represented by horned animals. They make war on the 'Saints', but the time of their hegemony is measured. The last enemy will soon be vanquished—Antiochus IV 'will be broken without the intervention of any human hand' (v.25).[1]

Yet there are substantial differences to be noted. The tone has become more sombre, the attacks against the integrity of the People and against God's honour are graver, and, above all, one after another they are crowned with success. The evil one uses clever delusions and many are taken in by them.

Chapter 8 is also distinguished from the preceding chapter by its language: we have returned to Hebrew from Aramaic and the style has suffered. The diagnosis given by criticism oscillates between attributing this text to a different author and the impression of being in the presence of a very spoiled Hebrew text. In fact, however, the similar para-historical information in the two parts of this book (Daniel A and Daniel B) concerning Belshazzar and Darius the Mede militate in favour of a single Author or Redactor.

In this second vision, Daniel the seer—this time in a state of wakefulness—is transported to a specific location: the bank of the artificial river Ulai at Susa.[2] We may see in this detail a reminiscence of the days of the Exile when the Jewish diaspora often found itself at the banks of flowing rivers.[3] Ezekiel, whom the Author is imitating, had himself also been transported to the bank of a river. We can, moreover, ask whether

---

[1] A. Bentzen, op. cit., p. 58, writes, 'For me, it is probable that ch. 8 is an actualizing explanation of pre-Maccabean material from ch. 7.'

[2] For this genre of ubiquity, see 2 Kings 2.16 (Elijah); Ezek. 8.3.

[3] This is the opinion of A. Bentzen, op. cit., ad loc. Cf. Ps. 137.

there is not a cryptic indication in the name of the river chosen as the site of the 'Vision for the end time' (v.17)? In Hebrew, אוּלַי[4] signifies 'perhaps', an 'expression of hope, prayer, and dread', according to the dictionary by Köhler-Baumgartner (sub voc.). In this way, the vision, which has so many other symbolic elements, expresses the possibility of a miraculous reversal of the situation.

In parallel with chapter 7, the empires are represented as animals, in this case, a ram and a he-goat. In astrological geography,[5] the ram represents Persia (κριός) and Syria is represented by a he-goat (αἰγόκερως).[6] By transposition, the goat here signifies Greece, the adopted homeland, at least on a spiritual plane, of the philhellene Syrian king, Antiochus IV.

Text 8. 1–14

(1) In the third year of the reign of King Belshazzar, a vision appeared to me, Daniel, after the one which had appeared to me previously. (2) I watched in the course of this vision and behold that in what I was watching, I was at Susa, the capital, in the province of Elam. I was watching in the course of this vision and I myself was near the river Ulai. (3) I lifted up my eyes and saw a ram standing before the river. He had two horns and his two horns were high, but one was higher than the other. The higher one grew up last. (4) I watched the ram strike out toward the West, the North, and the South, and no animal could stand before him nor could anyone deliver from his power. He acted as he pleased and grew larger. (5) Behold what I discerned: a he-goat came from the West, through the whole earth without touching the earth, and this goat had a remarkable horn between his eyes. (6) He came up to the ram with two horns whom I had seen standing before the river and he charged him with his furious power. (7) I watched him come upon the ram and he became enraged against him. He struck the ram and broke his two horns, and the ram did not have the strength to stand before him. He threw him down and trampled him and there was no one to deliver the ram from his power. (8) The goat grew enormously and while he was full of might, the great horn was broken and in its place arose four remarkable (horns) toward the four winds of heaven. (9) From one of them, another horn, a little one, came out which grew exceedingly toward the South, toward the East, and toward the magnificent (land). (10) It grew up to the army of heaven and cast down to earth a

---

[4] With *patach* and not *qametz* as here; but in vv.2 and 16 where the word appears we have either *Sof passuq* or *atnach*!

[5] It dates from Babylonian times.

[6] According to E. Dhorme, the he-goat is the symbolic animal of the god Amurru, known from the texts from Ras-Shamra as being *Qdsh-w-'mrr* (Qadesh-and-Amurru). See *L'Evolution Religieuse d'Israël* (Brussels 1937), p. 106; quoted by A. Bentzen, op. cit., p. 69.

part of that army and some of the stars which it trampled. (11) It grew up to the Prince of this army, taking away from him the regular offering and over-throwing the foundations of his sanctuary. (12) Beyond the regular offering, this army was given over because of its transgression. (The horn) cast the Truth down to earth and whatever it undertook, it succeeded. (13) I heard a particular Saint speaking. This particular Saint said to the individual who had asked: 'How long is this vision of the regular offering, of devastating transgression, of the sanctuary and the army given over to being trampled?' (14) He told me: 'For two thousand three hundred evenings and mornings; then the sanctuary will be re-established within its rights.'

Critical Notes 8. 1–14

V.1 חזון נראה: H. L. Ginsberg notes that the first word signifies 'vision', but also 'oracle', and the second, in the nominal form מראה, 'appearance, aspect' (e.g., in 10.6), but above all 'hearing, audition' (see 8.16, 26a, 27b; 9.23; 10.1). He attributes this situation, which is peculiar to Daniel in Hebrew, to the influence of Aramaic.

V.2 ויהי בראתי: *del.* in LXX; Θ; Pesh; Vul.—אובל אולי: LXX, Pesh., Vul.: אבול = door.—אולי: *del.* in Θ who just reads Οὐβὰλ in this chapter. אובל = יובל (Jer. 17.8).—LXX: ἐν τῷ ὁράματι τοῦ ἐνυπνίου μου.

V.3 קרנין: (see v.7) the vocalization here follows the analogy of the plural although the form is in the dual.

V.4 מנגח: cf. the literal meaning: Exod. 21.28, and the figurative meaning: Dan. 11.40.—יעמדו לפני: see Judg. 2.14; 2 Kings 10.4; Dan. 8.7; 11.16.—ואין מציל: LXX and Θ assume המציל. The same situation occurs in v.7.—ועשה כרצנו: see 11.3, 16, 36; Esth. 9.5.—והגדיל: see vv.8, 11, 25. Arrogance as in Ps. 55.12; Lam. 1.9.— LXX adds to the three cardinal points enumerated by the MT: πρὸς ἀνατολάς.

V.5 הייתי מבין והנה: too literal a translation in Heb. of the Aramaic משתכל הוית ואלו in 7.8.—צפיר־העזים: late Heb. (see Ezra 8.35; 2 Chron. 29.21; in Aramaic Ezra 6.17).—ואין נוגע: see Isa. 41.3 for Cyrus. We should not correct to ואיננו נוגע for the same formula is in v.27: אין מבין instead of ואיננו מבין of v.26b. H. L. Ginsberg (pp. 55–8) comments that Aramaic influence is manifest here. Regarding the idea involved here, Jeffery, op. cit. ad. loc., refers to Homer, *Iliad* XX, 226–9.—חזות: *del.*, in Θ; LXX has read אחת = ἕν. But Vul. = MT. Re this idea, see 2 Sam. 23.21; 1 Chron. 11.23: איש מראה. Ibn Ezra understands the word as coming from the root חז״ז: to complicate, ramify.

V.7 Here we find expressions similar to those in v.4. On ואין מציל,
see Isa. 5.29; Hos. 5.14.—ויתמרמר: see 11.11.—וירמסהו: see 2 Kings
14.9; the Hebrew corresponding to the Aramaic verb used in
7.7, 19.

V.8 חזות: see v.5. Here the LXX read 'other' (אחרת), a reading accepted
by many critics. לארבע רוחות השמים: see 7.2; 11.4.

V.9 מצעירה: difficult. It is better to ignore the preposition (also in the
Greek). Cf. 7.8: ואל הצבי—קרן אחרי זעירה. the LXX read הצפון,
which is an indirect confirmation of the MT.—תגדל יתר: see Isa.
56.12. Cf. the Aramaic יתירה in Dan. 3.22; 7.7, 19.

V.11 LXX: 'confused text' (Charles, p. 205). Θ is completely different
from the MT.—הגדיל: instead of the expected feminine; we have
passed from metaphor to the symbolized reality.—הרים: Qr:
הורם.—התמיד: for עולת התמיד, see Exod. 29.42; Ezek. 46.15; etc. Cf.
Dan. 11.31; 12.11.—מכון: see Ezra 3.3; Ps. 89.15. H. L. Ginsberg
suggests reading the first word of v.12 with v.11 and seeing in the
final *waw* of מקדשו a dittography of the *waw* of וצבא. It is also
necessary to suppress the word מכון where it occurs (v.11bβ) and
to transpose it to v.11bα. Read וממכונו instead of וממנו. Also מכון
must be introduced in 12aα between על and התמיד ('and it set up
upon [the stand of] the daily sacrifice an offence'; see 1 Macc.
1.54: 'they erected a desolating sacrilege upon the altar of burnt
offering').

V.12 תנתן: צבא is sometimes feminine, see Isa. 40.2.—והצליחה: see 2
Chron. 31.21: עשה והצליח.

V.13 פלמוני: hapax; contraction of פלני and אלמני.—שמם: abbreviated
po'el participle, for משמם; see Ges.-Kau. par. 52s; 55c; the reason
for the contraction is undoubtedly the assonance with (Baal)
Shamem. (See our commentary.)

V.14 אלי: LXX, Θ: 'to it'.—נצדק: LXX, Θ, Pesh., Vul.: 'will be purified'.
For the root צדק in Daniel, see 9.7, 14, 16, 18, 24; 12.3. See our
commentary on 7.22. For H. L. Ginsberg, *Studies*, p. 42, the text
of the versions is correct, the original Aramaic having been
ידקי (on the basis of the study by F. Zimmermann, 'The Aramaic
Origin of Dan. 8.12', *JBL*, 57 (1938), pp. 258–72).

Commentary

Like the vision in chapter 7, the one in chapter 8 is dated: 'in the third
year of King Belshazzar' (v.1). Here as was previously the case, this
date is arbitrary. At most it indicates that a lapse of time (two years?) has
occurred between the redaction of these two chapters and, by implica-

tion, that the announced miraculous event has not yet taken place. Something must therefore be added to the first vision (chapter 7) which will allow the reader to explain to himself the delay before the time of its accomplishment.

The seer is transported to Susa in Elam[7] (v.2), to the bank of the Ulai canal (יובל = אובל) whose classical name was Eulaeus.[8] Susa is here called a בירה, a fortified city, which corresponds to the historical situation after 521 when Darius I reconstructed the city which had been destroyed in 645. Elam was a Median, not a Babylonian province (see Esth. 1.2; 9.12; Neh. 1.1). It remained a key position in the ancient Orient for 200 years.

The telling of the vision begins in v.3. Daniel sees a ram whose two unequal horns represent Persia and Media, the first prevailing over the second, even though it came after it historically speaking (see v.20). Ezekiel (see 39.18) and Zechariah (see 10.3) had already employed the symbolism of rams and he-goats to designate princes (see also 1 Enoch 90.13ff.). M. Delcor[9] quotes the testimony of Ammianus Marcellinus (10.1) who says that the Persian king marched at the head of his troops with a gold head of a ram as a diadem.[10]

According to v.4, the Persian conquests extended in all directions, but the east is not mentioned (except in the LXX). We can see in this the particular point of view of a Palestinian for whom Persia lay to the east. Its oriental conquests would not interest such a person (see Isa. 41.2).[11] It is historically correct that Persia enlarged its frontiers at the expense of its neighbours: Cambyses (529–522) pushed toward the south as far as Egypt; Darius (522–486) went toward the north into Scythia and toward the west as far as Greece in 492–490. In 480, Xerxes sacked Athens (see Dan. 11.2).

But Persian strength ran into an insurmountable obstacle along the way, a one horned 'he-goat' coming from the west (v.5). We will quote J. Steinmann[12]: 'This he-goat, bearing one horn between its eyes—and probably wings since it flies over the whole earth—is a sort of unicorn, the symbol for Alexander the Great. The fight between the ram and the

---

[7] For Josephus, *Ant.* X, XI, 7, Daniel was physically in Elam where he had built himself an 'elegant tower' at Ecbatane. Elam is the modern Khuzistan.

[8] See Pliny, *Natural History*, 6, 27.

[9] Op. cit., p. 170.

[10] Archaeology has recovered such heads. See M. Avi-Yonah and E. G. Kraeling, *Our Living Bible* (Jerusalem 1962), pp. 224–5. From a psychological point of view, the ram is the 'symbol of the ferocious and creative forces of nature, but which also . . . touches the problems of the spirit . . . (it) seems to be related to the principle of order' (E. Aeppli, *Les Rêves*, p. 269).

[11] They are not ignored by Esth. 1.1.

[12] Op. cit., p. 97.

he-goat is an allegory for the struggle between the Macedonian and Darius III Codomannus.'[13] The total defeat which he inflicts on the ram (v.7) refers to the decisive battle at Issus in 333 following his victory at Granicus in 334. The fatal blow was struck in 331 at Gaugamela near the city of Arbela, to the east of Nineveh. Dan. 11.3–4 alludes to these events.

Just as suddenly as he appeared on the historical scene, Alexander disappeared, dying suddenly at Babylon in 323. His empire broke up into four 'Diadochies' with one of Alexander's generals at each of their heads. We may therefore follow Jerome[14] when he recognizes in the four 'horns': Ptolemy (Egypt): Philip (Macedonia); Seleucus (Syria and Babylon); and Antigonus (Asia Minor).[15] The rivalry between them and their successors lasted for more than twenty years until the Battle of Ipsus in 301 confirmed the distribution of territory among Ptolemy (Egypt); Seleuchus (Syria-Babylonia); Lysimachus (Asia Minor); and Cassander (Macedonia–Greece). The Author concentrates his attention on the Seleucid Kingdom and more particularly its last representative, the perverse Antiochus IV (v.9). The information in this verse is correct: Antiochus effectively made war in the south against Egypt,[16] in the east against the Persians and the Parthians,[17] and against Palestine, here called 'the magnificent (land)'. We know too what measures of religious persecution against Judaism were inaugurated by the campaign against Jerusalem (see Dan. 11.16, 41, 45), the centre of space and time for the Author. 'The magnificent land', he calls it, paraphrasing his predecessors (see Jer. 3.19; Ezek. 20.6, 15; 27.3; Isa. 4.2; 13.19; Zech. 7.14; Mal. 3.12; Ps. 50.2; 85.10; 106.24; 122. 2–9; 1 Enoch 89.40; 90.20; etc.).[18]

In the movement of his lyrical flight, and in conformity with the ideology from chapter 7, the Author passes from 'the magnificent (land)' to its transcendent and ultimate dimension: 'the army of heaven' (v.10). Here, as in the preceding chapter, it would be an error to fall into mythology. The heavenly army does not represent purely spiritual beings in opposition to men. They are heavenly beings to whom are joined the Saints of Israel, who have become angelic because this was

---

[13] See the statues of Alexander wearing the horns of his mythical father, Zeus Ammon.
[14] Migne, *P. L.* xxv, cols. 536, 539.
[15] Others think of a later date, following the elimination of Philip (317); they substitute Cassander (Macedonia and Greece) for him.
[16] See Dan. 11.25–30; 1 Macc. 1.16–20; 2 Macc. 5.1–14.
[17] See 1 Macc. 3.27–37; 6.1–17; 2 Macc. 9.1–4; Dan. 11.44.
[18] There is no place, therefore, with O. Plöger, op. cit., *ad* v.7, for drawing conclusions insufficiently founded on the absence of any commitment of the Author to one or the other parties involved. For Plöger, this is a sign of dualism and of flexible politics in Palestine during this period!

always their true identity. Similarly as regards the stars which in Mesopotamia were identified with the gods,[19] but which here designate the Saints (see 12.3; Matt. 13.43; 1 Enoch 46.7; 43.1–4).[20] Hence, in this verse 10 as in chapter 7, it is a question of the profanation of the Temple by Antiochus IV and, as well, of the correspondence between heaven and earth. Because such an intimate relation exists with the heavens, Antiochus' action is an attack on the divine majesty (see 11.36).

The Author's process of demythologization is to be noted (cf. p. 122, n. 1 above). The heavens are not peopled with divinities; those who surround the divine throne are the Saints of Israel.[21] But, as a corollary, God is truly struck in the person of his Elect; antisemitism is deicide.

This reading allows us to understand the ambivalence in v.11—the 'prince of this army' no doubt makes one think of God himself (see *Adonai Ṣebaoth*). However, Charles (p. 204, but cf. p. 207!), Montgomery (ad loc.), and above all M. A. Beek[22] have suggested seeing in the prince the High Priest Onias III assassinated in 171 by order of Antiochus (see 2 Macc. 4.33–5; 1 Enoch 90.8); Ephrem and H. Grotius[23] had already put forth the same suggestion and it is correct that some biblical texts clearly allow us to understand שר in the sense of '(High) Priest'. For example, 1 Chron. 24.5 cites among the servants in the Temple: שרי קודש ושרי הארהים; and Ezra 8.24: שרי הכהנים. Note also 1 Chron. 16.15: שרי הלויים. If, on the other hand, we take into account the fact that in the Book of Daniel the word שר always designates an angel,[24] it is clear that we must think not only of the High Priest, but also of the archangel Michael, the prince of Israel (see 10.21).[25] In short, we rediscover exactly the same situation as encountered in chapter 7 as regards the 'son of man', *and indeed, we believe it is a question of the same personage*. That the People should here be called 'his sanctuary' ought not to surprise us. The Temple profaned is not just an edifice in Jerusalem for the Author, it is also the people of the Saints, just as we saw in chapter 7.[26]

[19] The biblical texts warn us against any divinization of 'the army of the heavens', see Deut. 4.19; 2 Kings 17.16; Jer. 8.2; Zeph. 1.5.
[20] Vv.2 and 4: '. . . and (I saw) their revolutions *according to the number of the angels* . . . such were the names of the Saints *who dwell on earth* and believe in the name of the Lord of Spirits for ever.'
[21] There is probably also an allusion to the self-deification of Antiochus. Towards the end of his reign, he had coins struck bearing his head capped by a star; see 2 Macc. 9.10.
[22] M. A. Beek, *Das Danielbuch* (Leyden 1935), p. 80.
[23] *Annotationes in Vetus et Novum Testamentum* (London 1727).
[24] See Dan. 10.13, 20, 21; 12.1. Dan. 8.25 is problematic, see our commentary. See also the parallel text in Josh. 5.14.
[25] Targ. Ps. 137.7: Michael is the prince of Jerusalem. Ibn Ezra sees Michael also in Dan. 8.11.
[26] Note that the general theme of this verse is taken up again in 11.31.

E. Heaton says concerning the following verse that 'the meaning of the first half of v.12 is lost beyond recall' (p. 195). Other authors, as well, consider vv.11–13 as among the most difficult in Daniel.[27] We must proceed systematically. The term צבא was just used in the sense of people (the Saints) in v.11. It is repeated in v.13 in a commentary which leaves no doubt as to this meaning. In v.24 what it represents is explicitly stated: 'the people of the Saints'. There is no place here, therefore, for seeing an army of occupation in the pay of Antiochus. On the other hand, תנתן is difficult but not impossible to understand. Its meaning depends on its governing subject. Here it signifies 'to be given over' (and not 'to be posted', etc. as, for example, M. Delcor believes).

Von Lengerke[28] understands the following words as signifying: '. . . with the perpetual sacrifice because of iniquity'. B. N. Wambacq paraphrases them as 'an army (that is, the stars representing the pious Jews, see 10.3) was given over (to the enemy's power) with the daily sacrifice, through violence or to be treated with violence . . .'.[29] For the most part we follow this reading: 'Beyond the perpetual sacrifice, this army was given over because of its transgression.'

The remainder of the verse, in direct style, returns to the description of the profanation by the 'horn': 'it cast "The Truth" down to earth, and in whatever it undertook, it succeeded.' 'The Truth' is in quotation marks here because it is not a question of a concept, but rather as Malachi 2.6 indicates, the Torah[30] itself. In fact, Antiochus had all the sacred book which could be found burned (see 1 Macc. 1.54ff.).

With v.13 we face a new problem. Daniel speaks in the first person: 'I heard a particular Saint speaking.' It is clear that Daniel is singling out one of the 'Saints' from 'the army' which had been spoken of in the preceding verses.[31] It is not self-evidently true that it is a question of an angel as most commentators have believed, but rather a question of an 'angelized' Saint, if we may use such a phrase. The remainder of the verse is even more difficult. We believe the second אחד קדוש should be understood as designating the same individual as before:[32] 'and this

[27] See Charles, op. cit., p. 204.
[28] Quoted by Charles, p. 207. Charles rejects this reading on the basis of a specious argument that a 'natural community' between the terms assembled by the preposition would be required. This is to fail to understand apocalyptic licence.
[29] B. N. Wambacq, *Jahve Seba'ot* (1947), pp. 126–7. For McNamara, op. cit., p. 666, par. 535s, 'this appears to be the best understanding of the text; cf. 24'. We will also quote the reading by Rashi (followed by several critics): צבא as in Job 7.1; 14.4 (also Isa. 40.2) signifies a 'fixed time'; 'and a precise time was given for rejecting the daily sacrifice due to their transgression'.
[30] See Rom. 2.20. See also Rashi, Ibn Ezra, etc. on this verse.
[31] In this way the unorthodox construction אחד קדוש is justified. It may be translated 'one of the Saints'.
[32] *Sic* in *Mekor Hayim* (Mistranslations and Difficult Passages of the O.T.) by Benjamin Marcus (Dublin 1851).

particular Saint spoke to the individual (namely Daniel) who had asked . . .[33] he told *me*: for 2,300 evenings and mornings, etc.' (v.14).[34]

The terms of the question posed by the seer are not put together in terms of orthodox grammar. There are definite articles where there should not be, and they are absent where they should be. Yet the meaning is clear. Daniel refers to those elements of his vision which are a problem. Note the introduction of a new term שמם devastator, which prepares a subsequent development. Rashi had already understood that an allusion is being made here to the idol installed on the altar of the Temple at Jerusalem in December 167 by Antiochus, which other texts call שקוצים משמם (Dan. 9.27) or שקוץ שומם (11.31; 12.11; 1 Macc. 1.54) in assonance with the Baal Shamin of the Syrians who had become Zeus Olympios. We may also think with H. H. Rowley[35] that שמם 'has associations . . . with the idea of madness, and it may be that there is a further punning reference to Antiochus in the thought of the "abomination of the Madman"'.[36]

We indicated with regard to v.12 the explanatory association of 'the army' with 'the sanctuary' and, in v.24, with 'the people of the Saints'. For the Author, these are three aspects of one and the same reality.[37]

The point of the question is found in its first words: 'How long?' This is the question *par excellence* of the apocalypse, the reason the Author wrote chapter 8; and yet this painful question is not a new one for Israel (see Isa. 6.11; Jer. 12.4; Zech. 1.12; Ps. 6.3; 80.4; 90.13).

The answer in v.14 is 2,300 evenings and mornings by which we should understand 2,300 twice daily perpetual sacrifices or 1,150 days. In relation to 7.25, this computation is four months shorter, further proof that chapter 8 was written after chapter 7. We do not believe that much, if anything, is to be gained by ingenious calculations designed to defend the exactness of the number 1,150, as we are offered, for example,

[33] See v.16 where Daniel is designated with an equal impreciseness הלז equivalent to פלוני here. Re these expressions, see, on the one hand, 1 Sam. 21.3; 1 Kings 6.8; Ruth 4.1; on the other hand, Judg. 6.20; 1 Sam. 17.26; 2 Kings 4.25; etc. See also C. Colpe (*TWNT* VIII, p. 403) on the parallel expression: ההוא גברא, 'that man' = 'I'.

[34] Aquilas, followed by *Gen. R.* 21.1, sees in 'the individual' (lit.: 'someone') the name of an angel identified with 'the one who is in the interior' (*penimi*), that is, Adam. The versions for v.14 have read 'to him' instead of 'to me', evidently on the basis of their error in reading v.13. They have been followed by a surprising number of modern commentators.

[35] H. H. Rowley, *The Relevance of Apocalyptic* (London 1963)[3], p. 52.

[36] It will be recalled that the surname 'Epimanes', madman, was given to Antiochus in some settings contemporary with the king (see our Introduction).

[37] We do not follow Geo Widengren, 'Early Hebrew Myths and Their Interpretation', in *Myth, Ritual and Kingship* (Oxford 1958), pp. 149ff., who places Dan. 8.13 on the same plane as diverse other texts where the expression בני אלהים appears, interpreted after the literature from Ugarit, as designating gods.

by C. Schedl[38] or A. Lods.[39] Regarding this whole question, see our commentary on vv.12.7, 11, and 12 below. The central message, whatever the numbers proposed to establish it, is that there is a limit to the revolt against God, an end to the suffering of the Saints.[40]

From this analysis of vv.13–14, we will maintain their authenticity against the opinion of H. L. Ginsberg. They are the heart of chapter 8.

Text 8. 15–27

(15) Now, when I, Daniel, had watched this vision and was seeking to understand it, behold an appearance like someone fully man stood before me. (16) And I heard a man's voice in the middle of the Ulai which called and said: 'Gabriel, make this one understand the vision!' (17) He came close to the place where I stood and as he came, I was terrified and fell upon my face. He said to me: 'Understand, son of man, for the vision is for the end time.' (18) While he was speaking to me, I fell into lethargy, my face against the ground. He touched me and set me upright in the place where I stood. (19) Then he said: 'I am going to make you know what will happen at the end of the wrath, for the end is for a determined period. (20) The ram with two horns which you saw—they are the kings of Media and Persia. (21) The shaggy he-goat is the king of Greece. The great horn which he had between his eyes is the first king. (22) Once broken, the four which arose in its place are the four kingdoms which will arise from that nation, but without its strength. (23) At the end of their reign, when the transgressors will have completed (their sinning)

an impudent king, expert in cunning, will arise.

(24) His power will increase, but not by his own strength, he will cause stupendous destructions and succeed at what he undertakes; he will destroy the powerful, the people of the Saints.

(25) He will have superior skills at his disposal, he will succeed in his deceptions,

he will grow in his heart and in a time of peace destroy many,

he will rise up against the Prince of princes. He will be broken without the intervention of any hand.

(26) And the vision of evenings and mornings as it has been told is the truth.

As for you, keep this vision secret, for it concerns distant days.'

[38] *B.Z.*, n.s. 8 (1964), pp. 102–3.
[39] A. Lods, op. cit., p. 845. (Lods quotes Cornell who suggests to begin counting from the suspension of the cultus at Jerusalem at the order of Antiochus.) Rashi gives himself over to more knowledgeable calculations (see ad loc.).
[40] O. Plöger, op. cit., ad loc., is probably correct in thinking that the Temple had not yet been purified at the moment when ch. 8 was written, but 'the Maccabean victories at Beth-Horon-Higher conveyed the certitude that the final victory was not far off'.

(27) Then I, Daniel, fainted and was ill for days. When I arose, I occupied myself with the king's affairs. I was appalled at the vision, not having understood it.

Critical Notes 8. 15–27

V.15 ואבקשה בינה: has its Aramaic correspondence in 7.19. See our commentary.—כמראה גבר: LXX: ὡς ὅρασις ἀνθρώπου (Θ: ἀνδρός).

V.17 נבעת: the niphal is only found in late texts: 1 Chron. 21.30; Esth. 7.6—עת קץ: see 11.35, 40; 12.4, 9; resembles Ezekiel: עון קץ (21, 30, 34; 35.5). See Hab. 2.3 and Amos 8.2; cf. 2 Baruch 29.8; 59.4.

V.18 נרדמתי: see Gen. 2.21; 15.12 (where the term תרדמה is translated as ἔκστασις by the LXX and by Philo: *Quis rerum divinarum heres* 258).—ויעמידני: LXX: ἤγειρε, which would be a hapax in translating עמ"ד. It is therefore probable, following Charles, that the LXX read יעירני: 'he awakened me'. Θ has simply ἔστησε = MT.

V.19 מועד קץ: see 1 Qp Hab XI.6: ובקץ מועד.

V.21 וצפיר השעיר: LXX, Θ, Pesh., Vul., Hippolytus: צפיר העזים, as in v.8. See Charles, p. 216: 'Since צפיר is a loan-word from the Aramaic (see Ezra 6.17 . . .) some scribe added the Hebrew synonym: השעיר. . . .'

V.22 מגוי: every version except Pesh. has 'of his nation'. H. L. Ginsberg, מקרבו = מן גוה.—יעמדנה: 'androgynous' form say the ancient Jewish grammarians; E. König, *Hist.-Krit. Lehrg. der heb. Sprache*, 2 vols. (1881, 1885), thinks the hybrid form is explicable by the duality of intention: kingdoms (fem.) and kings (masc.). H. L. Ginsberg, op. cit., pp. 56–7, sees in יעמדנה a poor Hebrew translation of the Aramaic יְקוּמָן or some similar form of the root קום. There is a clear proof of the matter, he says, in 11.17b (with עמד), citing Isa. 7.7 (with קום). But the argument is incomplete for עמד is used in late Hebrew with the sense of קום: see Neh. 7.65 = Ezra 2.63; Ecclus. 47.1, 12; 1 Chron. 20.4 (cf. Ps. 27.3); cf. Dan. 12.13.

V.23 עז פנים: see Deut. 28.50; in Prov. 7.17, the expression applies to the impudent boldness of prostitutes.—מבין חידות: Bevan, op. cit., ad loc., gives the interesting translation: 'skilled in double dealing' see v.25; 11.21 (for the word חידות, see Judg. 14.12; 1 Kings 10.1; etc.).—כהתם הפשעים: every version understands 'sins', not 'sinners' (see 9.24), in conformity with Gen. 15.16 (see 2 Macc. 6.14; 1 Thess. 2.16), says Montgomery.—כהתם is understood by LXX, Θ, כָּתֹם: πληρουμένων τῶν ἁμαρτιῶν αὐτῶν (cf. Pesh. and Vul., but without the suffix). Charles is of the opinion that כהתם may be retained, but we should read 'sins' in any case.

V.24 Eliminated by M. Noth (see *Ges. Stud.*, p. 275, n. 7) in his discussion of the meaning to be given to the term 'Saints' in Daniel: '. . . *die textlich unsichere Stelle Dan.* 8.24.'—ולא בכחו: *del.* in Θ and LXX.—ונפלאות ישחית: lit.: 'he shall destroy wonderfully': Bevan, op. cit., p. 139, proposes to emend ישחית to ישיח: 'he shall utter monstrous things' (see 11.36).—LXX v.24d–25b: 'he will destroy the powerful; he will work his ruses against the saints, his treacherous conduct will succeed'.

V.25 See LXX v.24.

V.26 אתה סתם החזון: LXX: νῦν πεφραγμένον = סתם החזון; עתה סתם החזון; however, cf. 12.4.—לימים רבים: the same expression occurs in Ezek. 12.27. See Dan. 8.17, 19; 10.14.—The whole verse is built on the model of Hab. 2.2–3.

V.27 נהייתי: see 2.1 = to faint, pass out. Here, as there, the form is defective for H. L. Ginsberg, op. cit., pp. 58–9, who thinks it is a poor Heb. translation of the Aramaic אֶתְוַהֵת, the ethpaal of תוה (3.24): 'I was bewildered' (see 7.28b).—Note that the niphal of היה appears in Dan. 12.1; Judg. 19.30; Mic. 2.4.—Rashi and Redaq here see the root היה = destruction, as in Job 6.2; 30.13.— ואין מבין: LXX, Θ, Pesh., Rashi, older Protestant commentators, and many moderns: 'no one understood'; but the sense of the expression is not the same for all the interpreters. Rashi: no one perceived the state of Daniel's spirit, because he controlled himself before the eunuch. Vul.: 'There was no one to interpret' (= Ibn Ezra; Saadia). Montgomery, referring to 12.5, prefers: 'I heard and could not understand' (p. 355).

Commentary

A new development begins in v.15: the explanation of the vision. It is in parallel with the explanation in chapter 7 and takes up again elements (such as 'appearance like that of a man') which, consequently, are not so mysterious as they might appear to be at first glance. Here we have כמראה־גבר and not כמראה אדם as in Dan. 10.18,[41] due to the name of this personage given in v.16: *Gabriel*. One cannot fail to think of Dan. 7.13: 'like a son of man'. What is more, the ambiguity introduced by what seems to be the identification of the 'son of man' from chapter 7 with an angelic personage here is carefully cultivated in the following verses. Another divine being addresses himself to Gabriel in v.16 with a קול אדם: an Adamic (human) voice. An order—or permission—is given to Gabriel[42] to explain the vision to 'this particular man' who is Daniel

[41] Ezek. 1.26 served as a model here as in so many other places in chs. 7—8 of Daniel. We note with Charles, p. 213, that in the Ethiopian version of Enoch the 'son of man' is *filius viri* in 6.25; 69.29; and 71.14; and *filius hominis* in 46.2, 3, 4; and 48.2.
[42] Called 'the man Gabriel' in 9.21 (which is certainly from the same hand).

(v.16). Now, in v.17, he is called בֶּן־אָדָם (son of man). The three personages here, therefore, are bound together by an 'Adamic' tie which would be totally incomprehensible if we did not have chapter 7 about the 'son of man' whose inclusive character we have shown.

'I was seeking (discernment)' from the Hebrew verb בקש is also found in this same form אבקשה *with a liturgical connotation* in Ps. 122.9 and Ezra 8.23 (in the latter instance in the first person plural). In Song of Sol. 3.2 and 4 Qp Nah 3.6 the cultic dimension is less apparent but not impossible. Another point of contact with the backdrop of Dan. 7 is the expression 'stood before me' which is modelled on Josh. 5.13 which we cited as in parallel with 8.11–12 and in connection with 'the Saints' in the preceding chapter.

The Adamic voice in v.16 leaves commentators in total perplexity. It is a question, they believe, of the voice of an angel or of God. In fact, it is the voice of the central personage in chapters 7—8. He dispatches Gabriel toward Daniel because Gabriel is the revelatory archangel, the official spokesman, so to speak, of the heavenly world. This is the first time in Scripture that an angel is designated by name. In the rest of the book, Gabriel and Michael are both mentioned by name (9.21; 10.13, 21; 12.1). O. Plöger has intuited the essential bond between Daniel the seer and the heavenly beings mentioned in this chapter. He writes: 'The parallel between the two names of the angels Gabriel and Michael with the name Daniel allows us to assume that this onomastic kinship establishes a close relation between the seer, judged worthy of so great a revelation, and the representatives of the heavenly world. This correspondence is already indicated in chapter 7 in an allusive way, but it is certainly looked for in chapter 12 with a firm hope for "Israel".'[43]

Our interpretation of these verses 15–16 will have a direct influence on our reading of other texts such as Daniel 10.5, 16; 12.6ff.[44] Throughout Daniel B themes are repeated and respond to one another. The river from which comes the numinous voice, for example. We find it again in 12.6–7 in a similar context with a similar import (see ad loc.); 10.4 is not so far away either.[45]

Like Ezekiel (see 1.28; 2.1–2; etc.), whom Daniel closely imitates throughout this chapter, the Seer is terrified and falls on his face before being set upright again (v.17).[46] Slotki (op. cit.) comments that the only

[43] Op. cit., p. 131.
[44] See ad loc. in our commentary.
[45] See our commentary on ch. 2.
[46] Among the Scriptural parallels, see Josh. 5.14; Ezek. 3.23; 43.4; Rev. 1.17; 1 Enoch 14.14, 24; 2 Esdras 10.29ff.; Apoc. Ab. 10 (cited by Jeffrey, op. cit., ad loc.). It is to be noted, with C. Colpe (*TWNT* VIII, p. 418, n. 151) that Dan. 8.17 is the only text with Ezek. where a 'prophet' is called 'ben-adam'.

prophet to have remained upright in dialogue with God is Moses, all the others prostrate themselves.

The 'time of the end' is a development of the prophetic expression 'the latter days' (אחרית הימים)[47] which designates the judgement of Israel's enemies, the restoration of the People and their institutions, and the advent of the messianic era in the large sense of this term. All this, according to Daniel, depends on one thing: the destruction of Antiochus IV Epiphanes and his reign; it will not be delayed.

The repetition in the next verse (v.18) of the theme of prostration is surprising. It has led some critics, especially H. L. Ginsberg, to distinguish two different authors in verses 17 and 18. In fact, there is not repetition in 'fall on his face' in v.17 and 'fall into lethargy' in v.18, but a passage to a new idea. Ginsberg sees an Aramaic root דמך (to be in bed, to sleep) in the second verb poorly translated into Hebrew. The text should have 'to fall' (נפל) or 'to prostrate oneself' (השתחוה) on the model of Gen. 19.1. In short, there is no progression from v.17 to v.18.[48] But, for us, this is to miss the meaning of the text. The 'second state' of sleep is the indispensable condition if one is to have visionary experiences.[49] The Testament of Reuben cites an 'eighth' human sense which is 'the hypnotic spirit by which the ecstasy of nature is produced' (3.1). This particular kind of sleep may overtake the seer at the most unexpected moment and certainly has nothing to do with boredom: 'I was lamenting over the race of the sons of men and I prayed to the Lord to be saved. Then the "sleep" fell over me and I saw a high mountain and I was on it. And behold the heavens opened and the angel of the Lord said to me, Levi, Levi, come in!' (T. Levi, 2.5). The visionary has the appearance of a dead εἰκὼν τοῦ θανάτου (T. Reuben, 3.1; cf. Rev. 1.17) and this clarifies the second part of Dan. 8.18: the angel touches Daniel and puts him back on his feet—he gives him back his life. This miraculous touch is also found in Dan. 9.21; 10.10, 16, 18. Its model may be found, for example, in Isa. 6.7; Jer. 1.9; or Ezra 1.1, 5, but this theme is more deeply exploited in literature contemporary with or subsequent to Daniel (see 1 Enoch 60.3; 4 Esdras 5.14, 15; Rev. 1.17; cf. the Gospels where Jesus is frequently described as touching the ill to heal them).[50]

---

[47] We will cite, following E. Heaton, p. 197; Hos. 3.5; Isa. 2.2; Mic. 4.1; Jer. 23.20; 30.24; 48.47; 49.39; Ezek. 38.16; cf. 8.19, 23; 10.14; 12.8.

[48] H. L. Ginsberg, op. cit., p. 59.

[49] Our comments on ecstasy are inspired by the study by R. Eppel, Le Piétisme juif dans les Testaments des XII Patriarches (Paris 1930), p. 173.

[50] To cite only the Gospel of Matthew, see 8.15; 9.20, 21, 29; 14.36; 17.7; 20.34. Note again the use of this cultic theme in Dan. 8. We may say the same thing about prostration; see R. E. Clements, Prophecy and Covenant (1965), pp. 7–8; J. Lindblom, Prophecy in Ancient Israel (1962), p. 80; A. R. Johnson, The Cultic Prophet in Ancient Israel (1962)².

Except for Hos. 7.16, the term 'wrath' which we find in v.19 always designates the wrath of God.[51] It is given ample development in chapters 9 and 11.36. Unleashed by the reign of the transgressors (see v.23), its span reaches to the end of time, which is determined, that is, in sight, near, and certain; see 11.27, 35–6; 12.

There is little to be said about vv.20–1 which identify both the ram and the he-goat. The only new element is the term 'shaggy' in v.21, which perhaps[52] is an allusion to Macedonia in the form of a wood demon, a satyr. 'The first king' is Alexander the Great, 'the four' in v.22 are the Diadochi who succeeded him, but who had nothing in common with their master.

We have encountered several times now the apocalyptic motif that salvation will irrupt during the paroxysm of transgression. The same idea is again expressed in v.23, though we will not dwell upon it here.[53] Antiochus, the incarnation of evil, is successful to an incredible extent, even managing for a time to outwit the Saints (see 1 Macc. 1.30) however spiritually powerful they may be (v.24; cf. 7.25). Indeed, we read—both with ancient and modern commentators[54]—'the people of the Saints' as in apposition[55] to 'the powerful'.

This, by the way, is just one difficulty in a text which abounds in them. The expression 'but not by his (own) force' seems only to be an addition on the model of v.22. We will see that it is nothing of the sort. Theodotion, Ephrem, the Peshitta, Rashi, Ibn Ezra, and Vatablus[56] understand: by divine permission, because God so desires it.[57] This reading not only makes sense, it is probably the best one available, as we will attempt to demonstrate.

To do so, we must take v.25 into consideration and note the perfect parallelism between the elements of these two verses. V.24: (a) 'His power (b) will increase, (c) but not by his own strength, (d) he will cause destructions (e) stupendous (f) and succeed at what he undertakes; (d') he will destroy (g) the powerful, (h) the people of the Saints.' V.25: (a') 'He will have qualifications at his disposal, (b') superior, (f') he will succeed (e') in his deceptions, (b'') he will grow (a'') in his heart and (e'') in a time of peace (d'') destroy (g') many, (b''') he will rise up (h')

---

[51] See Isa. 10.5, 25; 26.20; Jer. 10.10; 15.17; Lam. 2.6; Ezek. 21.36; 22.31; Nah. 1.6; Zeph. 3.8; 1 Macc. 1.64. Montgomery sees in Dan. 8.19 an anthologizing reuse of Isa. 10.25 and 26.20.

[52] With Montgomery, ad loc.

[53] See our Introduction; cf. 2 Macc. 6.14.

[54] For example, Ibn Ezra, O. Plöger, etc.   [55] But not a gloss, see *infra*.

[56] See Montgomery, p. 350.

[57] We may also understand, following a suggestion from Jeffrey, op. cit., p. 481, that Antiochus' grandeur is not due to real strength, but only to intrigues unworthy of a king.

against the Prince of princes. (c′) He will be broken without the intervention of any hand.'

To 'but not by his own strength' in v.24 corresponds the 'he will be broken' in v.25, and these two condemnatory expressions of the evil one provide the framework for these two verses. There will be neither an armed uprising by Israel[58] nor the prodigious intervention of a *deus ex machina*. The rotten fruit will fall and reveal its putrefaction to everyone: ישבר: he will be broken.[59] In fact, Antiochus did not die a violent death, but 'of grief due to his military failures (1 Macc. 6.8–16; 2 Macc. 9) . . . which exactly recalls the destruction of the composite statue by a stone which detaches itself without the aid of any human hand, 2.34.'[60]

The king tries to outwit everyone, including 'the Prince of princes'. He uses שכל and מרמה. The first term usually has a positive connotation: 'comprehension, understanding'; here we should clearly understand 'slickness'. The second word designates using falsehoods to trick someone: Amos 8.5 (false balances); Mic. 6.11 (deceitful weights); etc. The Author has already noticed, with the painful surprise of a wise man confronted with the triumph of evil, that the tyrant's ruses are successful: והצליח. The form of this word is unexpected. Rashi understands: 'because he is successful and prospering, he keeps at hand deceitfulness'. The second verb in the factitive: יגדיל, lacks a direct complement. Bevan translates it as 'he shall devise great things' (p. 140); Delcor seems to us closer to the text in understanding 'he will grow in his heart'.

The next element: 'and in a time of peace[61] (he will) destroy many' is generally viewed as a direct historical reference to the arrival of the Mysarch Apollonius, an envoy from Antiochus, in Jerusalem in Spring 167. 1 Macc. 1.30 recounts how this official 'gained the confidence of the inhabitants through his friendly words; then he suddenly fell on the city, inflicting a great disaster upon it. . . .' So we have one valuable chronological index for dating the composition of chapter 8 of Daniel.

In Hebrew, רבים, 'a multitude', designates a precise sociological reality in the following passages of Daniel: 8.25; 11.14, 34, 44; 12.2, 4, 10. With the article, הרבים: 9.27; 11.33, 39; 12.3. In other words, the term was becoming a technical one.[62] At Qumran it refers to the elect community, excluding novices, see 1 QS 6.20–3. The רבים share in 'the community table' in parallel with the meal shared by the priests in the Temple; see Exod. 24.11. The term 'the numerous ones' at Qumran,

[58] Re the Author's attitude toward the Maccabees, see our Introduction.
[59] Charles, p. 220, notes that the term is used for the destruction of a kingdom (Jer. 48.4), or an army (2 Chron. 14.13), or an individual (Jer. 17.18).
[60] P. J. de Menasce, *Daniel*, p. 66. On the death of Antiochus, see our commentary on Dan. 11.40–5.
[61] 11.21 also insists on this fact.
[62] We will return to this theme *infra*; see in particular our commentary on 12.3.

therefore, has a priestly, or at least cultic, dimension. In Daniel, it is difficult to say whether this dimension is present each time the term is used, but it is perhaps not by chance that the 'Prince of princes' is appropriately mentioned in this context. Those exegetes who see God himself in the 'Prince of the army' in v.11, interpret the 'Prince of princes' here in the same way. To us, the parallel between the 'powerful' in v.24 and the 'multitude' in v.25,[63] on the one hand, and between 'the people of the Saints' (v.24) and 'the Prince of princes' (v.25),[64] on the other, indicates what direction the identification must take. The Prince, here as in v.11, designates the transcendent personification of 'the people of the Saints'. He is the central personage in chapters 7 and 8, the 'son of man' enthroned at God's side in the heavenly Temple. This accounts for the many cultic terms in these two chapters. The title 'Prince of princes' which is here attributed to this personage signifies that he is the chief of the angels (see Dan. 10.20; 12.1). The motif of the angels' submission to Man is an important eschatological theme for Judaism.[65]

The angelic explanation ends with a solemn affirmation of the truth of the מראה הערב והבקר (v.26) which must be understood in terms of what was said in v.14. There are numerous parallels in Scripture for such an assurance (see Dan. 10.1; 11.2; 12.7; Rev. 21.5; 22.6, 8). Its import is clear: it is a question of responding as firmly as possible to the anguish felt by Israel or the Church in times of persecution. This is, moreover, the same goal as expressed by the order to 'keep the vision secret'. In the first place, it explains how such an ancient revelation—from sixth century Babylonia—could remain unknown for such a long time, and, in the second place, it shows why this revelation is trustworthy. Furthermore, its secrets will not be deciphered until the very last days.[66] They are only passed on to 'those who have a heart capable of guarding such mysteries' (4 Esdras 12.38; cf. 14.5ff.; see Dan. 12.10). Here is the origin of a whole pseudonymous literature which flourished during the 'intertestamental' period.[67]

Chapter 8 ends on a vivid note with, it might seem, little import (v.27). With O. Plöger (ad loc.), however, retrospective reflection on v.2 has its place here. V.2 did not refer to a physical removal to Susa, but to a spiritual transference. At the end of this 'trip', Daniel recognizes that his understanding of his vision does not reach its depths. Each element in it has been explained to him by the angel Gabriel, but their synthesis

---

[63] g and g' in our schema *supra*.
[64] h and h' of our schema.
[65] See 1 Enoch 14.21; 15.2; 41.9; 55.4; 61.8–9; Life of Adam and Eve, p. 14 (cf. *Gen. R.* VIII; XXI); Asc. of Isa. 1.27–38; *Deut. R.* 1; *j. Shab.* VI. 8d; etc; Heb. 1.13–14.
[66] Similarly at Qumran, see 1 Qp Hab 8.1, 2; cf. 2.7–8.
[67] See 1 Enoch 1.2; 104.12, 13; 2 Enoch 33.9–10; 35.3; 4 Esdras 14.46.

escapes him. By means of this subterfuge, chapter 8 calls for a continuation which will be given in chapter 9. In Dan. 9.22, the angel Gabriel announces that he has come to give Daniel total understanding. We must turn therefore to the next chapter to discover what more there is to be learned.

9 The Seventy Weeks of Years

Text 9. 1–19

(1) In the first year of Darius, son of Ahasuerus, of the race of Medes, who had been made king over the kingdom of the Chaldeans, (2) in the first year of his reign, I, Daniel, was considering in the Books the number of years which according to the word of the Lord to the prophet Jeremiah were to be accomplished for the ruins of Jerusalem: seventy years. (3) I turned my face toward the Lord God in quest of prayer and supplications[1] through fasting and with sackcloth and ashes. (4) I prayed to the Lord my God and I confessed, saying: 'Ah! Lord, you, the great and terrible God who keeps the covenant and is faithful toward those who love him and keep his commandments! (5) We have sinned, we have done wrong, we have been impious and rebellious, we have gone astray from your commandments and decisions. (6) We have not listened to your servants the prophets who spoke in your name to our kings, princes, and fathers, and to all the people of the land. (7) To you, Lord, belongs justice and to us disgrace on our heads, in this day, to the men of Judah and the inhabitants of Jerusalem, to all of Israel, to those who are near and those far away, in every country where you have driven them because of the forfeiture which they have committed against you. (8) Lord, the disgrace is on our head, on our kings, princes, and fathers because we have sinned against you. (9) To the Lord our God belong tenderness and pardon, for we have been rebels against him. (10) We have not listened to the voice of the Lord our God by walking according to his instructions (תורות), which he had set before us through his servants the prophets. (11) All Israel has transgressed your Instruction (תורה) and gone astray without hearing your voice. Hence the curse and the imprecation written in the Instruction (תורה) of Moses, God's servant, have been cast upon us, for we have sinned against him: (12) God has carried out the words he spoke against us and against the rulers who ruled us, by bringing against us so great a calamity that nowhere under all heavens has such a thing been done as has been done to Jerusalem. (13) As it is written in the Instruction (תורה) of Moses, all this calamity has come upon us; and we have not appeased the face of the Lord our God by turning away from our wrong doings and being attentive to your Truth. (14) The Lord has kept watch over this calamity and made it come upon us; for the Lord our God is just in all the works which he has done, but we have not listened to his voice. (15) And now, Lord our God, who brought your people out of the land of Egypt with a mighty hand and who made yourself a fame as you

---

[1] We may also understand 'to seek it by prayer, etc.', but the preposition 'by' is missing in the text (see, however, Joüon, *Grammaire*, 126b; K. Brockelmann, *Hebr. Syntax*, par. 102, 104, cf. par. 90d).

have today, we have been sinners and impious. (16) Lord, according to all
your righteous acts, let your anger and furor be turned away from Jerusalem,
your city, your holy mountain; for, because of our sins and the wrong doings
of our fathers, Jerusalem and your people are the object of insults by all who
surround us. (17) Now therefore, hear, O our God, the prayer of your servant
and his supplications. Make your face shine upon your devastated sanctuary
for the Lord's sake. (18) O my God, give ear and hear! Open your eyes and
see our devastation, and the city upon which your name is invoked! It is not
because of our righteous acts that we lay down our supplications before you,
but because of your great tenderness. (19) Lord, listen! Lord, pardon! Lord,
be attentive and act, do not delay! For your own sake O my God, for your
name is invoked upon your city and your people.'

Critical Notes 9. 1–18

V.1 זרע: see 2 Kings 17.20: 'race of Israel'; Jer. 23.8: 'race of the house
of Israel'; see Isa. 41.8; Ezra 2.59; 9.2: 'holy race'; etc.—המלך:
probably a misunderstanding of the original Aramaic אמלך
(aphel) he became king. Θ: reigned.

V.2 The date repeated by the MT and LXX is omitted by Θ (also by
the ms. B of the LXX).—בינותי: irregular or faulty form.—חרבות:
the word often is applied to the devastation of the holy land, see
Lev. 26.31; Isa. 44.26; Ezek. 36.10. Θ: 'to bring about the ruin of'.

V.3 ואתנה את פני: see 10.15; but 11.17a: שם פנים. Cf. 2 Chron. 20.3. There
is perhaps an allusion here to the fact that one turned toward
Jerusalem to pray (see 6.11).—תחנונים: Heb. corresponding to the
Aramaic of Dan. 6.12. See Jer. 3.21, 'and frequently in later
books' (J. Montgomery, p. 361).

V.4 It is noteworthy that the Greek text of Baruch 1.15ff. is closer to
the MT of Dan. 9 than is the LXX text of this same passage. We
may conclude that the Greek translation of the Prayer of Baruch
(see B. N. Wambacq, op. cit., p. 464) followed the Θ version of
Dan. 9.—ואתודה: confession of faith or sins; the two themes are
fused in the prayer. For the absolute form of this verb, see Ezra
10.1 and Neh. 9.3.—האל הגדול והנורא: see Neh. 1.5. In Neh. 9.32, we
find האל הגדול הגבור והנורא. Rashi comments that it was not
appropriate to call God גבור at a time when his redemptive
power had not been revealed. See Deut. 7.21.—שמר הברית והחסד:
see Deut. 7.9, 12. . . . The combination ברית וחסד appears seven
times in the MT. Cf. 1 QS 1.8: בברית חסד.—The use of the third
person is a problem and the LXX, Θ, and Vul. replace it with the
second person (see v.5). The MT, however, is supported by the
parallel in Neh. 1.5 responsible for the present form of the
textus receptus.

V.5 וסור: absolute infinitive in place of a conjugated form.

V.7 See I Baruch 1.15.

V.8 אדני: many mss.: יהוה (so Ginsburg, Baer).—See I Baruch 1.16, 17.

V.9 הסלחות: Neh. 9.17: pardon within the structure of the Covenant. —See I Baruch 1.18.

V.10 בתורתיו: ancient plural, borrowed from Jer. 32.33; also the same in Ps. 105.45. The parallel text of I Baruch 1.18 in Greek shows that the plural was understood as designating the prescriptions of the Law (προστάγμασιν).

V.11 'The curse and the imprecation': see Num. 5.21; Neh. 10.29 (cf. the curses and menaces in Deut. 27—8). We may understand a hendiadys: 'the curse (pronounced under) oath'.—ותתך: a verb expressing the outpouring of divine anger, see Jer. 7.20; 42.18; 44.6; 2 Chron. 12.7; 34.21, 25. The literal meaning of the verb נת״ך is to pour out or cast metal.—See I Baruch 1.19c–20; cf. Jer. 18.10; 42.13; Neh. 10.30; Deut. 29.20; 34.5.

V.12 See I Baruch 2.1, 2.—Ketib: 'his words' = Θ.—Qr.: 'his word'.— a calamity, etc.: Θ: 'evils'.—תחת כל השמים: = Deut. 2.5; 4.19; Job 28.24 . . ., cf. Dan. 7.27.

V.13 See I Baruch 2.7. The Greek word here for חלינו is δεήθημεν (to beg).—בתורת משה: LXX: διαθήκη which in Greek has the sense of an ordinance (in Ecclus. διαθήκη most times translates חוק).

V.14 See I Baruch 2.9, 10.—Phraseology of Jer. 1.12; 31.28; 44.27.— על הרעה: del. in Θ.

V.15 אשר הוצאת: see E. Schild, 'On Exodus III.14—I am that I am', VT (1954), pp. 296–302: in our text, 'the governing substantive may be equated with the personal pronoun' (p. 298).—See I Baruch 2.11–12.—Cf. Jer. 32.21: 'with a strong hand and an outstretched arm'. In Dan. 9.15, the MT, Θ, and Pesh. have 'with a strong hand', while the LXX has 'with an outstretched arm'.

V.16 בכל צדקתך: Θ: 'in all your mercy'. In the parallel text of I Baruch 2.12d, the term is translated by δικαιώμασιν, commandments (in the LXX, too, δικαίωμα sometimes renders צדקה).—בחטאינו: Θ omits the preposition.

V.17 'For the Lord's sake': the versions have: 'for your sake, Lord'. The LXX has: 'for the sake of your servants, Lord'. Θ has at the beginning of the verse: 'hear, O Lord our God'. Regarding this expression, see Jer. 14.7–9; Isa. 48.9–11; Ezek. 20.44—Verse 17a is found in I Baruch 2.14.

V.18 'My God': LXX: κύριε, as in 2 Kings 19.16; I Baruch 2.16. Θ: ὁ Θεός μου.—פקחה: Qr. פקח. The Kt. is not impossible, see שמעה in 4.19. We may also think of an abbreviation of ה״ פקח (for פקח יהוה), reminiscent of 2 Kings 19.16 = Isa. 37.17. Cf. Gen. 21.19;

Isa. 42.7—מפילים תחנונינו לפניך: an expression only found elsewhere in Jer. (38.26; 42.2, 9; 36.7; 37.20). Hermann: εὔχομαι, *TWNT*: 'to pour out supplications before God'. Cf. the use of the verb נפל לפני or נפל: Jer. 36.7; 37.20; 38.20; 42.2, 9; Dan. 9.20.

Commentary

Chapter 9 turns a new page in Daniel B. Its point of departure is no longer a dream or a vision but a text from Jeremiah. Daniel 9 inaugurates a literary genre which grew to have great importance in many sectors of Judaism: the *pesher* or midrashic actualization of prophetic writings. Another example of it may be found in Dan. 11.33ff. on Isa. 52. And the manuscripts from Qumran sufficiently illustrate its use in Judaism in the time just prior to the Christian era.[2] It is remarkable how in the opinion of the Israelites in the second century BCE prophecy became a sort of cryptic message concerning the end of time.

Jer. 25.11–14 and 29.10 symbolically place the end of the tribulation of Exile and the inauguration of the Restoration after a symbolic time-span of ten sabbatical cycles (cf. Lev. 25.2–7; Deut. 15.1–11), or the total number of years of existence of a vigorous man (see Ps. 90.10; Isa. 23.15). We may also think of the 'sabbath' the land takes for herself when it has not been accorded by men (Lev. 26.34ff.; 2 Chron. 36.20, 21). Then, Israel's return to her status of spouse means, in the Exilic prophets' expectation, a second Exodus surpassing the first one in that it will really be eschatological.

The prophetic promise nourished the fervour of the ancient exiled Israelites who, at the time of Haggai, Zechariah, Malachi, Ezra, and Nehemiah, intransigently denounced the interdicts which delayed the fulfilment. And yet, with incomprehension, almost incredulity, the Jews watched the great Day of the Lord fade into the distance. In their days, the great prophets had energetically denounced their people's unfaithfulness to the Covenant. Israel was definitely responsible for the triumph of evil.[3] But in the time of Daniel, the Seer no longer addresses reproaches to the community—for meanwhile the people had become a church—but only consolations and promises. Evil is no longer in Israel's heart, but in the heart of Antiochus IV Epiphanes. The confession of sin is still present, to be sure, but it has acquired a supplementary character, something like the prerequisite for the presentation of divine secrets, a sort of initiation rite.[4]

---

[2] See 1 Qp Hab (pesher on Hab. 1—2); 4 Qp Nah (on Nahum); 4 Qp Mic (on Micah); 3 Q4 (on Isaiah); etc.

[3] See Ezek. 16; 20.

[4] We distinguish between the content of the prayer of confession in ch. 9 and its framework in vv.3–4 and 21–2 which indicates the spirit in which the confession was

By means of this internal 'preparation', Daniel is a 'favoured man' and he receives the explanation of the divine mysteries concerning the end of time. He comes to understand that the seventy years spoken of by Jeremiah in fact signify seventy weeks of years; that is, not ten sabbatical cycles (see *supra*), but ten times seven sabbaths of years, followed by the Jubilee (see Lev. 25.8–18). In brief, Daniel announces the coming of the ultimate Jubilee, the Eschaton. It is near to hand. Of the seventy weeks (*sic*) from Jeremiah's oracle, seven have passed from the beginning of the Captivity (587) to the enthronement of the High Priest Joshua (538; see Hag. 1.1, 14; Zech. 3.1ff.).[5] Sixty-two more weeks, or 434 years, correspond to the lapse of time between 605, the date of the oracle in Jer. 25.1, 11, and 171, the year of the murder of the second 'anointed one', the High Priest Onias III.[6] Of the last week, half of it has passed, it encompassed the time between the death of Onias III and Antiochus' coercive measures. A half week more (from 168 to 165), and 'the decreed destruction will be poured out upon the destroyer'.

The fragments which frame vv.4–20 seem to be the fruit of a translation from the original Aramaic into Hebrew.[7] They were composed at a late date which is difficult to determine. 9.21 presupposes 8.16, and 9.27b is in parallel with 7.25; 8.14; and 12.7. So it appears that we should think of a date between 166 and 164 for vv.1–3 and 21–7. The beautiful prayer of confession in vv.4–20 has been transmitted to us in its original language. In relation to the general vocabulary of Daniel B it presents many difficulties which clearly distinguish this fragment from the remainder of the book. We will point them out in the course of our commentary. It is equally difficult to date this text precisely. There are several interesting points, however: the city of Jerusalem and its Temple are destroyed (see vv.12, 16, 17, 18); this is a punishment merited by the people for they have sinned shamelessly (v.7). They have been dispersed among the nations because of their transgression (ibid.). At the heart of Israel's life is the Covenant (v.4), or, in the terms preferred by the Author, the Torah or Toroth (*passim*, see esp. vv.5, 10). As in Deut-

---

inserted into this chapter. In the second century, the recognition of collective sin was tempered by the then triumphant individualism throughout the civilized world. For their part, the Exilic prophets are both witnesses to and protagonists of this fact (see Jer. 31.29–30; Ezek. 18.1ff.).

[5] We might also think of Cyrus, called my 'anointed' in Isa. 44.28; 45.1. But the parallelism with v.26 where it is a question of the High Priest Onias militates in favour of Joshua here. Besides, the term 'anointed' is applied to the High Priest in the post-exilic writings, see Lev. 4.3, 5, 16; 6.15. E. Jenni, in his article 'Messiah' in *The Interpreter's Dictionary of the Bible*, vol. 3, p. 360, cites Dan. 9.25–6 with the texts from Leviticus in this same sense.

[6] See Ramir Augé, op. cit., ad loc.; reviewed by R. Tournay in *RB*, LXII, p. 289. See also A. Jeffery, op. cit., on Dan. 9.26.

[7] See H. L. Ginsberg, op. cit., pp. 41ff.

eronomy, it is 'the Torah of Moses' (v.11). He, like all the prophets, is a 'Servant of the Lord' (vv.6, 10, 11) and the Torah strangely dispenses with the priests for its transmission (*contra* Jer. 18.18); it is 'presented through the intermediary of his servants, the prophets' (v.10).[8] The social structures of the people comprise kings, judges-governors, princes, fathers, and the 'people of the land' (vv.6, 12); once again the absence of priests is noteworthy. The 'summary of the Law' is the one already cited from the Book of Deuteronomy (v.11). The Lord keeps watch over the accomplishment of his Word (cf. Jer. 1.12), which is why his threat is brought into action (v.14).

We are led therefore to see the origin of this Prayer as some time around 600, that is after the 'discovery' of the Deuteronomy book and the beginning of Jeremiah's preaching, but before the Restoration under Cyrus. The parallel between our text and the prayer in Baruch (1.15—2.19)[9] does not allow us to attain any better chronological precision since 1 Baruch 1.15ff. is later than Dan. 9 as B. N. Wambacq[10] has shown. The reminiscences in Dan. 9 of earlier pieces from the same period will be discussed below (see our commentary on Dan. 9.4).

According to the Author's factitious chronology, the episode reported in chapter 9 took place just after the end of the Babylonian era and the beginning of the Median period (v.1), that is, at the moment when Jeremiah's prophecy of the restoration should have found its realization (Jer. 25.11; 29.10). Regarding Darius 'the Mede', Belshazzar's successor in universal dominance, see our commentary on Dan. 6.1, and for the 'Chaldeans', see our commentary on Dan. 1.4. Xerxes (or Ahasuerus) is the Xerxes of classical literature, Darius' successor, not his father. He reigned from 485–465 and is the king in Esth. 1.1 and Ezra 4.6.

The insistence on the date in v.2 is explained by the restless expectation due to Jeremiah's prophecy. Since events did not confirm the validity of this hope it was normal that one should turn to the texts which gave rise to it. This is the first time in the Bible that 'books' are spoken of in the sense of 'Scriptures'.[11] So we have here an important testimony to the progressive canonization of the books which were to form the Hebrew Bible two centuries later.[12] It is also noteworthy that the word

[8] 1 Baruch 1.16 associates the prophets with the reprobation of the priests. Recall also that both were opposed to Jeremiah. See the parallel text to Dan. 9.8 and 1 Baruch 1.15–16 in Jet. 32.32. Re the Prayer of Baruch, see *infra*.
[9] The Prayer of Baruch continues on to 3.8, but after 2.19 it is no longer in parallel with Dan. 9.
[10] 'Les prières de Baruch (1.15—2.19) et de Daniel (9.5–19)', *Biblica* (1959), pp. 463–75. For more details on the Deuteronomistic character of the Prayer here and on its literary genre, see our 'The Liturgical Prayer in Daniel 9' to appear in *HUCA* (Cincinnati 1978).
[11] See 2 Pet. 1.19; 1 Pet. 1.10; Rev. 1.3; but above all, Ecclus., prologue and 49.7ff.
[12] Re this question, see our 'La Tradition dans le Bas-Judaisme', *RHPR*, no. 1 (1960).

ספרים equally designates the heavenly tablets in Daniel B (see 10.21; 12.1).[13] We are near to the origin of speculation about the concomitance of earthly and heavenly events. The same idea is found in vv.24ff. and in Dan. 10 as well. In this sense, what Jeremiah wrote (25.11ff.; 29.10), is only a copy of what the divine tablets contain. There is no place for an error by the prophet, therefore, when he speaks of 'seventy years' during which time 'the whole land will lie in ruins and desolation'. Just as they were witnesses to the national degradation, so Daniel's contemporaries also looked for the imminent fulfilment of the promise. The one was as certain as the other.

The sole difficulty was the number put forth by the prophet: 'seventy years'.[14] The apocalyptic writer was so bothered by it that he undertook spiritual exercises in order to learn the meaning of the text, if possible (v.3). In so doing, he indicates to his readers 'the good use'—as Pascal puts it—of the delay before the end, i.e., repentance.

The use for the first time in the Book of Daniel of the tetragrammaton[15] is to be noted. This fact about the text is important for it has been cited in support of contradictory theses. For B. W. Jones,[16] for example, we may not reject the prayer in vv.4–20 as inauthentic on the basis of its reference to God as YHWH. In v.2, the Author already uses the tetragrammaton along with a quotation from Jeremiah. At the other extreme, R. H. Charles changes v.2 to read Elohim 'since 9.4–20 did not belong originally to the text' (p. 225). In doing this he is following von Gall[17] et al. Our own position is as follows. The prayer is a liturgical fragment of a seventh-century origin (see our introduction to this chapter), but it was used by the very Author of chapter 9 of Daniel and not inserted after the fact.[18] The whole of chapter 9 is built upon the basis of this confes-

---

[13] See Exod. 32.32; Ps. 139.16; I Enoch 81.1, 2; 93.2; 103.2; 106.19; Jub. 3.10ff., 31; 4.5, 32, etc.; Test. of Levi 5.4; Test. of Asher 7.5; etc.

[14] The number 70 plays an important role in Scripture, see Gen. 50.3: 70 days of mourning among the Egyptians upon the death of Joseph; Exod. 1.5: 'all the offspring of Jacob were 70 persons'; Exod. 24.1, 9; Num. 11.16, 24f.: the 70 elders assisting Moses in the desert; etc. We also find '70 years' in an inscription from Asarhaddon: 'Even though he had written 70 years (on the tablets of fate) as being the period of its depopulation, Marduk the Merciful, after his heart had calmed down, changed the numerals, ordering its reconstruction in the eleventh year' (see R. Borger, Die Inschriften Asarhaddons, König von Assyrien (Graz 1956), p. 15).

[15] See, however, Dan. 1.2: אדני.

[16] 'The Prayer in Dan. IX', VT, 18 (1968), pp. 488–93.

[17] A. von Gall, Die Einheitlichkeit des Buches Daniel (Giessen 1895), pp. 123–6.

[18] O. Plöger rightly thinks that, even if Dan. 9 borrowed a pre-existing prayer for his own use, its insertion in the present context gives to it a new meaning (p. 49). Like Chron., Dan. stumbles on the 70 years of Jer. 25.11 etc. (cf. 2 Chron. 36.21), but for the former, those 70 years came to an end with the reign of Cyrus. Dan. 9 against that backdrop sounds like a protest (ibid.). It is, however, remarkable, continues Plöger, that to the Maccabean outgrowth of Chron. conception, and to their Hassidic (later, Pharisaic and Essene) opponents, 'there was a common root of faith and piety such

sion[19] which here plays the role taken in the other chapters of Daniel B by the *details* of the visions.[20] Daniel's reuse of this liturgical prayer is so little 'clumsy' (cf. Charles who speaks of the prayer as 'unskillfully interpolated before 145 BC') that B. W. Jones could discover at least a half dozen linguistic parallels between it and its framework within the text.

The notion of hidden truth plays an important role in the Book of Daniel. It must be discovered in a premonitory dream, a strange writing on the wall of a palace, or a mysterious voice from heaven mixed with the din of the waters of a mighty river. In chapter 9, such truth is hidden in a prophetic text and to discover it one must submit himself to a similar spiritual preparation as in the preceding instances of revelation. Consequently, in v.3 the Seer applies himself ('I turned my face toward the Lord') to the quest for the solution to the mystery. In our text there is a telescoping of several levels of its logical structure. The object of the verb בקש is normally God. In Amos 8.12, however, it is used with 'the Word of the Lord', which constitutes a parallel to our text. But Zeph. 2.3 most interests us here for בקש there is used with the Lord, justice, and humility as its objects. So we should understand that Daniel seeks a way of preparation suitable to the quest for the mystery of the Scriptures. A. Bentzen insists on this fact that the prayer, not God, is the object of Daniel's search (cf. Rom. 8.27). Jeffery opposes this view, suggesting that Daniel turns to prayer as a means of obtaining spiritual inspiration. We may, indeed, also understand Dan. 9.3 by supplying a personal pronoun at the accusative and the prepositions: 'in seeking *him through* prayer, etc.'.

Hence as G. F. Moore comments, most of the terms employed here (vv.3ff.) belong to the technical language of Jewish liturgy.[21] They

---

as it manifests itself in the prayer of Ezra 9 and Dan. 9 . . .' (ibid.). ('Reden und Gebete im deuteronomistischen und chronistischen Geschichtswerk', in *Festschrift für Günther Dehn*, Wilhelm Schneemelcher (Neukirchen 1957), pp. 35–49.)

[19] See McNamara, op. cit., p. 667, par. 536c: 'This prayer introduces the vision of 24–7 as it gives the theological reason why Israel is punished, and why the period of tribulation spoken of by Jeremiah has now been prolonged sevenfold. It is not, then, an interpolation as has been suggested by some (Marti, 64; Charles, 226f.; Göttsberger, 69; Bentzen, 41f.).'

[20] Thus in Dan. 8, the vision really concerns the 'evenings and the mornings' and not the 'ram and the he-goat'. Similarly here, the angel-interpreter's explanation has to do with the text from Jeremiah and not the prayer from vv.4–20, although it does play a role in the angelic discourse (v.23). It is inexact, with B. W. Jones, op. cit., to conclude that the prayer of Daniel is rejected by God and to trace a parallel with Job's questions which received no answer. If v.23 says, 'at the beginning of your supplications', it is not meant to indicate that the rest went unheard, but is rather a manner of emphasizing the promptness of the divine response to the supplications of the 'favoured man' (cf. Isa. 65.24). The same accent on rapidity is clearly marked in v.20 and 21.

[21] Op. cit. I, p. 500, n. 3.

provide an appropriate introduction to the language of the prayer which follows. The combination of fasting, sackcloth, and ashes is also found in a very similar context in Neh. 9.1. These spiritual exercises usually express mourning (the expression 'sackcloth and ashes' is found in Jonah 3.6; Esth. 4.1–4; Matt. 11.21; *Taan.* 16a). As for fasting, it is sometimes envisioned as preparation for receiving a revelation (see Exod. 34.28; Deut. 9.9; Esth. 4.6; Dan. 10.3; 4 Esdras 5.13, 20; 2 Baruch 20.5, 6; Hermas: *Shepherd* 6.1; cf. Asc. of Is. 2.10, 11). It became a regular exercise of piety in post-exilic Judaism. Judith spends long hours in fasting and other forms of mortification (see 8.5, 6); so do the patriarchs in the Testaments (Test. of Reuben 1.10; Test. of Juda 15.4; Test. of Sim. 3.4; Test. of Jos. 3.4; 9.2; etc.).

For Th. Chary,[22] the prayer which follows, beginning in v.4, has 'a clear cultic character. It is presented as a collective lamentation for a day of fasting and public expiation. Its resemblance to all the other instances of this same category has been noted by every exegete: 1 Kings 8; Ezra 9.6–15; Neh. 9.6–37; 1 Bar. 1.15—3.8. . . . (We find in it) frequent recourse to Jeremiah, a characteristic feature of Maccabean literature: 2 Macc. 2.1–12; 1 Bar. 1.15—3.8.' We have already stated above our opinion as to the language and date of this fragment.[23] The late expressions in the Book of Daniel are not found here. On the contrary, its composition is rather inspired by Deuteronomy and Jeremiah.[24] There are no Aramaisms and the style is 'synagogal' (see the many majestic synonyms applied to God by the speaker). Furthermore, it became part of the official Jewish liturgy for the daily morning office and for days of fasting, particularly Yom Kippur.

We have here the good fortune of being able to follow the evolution of an anthological liturgical text in the post-exilic literature. Indeed, Dan. 9.4ff. is a mosaic of quotations from Deuteronomy and Jeremiah, and occasionally from 1 Kings, Leviticus, and Ezekiel.[25] So we have a *terminus a quo* for dating this text (see *supra*). What is more, we find at each step along the way the text of Neh. 9 and—as is the case in v.4 of Dan. 9—Neh. 1.5.[26]

In contrast to the loyalty of God to the Covenant (v.4), v.5 lists five

---

[22] Th. Chary, *Les Prophètes et le Culte à partir de l'Exil* (Tournai 1955), p. 259.

[23] See our introduction to this chapter.

[24] The same opinion is found, for example, in S. R. Driver, *An Introduction to the Literature of the O.T.* (Cleveland 1963), 7th printing, p. 507.

[25] See our commentary on the following verses.

[26] See also Dan. 9.17a in parallel with Neh. 1.6, 11. The linguistic couple 'great and terrible' in Dan. 9.4 has a Deuteronomistic origin, as F. M. Cross has shown in *Canaanite Myth . . .*, p. 254. He refers to: '2 Sam. 7.23 (revised by 1 Chron. 17.21); see Deut. 10.21; compare Deut. 1.19; 7.21; 8.15; 10.17; Ps. 99.3; Joel 3.4; Mal. 3.23; Neh. 9.32; and Dan. 9.4'. On those parallels and others, see our article mentioned above in note 10.

terms expressing the community's transgressions. This use of contrasting themes is well known in Scripture, especially in the Deuteronomic and Deuteronomistic literature (see 1 Kings 8.47 and Deut. 17.20; see also Ps. 106.6; 1 Baruch 2.12; 1 QS 1.24–5).

Vv.6–7 are an anthology of older texts, particularly from Jeremiah.[27] The expression 'those who are near' (cf. v.16: 'all who surround us') in v.7 requires comment. It indicates that the original author of this poem was in Jerusalem and not in Babylon or Susa as in the fiction maintained by the Book of Daniel. Only a Judean author could simply affirm that the dispersion (important because it concerned several countries) was a divine punishment. *This also accounts for the absence of priests and prophets from the guilty social classes.*

Vv.8–9 are 'expansions of the introductory clauses in 9.7' (Charles, p. 229). They restate in more or less similar terms what had been said above. Neh. 9.17, to which Psalm 130.4 must be added, is in the background. We may, certainly, with Bevan think that in speaking of kings, the Author envisages the past history of the people and so 'confesses that from of old his people have been transgressors',[28] but since the text is not a composition from the second century, this judgement does not add much to our understanding of it.

V.10 is a variation on Jer. 3.13; 26.4; 32.23; and 44.10, 23 (cf. Deut. 4.8; 11.32; Jer. 9.13). The preponderant role attributed to the prophets in this prayer is to be noted. They are twice called the 'servants of the Lord' (vv.6 and 10), a title frequently applied to Moses, as the next verse recalls, 'Moses, God's servant' (cf. Deut. 34.5; Josh. 1.13; 8.31, 33; 11.12; etc.). This is why the text takes for granted that the prophets had no other mission and no other *raison d'être* than to transmit 'the Torah of Moses' (v.11). Regarding this expression, cf. Dan. 9.13; additions to Dan. 13.3, 62.[29]

B. N. Wambacq sees a new sentence beginning with v.11e: 'Because we have sinned against him, [v.12] he has carried out his word. . . .' Such a cutting up of the text is contrary to the Masoretic Text, the LXX, and the Vulgate, but it should be noticed that at this point we pass from the second to the third person singular.

The reuse of earlier texts in vv.12–13 is more subtle. The expression 'he has carried out his words' has a parallel in Neh. 9.8 (cf. Deut. 9.5), and 'by bringing against us so great a calamity' has one in Jer. 35.17;

[27] V.6a: cf. Jer. 7.25; 25.4; 26.5; v.6b: cf. Jer. 44.4, 21; Neh. 9.32, 34; v.7a: cf. Jer. 7.19; Isa. 9.7; v.7b: cf. Jer. 4.4; 11.2, 9; v.7c: cf. 1 Kings 8.46; Jer. 25.26; Isa. 57.19; v.7d: cf. 1 Kings 8.46–7; v.7e: cf. Lev. 26.40; Ezek. 17.20; 1 Chron. 10.13.
[28] A. A. Bevan: op. cit., p. 150.
[29] In other books, see Josh. 8.31; 1 Kings 2.3; 2 Kings 14.6; 23.25; Mal. 3.22; 2 Chron. 23.18; 25.4; 30.16; 35.12; Ezra 1.7, 8; 6.18; 7.6; 8.1; Neh. 8.14; 9.14; 10.29; 13.1; Tobit 7.10; 1 Baruch 2.2; Ecclus. 24.22; 2 Macc. 7.30.

36.31. The use of the word 'judges' is somewhat unexpected. The parallel text in 1 Baruch 2.1 demonstrates the ambiguity of this term. 'For Daniel, the "judges" seem to be those who actually govern; for Baruch, those who were historically known under the name "judges".'[30] In support of the former interpretation, see Amos 2.3 and Ps. 2.10.

What is really unprecedented in the catastrophe which has struck Jerusalem is that the Temple has been destroyed (the meaning of the text in the sixth century) or profaned (the meaning in the second century), which amounts to the same thing (see vv.17, 18). But even this calamity which surpasses all understanding in Israel, even the destruction or desolation of the Holy House, was not only permitted by God but was written down in advance in the Torah.[31] In conformity with Scripture in general, Israel is held responsible for not having repented, consequently for not having changed the course of events: 'we have not appeased the face of the Lord, our God'. The expression *hillah penei YHWH* probably means, on the basis of its parallel in Arabic, 'to remove God's face'. Its origin goes back to a common stock in the history of religions when the petitioner rubs the image of a god to entreat his favour. The concept was taken up by Israel by means of a demythologizing process: one caresses the face of the Living God to erase the wrinkles caused by his displeasure. To do this, man has at his disposition prayer,[32] sacrifice,[33] fasting,[34] the cultus,[35] or right conduct (see Ps. 119.58).[36] Then God's face shines (see here, v.17).

The context is plainly that of the Covenant. This framework explains the 'Lord's keeping watch over this calamity' (v.14). According to Slotki's definition,[37] שָׁקַד signifies 'being on the alert to bring about the speedy realization of a purpose, good or bad (see Jer. 1.12)'. Our present knowledge of texts of international covenant treaties in the ancient Near East considerably clarifies the *Sitz im Leben* of v.14. The most terrible threats of divine intervention in case of any breaking of the treaty figured in the contract. The gods were witnesses to the concluding of the covenant and guaranteed its execution on pain of sanctions. Thus, from the preceding verse (v.13), we could with Klaus Baltzer[38] draw a comparison with the treaty between Shuppiluliumash, king of Hatti, and

---

[30] B. N. Wambacq, op. cit., p. 469.
[31] V.13 here inaugurates the expression which became so common in the N.T. and in Rabbinic literature: 'as it is written'.
[32] See Exod. 32.11; 1 Kings 13.6; 2 Kings 13.4; 2 Chron. 33.12.
[33] 1 Sam. 13.12; Mal. 1.9.
[34] Zech. 7.2.   [35] Zech. 8.21–2.
[36] See *TWNT* II, pp. 782–99 (J. Herrmann): εὔχομαι (in the O.T.).
[37] Op. cit., ad loc.
[38] *The Covenant Formulary in O.T., Jewish, and Early Christian Writings*, tr. David E. Green (Philadelphia 1971), p. 49, n. 55.

Tetti, king of Nuhashshi, vol. IV, 46–7: 'All the words of this treaty and of this oath, if he transgresses the oath . . .' (a malediction follows).

God is just, he remains faithful to his Word as given, he is the guarantor of the Covenant with his People. The confession of sins is based on this conviction (see Ezra 9.15; Neh. 9.8, 32, 33; Deut. 32.4, 5; Jer. 12.1). God is צדיק, that is, he acts in conformity with the Covenant. He is the prosecutor as well as the only one who may delay the application of the curse following from rupture of the contract. This is why the confession of sins becomes a prayer for forgiveness and, at the same time, for the renewal of the Covenant.[39] So it is normal that the Author refers to the *Urtheophanie* of the Exodus in v.15. The wording of this verse is largely inspired by Jer. 32.20–1; Neh. 9.10; and Deut. 6.21. Regarding this theocentric motif of the salvation of Israel ('you made yourself a fame', lit.: 'a name'), see also Isa. 63.12, 14; 2 Sam. 7.23. The memory of the Exodus is present throughout Scripture up to Dan. 9.15.[40]

The anthologizing process continues in v.16. 'According to all your righteous acts' has its parallel in Ps. 103.6. In E. Heaton's words, 'The Jews associated the righteousness of God with specific acts (cf. Judg. 5.11; 1 Sam. 12.7; Mic. 6.5; Ps. 103.6) by which they were redeemed from the oppressors and vindicated in the eyes of the world (cf. 4.27; Isa. 46.13; 51.6; 54.14; Ps. 98.2; 103.17)'.[41] 'Let your anger and furor be turned away', see Num. 25.4; Isa. 19.1; Jer. 23.30; 30.24. 'Your city', see v.19; cf. Isa. 45.13. 'Your holy mountain' (also in v.20), see Ps. 2.6; 15.1; 43.3. It is located at the centre of the earth and the Sanctuary is built upon it (Ps. 48.2); it is the universal rallying-point at the end of time (Isa. 2.2ff.; 27.13; 66.20; Obad. 21; Mic. 4.7). 'Because of our sins and the faults of our fathers', see Neh. 9.2. Regarding collective guilt across the generations, see such texts as Isa. 65.7 and Jer. 14.20. 'An object of insults for all who surround us', see Ezek. 25.3, 6, 8; 35.10, 12, 13; Ps. 44.14; 79.4. Note here once again the point of view of an inhabitant of Jerusalem in contradiction to Daniel's situation as presented in this book.[42] The sarcasm of the nations (Ammonites, Moabites, Edomites) after the catastrophe of 586, was deeply resented by the Jews (see Ezek. 25.4ff.; 21.33ff.).

The first part of v.17 closely recalls Solomon's prayer for the dedication of the Temple (1 Kings 8.28; cf. Neh. 1.6, 11; Ps. 130.2). It is also the Temple liturgy and, more precisely, the Aaronic benediction from Num. 6.25 (cf. Ps. 80.4, 8, 20) which is repeated in the expression 'make your face shine . . .'. In all these texts it is a question of God's mercy and

[39] See Exod. 34.10; Neh. 10; Ezra 19.2, 14; 1 QS 1.18—2.18. K. Baltzer places Dan. 9 in this category (op. cit., pp. 48ff.).
[40] See D. Daube, *The Exodus Pattern in the Bible* (London 1963).
[41] Op. cit., p. 208.   [42] But see *infra* re v.20.

pardon. The 'devastated sanctuary' no doubt designates the Temple in Jerusalem destroyed by Nebuchadnezzar in 587 (see Lam. 5.18). That catastrophe finds its correspondence, for the Author, in the profanation of the Temple by Antiochus (see 8.13; 1 Macc. 4.38). He is the 'devastator' *par excellence* (see 9.27). The theme of devastation recurs five times in this chapter (see vv.18, 26, 27).[43] There is a crescendo in the movement up to v.27 where the apex is attained with the mention of שקוצים משמם. In the primitive hymn this is an alien element which has no parallel in Scripture. It was added by the Author in the second century. Note also the finale in the third person: 'for the Lord's sake' is a stereotype. There is no reason to change it to the second person following the versions.[44]

Except for the mention of 'my God' instead of 'Lord', the first part of v.18 is a quotation of 2 Kings 19.16 (Hezekiah's prayer, Isa. 37.17; cf. Neh. 9.19, 27, 31). But once again in this verse the element of 'devastation' has been added by the Author. It makes the transition to the second part of the sentence a bit awkward. Jerusalem is 'the city upon which your name is invoked'[45] (cf. v.19). Montgomery refers to 2 Sam. 12.28 as indicating the meaning of this expression: the city of which God is the proprietor.[46] This phrasing is Deuteronomic; it is used concerning Israel, Jerusalem, and the Temple.[47] This verse is a good illustration of post-exilic Israel's conception of divine justice, the juridic element only coming into play secondarily. Everything depends on the grace of God upon which Daniel is now calling. רחמים רבים appears frequently in liturgical passages (see 2 Sam. 24.14; Ps. 119.156; Neh. 9.19, 27, 31; Baruch 2.27; Ecclus. 3.20). Basically, the substantive רחם expresses a father's recognition of a newly born child as his own (see Gen. 30.3; 38.12; Ps. 2.7). Within the framework of the Covenant, as here, or above in v.9, the dominant nuance is that of forgiveness (see Deut. 13.18; 1 Kings 8.5; Jer. 42.2; Mic. 7.19; Ps. 51.3; 79.8; Prov. 28.13).

V.19 is the finale and apex of the prayer.[48] In pathetic terms, the

---

[43] See also 11.13; 12.11.

[44] So Montgomery, op. cit., ad loc. Cf. *Ber.* 7b: 'R. Johanan said in the name of R. Simon bar Yohai: Since the creation, no one called the Lord "master", until the day when Abraham came and invoked him as such (Gen. 15.8). . . . Rab said that Daniel was not hearkened to except for the love of Abraham, as it is said (Dan. 9.17) . . . for the love of *my Lord*! He should have said: for the love of Abraham who called you Lord.'

[45] Or, according to Th. Chary, op. cit., p. 262: 'the city which is called by your Name'.

[46] See Deut. 28.10; Isa. 4.1; Amos 9.12; Jer. 7.10. M. Delcor, p. 193, following R. de Vaux, *Festschrift L. Rost* (Berlin 1967), p. 221, recalls that already at El Amarna, 'to place his name on a country' meant to take possession of it.

[47] See Deut. 28.10; 1 Kings 8.43; Jer. 7.10; 14.9; 25.9; Isa. 63.19.

[48] In this verse there is a reminiscence of 1 Kings 8.30, 34, 36, and Ps. 40.17. There are also elements from the preceding verses: 'for your own sake', see v.17; 'your name is invoked on your city', see v.18.

speaker supplicates God to have pity on himself by forgiving his partner in the Covenant. Only a profound sentiment of love could dictate such accents in such a true tone. This verse has been called the *Kyrie eleison* of the Jewish Scriptures.

Text 9. 20–27

(20) I was still speaking, praying and confessing my sin and the sin of my people Israel, laying down my supplication before the Lord my God, for[49] the holy mountain of my God; (21) I was still speaking in prayer, when Gabriel, the very man whom I had seen earlier in vision, came close to me by a swift flight at the moment of the evening offering. (22) He instructed me and spoke with me, saying: 'Daniel, I am now come out to give you discernment and understanding. (23) At the beginning of your supplications, a word went out and I am come to announce it to you, for you are the favoured man! Understand the word and comprehend the apparition! (24) It has been fixed seventy weeks for your people and your holy city in order to stop the crimes and end the sinning, to expiate the wrong and bring about eternal justice, to seal vision and prophet, to anoint a Holy of Holies.

(25) Know therefore and discern:
From the time a word went forth for the Return and for the Reconstruction of Jerusalem
until a messiah-chief, there will be seven weeks,
during sixty two weeks will occur the Return and Reconstruction, with squares and moats
but in the distress of times.
(26) And after sixty two weeks a messiah will be cut off without anyone (to console) him.
The people of a chief to come will destroy the city and the sanctuary
but he will end up by being swept away and up to the end of the war devastations are decreed.
(27) He will impose a covenant on many, for one week,
and during half of the week he will end sacrifice and offering;
on the wing of abominations will be a destroyer and this will continue until the decreed destruction is poured out upon the destroyer.'

Critical Notes 9. 20–27

V.20 'My sin and the sin': LXX, Θ, Pesh., and Vul. have 'my sins and the sins'.

V.21 'By a swift flight': LXX paraphrases: τάχει φερόμενος; Θ:

---

[49] Or 'on'.

πετόμενος; Vul.: *cito volans*. The Pesh. glosses: 'flew in flying, and flew above, and came from the sky, and came up near to me'. Saadia, Rashi, Jephet, etc.: the two words have an identical root: 'flew in flying'. Ibn Ezra was the first to give to the root the sense of 'to be troubled': he was 'troubled by his long flight'.— נגע אלי: see 8.7; Mic. 1.9; Jer. 51.9; 'to come close to'. Θ: 'to touch', see 8.18; 10.16.—כעֵת: as soon as, see 1 Sam. 9.13, and not, as in Θ, 'about the hour (of the evening sacrifice)'; cf. Acts 9.3, influenced by Θ.

V.22 ויבן: *lectio difficilior*. LXX and Pesh.: 'he came' (ויבא). But Θ and Vul. have 'he instructed me' (ויבנני). 'I am now come' indicates the officiality of the visit and introduces the terms of a message, cf. Josh. 5.13–15; 2 Sam. 14.15ff.

V.23 חמדות: understood: איש as in 10.11, 19; cf. 2 Sam. 26.6: '(man of) nothing'. Here, LXX, Θ, Pesh., Vul. have the word 'man'.

V.24 שבעים: everywhere else we find a feminine form: שבעות. In the given form, there is a word play with the following term.— נחתך: hapax. It is also found in the Mishnah and Talmud, however, with the sense of 'to decide'.—לכלא: some mss. of Θ presuppose לבלא (see Tertullian, *Adv. Jud.* VIII, *inveteretur delictum*, cited by Charles, p. 237).—ולחתם: Kt. (cf. Θ: τοῦ σφραγίσαιἁμαρτίας); Qr.: ולהתם (cf. A: τοῦ τελειῶσαι τὴν ἀθεσίαν; cf. Vul.; Pesh.; LXX (?). Cf. also 8.23).—ולכפר עון: LXX, Vul.; read: למחות עון (cf. Ps. 51.11, etc.).—ולמשח קדש קדשים: Vul.: personal interpretation: *et ungatur sanctus sanctorum*; similarly Hippolytus IV, 32 (= Son of God); Pesh. is similar; also Jewish exegesis (see *Gen. R.* 14.18, Ibn Ezra; Nachmanides).

V.25 להשיב ולבנות: ms. J in the Taylor-Schechter collection in Palestinian punctuation (see P. Kahle, *Masoreten des Westens* II (Stuttgart 1930), pp. 72ff.): להשיב לבנות. Pesh. and Vul.: 'to reconstruct'. Ewald: 'to restore and to construct'. Bevan: 'to people and to build'. Marti: 'to bring back "Jerusalem" and to reconstruct' (Jerusalem in the sense of the exiled people). LXX and Θ: להשיב = ἀποκριθῆναι!—רחוב וחרוץ: Pesh.: רחוב וחוץ (see Prov. 1.20; 7.12; Isa. 15.3; Jer. 5.1). LXX and Θ: an impossible translation. The Aramaic inscription of Zakkur (eighth century BCE) illustrates the use of the word חרץ (written without *waw*) twice on the face A line 10 of the document. (See J. C. L. Gibson: *Textbook of Syrian Semitic Inscriptions*, II, *Aramaic Inscriptions* (Oxford 1975), no. 5, pp. 6–17.) The term clearly means 'entrenchment'.—ובצוק עתים Vul.: *in angustia temporum*. Θ: 'the times are run out'!

V.26 In the Taylor-Schechter ms. J are the following variations: עם נגיד: Θ read: מלחמה.—מלחמות instead of מלחמה; יכרת instead of יכרית

עָם; there is a composite text in the LXX and Vul. A has עַם.—The LXX combines הבא וקצו and reads ובא קצו.—וקצו בשטף: Θ: 'they will be cut off by a deluge'.—"ועד קץ וגמ: Θ: 'and until the end of a shortened war, (there will be) disappearances'. LXX: 'its end will come with wrath, and until the fulfilment, they will fight the fight'. Pesh.: 'and until the end of the war, decrees of destruction' (= MT).

V.27 הגביר: in a transitive sense ('to fortify'), see 1 QH 8.35.—ישבית: Vul., A Σ: ישבת.—משמם: poel participle; Θ: 'the devastated abomination', cf. Dan. 8.13. Rashi too understands the passive form. Tradition made שמם a synonym of שממה. שמם is either 'devastated' or 'devastator'. Ibn Ezra and Ps. Saadia understand the active.—כלה ונחרצה: hendiadys. See Isa. 10.23; 28.32.

Commentary

We come to the second part of chapter 9 in v.20. It is a résumé of what has gone before. The central element is Zion. Daniel has prayed for Zion and, through it, for God himself. In this way the Author is exercising what Paul will subsequently call the 'ministry of reconciliation'[50] to re-establish loving relations between the Creator and the creature.

There is a certain ambiguity in the preposition על in על הר־קדש אלהי. It may be understood as indicating the prayer's object ('for the Mountain, etc.') or the place where the speaker is ('on the mountain, etc.'). In favour of the latter reading is the fact that v.21 indicates the moment of the angelic intervention as the time of the 'evening offering', which is to say, the time when the sacrifice of מנחה is brought to the Temple (see Exod. 29.41; 1 Chron. 23.30; Num. 28.4; Lev. 6.12ff.). In fact, there is a new telescoping of two realities which the Author unites here: the Temple is heavenly and earthly, transcending space as the cultus transcends time. Finding himself in Babylon during the reign of Darius, Daniel turns toward Jerusalem ('toward the Lord God', v.3) at the moment of the evening offering,[51] and, in effect, he is in the Temple, offering the minḥah. The message to the reader in the second century is

[50] 1 Cor. 5.18.

[51] Minḥah is offered in the middle of the afternoon. It is the most important sacrifice of the day. See 2 Kings 16.15; Acts 3.1; 10.3. Under Antiochus' persecutions, it was forbidden, see Dan. 8.11.

The singular form of the word minḥah is a problem, for Exod. 29.38–42 and Num. 28.3–8 say that there is a double offering. We should probably accept Th. Chary's judgement, op. cit., p. 258, that 'it is highly probable that in the past the evening sacrifice only consisted of one oblation: 2 Kings 16.15. We would then have a better understanding of the expression minḥat-'ereb which is utilized several times in the Bible: Ezra 9.4, 5; Ps. 141.2 and up to Dan. 9.21. The more archaic expression was conserved despite the change in the rite.'

clear: Antiochus' interdiction against offering the sacrifice (8.11, etc.) and his profaning the Temple are insupportable and God is going to end this blasphemy; but, in truth, nothing and no one may act in any way against the Temple and its divine office.

V.20 is a rather awkward transition from Daniel's prayer to the arrival of the angel. V.21 follows naturally upon v.3. Nevertheless, we do not think the prayer was added after the fact (see *supra*). Porteous[52] sees a 'touch of the grotesque' in the fact that the angel flies to Daniel 'by a swift flight'. This judgement is too strong for what constitutes only a weakness in the Author's style. Furthermore, it explains nothing. The representing of angels with wings had been part of popular imagery for a long time, inspired perhaps by the sculptures of winged demons in Egypt, and Mesopotamia. We may also understand מעף ביעף by seeing in the second word the meaning 'to be fatigued'.[53] Then referring back to 8.17–18, the translation would be: 'whom I had seen earlier in my vision when I was exhausted'. But this would be to give the verbs in 8.17–18 a meaning which they have only quite secondarily. It is better to retain the traditional reading. After all, this is not the first instance in Scripture where angels are seen flying (see Isa. 6.2, 6; Ezek. 1.6, 14), and no one, to our knowledge, has ever thought of these texts as having 'a touch of the grotesque'.[54] R. Hammer (op. cit., p. 98) cites 1 Chron. 21.16 in that connection. It is true that this text does not say whether the angel seen by David was or was not winged. As such it is, however, an interesting text as it attributes to the angel 'a similar mediatorial role; he is the bearer of the divine message'.

The angel-interpreter from chapter 8[55] is here too named Gabriel. Chapter 9 presupposes at least vv.15–16 of chapter 8 which is a weighty argument in favour of a single Author for these two chapters. Moreover, Gabriel is here called 'the man' (האיש), that is not just the one who appeared in human form in 8.15–16 ('the one whom I had seen earlier in my vision'), but also the one who constitutes a transcendent link between Man and man, as we saw with regard to chapters 7 and 8.[56]

[52] Op. cit., p. 139.
[53] Against the versions.
[54] See also 1 Enoch 61.1. On the basis of Isa. 6 and Ezek. 1, we do not believe it is legitimate at the time of Daniel to make a radical distinction between cherubim and seraphim, on the one hand, and the angels, on the other (as, for example, Charles does, op. cit., p. 235).
[55] See 8.15–16.
[56] From the designation of Gabriel as a 'man', *Ber.* 4b draws the conclusion that he was inferior to the archangel Michael. What is more, Gabriel had to come in two bounds ('he flew in flying'), while Michael comes in one (Dan. 10.20).

We may retain from this the process of demythologization of the angel who is a 'man' in intentional opposition to his 'swift flight'. On the level of the vision he is an angel, on the level of encounter and dialogue, a man.

One of the most important contributions of the Book of Daniel is its novel insistence on the linking of faith to understanding, by which is meant the comprehension of the 'mysteries' (or: signs, sacraments) of God's work in history. This is why the Book of Daniel has so many points in common with Wisdom.[57] In both cases it is a question of comprehending a message addressed to all men. The only condition for having one's eyes opened is תשובה (repentance, expressed here by the prayer of confession). From the same perspective, Isa. 52.13, 15 speaks of obtaining understanding and the success which depends on it: ישכיל; התבונגו. Understanding is a communication, a gift, the fruit of the Encounter with God. Gabriel says, 'I am come out to you';[58] he brings Daniel something heavenly, an offer to participate in the mystery.

Prayers need not pile up words to be understood.[59] From the beginning of Daniel's supplications, he was hearkened to, says v.23. 'A word went out' is the expression of a commandment (see Isa. 7.8; 9.7; 55.11). God has ordered a response to Daniel's repentance; Jeremiah's oracle is about to be understood, Daniel's vision about to be clarified: 'Seventy weeks (of years)', this is the meaning of Jer. 29.10.[60]

Th. Chary has commented that v.24, even though it stands at the head of the angelic revelation, is really a conclusion with vv. 25–7 giving the details for the period under consideration. The eschatological blessings are described first, before the steps which lead to them are spoken of. One is reminded of Jer. 31.34c and Ezek. 36.25. A period of seventy sabbath years must occur.[61] We have discussed this notion at the beginning of this chapter and refer the reader to those comments. It is a clear example of the midrashic actualization of the Scriptures (a *pesher*). In the same vein, 1 Macc. 1.54; 1 Enoch 89.68—90.27; and Testament of Levi 16–17 make the text of Daniel 'contemporary': the calculation ends with the Hasmonean dynasty. The New Testament sees the announcement of the Kingdom of God inaugurated by Jesus (Matt. 25.15 = Mark 13.14; 2 Thess. 2.4). Josephus reads here the destruction of Jerusalem in 70 CE (see *Ant.* X, XI, 7; *B.J.* IV, V, 2). In so doing he is in agreement with the Rabbinic texts (see *Seder Olam*, ch. 30 = *A.Z.*

---

[57] We may say that with Daniel, Wisdom, which until then, only occupied itself with problems of a general order, undertook a synthesis of Deuteronomic and prophetic perspectives.

[58] Ibn Ezra: 'I came out of a group of angels, or out of a heavenly palace'.

[59] See Matt. 6.7.

[60] See our commentary on v.2; cf. Jub. 11.16; 12.15; 19.1, 7, 11, 12 . . . 1 Enoch 93.9, 10; 91.12; 4 Esdras 14.11; 2 Baruch 53.72; Ass. of Moses 10.12–13. O. Betz, *What do we Know about Jesus?* (London 1968), p. 47, insists on the fact that Jesus thought in an apocalyptic manner. Mark 9.1, for example, indicates that Jesus had an apocalyptic calendar and it may be that Dan. 9.24–7 is decisive here as in all of Judaism at that time.

[61] See 2 Chron. 36.21; Lev. 26.34, 35.

8b–9a). Jewish commentators during the Middle Ages closely followed their model: Rashi, Ibn Ezra, Ps. Saadia, Abarbanel. For the first two, the 'cut off messiah' in v.26 is King Agrippa. Patristic exegesis, in its calculations on Daniel 9, saw this happening in the second century CE. More objective, the pagan Porphyry sees a *vaticinium ex eventu* on the Maccabean period.

'For *your* people and *your* holy city' indicates the esteem in which the hero, the 'favoured man', is held. He represents the true Israel (cf. Bevan).

'The sinning' points to the desecration of the Temple by Antiochus as is evident from 8.12, 13, 23. The three terms פשע, חטאה, and עון are classic in Scripture for designating sin.[62] To this sombre trilogy correspond three positive elements: the bringing about of eternal justice, the 'seal on the vision and the prophet', and the anointing of a Holy of Holies.

The expression לכפר עון appears only here in Scripture (see our critical notes). We accept McNamara's simple explanation: 'appeasing God, offended by sin'.[63] Montgomery quotes S. R. Driver: 'When, as here, the reference is to sin, or iniquity, the mng. differs, acc. as the subj. is the priest or God; in the former case the mng. is to *cover* or *screen* the sinner by means (usually) of a propitiatory sacrifice, and it is then generally rendered *make atonement* or *reconciliation* for . . .; in the latter case it means *to treat as covered, to pardon* or *cancel.* . . .'[64]

Charles, who energetically militates against the Masoretic text on this point, and who proposes to replace כפר by מחה (see pp. 238, 241), has not seen the close relation between the jubilary division of time in Dan. 9 and the Great Day of Forgiveness *Yōm ha-kippurim*.[65] Indeed, on the tenth day of the seventh month, in the Jubilee Year, the horn resounds, proclaiming freedom to every Israelite in bondage and restoring to their lands those who had been forced to flee them. The Jubilee shows that no man has ultimate authority over another man. There is no doubt that an eschatological accent here has been taken up by Daniel.

We should probably see the following expression, 'eternal justice'—which has no parallel in Scripture—in the perspective indicated by Bevan: 'The words כפר and צדק are both *legal* terms, by the "atoning of sin" and the "bringing in of everlasting righteousness" is meant the termination of that controversy or suit (ריב) which God has with his people (see Isa. 27.9)'.[66] Note that we find עלמים quite frequently in 1

---

[62] See S. Lyonnet, *De Peccato et Redemptione* (Rome 1957), I, pp. 38–40 = *V. Dom.* 35 (1957), pp. 74–6.
[63] Op. cit., par. 536 h.   [64] Montgomery, p. 374.
[65] See Lev. 25.8ff.; 27.17ff.; Num. 36.4.   [66] Op. cit., ad loc., p. 154.

QS to designate the eternity of understanding or peace (2.3, 4), of the community or the people (2.23, 25; 13.9), of the covenant (4.22), of good will (4.3), etc. In 11 QPs[a], we find exactly the same terms as in Daniel.[67]

We passed over the expression 'end the sinning', or in the *Ketib*, 'seal the sinning', because it presents a vocabulary similar to 'seal the vision and prophet'.[68] The parallel to 8.23 indicates that we should probably prefer the *Qere* (used in our translation) and assume that there is some contamination of the first part of the verse from the second part. As for the seal on the vision and the prophet, the expression is unusual. One puts a seal on a document (see 1 Kings 21.8; Jer. 32.10, 11, 49; Dan. 6.17; 12.4, 9); yet we find a metaphorical use of this term in John 3.33; 6.27; 2 Cor. 1.22; Eph. 1.13; etc., where living beings are at issue: they are confirmed in their role or justified in their action.[69] History reaches its peak at the end. At that moment, both the 'vision' and the 'prophet' are sealed. There is no longer any hiatus between them, there is nothing more to add to or to subtract from the prophetic testimony. Daniel is conscious of ending prophecy in Israel once and for all and this gives his book a unique character which cannot fail to impress the reader.

Normally, the 'Holy of Holies' refers to a material object, altar, or Temple (see Exod. 29.36; 30.26ff.; 40.9; Ezek. 43.8, 9–12; 37.26–8). But in a late text, 1 Chron. 23.13, the expression should perhaps be interpreted in a personal sense: Aaron himself being referred to as the 'Holy of Holies'.[70] Such an interpretation is rejected by some;[71] it is, however, adopted by the Vulgate, Peshitta, and Hippolytus (see our critical notes). Annie Jaubert[72] is strongly attracted to it: '. . . nothing permits us to affirm that during the time of the Hassideans, the group of the faithful already considered itself as a sanctuary; a doctrine which was later to be held by the community at Qumran. However, it would be seductive to interpret the anointing promised to the Holy of Holies in

---

[67] See M. Delcor, 'L'hymne à Sion du rouleau des Psaumes de la grotte 11 de Qumrân', *RQ*, 21 (1967), pp. 84ff.

[68] See our critical notes.

[69] So Ibn Ezra and most commentators. But since the seal is a signature at the bottom of something, Jephet and Pseudo-Saadia retain the sense of to end or conclude for 'no prophet has arisen since the Second Temple'. We may find the same hesitation between לחתם and להתם (which justifies the interpretations of the last commentators cited) that we have seen concerning ולחתם חטאות in this same verse (see our critical notes).

[70] See F. Michaeli, op. cit., p. 119, n. 2: 'the expression *holy of holies* may not designate the most holy place in the sanctuary, but Aaron himself; he would be consecrated as holy of holies.'

[71] Th. Chary, op. cit., p. 272: 'We must understand the Temple for the "Holy of Holies" which receives an anointing. The expression *qodeš qodašim* never applies to human beings. The only possible exception, 1 Chr. 23.13, depends on an uncertain text (Göttsberger, *Chronik*, p. 86).' Cf. M. Delcor, p. 196; J. Montgomery, ad loc.; Charles, p. 242, E. Heaton, p. 213.

[72] Annie Jaubert, op. cit., p. 84.

the famous prophecy of the seventy weeks (9.24) in this sense. In that case, the expression "Holy of Holies" not only designates the restored Temple, but also the faithful priesthood around whom is gathered the community of Israel.'[73] J. de Menasce turns up his nose at any timidity on this point: 1 Chron. 23.13 concerns 'the priestly consecration of Aaron and his sons'.[74]

We believe J. de Menasce is correct. We see confirmation of this in the very structure of the text and in the identification constantly established by Daniel since chapter 7 between the Temple and the People. We saw the most recent instance of this in vv.20–1. It is again the doctrine from chapter 7 which is determinative. The Temple in Jerusalem was defiled by Antiochus, but the 'Adamic' Temple cannot be debased, once again understanding that there can be no dichotomy between the two aspects of a single reality. When the Temple in Jerusalem is purified—anointed by an ultimate anointing—the People-sanctuary will at the same instant be restored to its perfect priesthood.[75]

The structure of the text, we said, points in the same direction. The 'seventy weeks' are divided, in vv.25–7, into three parts. Each slice of history so distinguished ends with mention of an event concerning a 'messiah' (or 'anointed one'):

(1) v.25: '. . . until a messiah, there will be seven weeks'.
(2) v.26: 'after sixty-two weeks a messiah will be cut off'.
(3) v.24 (really the conclusion of this pericope): 'He has fixed seventy weeks . . . to make a Holy of Holies messiah.'

In chapter 9, as earlier in chapter 7, it is clear that the Author has a plainly priestly conception of history and eschatology. His 'messianic' expectation is centred on the person of the High Priest, who in v.25 is called the messiah-chief. This, says S. Mowinckel,[76] is the 'anointed-priest', the High Priest as in Lev. 4.3, 5, 16; 6.15.[77] J. Coppens[78] adds that the term 'prince' (= chief) serves to designate a high personage, and he cites Dan. 11.2; Neh. 11.11; 1 Chron. 9.11; and 2 Chron. 31.8. He sees here an exalting of the priesthood at the expense of the royal power. Therefore we rediscover the cautious, yet present, messianism

[73] The author continues by quoting 1 Chron. 23.13 and by concluding that from Chronicles to Qumran, the line runs through Daniel.
[74] J. de Menasce, op. cit., p. 71, n. e.
[75] 'It is necessary to emphasize', says A. Jaubert (p. 84), 'the deliberate comparison of the saints and the sanctuary in 1 Macc. 1.46, "the king wrote to defile the sanctuary and the saints". . . . "Your Name was invoked upon your city and your people", recalls the supplication in Daniel 9.19.'
[76] Op. cit., p. 6.
[77] And not 16.15 (sic). In Ecclus. 45.24, προστάτης designates the High Priest; cf. Josephus, Ant. XII, IV, 2; BJ IV, V, 2; 1 Macc. 13.42.
[78] NRTh, 90, pp. 35–6.

of the Author. His timidity is due to the deviation he brings to this notion: we pass from a hope for the Davidic line to a priestly type of eschatology. See our commentary on chapters 7 and 8.

'From the time a word went forth, etc.': it is a question of Jeremiah's oracle which stands at the centre of this chapter of Daniel. The beginning of the Exile, 587, is the point of departure for the calculation. 'Seven weeks' pass until the enthronement of Joshua (538; see our introduction to this chapter). But this is only one step toward the final light when the moment of להשיב ולבנות will come. This is a difficult expression. It cannot simply be translated by 'reconstruct' as in the Peshitta and Vulgate (see our critical notes), which presuppose an equivalence between the hiphil (להשיב) and the qal (לשוב). In fact, it is an elliptical construction deriving from the usage which became technical in the exilic prophets where it designates the return of the captives (see Jer. 12.15). The verb השיב is often followed by the substantive שבות which is in assonance with it. השיב את שבות is an expression rich in meaning. It is the return of the exiles to Zion and also the correspondence of the *Endzeit* to the *Urzeit*[79] (see Jer. 32.44; 33.7, 11, 26 (Qr.); 49.6, 39 (Qr.); Ezek. 39.25; Joel 4.1; Lam. 2.14). Daniel adopts the verb in the hiphil and leaves it without an object because its implication is immediately understood. A bit further on in the same verse, we have תשוב ונבנתה in parallel to its beginning. We should understand that it is a question here of the return of the exiles and the reconstruction of Jerusalem. Elsewhere, the prophets of the Exile also use the qal of this verb: שב את שבות (see Jer. 29.14; 30.3, 18; 31.23; 48.47; Ezek. 16.53; 29.14; etc.; cf. Deut. 30.3).

The second historical era is longer. It lasts 'sixty-two weeks' of years or 434 years, and runs from 605 (the date of Jeremiah's oracle, see 25.1, 11) to 171 which is spoken of in the next verse. These 434 years are characterized by the Author as a time of restoration.

But at the end of this period, a series of catastrophes strikes the city, the sanctuary, and its head (v.26). The text of this verse is almost impossible to understand, its style being so truncated. The reader is obliged to fill in the blanks left by the Author in his attempt to be allusive. It is clearly tempting to alter the text in order to make it more readable. A. Kamphausen, quoted by Montgomery (p. 377), warns us against such emendations: 'The more the difficulties in understanding an important passage of the Book of Daniel accumulate, the less we are permitted to make an attempt at overcoming them by mere alteration of the text. In such cases the text has been transmitted with special care.' The versions, in their fashion, confirm this judgement.

---

[79] Re this notion of the *Urzeit-Endzeit*, see our commentary on ch. 7.

The 'messiah' in question here, we saw above, is Onias III, assassinated on the urging of the usurper High Priest, Menelaus, in 171. His
death marks the beginning of the persecutions which lasted until 168.
Onias is 'cut off', a term used for persons in Gen. 9.11 and Lev. 7.20,
for example, where it technically refers to the death penalty. Regarding
the death of Onias, see Dan. 11.22; 2 Macc. 4.7ff.[80] The next words in
this verse seem to indicate the injustice of Menelaus' act, but ואין לו is
very obscure. We can think of quite a few different ways to complete this
hanging sentence.[81] Theodotion added κρῖμα: 'and there was nothing
left in him (as a matter) of judgement'. The Vulgate, according to
Jerome's commentary, had 'and the people who denied him will no
longer exist'. Montgomery, after Θ, has: 'there was nothing against
him'. The 'Jerusalem Bible' translates: 'but not for himself'. Jeffery
compares this passage to Ezek. 21.32, interpreting it as he was no longer
remembered—in our opinion, the least satisfactory solution for, on the
contrary, Onias III was afterwards idealized. The Peshitta imagines that
Jerusalem is the subject: 'she will have him no more'. McNamara (par.
536l, p. 669) rearranges the text: 'With some Heb. mss. we may suppress
the word, "and", join "the city" with the preceding, and read: "he shall
be cut down while he does not possess (i.e., is away from) the city"'.
Other complements have also been imagined: 'and he did not have any
possessions'; or 'no malignity' (ואין און לו as a dittography); or 'without
any heir'; etc. For our part, we establish a parallel with the phenomenon
seen above on the subject of the verb השיב which had to be completed as
השיב שבות following the expression from the exilic prophets. When they
addressed an elegy to the beloved city destroyed by the barbarians, they
used a stereotype phrase to sum up Zion's desperate situation
אין מנחם לה: 'she has none to console her' (see Lam. 1.2, 9, 16, 17, 21).
Similarly when Nahum wanted to show the total dereliction of Nineveh,
he asked: 'who then will have compassion on her? Where will I find
someone to comfort you?' Ecclesiastes, in the same vein, remarks bitterly,
twice in the same verse, that the oppressed 'have no one to comfort
them'.[82] If this solution is well founded as concerns Dan. 9.26, it

[80] According to J. Wellhausen, *Israel und jüd. Gesch.*, p. 235, and H. Willrich, *Juden und
Griechen* (1895), pp. 77ff., the official version of the facts cannot be reconciled with the
historical reality (cf. S. Zeitlin, *The History of the Second Jewish Commonwealth*
(1933), pp. 26ff.; J. Seeligmann, *The LXX Version of Isaiah*, pp. 91ff.). 2 Macc. would
have transferred to Onias the story of the tragic death of the son of Seleucus under
the blows of Andronicus (Diodorus XXX, 7.2). For V. Tcherikover, op. cit., p. 469,
n. 40, both stories may be authentic and 2 Macc. might have borrowed the details of
the murder of Onias from the report about the death of Seleucus' son. Onias was
subsequently idealized (see 2 Macc. 15.12ff.) and his tragic death had something to
do with it.

[81] Unless, with Rashi, we do equate ואין דו and ואיננו: 'and he was no more'; cf. LXX.

[82] We may also, on the model of Dan. 11.45, supply the term *'ozer*: 'without anyone

emphasizes once again the intimate association the Author establishes between the High Priest, the Holy City, the People, and the transcendent Destiny of Israel. This fact is further confirmed by the next part of the verse which immediately following the cut off 'messiah' speaks of the city and the Temple destroyed (by Antiochus IV). Now it is noteworthy that the destroyer should also be a נגיד, a chief, like the High Priest in v.25. For Daniel, Israel's oppressor usurps its dignity. This is why the persecutor's henchmen are called a עם, a people, just as Israel is a עם (cf. v.24).[83]

The ambiguity continues with the verb 'to destroy'. The profaning of the Temple or the 'cutting off' of the High Priest are a destruction even though, as Montgomery points out (ad loc.), the Greeks destroyed very little in Jerusalem. In 8.24–5, as well, the subject of the same verb is Antiochus.

'He will end up by being swept away': Montgomery objects that the Masoretic Text here anticipates Antiochus' end which will not be described until v.27. It is possible, he says, that the reference is to the end of the city and the sanctuary (if the pronoun in the masculine is made to refer to the prior antecedent).[84] Our reading based on a telescoping of the personal and impersonal in the description of the High Priest and his enemy allows us to avoid a subjective choice between such indissociable elements. The cataclysm, literally 'the inundation, the deluge', could signify the overflowing of the divine judgement (see Nah. 1.8), but we prefer G. von Rad's proposal[85] to see an allusion here to Isa. 10.22: 'destruction is decreed, sweeping [everything] away with righteousness'.[86] In this way the next part of the verse is also clarified—it is decidedly full of allusions to the prophetic message—'and up to the end of the war, devastations are decreed'. (See Isa. 10.23: 'for an extermination is decreed'. Daniel replaced the substantive כלה [extermination] by שממות for obvious reasons, the Author recalling by successive touches the theme שמם until finally he zeros in on it in his final verse by mentioning it twice thereby granting it the ultimate place in this chapter.)

The countdown until the end of time continues in v.27. Antiochus' impiety is brought to its paroxysm. Even the 'multitude' in Jerusalem[87] will be won over by the tyrant's demagogy. The Author uses the

---

coming to his aid' (see H. Graetz, 'Beiträge zur Sach- und Wörtererklärung des Buches Daniels', MGWJ, 20 (1871), pp. 339–52; 385–406; 433–49). The overall meaning stays the same.

[83] See our critical notes.   [84] Op. cit., p. 384.

[85] G. von Rad, Theology II, p. 314.

[86] Von Rad adds, 'for the very next verse to that (Is. X.23) is used in the same passage in Daniel . . .' (ibid.).

[87] Re this notion of a 'multitude', see our commentary on 8.25 where we point out its technical meaning as largely confirmed by Qumran (see, e.g., 1 QS 6.1, 8, 20–3).

positive term בְּרִית (covenant) in the same spirit that he says of Antiochus that he is a נָגִיד (chief) as the messiah-high priest is a נָגִיד.[88] Concerning the political support Antiochus found among some Jews, see 11.30, 32; 1 Macc. 1.10–15, 31, 45, 55; 2 Macc. 4.12ff. In 1 Macc. 1.11, 'the multitude' (of Hellenized Jews) decides to enter a 'covenant' with the neighbouring nations. They are the inconstant mass whose convictions are 'tossed to and fro and carried about by every wind of doctrine'.[89] R. H. Charles, however, recalls that the Hebrew in Daniel B is translated from Aramaic. At the basis of our expression one could see וקים יתקף playing on the double sense of קְיָם: covenant or statute, and in fact it is the second term of this alternative which is correct here: Antiochus will proclaim a harsh law against the multitude. Taking everything into consideration, our preference goes to this reconstruction of the primitive text[90] despite the support accorded the Masoretic Text by all the versions. We believe the Masoretic Text is here an erroneous, but not a corrupt, translation from the original Aramaic.

The ultimate goal of the persecutor's iniquitous statutes is attained when every sacrifice is prohibited (this is what 'sacrifice and offering' signifies, see Ps. 40.6).[91] In their place, Antiochus has installed an idol עַל כְּנַף. This expression is not clear. Theodotion translates it as the Temple, as do the LXX and the Vulgate. כְּנַף designates any projecting extremity. In the Gospels it is interpreted as the pinnacle of the Temple (see Matt. 4.5; Luke 4.9; also the versions A and Q of Theodotion for this verse). However, 1 Macc. 1.54 (cf. 2 Macc. 6.2) clarifies our passage: on the altar of burnt offerings at Jerusalem, Antiochus had constructed an altar or a sacred stone to Zeus Olympios. Josephus (Ant. XII, V, 4) adds: 'when the king had built an idol altar upon God's altar, he slew swine upon it'. Elias Bickermann[92] has pointed out that the installation of a new cultus presupposes the prior destruction of the altar (see Judg. 6.25; 2 Macc. 14.32). Here, however, the enterprise is even more insidious. Antiochus wants 'no doubt to mark the continuity of the cultus despite the apparent change in the divinity to whom it is addressed —the Most High God of the Jews (2 Macc. 3.31, 36) appeared to him to be identical with the Olympian Zeus (2 Macc. 6.2). In syncretistic conceptions, the latter is none other than the Syrian god Baal Shamin, "the master of the Heavens".'[93]

[88] See our commentary on v.26.   [89] Eph. 4.14 (R.S.V.).
[90] Our translation, as is evident, respects the MT as it has come down to us. It is also this text and no other which was commented on by Rashi, Ibn Ezra, Jephet, seeing in the covenant mentioned in this verse the treaty between the Jews and the Romans.
[91] From 15 Kislev (7 December) 167 to 25 Kislev (14 December) 164; see 1 Macc. 1.59; 4.52ff.
[92] Der Gott der Makkabäer (Berlin 1937), p. 105.
[93] M. Delcor, op. cit., p. 167.

We follow M. Delcor when he sees in כנף an equivalent of קרן and explains the necessary demolition of the 'horns' of the Jewish altar in order to install another 'abominable' stage on it (see Judith 9.8).[94] As for the replacement by the Author of a word as current as קרן by כנף, it seems to us that O. Eissfeldt has given us a plausible reason.[95] A god at Ugarit is called *B'l Knp*.[96] Jeffery adds that the Baal Shamin of the Syrians was generally represented on monuments in the form of an eagle.[97] In our opinion, therefore, the word 'wing' is a word play on both the corners of the altar to YHWH and the wings of the 'abominations'.

The next expression is another linguistic 'impossibility'. The first word is in the plural while its predicate is in the singular: שקוצים משמם. Thus many have sought to correct the text by 're-establishing' the singular שקוץ, seeing in the plural the mark of a dittography with the first letter of the following word. The versions seem to support this 'restoration'.[98] On the other hand, the word 'abomination' reappears in the same expression in 11.31 and 12.11, both times in the singular. The Masoretic editors resolved the problem by attaching שקוצים to the preceding word. Our translation (*of the MT*) takes account of this punctuation: 'on the wing of the abominations will be a destroyer'. This is an elegant solution, but with the disadvantage of cutting off an expression which appears here just as it does in 11.31 and 12.11. The versions were not fooled, not here or in 1 Macc. 1.54, 59 or Mark 13.14 (cf. Matt. 24.15). We believe the plural could be maintained if we see in our term a substitute for the single word in Hebrew which, even though it is in the plural governs a singular verb or predicate: *Elohim*. Antiochus' idol pretends to be the Jews' *Elohim*, but is only שקוצים. It pretends to represent the *El Elyon* of Israel and the *Ba'al Shamin* of Syria, but it is only משמם, frightening, destructive,[99] in the image of its author, Antiochus 'the devastator'.

---

[94] Ibid., p. 201.
[95] O. Eissfeldt, 'Die Flügelsonne als Kunstlerisches Motiv und als Religiöses Symbol', *Kleine Schriften* II (Tubingen 1963), pp. 416–19.
[96] Literally 'having wing(s), a winged being'. See C. Gordon, *Ugaritic Textbook* (Rome 1955), text 9, line 6.
[97] Jeffery, op. cit., ad loc.
[98] But it must be said that, no more than in a modern language, neither Greek nor Latin would allow such a grammatical monstrosity as we find in the MT.
[99] Thus the infamous בשת (shame) was substituted for Ba'al in Hos. 9.10; Jer. 3.24; 11.13; etc.

10–12 The Great Final Vision

Chapters 10—12 constitute a literary unit. They report the fourth and last vision in Daniel B, centred as in chapter 9 on a prophetic word, this time from Second Isaiah. Jerusalem's bondage is ended, the prophet announced; the restoration is imminent. Now 'there will be a great slavery' (Dan. 10.1) and it is only 'in the vision' that one may 'understand' it (ibid.). Therefore the Seer prepares himself for ecstasy and he has a revelation from the personage already encountered in the preceding chapters, the one whom Dan. 7.13 called 'son of man'. He is going to give the meaning of Scripture, but once again an angel-interpreter must intervene and bring about the visionary's understanding. Thus Gabriel stands alongside Daniel and the 'son of man' as the third personage in chapter 10. There is also a fourth one in the person of the archangel Michael whose battle against 'the principalities and powers'[1] is described beginning in 10.13.

Before the End—whose arrival is imminent—there will be great historic, cosmic, and heavenly overturnings and reversals. What happens on earth, with Israel at the centre of these events, is a replica of the war waged among the guardian angels of the peoples in the transcendent spheres. For each nation has a heavenly or angelic dimension, as does man, who is not exhausted by his visible material dimension.[2]

In other words, what the people of Israel experience during the dark years of the reign of Antiochus IV is not just a series of minor events of little importance. Heaven and earth are profoundly affected by them. What is ultimately at issue is the Kingdom (= reign, sovereignty) of God itself.

Chapter 10 is an introduction to chapter 11. The essential part begins in 11.2 with a detailed description of history ending in the period of Antiochus IV. The historical retrospective in Dan. 10 goes back to the days of the Persian Empire since the Seer is deemed to have lived in that time. This provides the opportunity for showing that the guardian angel of Israel has fought with the angels representing Persia and Greece in succession. One after another Israel's enemies are defeated by Michael. He 'neither slumbers nor sleeps'. He is on the battlefield and Israel may rest assured of his final victory which is announced in advance by the very events which have brought the people to this point. It is also inscribed in 'the book of truth' (v.21) which is in God's hands. 'What

[1] Eph. 6.12.
[2] See our commentary on ch. 7.

will happen to your people in the last days' (v.14) is written down there. We have already encountered this book of destinies (see 7.10) and we will meet it again in 12.1. The most terrible historical events cannot take God or his servants by surprise; even catastrophe only helps to realize God's plan.

Given this perspective, no chronological framework could be more appropriate than the one furnished in v.1: 'In the third year of Cyrus, king of Persia'.[3] This is the time of redemption, of *ge'ulah* (see Isa. 41.14; 43.1, 14; 44.6, 22–4; etc.); the time of the ultimate Exodus (see Isa. 40.3ff.). The 'great slavery' (Dan. 10.1) of Jerusalem is ended (see Isa. 40.2). H. L. Ginsberg[4] has shown that chapters 10—12 of Daniel are a complete midrash of Isaiah. We will return to this point in regard to chapter 11. Other prophetic books have also added their influence, above all Ezekiel (cf. vv.4–10 and Ezek. 1 and 10); Habakkuk (cf. v.14 and Hab. 2.3; also Dan. 8.26); and Joshua (cf. v.19 and Josh. 1.6–7; cf. also Deut. 31.7, 23).

Within the literary unit constituted by chapters 10—12, it is useful to distinguish:

(a) the prologue: Dan. 10.1—11.2a;
(b) the revelation: Dan. 11.2b—12.4;
(c) the epilogue: Dan. 12.5–13.

It is clear that chapters 10—12 were written after chapter 9 (see 11.1, corresponding to the interval of three years between 9.1 and 10.1; the angel-interpreter identified with Gabriel on the basis of 9.21). What is more, there are many different points of contact with Daniel 8 as well (cf. 10.9 and 8.18; 12.4 and 8.26; etc.).[5]

Text 10. 1–14

(1) In the third year of Cyrus, king of Persia, a word was revealed to Daniel, who was called Belteshazzar. This word is true: there will be a great slavery. As for the understanding of this word, it is in the apparition. (2) In those days, I, Daniel, was in mourning for three weeks: (3) I ate no delicacies, no meat or wine entered my mouth, and I did not perfume myself until the end of the three weeks. (4) The twenty-fourth day of the first month, I found myself on the bank of the great river, the Tigris. (5) I lifted up my eyes and looked, and behold there was a man clothed in linen; there was a belt of gold from Uphaz around his loins. (6) His body was like chrysolite, his face like

---

[3] Or, according to the LXX, 'in the first year', that is the year of the decree by Cyrus liberating the peoples in Exile.
[4] 'The Oldest Interpretation of the Suffering Servant', *VT*, 3:4 (1953), pp. 400–4; 'Daniel' (additions) in *Encyclopaedia Biblica* (in Heb.), vol. 2, cols. 949–52.
[5] See *infra*, our commentary.

the appearance of lightning, his eyes like flaming torches, his arms and legs like the sparkle of burnished brass, and the sound of his words like the sound of a multitude. (7) I, Daniel, I alone saw the apparition; the men who were with me did not see the apparition, but a great terror fell upon them and they fled to hide themselves. (8) I remained alone and saw this great apparition. No strength remained in me; my fine appearance was upset and fell apart and I retained no strength. (9) I heard the sound of his words and when I heard the sound of his words, I fell in lethargy on my face, face to the ground. (10) But behold a hand touched me; it set me, trembling, on my knees and the palms of my hands. (11) He said to me: 'Daniel, favoured man, understand the words I am saying to you and stand fast at your post, for now am I sent to you'. While he was speaking this word to me, I stood up trembling. (12) He said to me: 'Fear not, Daniel, for since the first day when you have had a heart to understand and to humiliate yourself before your God, your words have been heard, and it is because of your words that I have come. (13) The prince of the kingdom of Persia opposed me for twenty-one days, but behold Michael, one of the chief princes, came to my aid, and I remain there near the kings of Persia. (14) I am come to make you know what will happen to your people in the last days; "for there is still a vision for those days".'

Critical Notes 10. 1–14

V.1 LXX: 'the first year'; see Dan. 1.21.—הדבר: LXX: 'the vision and the word'.—צבא: the versions have: δύναμις, *fortitudo*, etc.

V.3 Ms. Taylor-Schechter has the variation: וסוך לא סחתי (*sic*); see P. Kahle, op. cit., p. 73; for H. L. Ginsberg, the Aramaic model was probably ומשח לא משחת (see the parallels in Deut. 28.40 and Mic. 6.15) which in Heb. would be rather: עד מלאת.—ושמן לא סכתי: see Jer. 29.

V.4 הוא חדקל: Pesh.: Euphrates.

V.5 אופז: in general, the versions understood this term as a place name. It is also found in Jer. 10.9. But the LXX has the impossible text: ἐκ μέσου αὐτοῦ φάς. The Pesh.: 'in honour of the praise'. It has also been proposed, on the basis of Song of Sol. 5.11, where the word designates pure gold, to read ופז here (Montgomery). Another emendation: אופיר (see Gen. 10.29).

V.6 כתרשיש: paraphrased by Pesh.: 'his appearance was different and there is nothing like him'.—מרגלותיו: only here and in Ruth 3.4ff.—קלל: the meaning is not certain. It is found again in Ezek. 1.7. Vss.: 'shining'; Rev. 1.15: 'purified by fire'.—המון: a deep sound. It recapitulates the terms in Ezek. 1.24. Cf. Isa. 13.4; 33.3.

V.7 בהחבא: LXX: ἐν σπουδῇ; Θ: ἐν φόβῳ.

V.8 ולא נשאר בי כח: see 1 Sam. 28.20.—עצרתי כח: see 10.16; 11.6; 1 Chron. 29.14; 2 Chron. 2.5; 13.20; 22.9.

V.9 וכשמעי את־קול־דבריו: should be omitted according to the Kennicott and Rossi variations; the same for LXX and Pesh.—ואני הייתי: Θ, Pesh., Vul. omit ואני.—ופני: not found in 8.18.

V.10 ותניעני: Θ and LXX: ותעירני (ἤγειρέ με), as in 11.25. 6 Q Dan has להניעני (cf. *Discoveries* . . ., III, pp. 114–16). See the parallel of Ezek. 1.28; 2.1.—כפות ידי: *del.* in Θ.

V.12 נתת את לבך: a late expression found only in Eccles. and Chron. Contrast with 1.8. LXX: ἔδωκας τὸ πρόσωπόν σου διανοθῆναι (cf. Dan. 9.3, 10.15).

V.13 מיכאל: see 10.21; 12.1. M. Delcor (op. cit., p. 46) suggests that this name is perhaps a different vocalization and slight consonantal modification of *MKL*, a Canaanite divinity from a stele at Beth-Shean of the 15th century BCE, as well as some late syllabic Phoenician inscriptions on Cyprus where *MKL* is associated with Resheph. For E. Lipinski, on the contrary, the angel 'Michael' has nothing to do with Resheph of Cyprus (Personal communication).—ואני נותרתי: LXX and Θ = והותרתיו. It has to be noted that in the following verse Daniel's interlocutor comes toward him, which means that he did not remain near the kings of Persia (see F. Michaeli in the *Pléiade Bible*, ad loc.). H. L. Ginsberg, op. cit., pp. 60–1, thinks there was some confusion in the translation to Hebrew from Aramaic: ודנה אשתאר or אותותר, which are third person forms, but easily mistaken for first person forms in Hebrew. Other critics see no need for a correction. Rashi comments: 'to reduce the Persian prince to silence'. The 'metsudath David': 'I remained alone' (until Michael came to console me). Ehrlich: 'I was superfluous' (after Michael arrived). Bevan (p. 168): 'whereas I had been left (alone) there (contending) with the kings of Persia'. For us, the meaning is: '(thus) I was delayed', completed by the following verse: 'but (now) I have come . . .' (see Pesh.).—אצל מלכי פרס: LXX and Θ: 'near the *prince* of the kings of Persia'.

V.14 להבינך: see 8.16; 9.22, 23.

Commentary

With v.1 we are in 'the third year of Cyrus, king of Persia',[6] that is, about 536–535. The title 'king of Persia' is common to all the Achaemenids; but as concerns Cyrus, the documents give him the title only *before* his conquest of Babylon and *at the end* of the Persian period or beginning of the Greek period—for example, the Book of Ezra. Earlier he is the 'king

---

[6] Rashi comments: 'In the third year that Daniel was favoured at Cyrus' court'.

of Babylon' (see the ancient document quoted in Ezra 5.13). Most often one finds 'the (great) king', 'the king of kings', 'the king of nations', etc.[7] So it is during the reign of this king, the conqueror of Babylon and 'messiah' according to Isa. 45.1, that the word is נגלה, revealed to Daniel. The use of this verb with its rich meaning in Second Isaiah (see 40.5; 53.1; 56.1 and also 47.2; 57.8) is well known. The midrash on Isaiah begins with this verse.[8] According to a tendency much affirmed in the Book of Daniel, the term 'word' becomes almost synonymous with 'mystery' and גלה with the revelation of mystery. Since 9.2 דבר designated the Word of God to Jeremiah, it is tempting to see in the דבר in Dan. 10.1 reference to another prophecy, in this case Isa. 40. Dan. 10 is going to show us on what 'true' basis the prophet could have announced the end of Jerusalem's 'great slavery'. Indeed, we understand the terms וצבא גדול as a succinct and allusive résumé of Isa. 40.2.[9] As in chapter 9, the Author here too bends over the prophetic 'books' and, at first, does not know how to understand Isaiah's oracle about the end of Jerusalem's tribulation. Again, as in chapter 9, illumination is given Daniel by an angel-interpreter following a suitable spiritual preparation (vv.16ff.). In Dan. 9, however, the prayer of confession took the place of the vision; in chapter 10 the normal sequence is re-established: before the interpretation Daniel receives a vision.

The parallelism with the preceding chapter becomes clearer at the end of the verse. It repeats almost *verbatim* 9.23b where it was a question of an angelic command: 'Understand the word and comprehend the apparition.' What is more, the Author does not bother to place the verbs from 9.23 which he quotes in 10.1 in a form suitable to their new context. The translator can only lightly paraphrase them or put the cut off citation in quotation marks. So it is chapter 9 which serves as the Author's rough draft. Let us signal here that this kinship between the two visions will permit us to identify the personage in vv.16ff. with Gabriel.

Let us also signal some other ties to the preceding chapter: the mention of Daniel's Persian name recalls 1.7; 2.26; 4.5, 6, 15, 16; 5.12. As in chapter 8, the Seer finds himself on the bank of a river (although here it is his actual location), see v.4. The LXX[10] has the text 'in the first year of Cyrus, etc.' which closely recalls Dan. 1.21. The polarity word/vision

[7] See also S. R. Driver, *An Introduction to the Literature of the Old Testament*, p. 546.
[8] See the introduction to this chapter.
[9] See also Job 7.1; 14.14. Not having seen this, Bevan believes there is an allusion to a 'charge' or 'obligation laid upon Daniel' (cf. O. Plöger; Havernick: 'die Anstrengung' of the prophet Daniel). The Jewish commentators in the Middle Ages and the Protestants during the Reformation understood that it would be a long time before the end (Rashi, Redaq, Calvin).
[10] See our critical notes.

204

is in parallel with 9.23 as we saw above.[11] Even the use of the third person singular when Daniel speaks has its antecedent in 7.1. The 'truth' was mentioned in 8.26. And v.2 takes up again a motif from chapter 9: mortification preparatory to a vision. The 'sackcloth and ashes' of 9.3 are replaced here by the single word מתאבל (I was in mourning). See also v.12 (cf. 4 Esdras 5.13). This preparation lasts 'three weeks of days'; manifestly the Author added the term 'days' to prevent confusion with the 'week (of years)' from chapter 9. Similar expressions may be found in Gen. 41.1 ('two years of days'); Deut. 21.13 ('a month of days'); etc. Note that the traditional three days for sanctification (see Exod. 19.10–15; Ezra 4.16) are here expanded to three weeks. The rite, as in chapter 9, is particularly fitted for the Day of Atonement.[12] Daniel therefore eats no 'delicacies' (v.3).[13] In the original Hebrew the same term is only used again v.11 to designate Daniel, the 'favoured (man)'. Such food stands in contrast to that proper to Passover, as in Deut. 16.3 (לחם עני). As in chapter 1, Daniel consumes neither meat nor wine. He does not anoint himself with oil (see 2 Sam. 14.2; Isa. 61.3; Matt. 6.17; Judith 10.3). The delay of three weeks is mentioned again—it symbolizes the expectation of God's intervention to end tribulation (see v.12 and 11.1 read as 'since the first year of Darius', see ad loc.).

The 'Great River' in question in v.4, and from whose bank the Seer witnesses the vision as in chapter 8, is here specifically the Tigris. Everywhere else it designates the Euphrates (see Gen. 15.18; Josh. 1.4) next to which stood Babylon. The Tigris is just mentioned once elsewhere in the Bible, in Gen. 2.14. It may be that this unusual identification is an ancient gloss (from even before Theodotion!). Since the finale in 12.5–13[14] corresponds to the introit in chapter 10, the Tigris must also be understood to be in question there.

As in Ezekiel's call, the geographical and chronological framework is indicated first. It is surprising to learn that Daniel's fast continues until 24 Nisan,[15] that is, despite the rules of the Torah,[16] through a period which includes the feast of Passover.[17] Perhaps this is an allusion to the interdiction against celebrating this feast imposed by Antiochus: the pious man then resolved to fast and mortify himself instead.[18]

---

[11] On the subject of this polarity, let us quote what Montgomery says (p. 405): 'The word is impotent until divine grace unfolds the mystery'.
[12] See our commentary on ch. 9.
[13] This verse is utilized by Test. of Reuben 1.10.
[14] See O. Plöger, op. cit., p. 144.   [15] See Neh. 2.1; Ezra 3.7.
[16] This is why Ibn Ezra thought it was a question of the first month of the third year of the reign of Cyrus.
[17] Between the fifteenth and the twenty-first day of the month; see Deut. 16.3 which speaks of 'the bread of affliction' which we have contrasted to 'the bread of delicacies' in Dan. 10.3.
[18] See infra, our commentary on v.12.

One generally sees Gabriel in the personage in vv.5ff.[19] This is a mistake, however. The angel Gabriel does not appear until v.16. Here, the description of this second *dramatis persona* 'seems to transcend that given of Gabriel in the earlier chapters . . . (One is reminded) of some supernatural being superior to Gabriel and Michael and carefully distinguished by the writer from them' (Jeffery, p. 502). At an earlier date, Charles, too, had written: 'He is not to be identified with Gabriel.' One of the reasons advanced by this scholar is weighty: in 9.21 Daniel is not affected by Gabriel's appearance.[20] Here on the contrary, the Seer must be revived three times: 10.8, 9, 10, 15, 18, 19. J. de Menasce[21] is on the right path when he comments regarding the linen and gold: 'These two features are also found in the description of the Son of Man, Rev. 1.14–15 and 2.18; and cf. Ezek. 1.4 and 13.' The linen robe is a priestly vestment (Lev. 16.4, 23; 1 Sam. 2.18; Ezek. 9.2, 3, 11; 10.2, 6, 7).[22] The one wearing it here is called אִישׁ־אֶחָד with the same ambiguity as in 7.13. Yet it was this 'particular man' who was described in terms parallel to those which Ezek. 1 uses for the divine majesty. Regarding this astonishing association, we refer the reader to our commentary on chapter 7.[23]

The theophany-like description in v.6 is largely inspired by Ezek. 1 and 9 (see 1.7, 13, 14, 24, 28; 9.2, 3, 8, 11). Similar elements, originating from common sources, may be found in 2 Enoch 1.5; Rev. 1.14; and 19.12. In all these texts, there is a recall of the *Urtheophanie* at Sinai (Exod. 20.18). We might also think of Gen. 15.17 (Abraham's vision).

The word גְּוִיָּה used here is parallel to the term בָּשָׂר, flesh. Normally, however גְּוִיָּה designates a cadaver (see Judg. 14.8–9; 1 Sam. 31.10, 12; Nah. 3.3). In Ezek. 1.11 and 23 it refers to the bodies of transcendent beings.

The stone תַּרְשִׁישׁ (topaz or chrysolite) is so called from the name of the city from which the stone was exported, Tartessos in Spain. It is also mentioned in Ezek. 1.16, 24.

The consideration of some of the body's members is an anthropologic scheme well known in Scripture (see Ezek. 1; Ps. 94.9–11; 102.20–1;

[19] See A. Bentzen, N. Porteous, H. L. Ginsberg, etc.
[20] We would also add that in 10.16 Daniel is also not affected physically by Gabriel's intervention.
[21] Op. cit., p. 74, n.e.
[22] Here as in Dan. 12.6, 7 the LXX translates this as βύσσινα; by so doing, it brings the texts in Daniel into relation with the description given in 1 Chron. 15.27 of David's priestly garments at the time of the transference of the Ark to Jerusalem. This parallel should require our full attention.
[23] 'The man' in Dan. 10.5 has been compared to the anonymous angel in the Testaments of the XII Patriarchs (see Test. of Dan 6.1, 5; Test. of Benj. 6.1; Test. of Asher 6.6; Test. of Levi 5.6. He is the angel of peace, an intercessor, mediator, and source of consolation, and he fights for Israel). In fact, we believe it is a question of the angel Michael and the comparison is thus well founded.

135.16–17; Prov. 26.7–9; etc.). The זרעות (arms) are also found in 11.6a, 6b, 15, 22, 31.

In chapter 5, the Author had contrasted one man, the only one capable of reading the inscription on the wall, to a crowd of distinguished but foolish people. Here again, the Seer is alone although surrounded by people (vv.7–8).[24] This does not prevent the occurrence of a general feeling that something is happening that results in collective fear and trembling. Finally, everyone flees (cf. Dan. 5.6, 9; the texts in the Book of Acts mentioned above; Wisd. 17.14—18.4). Daniel sees what everyone should see.[25] It is not a question of an ecstatic vision (חזון), but an apparition (מראה). This latter term designates either a *phenomenon* (with דמות and תואר, see 1.15; 8.15; 10.6, 18), or an auditory manifestation (see 8.26 which refers to the conversation in vv.13–14 which precede it and not to the vision of the ram and the he-goat in vv.2–12; cf. 10.16).[26]

The vocabulary in v.8b is a problem. הוד, according to Montgomery, is 'the natural beauty of a living thing, its appropriate strength and grace'.[27] Prov. 5.9 may even lead us to think that it is sometimes a question of a man's virility.[28] On the other hand, נהפך is the Hebrew translation of the Aramaic ישתנון as we find it, for example, in 7.28 where the complete expression is וזיוי ישתנון. For H. L. Ginsberg,[29] v.8b is a bad translation of זיו which signifies 'splendour' and 'appearance'. The second term of the alternative, not the first, ought to have been chosen. In this way a perfect parallel with Dan. 7, which, as we signalled above, is determinative for understanding Dan. 10, is re-established.[30] Another direct influence, we have said (following H. L. Ginsberg), comes from Second Isaiah. The term משחת (translated 'fell apart') is drawn from Isa. 52.14 where it is a question of the appearance of the Servant of the Lord.

---

[24] Similarly, Elisha alone sees the armies of the Lord come to help Israel (2 Kings 6.14–17; cf. vv.18–20); Paul is the only beneficiary of the vision on the road to Damascus (Acts 6.7; 22.9; 26.13–14).

[25] See John 1.9, the light 'enlightens every man'.

[26] *Sanh.* 94a draws the conclusion from this that Daniel was both inferior and superior to a prophet. He was inferior to Haggai, Zechariah, and Malachi for 'they were prophets and he was not one. But he was their superior in that he saw the vision which they did not see'. Maimonides, too, argues from this text in Daniel that the prophetic vision is 'a state of agitation and terror which seizes the prophet while awake'. Three terms are used for this effect in Scripture: מראה (as here), יד־יהוה (see Ezek. 37.1), and מחזה (see Gen. 15.1; Num. 24.4, 16). The only other way to have a revelation is through the intermediary of an angel in a prophetic vision (see Num. 12.6) (*Guide for the Perplexed*, II, 41).

[27] Ad loc.

[28] See Prov. 5.9 in LXX Lucianus.

[29] *Studies . . .*, p. 41.

[30] See also Dan. 2.1; 5.6, 9.

V.9 recalls 8.18. It has the same unusual verb we discussed at that point in chapter 8.[31]

In regard to v.10, we once again[32] have the label 'grotesque' applied to an image in Daniel by a scholar.[33] We are not convinced, however, that one should lop off this feature, if only because it is not absent from the Jewish (or Christian) mystical tradition. One Hassidic story tells how Rabbi Sussya saw his petition to experience the fear of God granted in a dramatic manner: he threw himself under his bed and 'barked like a little dog'.[34]

But Daniel's animal posture—corresponding to the first section of chapter 7 with its four animals superseded by a Man—does not last. 'The man clothed in linen' gives him back his human dignity (v.11) and stands him back on his feet.[35] It is not a picturesque feature therefore when Daniel is called the 'favoured man' as in v.19 (cf. 9.23).[36] The word 'man' (איש) is at least as important as the other. It binds Daniel to the 'son of man' who is speaking to him.

The linguistic parallel to 8.17–18 continues, but the problematic is that of chapter 9. As is the case there, the response to the prayer has been delayed, although, again as in chapter 9, the prayer has been heard from the beginning of Daniel's mortifications, v.12. 'Now' the Man has been sent to Daniel, and this 'now' has the resonance of 'finally' as in 9.22 or in Josh. 5.14. Daniel's interlocutor says to him: 'Fear not', an exhortation also found in v.19 and throughout Scripture (see Gen. 15.1; 21.17; 26.24; etc.; cf. Ezek. 2.6; 3.9). It is a *formula revelationis*[37] which introduces a salvation oracle. More specifically, it is the priestly response to an individual lamentation; for example, Hannah's prayer of humiliation which the priest Eli responds to with a formula for peace. Lam. 3.57 demonstrates the technical value of this formula.

[31] Recall that H. L. Ginsberg sees an Aramaic verb (דמך) correctly translated in 8.17 by redactor, but incorrectly translated by another redactor in 8.18 and 10.9. We have not accepted his arguments, emphasizing instead the parallel with Test. of Reuben 2.3—3.1.

[32] See Porteous *ad* 9.21.

[33] Charles, op. cit., p. 261. On the contrary, in the reuse of Dan. 10.10 in 4 Esdras 5.14–15, this 'grotesque' element is absent. The scene is a repetition of Dan. 8.17–18.

[34] See M. Buber, *Die chassidischen Bücher* (Hellerau 1928), p. 439.

[35] It will be recalled that for L. Köhler, for example, man as 'the image of God' signifies that he stands upright on his feet, not on 'four paws', like the higher animals (see *ThZ* (1948), pp. 17ff.). Cf. Ovid, *Metamorphoses* 1.85: '. . . et erectos ad sidera tollere vultus'. As Mircea Eliade puts it (personal communication), the 'uprightness' of man, standing on his two feet, freed his hands for the act of prehension and, most importantly, turned his eyes from the ground toward the sky.

The imagery and message of Dan. 10.11 are already found in Ezek. 2.1 where, moreover, the prophet is called 'son of man' by God.

[36] In the N.T. the title is accorded to Mary (Luke 1.28: κεχαριτωμένη) and to the shepherds at Christmas (ἄνθρωποι εὐδοκίας), Luke 1.30; 2.14.

[37] See L. K. Schweitz, *ThZ* (1919), pp. 33–9.

We are therefore, here as in each instance where it is a question of the 'son of man', in a cultic framework.[38] This fact is confirmed by the presence of another technical term in this verse: להתענות. Humiliation, or mortification, says Montgomery (p. 411), is 'parallel to the phrase "afflict the soul (self)" in the regulations for the Day of Atonement, Lev. 16.29, etc., cf. Ps. 35.13'.[39] Daniel, in the light of the harsh times and the interdiction against celebrating Passover, has, in a way, transformed Pesaḥ into Yom Kippur, for even though one may prevent a population from eating foodstuffs, one cannot keep them from fasting![40]

So Daniel learns that his prayer has been heard since its commencement (cf. 9.21–3), but the message has taken twenty-one days to get to him because 'the (angelic) Prince of the Kingdom of Persia opposed' the 'son of man' (v.13) and was defeated thanks only to the intervention of Michael,[41] who is thus introduced as a fourth *dramatis persona* in Dan. 10.

V.14b depends on Hab. 2.2–3. The key word is *yamim* (days) which appears twice in this verse. Its association with חזון (vision) indicates, says H. L. Ginsberg,[42] that חזון has the sense of 'events which are to arrive during the term' (of the ימים). This misunderstanding in relation to Hab. 2.2–3 is based on the absence of an article before חזון and on the Masoretic reading עוד (still) instead of עד (testimony) which Ginsberg thinks must have been the original lesson.[43] We have placed this expression in quotation marks in our translation because it is a citation from Habakkuk whose meaning the 'son of man' is going to interpret along with the oracle from Deutero-Isaiah. Daniel is to be the beneficiary of the vision before 'those days' promised by the prophet Habakkuk. It begins in v.16 with the apparition of the angel-interpreter (Gabriel) and continues until the end of the Book of Daniel. Daniel takes up the favourite prophetic expression באחרית הימים[44] to designate those

---

[38] For S. Mowinckel, as is well known, the whole of Israelite eschatology is born in the framework of the cultus and, more specifically, of the cultic proclamation of God as King.

[39] See Ezra 8.21; 9.5.

[40] See *supra*, our commentary on v.4.

[41] In retrospect it is quite clear that we ought not to see Gabriel in Daniel's interlocutor, but rather the representative of Israel as in ch. 7. At the same time, Michael is distinct from the 'son of man' and the personification of his glorious dimension.

Angelic intercession on behalf of human beings can be found in 1 Enoch 9; 15.2; 89.76; 40.6; 47.2; 99.3, 16; 104.1; cf. Job 5.1; 33.23; Zech. 1.12. Cf. Tobit 12.12, 15; Test. of Levi 3.5; 5.6, 7; Rev. 8.3.

[42] *Studies . . .*, pp. 35–6.

[43] Re the Midrashic use of Hab. 2.2–3 in Daniel, see Dan. 8.17b, 26b; 10.14b (cf. 14a); 11.27b, 35b.

[44] See Isa. 2.2; Jer. 23.20; 30.24; 48.47; 49.39; Ezek. 38.16; Hos. 3.5; Mic. 4.1; cf. Num. 24.14; Deut. 4.30; 31.29. In Daniel this expression is in Aramaic in 2.28. However אחרית is used in construction with other substantives in Dan. 8.19, 23; 12.8. At Qumran, באחרית הימים appears quite frequently.

days. Its scriptural origin goes back to Gen. 49.1, the preamble to Jacob's blessings.[45]

Text 10. 15–21

(15) While he was speaking to me in these terms, I turned my face toward the ground and kept silent. (16) But someone having the likeness of the sons of men touched my lips; I opened my mouth and began to speak. I said to the one standing in front of me: 'My lord, because of the apparition, anxiety has seized me and I have no strength left. (17) How could this servant of my lord speak to my lord here when there is no strength and no breath left in me?' (18) Then, the one who had the appearance of a man touched me again and strengthened me. (19) Then he said to me: 'Fear not, favoured man! Peace be with you, be strong, yea, be strong!' And as he was speaking to me I regained my strength and I said: 'Let my lord speak, for you have strengthened me.' (20) He said: 'Do you know why I have come to you? Now I am about to take up again the war against the Prince of Persia and when I am gone, behold the Prince of Greece is coming. (21) But I will announce to you what is written in the Book of Truth. No one holds with me against these, except Michael, your Prince.'[46]

Critical Notes 10. 16–20

V.16 לנגדי: Ms. Taylor-Schechter: כנגדי (influence of Gen. 2.18?).—
לא עצותי כח.—בן אדם: LXX=אדם יַד כדמות *Θ*, Vul.=אדם.—כדמות בני אדם
see note to 10.8—צירים: the suffering of childbirth (see 1 Sam. 4.19; Isa. 13.8); used metaphorically: Isa. 21.3, here too after a frightening vision.

V.17 היך: only here and in 1 Chron. 13.12 (influenced by Palestinian Aramaic. Charles refers to Targ. Gen. 3.9; Job 21.34.)—אֲדֹנִי זֶה:
the two words are separated by disjunctive accents. In the second instance, on the contrary, they are intimately linked together: עִם־אֲדֹנִי זֶה. This is why Charles translates: 'how can so mean a servant of my lord talk with so great a one as my lord?'—מעתה:
LXX has read מעדתי ('I walk', see Ps. 18.37; 26.1). *Del.* in Pesh.; Vul. and 'Metsudath David' retain the habitual meaning, i.e., after having seen the angel in human form. Ehrlich gives the

[45] Here is Rashi's paraphrase: 'to tell you what you have not been told and what is yet to come during the many days which are given for the fixed time'.

[46] Or, following the order of elements of the text which has been suggested by several scholars:
20a He said to me: 'Do you know why I have come to you?
21a I will announce to you what is written in the Book of Truth.
20b Now I am about to take up again the war against the Prince of Persia and when I am gone, behold the Prince of Greece will come.
21b No one helps me against these ones, except Michael, your Prince.'

word a sense it often has in the Talmud: 'in these circumstances, hence' (adopted by Montgomery).

V.18 ויחזקתי: see Jeffery, ad loc.: the verb is used to speak of physical strength: Ps. 147.13; Ezek. 30.24; 34.4; Hos. 7.15; and of a moral or spiritual strength: Deut. 1.38; 3.28; 2 Sam. 11.25; Isa. 41.7.

V.19 חזק וחזק: many mss., LXX, Θ, Vul., and Pesh. have חזק ואמץ, as in Deut. 31.7, 23; Josh. 1.6–7; and also the epistolary formulas of the Greek Bible, see 2 Macc. 11.21; Acts 15.29. We note, however, that the corresponding Aramaic for חזק would be גבר on the basis of the name 'Gabriel'; see our commentary on Dan. 9.21.

V.20 כתב: Aramaism, see 5.7, 8, 15; 6.9, 10, 11, etc.—התחזק עמי: see 1 Chron. 11.10; 2 Chron. 16.9.

Commentary

V.15 serves as a transition to the second part of chapter 10. At the announcement of the vision preparatory to the end of time, Daniel is overcome by a feeling of incapacity and unworthiness. He prostrates himself on the ground[47] and loses his voice (cf. Exod. 3.26; 24.27). Only the angel's intervention, in v.16, allows him to see and hear the great final revelation. As was the case with the prophet Isaiah in the Temple, who knew himself to be impure and unworthy of God's favour, the angel touches Daniel's lips.[48] The new personage is someone 'having the likeness of the sons of men'. He is plainly distinguished from Daniel's preceding interlocutor. He does not upset the Visionary as does the 'son of man' in vv.5ff. On the contrary, his presence is reassuring. Daniel was 'seized with anxiety *because of the vision*' which was at issue in the preceding verses (see vv.6, 7a, 7b, 8). Moreover, vv.16–17 are an amplification of v.8 from which they borrow part of their vocabulary. Here, as everywhere else when Daniel described an apocalyptic vision, Ezekiel serves as the source of inspiration (see Ezek. 1.5, 10; 8.2; 10.1).

The last part of the verse is a repetition of v.8 (see *supra*). This is a way of emphasizing the Author's insignificance, as in **verse 17** as well. We should understand מעתה (translated: 'when') in the context indicated above: the announcement of the final vision takes Daniel's breath away.[49] There is no need therefore to give any unusual meaning to the expression מעתה (see our critical notes).

Once more in v.18, Daniel uses the term מראה (appearance, vision). It is the sixth time in this chapter. It was also a מראה־גבר which Daniel saw in 8.15, and we invite the reader to reconsider our comments on that

[47] With de Menasce and against most of the Anglo-American translators.
[48] See Isa. 6.7; Jer. 1.9; cf. Dan. 10.10, 18.
[49] See Josh. 2.11; 1 Kings 10.5.

verse. The Author even draws upon the Archangel Gabriel's name ('man of God') to describe him as having a human appearance.

We insisted above (see v.12) on the cultic import of the expression 'fear not' which we find again in v.19. This *formula revelationis*, we said, introduces the oracle of salvation which a priest pronounces in response to an individual lamentation. So the angel Gabriel, too, has a priestly function as does the 'son of man' in v.5ff. Even Daniel is a איש[50] like the 'son of man' and Gabriel! One could not be more explicit regarding the unity of these personages (Daniel standing for the Jewish people) which only the Seer's analysis can distinguish from one another.

Note that, as Plöger points out, except for one small intervention at the end of the book (12.8), this verse constitutes Daniel's final words in a direct style. From here on the heavenly messenger alone speaks.

The third part of the chapter begins in v.20. In fact, chapter 11 should have begun here. It is generally agreed that vv.10.20—11.1 are out of order. Following Montgomery (1927) and Ginsberg (1929), we ought to read the following order: 20a, 21a, 20b, 21b, 11.1. 10.21a is also found in 11.2a, and 11.1a should be understood[51] following Ginsberg as 'as for me (Gabriel), since the first year (משנת) of Darius the Mede, I have been standing near him (Michael) to strengthen and support him.'

For H. L. Ginsberg, the original Aramaic of v.20a had הא 'behold', but it was misunderstood as an interrogative in passing to Hebrew. Montgomery preserves the Masoretic Text, comparing it to Zech. 1.6 and Rev. 7.13. To the angel's question (?) responds the remainder of his discourse in v.21a: it is a revelation of what is recorded in 'the book of truth'. And it ought to be understood as a multi-dimensional reality as we indicated on the occasion of the ספרים (books) in Dan. 7.10 and 9.2. It refers not just to the heavenly tablets,[52] but to the prophetic Scriptures as well. In Dan. 9 the issue was Jeremiah's oracle of seventy weeks; here it is a question *as well* of the oracle of the Restoration in Deutero-Isaiah and Habakkuk's announcement of an ultimate vision. Indeed, Plöger (ad loc.) has judiciously brought together 11.1a and 9.1 where we find the same terms: 'in the first year of Darius, etc.'[53]

ועתה (and now) introduces the details of the revelation. Gabriel announces that he is going to return to combat with the 'prince of Persia' in whom we should see a fusion of the king and the guardian angel of that nation (cf. v.13). But when Gabriel goes (יוצא), 'the prince of Greece' will take advantage of his absence to come (בא) and occupy a

---

[50] See v.11 and our commentary.
[51] But not to transform the text, which faithfully repeats 9.1, see *infra*.
[52] Charles, p. 266. He refers to 1 Enoch 81.1, 2; Jub. 5.13; 23.30–2; 30.21–2; etc. See also Exod. 32.32; Isa. 4.3; Ps. 31.16; 69.29; etc. Cf. *R.h.Sh.* 16b.
[53] Plöger, however, believes that it is here exclusively a question of the oracle of the seventy years in Jeremiah.

place easily conquered since it is without support.[54] Israel cannot count on anyone. Greece, which was to deliver it from the hand of the Persians, has become its enemy (v.21b). Only 'Michael, your prince' is faithful, but he will suffice.

[54] It may be that H. L. Ginsberg is correct in thinking that at the basis of ואני יצא in v.20 there was some confusion between דנא in the original Aramaic and אנא: 'When this one (the angel of Persia) goes, the patron of Greece will arrive.'

11 Historical Retrospective

In chapter 11 we come to the heart of the message of the angel in human guise. In an enigmatic form[1] designed to establish the fiction of a prophecy *ante eventum*, and also perhaps to maintain a prudently esoteric manner, the angel presents the chronological unfolding of history between the fourth and second centuries BCE. In so doing, he shows that everything takes place according to a pre-established divine plan.

The historical allusions in this chapter are quite clear for the most part and our commentary will identify them as we proceed. We have here, Montgomery rightly says, the first Jewish attempt since the Table of Nations in Gen. 10 to trace a universal history.[2] Dating the Book of Daniel in its final redaction is greatly facilitated by the fact that we find in the fresco given in chapter 11 the description of the Temple profaned in 168 by Antiochus IV (v.31) and an allusion to the beginning of the Maccabean revolt (v.34). But the dedication of the purified Temple under Judas Maccabee in 165 is not mentioned. Nor was the angel's announcement of the sudden end of Epiphanes in a camp 'between the seas and the holy mountain of Magnificence' (v.45) realized. Antiochus IV died sometime in 164–163 on an expedition to the east of Gabai in Persia.

It is not the least of the paradoxes in the Book of Daniel that chapter 11 should be so 'Greek' in its genre. Ever since Aeschylus' *The Persians* (472), Greek poets pretended to retell history as though the related events were still to come.[3]

The structure of this chapter is as follows:

Introduction: a rapid evocation of the Persian period and the conquests of Alexander the Great (vv.1–4).

Part one: the Ptolemies and Seleucids up to the enthronement of Antiochus III (vv.5–9).

Part two: Antiochus III the Great (vv.10–19; v.20: Seleucus IV).

Part three: Antiochus IV (vv.21–45).

Text 11. 1–9

(1) As for me, in the first year of Darius the Mede, I was at my post in order

---

[1] This makes reading the original text extremely difficult.

[2] Montgomery compares this attempt to that of Polybius, who as a captive in Rome in 166 (that is, exactly at the time of the redaction of Dan. 11), tried to relate how almost the whole world could fall to the power of the Roman Empire within a span of 53 years (*Hist.* I, 1, 5).

[3] See E. Bickerman, *Four Strange Books . . .*, p. 117.

to give him strength and support. (2) Now therefore I will announce the truth to you. Behold three more kings are yet to arise for Persia, and the fourth will amass more wealth than they all, and when he is strong because of his wealth, he will rouse everything against the kingdom of Greece. (3) But a valiant king will arise; he will rule a great dominion in acting according to his will. (4) When he is well established, his kingdom will be broken up and divided to the four winds of heaven, without passing to his descendants nor according to the dominion he wielded, for his royalty will be uprooted and passed to others besides them. (5) The king of the South will become strong, but one of his princes will be stronger than he and wield a greater dominion than his own. (6) But after several years, they will become allies, and the daughter of the king of the South will come to the king of the North to carry out accords. But she will not retain the support of any arm and her offspring will not endure: she will be given up, she and they that brought her, her child and her support in those times. (7) A shoot of her roots will arise in his place, he will come against the army and enter the fortress of the king of the North; he will work against them and be stronger. (8) Even their gods, with their cast images and their precious objects of silver and gold, he will lead into captivity in Egypt. Then he will remain for several years far from the king of the North. (9) That one will come into the kingdom of the king of the South, then return to his own territory.

Critical Notes 11. 1–8

V.1 LXX: 'King Cyrus'; Θ: 'Cyrus'. ואני...המדי: Montgomery, Bentzen, Plöger: a gloss. V.1b should then be attached to 10.21 and לו must be read as לי (cf. Pesh.): Michael is the one who comes to help Gabriel. See our commentary on 10.21.

V.2 LXX and Θ: ἐπαναστήσεται πάσαις βασιλείαις (παντὶ βασιλεῖ) Ἑλλήνων. Bentzen (whom we are following in our translation of this passage) understands את in the sense of על as in Jer. 38.5— יעיר: 'set in motion', see Isa. 41.2, 25; 45.13; . . . Ezra 1.1, 5; 1 Chron. 5.26; 2 Chron. 21.16; 36.22.

V.3 כרצונו: see vv.16, 36; 8.4.—ממשל: only here and in 1 Chron. 26.6.

V.4 ותחץ: to divide into several parts. The only parallels are in Judg. 7.16 and 9.43 where it has a special military meaning.

V.5 ממשלתו: following Ehrlich, Montgomery suggests adding a מן of comparison: 'his reign is greater than his reign'. MT = LXX, Vul. The word is missing in Θ and Pesh.—נגב: Egypt, as in vv.6, 8, 9, . . .

V.6 תבוא אל: indicates a marriage, see Josh. 15.18; Judg. 12.9.— כח הזרוע: LXX makes the arm the subject and understands: 'this proceeding did not retain its strength' (= the marriage).—וזרוע: Θ, Σ, Vul.: זרועו: 'his seed'. Only this text makes sense. Similarly

215

in the following case: והילדה :Σ, Θ: ἡ νεᾶνις; adopted by von Gall, Marti, etc. (cf. our translation); Pesh. Vul.: 'his sons'.—ותנתן היא: 'she will be given up'; a use without any parallel in Scripture. This is why Charles, for example (p. 271), proposes ותותש which agrees with the metaphor in the preceding sentence. But, cf. Montgomery, ad loc.—ומחזקה בעתים: another translation sometimes proposed: 'he who supported her with the times' = an astrologer who guided her acts with the help of the stars (see Slotki, ad loc.). Montgomery appeals to the authority of the text of Θ here: 'he who had obtained her' = her husband; see v.21.

V.7 כנו: or על כנו is a term without parallel here and in vv.20, 21, and 38. In classical Heb. תחתיו (see Charles, p. 268).—ועשה בהם: see Jer. 18.23, to act hostilely.

V.8 עם כלי: Ms. Tayl.-Sch. ועם.—כלי חמדתם: see Jer. 25.34; Hos. 13.15. Ancient historians say there were about 2,500.—כסף וזהב: Ms. Tayl.-Sch.: זהב וכסף. The annals speak of 40,000 talents.—יביא: Ms. Tayl.-Sch.: יבוא.—יעמד: 'will abstain from attacking' or: 'will endure' (he will reign much longer than the king of the North). For the first solution, see Gen. 29.35. Θ: 'he will hold himself over the king of the North.'

Commentary

As we saw above concerning chapter 10, v.1 of Daniel 11 belongs to the preceding context rather than to the following one. The eschatological and 'heavenly' combat which it describes (continuing 10.13, 21) should be compared to texts in the same vein in Ezek. 38—39 (Gog); Joel 4; Zech. 12—13.6; Isa. 24—27 (apocalyptic); and the royal Psalms. The genre is thus an adaptation of 'the Divine Warrior Hymn', which draws on the ritual pattern of the conflict myth. Gabriel speaks. He was with Michael fighting for Israel, but left his angelic companion for a moment to come to reveal the truth to Daniel. We have seen how H. L. Ginsberg reconstructs this verse: 'and as for me [the angel-interpreter] since the first year [משנת] of Darius, I stood [עומד] to reinforce . . .' (in the original Aramaic text, the verb was למגבר, alluding to the angel Gabriel's name which does not appear in the MT.).[4]

V.2a is a quotation from 10.21a (see ad loc.). It ties the continuation of the discourse here with 10.20 where it had been interrupted. V.2 concerns the Persian period, but the four kings are difficult to identify. The fourth, defeated by Alexander the Great 'the valiant king' (v.3), is Darius III Codomannus. Some have also thought he may be Xerxes I (485–465) who consecrated his fabulous wealth to fighting the Greeks.[5]

---

[4] See his article 'Daniel' in the *Enc. Bibl.*, II, col. 693.
[5] Re Xerxes' wealth, see Esth. 1.4; Herodotus VII, 20–99.

That campaign ended with the disaster at Salamis in 480. 'The Kingdom of Greece' then should be taken in a large sense since Greece did not become a kingdom until the time of Philip and his son Alexander the Great. The four kings in succession might be as already suggested by Porphyry: Smerdis, Cambyses, Darius I, Xerxes.[6] But on the basis of Daniel 7.6 we think it is: Cyrus, Xerxes, Artaxerxes, and Darius III Codomannus.[7] The motif of great riches could perfectly well have been mentioned by the Author in telescoping chronologically distinct elements. By treating the whole Persian epoch in a single verse, such a thing seems almost inevitable.

Alexander the Great, the king in v.3, conquered Persia along with other countries between 334 and 330. He acted 'according to his will', this being the accomplishment of his dream, on a world scale, to dethrone all the gods and liberate the universe from the shadows of superstition. Aristotle, his teacher, had declared: 'The Greeks could rule the world if they just associated themselves into one political society.' This was Alexander's goal.

The next verse, v.4, recounts the astonishing fall of so great an empire and its division among the Diadochi. Its image is clearly constructed on the model of Dan. 8.8, which explains the terms 'will be broken up' which earlier referred to 'the horn'. As a consequence of this it has been suggested[8] that we read the first word as וכעצמו ('while it was full of might') as in 8.8. At the height of its power the empire disintegrates with the death of its sovereign and does not pass on to his descendants (אחריתו) as might have been expected. So the dream ended; what followed was no longer כמשלו, see 8.22.

The end of the verse is more difficult. To whom does 'to others besides them' allude? Who are these frustrated men: Alexander's sons (אחריתו) or the Diadochi (ארבע רוחות השמים)? In the latter case, it must refer to the secondary dynasties such as Cappadocia and Armenia who declared themselves independent during the century and a half following Alexander's death.

The allusions in v.5 are to Ptolemy I Soter (323–285), who was supplanted by the first of the Syrian Seleucids, Seleucus I Nicator (312–281), after the battle of Gaza in 312.[9] Seleucus then made himself master of Babylon in 311, inaugurating the 'Seleucid era'. He established his capital at Antioch (300) and died in 281. In the course of his reign and following it Palestine changed hands several times, but finally remained under the Ptolemies until 198.

---

[6] E. Bickerman, *Four Strange Books . . .*, agrees.
[7] See Montgomery, ad loc.   [8] With Gratz, Charles, etc.
[9] Seleucus had been general of the Egyptian armies in the war against the Diadochus Antigonus of Macedonia: מן שריו.

V.6 refers to the marriage which took place between Antiochus II of Syria and Berenice, the daughter of Ptolemy II of Egypt, about 250. Berenice, her husband, and their child were poisoned by Laodice, Antiochus' first wife whom he had repudiated. It was Antiochus' son by this princess who reigned in Syria under the name Seleucus II Callinice (246–226). He was immediately attacked by Ptolemy III Euergetes (247–221), Berenice's brother,[10] who gained a victory in 246 but did not carry through on it (see Dan. 2.41–3).

The quite fluid chronology in v.6 brings us to לקץ שנים, 'after several years', actually about thirty-five years. The text speaks of 'the king of the north' even though most of the Seleucid Empire lay to the east of Palestine.

As we have indicated, Ptolemy III's success, reported in v.7, led him to penetrate deeply into the Syrian kingdom, as far as Seleucia and even Babylon (במעוז מלך צפון). He carried off a considerable amount of booty (v.8), including the idols.[11] It is true that the Masoretic vocalization of the word נסכיהם causes a problem, for as such the word signifies 'libations'. It should have been נְסִיכֵיהֶם from the word נסך[12] (see Isa. 41.29; 48.4). Before leaving this verse let us also note the explicit mention of Egypt rather than an allusion to 'the south'.

There is no historical attestation to any attempt by the king of the north to get revenge (v.9). We only know that Seleucus was able to re-establish his power in his own land in 242.

Text 11. 10–45

(10) His sons will work themselves up; they will gather a great multitude of troops. One of them will advance, sweep them away and pass on; then he will return and work himself up as far as his fortress. (11) The king of the South will become enraged. He will come out to fight against him, against the king of the North, he will raise a great multitude and the multitude (against him) will be delivered into his power. (12) When that multitude will be carried away, his heart will be lifted up; he will make myriads fall, but will not triumph. (13) The king of the North will return and raise a multitude greater

---

[10] This is why v.7 speaks of 'a shoot of her roots' (i.e., Berenice).

[11] Y. Kaufmann, *The Religion of Israel*, p. 12, emphasizes this characteristic feature of Scripture which holds that the gods are only idols, incapable of movement, and must be carried from one place to another (see Jer. 47.52; Nah. 1.14; and above all Isa. 46.1–2; Jer. 48.7). Slotki (ad loc.) adds: 'The capture of these images implied that the conquered nation had nothing further to hope for since their greatest source of strength had gone over to the enemy.' Finally, for Jerome, these cast images included some brought from Egypt by Cambyses 280 years earlier. This is why Ptolemy III deserved the title 'Euergetes', doer of good works.

[12] Saadia and Rashi understand 'their dignitaries' following one possible meaning of the Masoretic punctuation.

than the first one. After some time, several years, he will advance with a great army and abundant supplies. (14) In those times, a multitude will rear up against the king of the South and the violent men of your own people will arise to accomplish a vision, but they will stumble. (15) The king of the North will come, he will cast up siegeworks and take a fortified city. The battalions of the South will not withstand him, nor its élite troops, they will not have the strength to withstand him. (16) He who will advance against him will do as he pleases; no one will stand before him and he will stop in the magnificent Land, holding destruction in his hand. (17) Having (in fact) conceived a plan to intervene with all the strength of his kingdom, he will make a show of uprightness in his actions. He will give him a daughter of women in order to destroy it (= Egypt), but this will not stand; it will not come to pass for him. (18) So he will turn his sights in the direction of the islands and take many of them; but a magistrate will put an end to his outrage without his being able to return the outrage of this latter one. (19) Then he will turn his sights in the direction of the citadels in his own land, but he will stumble, he will fall and not be found again. (20) Someone will arise in his place who will make an exactor pass through the Splendour of the kingdom, but in a few days he will be broken, though not by anger or war. (21) In his place will arise someone despicable to whom had not been given the honour of royalty: he will come in a time of security and take the kingship through smooth talk. (22) Swooping battalions will be swept away before him and broken, as well as a chief of a covenant. (23) Because they will be joined with him, he will use trickery; he will get under way and overcome with (the help of) a few people. (24) In a time of security, he will come into the fertile regions of the province and he will do what his fathers did not do, nor the fathers of his fathers: he will distribute to his men booty, spoils, and supplies, and he will plot against fortresses, and this (will continue) until a set time. (25) He will rouse his strength and courage against the king of the South with a great army. The king of the South will work himself up with a very large and powerful army, but he will not stand, for they will plot against him: (26) Those who eat at his table will break him, his army will be swept away and a great number of victims will fall. (27) The two kings, their hearts full of wickedness, will speak lies at the same table, but this will not succeed, for the end must come at its hour. (28) He will return to his land with great supplies. Having hostile intentions against the holy Covenant, he will carry them out, and then return to his own land. (29) When the hour comes, he will return against the South, but the end will not be like the beginning! (30) The ships of Kittim will come against him and he will be discouraged. Again, he will hurl curses and act against the holy Covenant; again he will be in collusion with those who abandon the holy Covenant. (31) Battalions come from him will take up position; they will profane the Sanctuary-Citadel, stopping the regular offering and setting up the devastating abomination. (32) Through his smooth talk, he will make the profaners of the Covenant apostasize themselves, but the people of those who know their God will take firm action; (33) the thoughtful ones among the people will instruct a multitude but they will stumble before the sword, the flames, the captivity and the looting, for some days. (34) When they are stumbling, they will receive a little help, a multitude will join them through smooth talk. (35) Among the thoughtful ones, there are some who will stumble in order to be refined, purified, and whitened until the time of the end, for it must come at its hour. (36) The king will do as he pleases, he will exalt himself and magnify himself beyond every god, and he will speak astonishing things against the God of gods. He will succeed until the (time of) curse is over, for what has been decreed will be executed. (37) He will have no regard for the gods of his fathers; he will not regard the Favourite of women or any divinity, for he will magnify himself above all. (38) He will glorify in his place the god of citadels; he will glorify a divinity unknown to his fathers, with gold and silver, with precious stones and jewels. (39) He will act against the fortifications of citadels with a foreign divinity; those who recognize him, he will cover with glory. He will give them dominion over the multitude and grant them lands as a reward. (40) At the time of the end the king of the South will confront him, but the king of the North will rush upon him with chariots, horsemen, and many ships, he will penetrate the lands, sweep them away, and pass on. (41) He will come into the magnificent Land and many others will stumble; these will escape his hand: Edom, Moab, and the élite of the sons of Ammon. (42) He will stretch his hand against the lands and the land of Egypt will not be able to escape. (43) He will have mastery over treasures of gold and silver and over all the jewels of Egypt, and the Libyans and the Ethiopians will march in his train. (44) News from the Orient and the North will frighten him; he will go out in a great furor to destroy and exterminate the multitude. (45) He will plant the tents of his palace between the seas and the holy mountain of Magnificence; he will come to his end without anyone to come to his aid.

Critical Notes 11. 10–45

V.10 וּבְנוֹ: Kt.; Qr.: וּבָנָיו. LXX has used the singular throughout this verse which, according to the MT, passes from the plural to the singular and back to the plural again. This reading is approved by H. L. Ginsberg and Montgomery, for example.—יִתְגָּרוּ: see v.25: 'to become worked up against' (see Deut. 2.5, 9, 19; 2 Kings 14.10).—וּבָא בוֹא: in classical Heb. this construction indicates the repetition or continuity of action (see Charles, p. 269).—וְשָׁטַף וְעָבַר: image of a conquering army; see Isa. 8.8; Jer. 47.2. Cf. vv.22, 26, 40.—מָעֻזֹּה: a word play with עַזָּה, Gaza, is seen here (it held out for two months against Alexander the Great), Antiochus' citadel.—The ms. Tayl.-Sch. presents the following

divergences: וׁבא בו instead of וׁבא בוא; ויתגרהו instead of ויתגרו;
על instead of עד.

V.II ויתמרמר: see 8.7.—עמו עם מלך: pure Aramaism, see 5.12 (but cf.
Josh. 1.2; Num. 32.33; Judg. 21.7 . . .).—והעמיד: Ptolemy.—
נתן בידו: see I Kings 20.28. This verse as well as others from this
chapter is used by 1 QM at Qumran in an anthology of texts of
the Scripture.

V.12 נשא: see 2.35; Isa. 40.24; 41.16; Job 32.22.—ירום לבבו: Qr., LXX, Θ,
Vul.: ורם; idem in the ms. Tayl.-Sch.—רבאות: Aramaic for
רבבות.

V.13 יבוא בוא: see v.10 and its note. Many mss., including Tayl.-
Sch. and LXX have: בו, adopted by Charles (see p. 272)—
ברכוש . . . בחיל: ms. Tayl.-Sch. וחיל . . . ורכוש. רכוש: see Gen.
14.11, 12; 2 Chron. 21.14. . . .

V.14 פריצים: Θ translates with λοιμοί, for which Acts 24.5 concerning
Paul clarifies the negative sense. For Montgomery, it is a
question of those who 'break' the Torah (see j.A.Z. 41a).—Ms.
Tayl.-Sch. has יעמדו instead of יעמודו; על מלך instead of אל מלך.

V.15 מלך הצפון: ms. Tayl.-Sch.: מלך הנגב! It also has אין כח instead of
ואין כח.—עיר הבצרות: the unique instance, normally we find
עיר מבצר. The masculine plural in Jer. 5.17 (עיר מבצרים) is also an
isolated instance.—זרעות: figurative for battalions (see vv.22,
31).—עם מבחרים: for the plural, see 2 Chron. 36.19.

V.16 ארץ־הצבי: Pesh.: 'Israel'; Vul. and A: 'a land of renown' (!).—
כלה: Saadia translates as 'sword' from the Arabic kallat = short
sword (cited by Montgomery). Mekor Hayim, op. cit., imitated
by Ewald on the basis of the parallel in Gen. 18.21: 'he will be
totally within his hand'. LXX and Θ: 'he will be destroyed'.

V.17 וישם פניו: to conceive a plan, see Gen. 31.21; 2 Kings 12.18; Jer.
42.15, 17.—בתקף: late Heb.; see Job 14.20; 15.24; Esth. 9.29; 10.2;
Eccles. 4.12; 6.10 (see Charles, p. 270); cf. Dan. 2.37; 4.27; etc.—
וישרים: LXX, Θ, Pesh., Vul. read: מישרים. Ibn Ezra follows this
reading: 'he will make peace with him'. But Rashi understands:
'he will fight even against the righteous men to be found on the
Egyptian side and win'. Mets. David: 'certain righteous men
(=Judeans) will come to his aid too and he will do (what he
pleases in Judea)'.—ובת הנשים יתן לו להשחיתה: see H. L. Ginsberg,
op. cit., p. 61: it is the Syriac expression 'yaḇ benešše' (see Bevan,
p. xii); to give in marriage. The original Aramaic was something close to: ובתה במשין יתן לה לחבלותה: 'and he will give him his
daughter in marriage in order to destroy him'. (ה־תה was taken
as feminine rather than masculine).—ולא תעמוד ולא לו תהיה: see
Isa. 7.7. עמד is used in the same sense as קום, see Esth. 3.4.—לו:

del. in LXX. The original strong meaning of היה was *cadere, evenire* (see Joüon, *Grammaire Hébraïque*, par. 111h).

V.18 Cf. ms. Taylor-Schechter: והשבית קצין חפר חרפתו.—Cf. ibid.: וישב פניו אל.—ישוב: Qr.: וישם (for Charles, Bevan, etc., this could indicate a change of subject, but this is not correct. It is necessary therefore to prefer the Kt.). חרפתו ישיב·לו: see Hos. 12.13.

V.19 ולא ימצא: see Ps. 37.10; Job 20.8.

V.20 מעביר: ms. Taylor-Schechter: מעמיד.—נוגש: see Zech. 9.8 (it is interesting to note that in the Talmud, the 'exactor' designates Mattathias and his sons!).

V.23 במעט גוי: see H. L. Ginsberg: 'barbarism' for במעת־עם or some other expression of this genre.

V.24 מדינה: Θ: 'the provinces'.—יחשב: ms. Taylor-Schechter: יחשב.—יחשב.—ועד עת: Θ: ἔως καιροῦ; but LXX: εἰς μάτην (=לשוא).—יבזור: only found elsewhere in Ps. 68.13.

V.26 ישטוף: 'will sweep away' (active) but the context clearly shows that it is a question of a disaster and not of a victory. Furthermore, the consonantal text of several Heb. mss. as well as that of the Pesh. and the Vul. give the passive. Regarding the use of this verb, see v.22 and our commentary.

V.27 ושניהם המלכים: not a Hebraic cast (an Aramaism).

V.28 על ברית קדש: ms. Taylor-Schechter: עד. Regarding this expression, see 1 QSb 1.2; CD 3.10; 5.12; 1 Qp Hab 2.3; 1 Macc. 1.15, 63; cf. Luke 1.72.

V.29 כראשנה וכאחרונה: see 1 Sam. 30.24; Ezek. 18.4.

V.30 כתים: Vul.: 'Romans', cf. LXX, Pesh., Targ. Jon.—ציים: *del.* in LXX, Θ.

V.31 והסירו התמיד: see 12.11; 8.11. For the importance of the continuity of the 'tamid' offering, see Neh. 10.33ff.—השקוץ משומם: idols are often called שקוץ, see 1 Kings 11.5, 7; Ezek. 20.7, 8; Jer. 4.1. . . .

V.32 יחניף: for the hiphil, see Num. 35.33; Jer. 3.2 (complement of direct object: ארץ); for the qal, see Jer. 3.9 (ibid.); for the niphal, see Jer. 31 (ibid.).

V.34 Ms. Taylor-Schechter: בחלק לקות (v.21). See LXX: 'and many in the city and many as in a heritage will join them'. חלקלקות already has been encountered in v.21.

V.36 Ms. Taylor-Schechter: על כל אלה.—אל אלים: see 2.47: אלה אלהין; cf. Deut. 10.17: אלהי האלהים.

V.39 אל נכר: see Deut. 32.12.—הכיר: Qr. יכיר (useless).

V.40 בארצות: LXX, Θ, Pesh.: בארץ.—ושטף ועבר: *del.* in LXX, Pesh.

222

V.41 ורבות: influenced by ארצות from v.40. Bevan, following de Wette, etc., proposes רְבּוֹת: 'tens of thousands'.

V.43 במכמני: hapax. On the basis of Arabic, we understand: 'what is hidden'.

V.45 אפדנו: del. in LXX, Θ, Pesh., and Vul. as substantive. Θ, A, Vul. see a proper name here. LXX: 'then'. 'Apadana' is an Old-Persian word designating an audience hall. It should be seen as the luxurious tent of a king on campaign.—בין ימים: the Mediterranean and the Dead Sea, or, following Charles, a poetical plural as in Judg. 5.17 and Deut. 33.19 = 'the Sea' (the Mediterranean).

Commentary

V.10 inaugurates the second part of chapter 11. It is here a question of the sons of Seleucus II: Seleucus III (226–223) and especially Antiochus III (223–187).[13] This latter king fought against the Ptolemies from 222 to 187. He brought Palestine as well as Tyre, Ptolemais, etc., under the Seleucid sceptre in 198. But before that there was a notable Egyptian reaction. The army of Ptolemy IV Philopator marched through Judea and met the Syrian troops in Lebanon, but the Egyptians were defeated and Antiochus III seized many of the Palestinian cities on both sides of the Jordan River (218). However, at the Battle of Raphia in 217 ('his fortress'?,[14] see v.10), Antiochus suffered huge losses.[15] The hostilities continued and were endemic until the accession to the throne of Ptolemy V Epiphanes (205–181).[16]

V.12 describes the effect of his victory at Raphia on Ptolemy IV. His heart, that is, his courage (see v.25), was renewed. The Syrian multitude had been carried away like chaff before the wind,[17] and the naturally weak and indolent character of Ptolemy was distracted for one short moment from its appetite for luxury and sensual pleasure. He reconquered Palestine but did not carry through on his victory (with Bevan, following Von Lengerke and Hitzig, we could translate ולא יעוז by 'he shall not shew himself strong' see p. 179), rapidly concluding a treaty with Antiochus and returning to Alexandria.

V.13. Twelve years after the Battle of Raphia, in 205, Antiochus III returned in force. He was supported by Philip V of Macedonia and

---

[13] But cf. our critical notes.
[14] But cf. our critical notes.
[15] The text says 'a great multitude of troops' for there were 60,000 Syrians opposed to 70,000 Egyptians at the Battle of Raphia. Antiochus lost about 10,000 killed and 4,000 taken prisoner. See 3 Macc. 1; Polybius V, 85.
[16] Ptolemy was only five years old at the time!
[17] According to the image in Dan. 2.35.

encouraged by internal struggles in Egypt. He invaded Phoenicia and Syria. Note the vague and mysterious indications of time which begin in this verse and continue throughout the remainder of the chapter (see vv.14, 20, 24, 27, 29, 35, 40; in v.45 there is a new use of the word קֵץ in another context where chronology is not totally absent either). All these expressions are in the service of the message that the related events are all steps on the way leading to the End.

In 200, Ptolemy V, who had succeeded his father at the age of five or six years old, regained Judea but suffered a total rout at Panion in 198 (see Josephus, *Ant.* XII, III, 3). From this time on, as we said above, Palestine passed definitively under Seleucid domination. Antiochus' reception at Jerusalem (see v.14) is described by Josephus as follows (*Ant.* XII, III, 3). 'The Jews, of their own accord, went over to him, and received him into the city and gave plentiful provision to all his army, and to his elephants, and readily assisted him when he besieged the (Egyptian) garrison which was in the citadel of Jerusalem.' Josephus goes on to report that Antiochus gave magnificent presents to the Temple. In fact, the king assured the financing for the sacrifices and for rebuilding the city. He exempted them from taxes for three years and reduced all subsequent taxes by a third. According to Josephus, there was even one clause specifying, 'let all of that nation live according to the laws of their own country'.

However, from the Author's historical perspective, those who revolted against Ptolemy were outlaws (פריצים; cf. Jer. 7.11). They were, in effect, 'modernists' who took sides with Syria. Apparently they were few in number, but influential and militarily strong. It seems as if the High Priest Simon the Just[18] was at the head of this party made up of the upper aristocratic and priestly classes, especially the Tobiads.[19] Let us note in passing that Simon is highly approved by ben Sirach (Ecclus. 50) who was a Sadducee. Bevan[20] is probably correct in thinking that in fact the faction said to be 'pro-Seleucid' entertained the hope of completely throwing off the foreign yoke and thus fulfilling the prophetic predictions. This would explain the end of this verse 'to accomplish a (the?) vision, but they will stumble' (cf. Ezek. 13.6).

The Egyptian defeat is described further in v.15. Allusion is made here to the taking of Sidon where the Egyptian general Scopas had retreated following the defeat at Panion (198). From this time on, Antiochus had

[18] We should probably accept G. F. Moore's conclusions that Simon the Just was the Simon from the end of the third century, beginning of the second century, and not the one from the beginning of the third century. See 'Simon the Just', *Jew. St. in Mem. of I. Abrahams* (1927), pp. 348ff.
[19] Their adversaries were the Oniads.
[20] Op. cit., ad loc.

a free hand in Palestine which v.16 (like 8.9 and 11.41) calls 'the magnificent Land'.[21]

V.17 is not easy to understand. Following the versions (see our critical notes) some read מישרים instead of וישרים: 'he will conclude an agreement with him'. But it is not necessary to alter the Masoretic Text on this point. It describes Antiochus' ruse. He plays the role of an honest, upright (ישרים) man in giving his daughter, Cleopatra, as a wife to Ptolemy V, although his real goal was to use her to better be able to destroy the Egyptian (see our critical notes). But 'this will not work', for Cleopatra adopted the Egyptian cause and called on Rome for help against the Seleucids when her father sent a fleet against the (Egyptian-controlled) coasts of Cilicia, Lycia, and Caria in Asia Minor.

This is the meaning of v.18. Taking advantage of the situation created by his daughter's marriage to Ptolemy, Antiochus turned toward the coastal regions of Syro-Palestine and Asia Minor in order to annex the Greek and Egyptian cities despite Rome's warnings. In 192, the Romans declared war against Antiochus and, for the first time in that region of the world, Rome in the person of Lucius Cornelius Scipio ('the magistrate') intervened, saving Egypt *in extremis*. The decisive battle took place in 190–189 at Magnesia on the Meander in Lydia (Turkey).[22] The time had come for the Romans to act, for Antiochus had even seized Greek territories north of Corinth. In 191 the Romans inflicted a serious defeat on him at Thermopylae. Perhaps there is an allusion in our verse to Antiochus' dry diplomatic response to the Romans before the battle. He told them to concern themselves with European affairs and to leave Asia to him (see Livy, XXXIII, 40).

Antiochus became a vassal of Rome under the terms of the peace treaty of Apamea (189). His son, the future Antiochus IV, was taken to Rome as a hostage and he himself had to pay a heavy tribute. Having resolved to pillage a temple of Bel at Elam to pay his debt, Antiochus III and his followers were assassinated by the local population (187). This is the historical background of v.19.

Seleucus IV Philopator (187–175), his son, succeeded him. He sent his head of finances, Heliodorus,[23] to Jerusalem[24] to seize the Temple treasure (v.40). Apparently the High Priest Onias III, a partisan of the Ptolemies, had not sent tribute to the Seleucid kings and a certain Simon,[25] trying to obtain the pontificate by intrigue, had reported to Seleucus IV that the Jerusalem Temple possessed much treasure.

---

[21] It is the presence of the Temple in the Land of Israel which gives it its magnificence; see A. Jaubert, op. cit., p. 85. Cf. Zech. 7.14; Ezek. 20.6, 15; 1 Enoch 89.40; 90.20.
[22] See Livy, XXXVII, 39–44.
[23] 'An exactor'.　　　[24] 'The Splendour of the Kingdom'.
[25] Simon belonged to the family of the Tobiads, the adversaries of the Oniads.

Heliodorus, however, was unable to carry out his mission. According to 2 Macc. 3, he was prevented from doing so by a supernatural apparition.[26] Onias III was in a difficult position. He resolved to go and plead his case in person before the king, but he died, poisoned on the urging of the High Priest Menelaus by the hand of Andronicus. Meanwhile Antiochus IV had returned from Rome where he had promised to re-establish the temple to Zeus Olympios in Athens. Seleucus' death was the occasion for the Hellenistic party in Jerusalem to carry out a sort of palace revolution with the help of Jason, the brother of Onias III. This Jason succeeded in having himself named High Priest in place of his brother by Antiochus to whom he promised enormous sums of money. With Jason, the Hellenizing party took power in Jerusalem (174–171). Jason proceeded to found a πόλις.

The 'despicable being' in v.21 is Antiochus IV. He had no right to the throne, but 'through tricks' he ousted Demetrius, his brother Seleucus IV's son. In 172, Menelaus, the brother of Simon the Tobiad, was able to strip Jason of the High Priesthood by promising Antiochus even more money. Not being a member of a priestly family, however, Menelaus' appointment gave rise to much opposition, even among the Hellenizers. He attained the height of his infamy when he dipped into the Temple treasure to have Onias III (the נגיד ברית in v.22)[27] assassinated.

The 'swooping battalions' in v.22 are literally 'flooding or inundating battalions'. We have already discussed this term in regard to 9.26 where it also appears in relation to Antiochus IV and Onias III on the basis of Isa. 10.22.[28] It is a question therefore of the forces of 'righteousness sweeping [everything] away', and not evidently of the forces of Israel's enemies.[29] In fact, Egyptian troops were defeated by Antiochus and Onias III was assassinated during the disorders brought about by this campaign, probably for being in collusion with the enemy (171).

Onias, as we have seen, was considered a saint by the people and even perhaps a messianic figure.[30] He is here called a 'chief of the covenant' corresponding to the 'anointed chief' (messiah) in 9.25. 2 Macc. 3.1 praises Onias for his 'piety and his severity toward wicked men'. Martin Noth[31] sees in the expression of our verse a sign of the edulcoration of the notion of the covenant as it is found in the more recent texts

[26] 'not by anger or war'.
[27] According to H. H. Rowley, '"The Prince of the Covenant" in Daniel 11.22', E.T., 55:43–4, pp. 24–7, it is not a question here of Onias but of the son of Seleucus IV supplanted by Antiochus. Apparently the prince was loved by the people.
[28] As we will see in what follows, the oracles of Isaiah, especially those in chs. 8, 10, 52, etc., play a determining role in this third vision of Daniel (see 10—12).
[29] Contra M. Delcor, op. cit., p. 235.
[30] See Dan. 9.26 which is interpreted in this sense by Θ.
[31] M. Noth, 'Die Gesetze im Pentateuch', Ges. St. z. A.T. (Munich 1957²), pp. 9–141.

of Scripture.[32] It will be recalled that the term ברית had been usually avoided by the prophets. It had probably taken on a syncretistic connotation and it is understandable that its use again in more recent texts would be rather timid. Qumran demonstrates the end of the process which begins here: 'the Covenant' designates the community.[33]

V.23 seems to indicate that the ultimate responsibility for the tyrant's easy victory depends on the collaborators in Jerusalem. Historical truth, then, may be on N. Bentwich's side when he writes: '(Antiochus IV) was less the promoter than the instrument of the policy which had its roots in the corruption of a part of the Jewish people.'[34]

Emil Schürer in turn writes: '. . . a section of the people (of Israel), including the upper class and the educated, readily gave their consent to the Hellenizing projects of Antiochus Epiphanes and even went beyond him in carrying them out.'[35] As for the king's character, it is well conveyed by Schürer in the following lines which conform to Polybius' testimony (XXVI, 10). '(Antiochus) was by nature a genuine despot, eccentric and undependable, sometimes extravagantly liberal, and fraternizing with the common people in an affected manner, at other times cruel and tyrannical.'

In any case, even Antiochus' allies came to regret their co-operation with him for it was founded on illusions. It was no better having Antiochus as a friend than as an enemy. The king saw to his own interests or those of his powerful courtiers alongside whom the Jewish collaborators had little weight. This idea is expressed in v.24 which insists on the division of the spoils from the richest provinces—or the 'central' province, Judea[36]—among those who could assist Antiochus in conquering Egypt (see the following verses; cf. 1 Macc. 1.16). As in vv.21 and 8.25, v.24 emphasizes that there was no provocation ('in a time of security') behind Antiochus' extortions. This seems to give us the key to the expression 'what his fathers did not do, nor the fathers of his fathers'. His worship of foreign gods stands in opposition to his own people's and his dynasty's past (cf. vv.36–9).

The 'fortresses' in question are Egypt's (see 1 Macc. 1.19) where

[32] Num. 25.12, 13 (a late addition to P); Mal. 2.4, 5, 8; Neh. 13.29: the tone is colourless in relation to the older texts.
[33] See Jubilees; 1 QM 14.4–5. In parallel with Jer. 34.10; Ezek. 16.8; 2 Chron. 15.12 . . ., but with a new meaning, see 1 QS 2.12, 18; 5.7, 8, 20, 21; CD 6.11; 1 QS 1.7–8; 3.11–12; 5.5–6; 6.14–15; 8.16–17 (cf. A. Jaubert, op. cit., pp. 182–4).
[34] *Hellenism* (1919), p. 93, quoted by H. H. Rowley, *The Relevance of Apocalyptic* (New York 1964), p. 37, n. 3.
[35] *A History of the Jewish People in the Time of Jesus*, ed. N. Glatzberg (New York 1961), p. 20.
[36] Bevan, op. cit., ad loc., identifies the fertility image here with the one in Dan. 8.24 and links it with Isa. 10.16 and Ps. 78.31. He translates: 'By stealth, he shall assail the mightiest of men of (each) province.'

resistance was organized with 'very large and powerful' means (v.25). But there was something rotten in Egypt. Ptolemy VI's generals betrayed him and handed the country over to Antiochus IV (v.26) in 170. Ptolemy VI Philometor, Antiochus' nephew since his mother, Cleopatra, was the Syrian's sister, had to give himself up to his uncle who pretended to treat him with friendship while pillaging Egypt (v.27a). The political conversations which occurred between these two men are qualified as full of 'wickedness' and 'lies' in v.27b. When the Alexandrians named Ptolemy VI's brother, Ptolemy Physcon, king of Egypt, Antiochus placed his prisoner under his 'protection'. V.27c ends with the expression well known to the readers of Daniel: 'for the end must come at its hour'. We have already discussed this quotation from Hab. 2.3 in our commentary on Dan. 8.17b, 26b, and 10.14b.

Meanwhile, the false news that Antiochus IV had died had spread through Jerusalem and Jason declared himself ruler of the city (in 170 or 169). On his return from Egypt, Antiochus punished the city because of this move (v.28).[37]

Antiochus undertook a second campaign against Egypt (v.29). But this undertaking was ended by a crushing defeat. In 168, the Roman consul Gaius Popilius Laenas met with Antiochus near Alexandria and informed him on behalf of the Roman Senate that he must pull back.[38] 'The ships of Kittim'[39] (v.30)—which is to say Rome—were threatening the Syrian coasts and Antiochus, 'discouraged', had to return home. He assuaged his rage against the Jews. He had barely left the city, however, when the rebellion began again (see 2 Macc. 5.22).

Apollonius, the head of his mercenaries, retook the city during a sabbath. He constructed the Acra citadel which became the centre of the Greek polis (see 1 Macc. 1.35–6; some inhabitants left the city, see also v.45). It is the Hellenized citizens of this polis that v.39 below speaks of. They are here called 'those who abandon the Holy Covenant',[40] see 1 Macc. 1.11–15, 43, 52.

[37] See 1 Macc. 1.20, 21–8; 2 Macc. 5.11–21; cf. Dan. 8.9b–10.
  According to V. Tcherikover, op. cit., p. 186, this first visit to Jerusalem was peaceful despite the pillaging of the Temple (cf. Josephus, C. Ap. II.83). It was only following the second campaign in Egypt in 168 that Antiochus' death was announced and a civil war broke out in Jerusalem (see 2 Macc. 5.6). Antiochus recaptured the city in a lightning attack (2 Macc. 5.11ff.), massacring 40,000 people and selling as many into slavery.
[38] See Polybius XXIX. 1; Livy XLIV.10; XLV.12.
[39] A quotation from Num. 24.3ff. The word 'Kittim' originally designated Cyprus, but by extension it came to designate all the Mediterranean countries west of Palestine (see Gen. 10.4; Isa. 23.1, 12; Jer. 2.10; 1 Qp Hab 2.12, 14; 3.4, 9 . . .; 1 QM 1.2, 4, 6, 9, 12, etc.).
[40] It is interesting to contrast this expression with Mattathias' war cry: 'Let everyone who is zealous for the Law and who supports the Covenant follow me!' (1 Macc. 2.27).

7 December, 168, Antiochus *in absentia* (whence the expression 'come from him') had his troops profane the Temple (v.31). For a period of three years the carrying out of the Jewish cultus was forbidden. An idol was erected and consecrated to Zeus Olympios and swine were sacrificed on the altar in Jerusalem. This is the 'devastating abomination' which we discussed in our commentary on 9.27; see also 12.11.[41]

'The Sanctuary-Citadel': or 'the Citadel of the Temple' (cf. v.10, מעוז) is also found in Neh. 2.8 (cf. 1 Macc. 1.31, 33). H. L. Ginsberg[42] recalls the words in 1 Macc. 1.46: '(the edict ordering) the defiling of the sanctuary *and the saints*' (cf. vv.48, 54), and sees in מעוז or מעזים in Daniel another designation of the saints on the basis of the Aramaic חסין (referring to the Essenes). There must have been some confusion with חֲסֵן (fortress). A. Bentzen has contested this reconstruction.[43]

V.32 reports dissension within the Jewish people. Parties were formed in Jerusalem which would be the origins of the Sadducees, the Hassidim, and later the Pharisees, Herodians, etc. The Author's sympathies clearly lie with the Hassidim.[44] They 'take firm action' and are called 'mighty warriors of Israel' in 1 Macc. 2.42. They are 'the thoughtful ones', capable of instructing 'a multitude' (v.33) and, in fact, there were many scribes in their ranks (see 1 Macc. 7.12). Despite their understanding (see 12.10), these teachers will fail. More exactly, they 'will stumble' (the root is *k.š.l.* and a word play with *s.k.l.* is clear). Through them, the Spirit is scoffed at by Antiochus. And, as in 1 Enoch 100.6; 104.12, understanding is justice as well.

As for their adversaries, they are described as מרשיעי ברים. This expression is also found in 1 QM 1.2 (cf. CD 20.26) to designate, as here, the Hellenizers. Antiochus 'will make them apostasize themselves through smooth talk' (see 1 Macc. 1.52).[45] This new tie to Qumran is not without interest. משכיל is perhaps the name taken by the head of the sect, see 1 QS 1.1, 3.13; 5.1.[46] And it is probable that this title was also assumed by his successors (see 9.12). The accent is on teaching the disciples and the discerning of who is worthy of such instruction.[47] In the Book of Daniel, we find the term משכיל in 11.35 and 12.3, 10. The hypothesis of a Hassidic Daniel which we have adopted thus makes sense. The *maskilim* instruct the *rabbim* (the multitude). This latter term appears in Dan. 8.25, (26); 11.(10), 14, 18, (26), 34, 44; 12.2, 4, 10;

---

[41] See 1 Macc. 1.57; Matt. 24.15.
[42] Op. cit., pp. 42–9.   [43] *Daniel*, p. 80.
[44] 'The people of those who know their God', see 8.24, 25, 27; 1 Macc. 1.65 (2.20, 29, 42); 2 Macc. 6.9; CD 6.2 (8.5); 20.27; cf. 3.10; 6.6; 19.9; 1 Qp Hab 5.7; 12.3–5.
[45] The term חלקות is found more than once at Qumran in the expression: דורשי החלקות, 'those who seek smooth things', see 4 Qp Nah 1.7; 2.2, 4; 3.3, 6–7; 4 Qp Is c li. 10.
[46] In mss. 2, 4, and 7 from cave IV.
[47] Besides, this root signifies having a just estimate of things.

and with the article in 9.(18), 27; 11.33, 39; 12.3.[48] At Qumran, *rabbim* is the elect community excluding novices: 1 QS 6.20–3.

The association of the *maskilim* with the *rabbim* is manifestly a reminiscence of Isa. 53. Similarly in Dan. 12.3, the allusion to the Song of the Suffering Servant is clear. H. L. Ginsberg has advanced the convincing thesis that in chapters 10—12 of Daniel we have 'the oldest interpretation of the suffering servant',[49] and it is a plainly collective interpretation. The martydom of the *Hassidim* in the second century (cf. 12.3) justifies the *rabbim*, the multitude, the people. These teachers thought they could make the people understand ('they will instruct') that Isa. 10.5–15 was not spoken just to the then king of Assyria, but to the present king as well (Dan. 11.36–7). Thus Isa. 14.24–7, too, is about to be fulfilled (Dan. 11.45) and that will be the end of the tyrant, Antiochus.

V. Tcherikover is probably correct to emphasize here that the Author does not put his trust in the Hasmoneans (see v.34: 'a little help'), but solely in God and in those who submit to martyrdom for 'the sanctification of the Name'.[50] This same author, in opposition to Charles, Montgomery, and others, thinks that those who co-operate 'through smooth talk' do not in fact join the Hasmoneans but the Hassidim. 'The grammatical subject has not changed from the beginning of the sentence.'[51] He thus understands בחלק לקות as signifying not 'tricks', but the twisting paths across the mountains which the resisters would have to resort to, see Ps. 35.6 and Jer. 23.12. The Hasmoneans, therefore, are not accused of being hypocrites in their attempt to aid the Pious, but of impotence.[52]

V.35 was explained above as being a midrash on Isa. 53. The martyrdom of the Hassidim is propitiatory. Their trials are described in terms for the 'purification of metals and the bleaching of cloth. See Rev. 3.18 (de Menasce). The last part of the verse is another reuse of Hab. 2.2–3; see our commentary on Dan. 8.17b, 26b; 10.14b. The Author here

---

[48] The verses listed in parentheses are instances where the word accompanies another predicate and therefore does not designate the sociological reality of Israel.

[49] See *VT*, 3 (1953), pp. 400–4. For another midrash on the Suffering Servant, see Wisd. 2.12–20; 3; 5. Cf., e.g., Dan. 11.32, 35; 12.3 and Wisd. 2.13; 3.6, 7.

[50] Op. cit., p. 198: 'He (Daniel) therefore regards them (the 'maskilim') rather than the Hasmoneans, who had not yet been able to reveal the full extent of their strength, as the true leaders of the nation.'

Thus, may we add, the book of Daniel uses the colourful imagery of the Holy War, but its message is a call to passive resistance (cf. 8.25; 2.34, 45; 11.32–35; 12.12). God is the One who will bring a solution to the crisis.

Re the martyrdom of the pious, A. Jaubert, op. cit., p. 78, refers to Ps. 44.18ff. which she considers to be an Asidean addition to an older fragment.

[51] Op. cit., p. 477, n. 37.

[52] For a different version of the facts, see 1 Macc. 2.42–8; 3.11ff.; 4.12–15.

inaugurates the theory which he will develop further in chapter 12 that the martyrs' sad end is not ultimate 'for there is another time fixed'.

In v.36 we have a new portrait of the abominable Antiochus. The height of blasphemy against the Lord is reached in the king's self-deification (see 1 Macc. 1.49; 2 Macc. 5.7ff.). He places himself above all the gods[53] (cf. Dan. 7.8, 20; see Dan. 8.4 and 11.3 on the king of Persia and Alexander the Great; and 11.16 on Antiochus the Great). According to our text he says נפלאות, 'monstrous things, revolting slanders',[54] see Daniel 8.24 and our commentary. For Daniel the revolt against God must reach its height for then the divine anger will be complete. So the Author quotes Isa. 10.23 (see *supra* concerning v.32) and repeats Dan. 9.27.

More objectively, Adam C. Welch observes that, 'the horde led by Alexander was not made up of Greek philosophers. . . . There was nothing left which such an Emperor could play in order to unite his kingdom except his own personality.'[55] This also holds for Antiochus IV. More ambitious than his predecessors, he replaced the Syrian gods of his fathers with Zeus Olympios whom he had represented with his own features (see vv.37–8).[56] 1 Macc. 1.41ff. even insinuates that Antiochus tried to set up a pagan monotheism, 'a thing unparalleled in the Graeco-Roman world before the third century CE,' says V. Tcherikover[57] who rejects this thesis as 'not credible' (p. 398). Yet we must not forget that the Jerusalem Temple was named the Temple of Zeus Olympios and the Jews were forced to celebrate *the king's* birthday there each month and to participate in the festive procession to honour Dionysos (see ibid., p. 196).

Antiochus' rejection of other divinities is especially well explained by L. Cerfaux and J. Tondriau: 'in order to realize the cult of the sovereigns, not only had the prestige of mortals to be extolled to the heavens (Alexander contributed powerfully to this), but the immortals had to be

[53] With J. J. Collins ('The Son of Man and the Saints . . .'.), it may be possible to distinguish between the heavenly beings spoken of in v.36 and associated with YHWH (i.e., the angelic host), and those mentioned in v.37 (the pagan gods). About the former ones, not only the Qumran scrolls are relevant, but also Ps. 82. About the latter ones, Julius Morgenstern ('The King-God among the Western Semites and the Meaning of Epiphanes', *V.T.* 10 (1960), no. 2, pp. 138–97) says that Antiochus shifted to a solar calendar, a fact which 'goes hand in hand with the development of empire' (p. 139). There was an identification of Baal Shamem with Melkart (Heracles) who, like the phoenix, dies and comes back from his ashes to life. 2 Macc. 4.18–20 shows that games were organized every 5 years in Tyre to honour Melkart. Sacrifices were offered to the god as to a dead hero. He was represented by the king, becoming on this occasion a divine epiphany. Antiochus IV took the title Epiphanes in 172. (The Samaritans sent him a letter calling him 'King Antiochus, god, Epiphanes', cf. Jos. *Ant.* XII.V.5.)
[54] Gesenius-Buhl (17th edn) ad loc.
[55] *Visions of the End* (London 1958), p. 67.
[56] In the N.T., Paul utilizes this text in his description of the Antichrist: 2 Thess. 2.4.
[57] Op. cit., p. 182.

devalued as well (the Olympian religion actually suffered this "devaluation")'.[58] Even 'the Favourite of women' thereby lost standing. This is Adonis-Tammuz (mentioned in Ezek. 8.14), one of the more popular fertility gods. As for 'the god of citadels',[59] he is probably Zeus. Antiochus built a magnificent temple to him at Antioch according to Livy XLI, 20. Our Author, however, is more interested in the supplanting of the God of Israel and he uses 'in his place' in reference to Zion's Temple rather than the plural 'in their place' (the other gods).

The 'foreign divinity' in v.39 could represent Antiochus himself according to O. Plöger. This is possible but not necessary. It will be recalled that in the 'Pamphlet against Nabonidus' (I.21; see *ANET*, 'Nabonidus and the Clergy of Babylon', p. 313a) Sin was a god whom 'none had seen in this country' (even though he was well-known elsewhere).

'The fortifications of citadels' no doubt refers to the Acra in Jerusalem (see 1 Macc. 1.33–4). It is possible that in the light of this latter text which speaks of a 'people of sinners' we should read here עַם (people) instead of עִם (with). This is V. Tcherikover's opinion. He sees them as new colonists, Antiochus' soldiers. 'Every *cleruchy* or *katoikia* in the Hellenistic period was military in its membership and organization . . . (*Ant.* XII, 159).'[60] He adds that this fact implied the confiscation of property, vexatious and violent acts with regard to the original inhabitants, taxes, and even expulsion from the city (see Thucydides I,114,3; II,70,4; IV,102,3).

Here the history properly speaking ends and the 'prophecy' begins. The events which occurred during the second half of 166 are not mentioned: the succeeding of Mattathias by his son Judas and the rout he inflicted upon the generals Lysias, Nicanor, and Gorgias.[61] This pericope opens on the inaccurate 'at the time of the end' (v.40). According to all the evidence Dan. 11 was written during the first part of 166.

There is no historical documentation of any total conquest of Egypt by Antiochus. The campaign described beginning in v.40 is a projection of Daniel's convictions into the future.[62] As in v.10, the invasion is a veritable inundation which recalls Isa. 8.7–8. Furthermore the eschatological dimensions are borrowed from other texts of Isaiah and Ezekiel (see Isa. 10.5ff.; 31.8–9; Ezek. 38—39 on Gog and Magog; etc.). It is possible that Antiochus' death, described in v.45, is an imitation of the

[58] *Le Culte des Souverains* . . ., p. 263.
[59] O. S. Rankin, 'The Festival of Hanukkah', in *The Labyrinth*, p. 198, quoting H. Gressmann, *Die hellenistische Gestirnreligion*, pp. 19–20, thinks it is rather a question of the god Kronos-Helios who was a warrior by nature (see Sib. III. 97–154). The astral element could have been regarded as a recent import in Daniel's time.
[60] Op. cit., p. 189.
[61] See 1 Macc. 3 and 4.   [62] Porphyry is not trustworthy here.

enemy 'falling upon the mountains of Israel' (Ezek. 39.4; cf. Zech. 14.2; Joel 3.2; Isa. 14.25). This eschatological aspect of the text did not escape the attention of the sectarians at Qumran. 1 QM is a midrash on our text.[63]

The open reference to the peoples of Edom, Moab, and Ammon in v.41 should not put us on the false scent. R. H. Charles believes it to be a later interpolation, but this need not be so, since, paradoxically, the nations mentioned add to the oracular dimension of the text. They are the almost mythical enemies of Israel. As if to emphasize this the Author uses the term ראשית (the élite) which sometimes applies to the nations when they are being considered mythologically (see Gen. 49.3; Num. 24.20; Jer. 49.35; Ps. 78.51; 105.36).[64] Besides there is a sort of irony here. The Jews' traditional enemies evidently escape the destruction by allying themselves with the persecutor. Their 'élite' is only good at evil. Their prowess is directed against 'the Magnificent Land' (cf. vv.16 and 8.9).

In v.43, the Libyan and Ethiopian nations[65] are mentioned who will consider Antiochus as their liberator from the Egyptian yoke. But whatever external aid he may call on, Antiochus once more[66] will receive bad news which will again interrupt his expedition in Egypt (v.44).[67] As before, the king will vent his rage against the Jews (designated by the term *rabbim*).

Historically, Antiochus' death occurred before the dedication of the Jerusalem Temple by Judas Maccabee on 14 December, 164; more exactly, he died sometime between 20 November and 19 December, 164,[68] at Tabae in Persia.[69]

[63] See in particular 1 QM 1.4–7; cf. Dupont-Sommer, *Ecrits Esséniens . . .,*[3] p. 185, n. 2.
[64] There is no need therefore to correct it to שארית (a remnant).
[65] Re these peoples, see Nah. 3.9; Jer. 46.9.
[66] See also Sennacherib's expedition into Palestine which was cut short, Isa. 37.7; 2 Kings 19.7.
[67] In fact, Antiochus had to turn his attention away from Egypt to deal with the Parthians and Armenians.
[68] See the British Museum table no. 35603 published by A. J. Sachs and D. J. Wiseman, 'A Babylonian King List of the Hellenistic Period', *Iraq*, 16 (1954), pp. 202–12.
[69] See Polybius XXXI.11 (1 Macc. 6.1–4; 2 Macc. 9.1–2). A propos the death of Antiochus as forecast by Daniel here, Stanley B. Frost evokes Shelley who, he says, 'saw so clearly in his *Prometheus Unbound*, (that) a tyrant whose hour of defeat is certain, is a tyrant already overthrown'. (*O.T. Apocalyptic* (London 1952), p. 241.)

12 Resurrection and Eschatology

The vision in chapter 11 which actually began in chapter 10 reaches its completion in chapter 12. The Book of Daniel has attained its ultimate goal in 11.44–5 with the description of the tyrant's end, but certain questions remain to be answered:

(a) How much time remains before the blessed end? It is true that this question had already been treated in chapter 9, but the explanation of the 'seventy weeks' (of years) left several details obscure.

(b) Who will be the beneficiaries of the divine parousia? Only those who are fortunate enough to be alive still when that Day comes? What of 'the faithful servants of YHWH who amid untold distresses had been true to their trust and held Israel together as YHWH's witness in the world'?[1] 'How could the social hope of a Messianic reign on earth be ethically complete, if those who had sacrificed little or nothing enjoyed it and those who had given all for it remained unblessed in the nether world?'[2] A related question concerns the ultimate fate of the wicked.

It is to these problems that the Author now turns. He does so by composing a piece with two parts: vv.1–4 deal with question (b), and vv.5–13 with question (a). The first verses are of an extraordinary thematic density. From the fact that their place is so appropriate in this context, they elevate the last part of the book to a very high level. It is difficult here to follow Paul Volz,[3] for whom Dan. 12.1–3 is a fragment of an old apocalypse inserted after the fact. It seems on the contrary that once again the Book of Jeremiah has inspired the Author. The expression עת צרה ('a time of anxiety') in v.1 is a quotation from Jeremiah 30.7: 'It is a time of anxiety for Jacob, yet he will emerge from it saved!' This chapter of Jeremiah continues by describing the miraculous liberation of the people: 'I will save you from afar. . . . For I am with you to save you, says the Lord. . . . I will restore the captives of the tents of Jacob and have pity on his dwellings; a city will be built on its ruins and a palace will be set up where it used to be. . . . I will multiply them (והרביתים), and they will not be diminished, etc.' It is clear that in Daniel's time the Hassidim read such prophecies not just as announcing the re-establishment of the Community after the Exile, but as the promise of a resurrec-

---

[1] H. E. Fosdick, *A Guide to Understanding the Bible* (New York 1938), pp. 270–1.
[2] Ibid.
[3] Paul Volz, *Die Eschatologie der jüdischen Gemeinde im neutestamentlichen Zeitalter* (Tübingen 1934), p. 11.

tion from the dead of those who had been faithful in Israel. Every life is inscribed in the Book (Dan. 12.2) and is important in the eyes of the Lord of history.[4]

The displacement of emphasis from the community as an entity to the community as composed of 'saints', 'thoughtful people', 'who justify the multitudes', is the fruit of an important socio-philosophical transformation. With Alexander's conquests and the creating of the Empire, man became a citizen of the world, of the *oikoumene*. And in a paradoxical, yet comprehensible way, this enlarging of men's horizons to universal dimensions had the consequence of atomizing society into individuals. In the process of the disintegrating of social structures which had been second nature to him, man found himself alone, hence unique, with particular problems which could no longer be resolved by collective solutions. The man of the Hellenistic period, says W. W. Tarn, 'was an individual, and as such needed new guidance'.[5] In a way we may say that the problem of coexistence between universal humanity and autonomous individuals inaugurated by Hellenism remains unresolved to this day. On the plane of their relation to each other, Daniel's recourse to the idea of a partial resurrection at the end of time creates as many, if not more, difficulties as it resolves.

The theme of the resurrection of the dead cannot be isolated from the rest of the book. It is not a question here of the intervention of a *deus ex machina*. The notion of resurrection is linked to the idea of the *People of Israel*, present throughout the book, either explicitly (see Dan. 12.1c) or implicitly by means of the personifications of Daniel and his companions, the 'son of man', and Michael. When we ignore this bond, the notion of resurrection becomes mythical. It rejoins the false Canaanite assurances of an uninterrupted cycle of life-death-rebirth. We must begin here if we are to understand

(a) why we do not find any expression of a resurrection of individuals except in late Biblical texts;

(b) and why the faith in 'resurrection, immortality, and eternal life'[6]

---

[4] This constitutes a decisive breakthrough brought about by the apocalypticists. Recall the above-mentioned article by J. J. Collins (cited in the commentary on Dan. 7, introduction): 'Apocalyptic Eschatology as the Transcendence of Death', *CBQ* 1974. In another paper published by *Biblical Research* the same year, Collins insists: '. . . hope for the transcendence of death is what decisively distinguishes apocalyptic from earlier prophecy' ('The Symbolism of Transcendence in Jewish Apocalyptic', p. 10).

[5] W. W. Tarn, *Hellenistic Civilization* (London 1927), p. 268.

[6] The title of a dissertation by George W. E. Nickelsburg, Jr., published in the 'Harvard Theological Series', no. 21 (Cambridge, Mass. 1972) (*Resurrection, Immortality, and Eternal Life in Inter-testamental Judaism*).

is very old in Israel but in a deliberately cautious form and always within the framework of the communal covenant.

Until just recently, biblical scholarship had held that the idea of eternal life for an individual appeared quite late in Israel. Hermann Gunkel,[7] for example, writes: 'Faith in the resurrection was not born from prophetic eschatology or the psalmist's piety. The prophets proclaim a hope *for the people*, not for the individual. The psalmists believe in a God who can only be praised "in the land of the living". We nowhere find the origin of faith in the resurrection, neither in the Old Testament nor in post-canonical Judaism. We only observe it where it is already developed and certain. Surely it was not born from "impressions", no faith finds its origin there. It is just as certain that it was not developed from religious reflections.[8] A representation such as hell testifies to this. It does not indicate some readily comprehensible speculation, but a wholly different origin. Thus this faith is a quite difficult enigma for the Old Testament scholar. . . .'[9]

Mitchell Dahood[10] has overturned this position which had been taken as firmly established. On the basis of linguistic parallels in the mythic texts from Ugarit (dating from about the thirteenth century BCE), Dahood sees faith in a personal life after death in some forty places in the Psalter.[11] He also refers to Prov. 14.32; 12.38; 16.2; 15.24; etc., not mentioning the other witnesses which traditionally were seen as ancestors of this notion (see Gen. 5.24 and 2 Kings 2.3, 5, 9; Deut. 32.39; 1 Sam. 26; Ps. 16.11; 17.15; 49.15; 73.24; Ezek. 37; etc.). Dahood's radical position has given rise to much vigorous protest (he discusses some of it in his introductions to vols. 2 and 3 of his commen-

---

[7] H. Gunkel, *Schöpfung und Chaos* (Göttingen 1895), p. 291, n. 2.

[8] *Sic.* We do not follow Gunkel on this point.

[9] The same opinion is shared by many scholars. See R. H. Charles, 'Eschatology', *EB*, vol. 2, 1901, col. 1355, for whom it seems that Isa. 26.19 is the first text (written very late but perhaps preceding Dan. 12) which speaks in the Hebrew Bible of individual resurrection. Cf. D. S. Russell, *The Method and Message . . .*, pp. 366ff., 369. He regrets that in Dan. 12 the *raison d'être* of the Resurrection, i.e., a continued communion with God, is lost from view. R. H. Charles, in the article already cited, speaks of a 'sort of eschatological property, a device by means of which the members of the nation are presented before God to receive their final award'. Mitchell Dahood, *Psalms*, The Anchor Bible (New York 1965–70), 3 vols., quotes the following as sharing the same perspective (in order to refute them): S. Mowinckel, *The Psalms in Israel's Worship*, I, p. 240 (Dahood, I, p. xxxvi); A. F. Kirkpatrick, *The Book of Psalms* (Cambridge 1903), p. xcv (Dahood, III, p. xlii); J. Hempel, *I.D.B.*, III, p. 951 (Dahood, III, p. xliii); J. H. Eaton, *Psalms: Introduction and Commentary* (London 1967), p. 40 (Dahood, ibid.).

[10] Op. cit. (See the preceding note.)

[11] True, already the Rabbis had read some Psalmic expressions as referring to resurrection (e.g., *Yalk. Ps.* 671; Targ. and Rashi on Ps. 73.20; etc.). Such a Rabbinic exegetical confirmation, however, must be assessed in keeping in mind the Pharisaic apologetics for the doctrine of resurrection.

tary on Psalms. If a technical discussion of all the positions being stated cannot be here undertaken, we do believe it indispensable for the understanding of Dan. 12 to draw the reader's attention to the fundamental message communicated by the notion of resurrection.

Thus as we indicated above, Israel's eschatological hopes are linked to the concept of the people of the Covenant. From this perspective, expressions such as 'you have brought my soul up from Sheol' (Ps. 30; 86; 103; Isa. 38.17) cannot be considered as hyperboles or symbols but must be understood as expressing existential realities, although as yet without any eschatological nuance.[12] In other texts, such as Hos. 6.1–3; 13.14; Ezek. 37.1–14; and Isa. 53.10ff. it is a question of national restoration. However, on the subject of Second Isaiah, R. Martin-Achard writes: 'We have the impression that he is groping. He has the presentiment that the Servant must escape death. He therefore affirms without being able to explain the modalities of an event which is beyond him.'[13] Today we can be more explicit thanks to our deeper knowledge of North-west Semitic literature. Second Isaiah, like so many other pre-exilic biblical writers, does not so much 'grope' as hesitate to give his faith in the ultimate victory of life over death a 'Canaanite' expression. M. Dahood is correct to emphasize the use by many of the psalmists of Ugaritic expressions and thus to demonstrate that Israel had a much more developed faith in eternal life than had previously thought to be the case. In this as in almost everything else, Canaan furnished Israel its means of expression.[14] Yet Dahood is wrong on two counts:

(a) He does not sufficiently recognize the originality—so fundamental in our opinion—of the Israelite notion of eternal life, whose corollary is the resurrection; and

(b) he does not draw decisive enough conclusions from the biblical writers' cautious reserve when they express their faith in Life before the second century BCE.

Both points indicate what is at issue here. For Canaan, survival was a fact of *nature*; for Israel it is an *historical* phenomenon. In other words,

---

[12] See C. Barth, *Die Errettung von Tode in den individuellen Klage und Dankliedern des A.T.* (Basel 1947), quoted by Robert Martin-Achard, *De la Mort à la Résurrection d'après l'A.T.* (Neuchâtel 1956), p. 55.

[13] R. Martin-Achard, op. cit., p. 95.

[14] It is well known how far M. Dahood pushes Israel's dependence on Ugarit concerning the vocabulary of the 'after-life'. חיים often means 'eternal life' (he cites a dozen Psalms, four passages from Proverbs, etc.) (*Psalms*, III, pp. xlvi–xlvii). אחרית signifies 'the future' or 'the future life'. Some Psalms speak of the Heavenly Banquet at the time of the after-life; there are 'references to the beatific vision'; etc. (see ibid., pp. xlvii–lii).

the affirmation in the myth from Ugarit (see especially 1 Aqht VI) of the 'resurrection' of Baal is an expression of faith in the natural cycles: what has been, will be. Israel's affirmation of the ultimate triumph[15] of Life is not the affirmation of an objective fact, it does not seek magically to protect the *status quo* against any alteration. It is a cry, an invocation, a prayer, a wager. It participates in Israel's 'work' (*'abodah*) of giving meaning to history in such a way that in the middle of despair there is hope, in the middle of death Life.

Its distance from Canaanite myth is such that its terms, here more than anywhere else, especially if we take into account the enormous naturistic temptation on Israel, could only have been utilized with an extreme circumspection by those circles which today we call 'Yahwist'.[16] It was necessary to avoid any misunderstanding in this matter, for it would jeopardize Israel's fragile edifice erected on the plane of being, not on the plane of having. When the psalmist praises God for having saved him from the 'snares of Sheol' and his 'soul (life) from death' (Ps. 116.3, 8, etc.),

(a) he speaks out of a personal historical situation,

(b) in this situation, the whole people may find a faithful image of its own experience;

(c) death and life, Sheol and 'the land of the living',[17] weakness and help (Ps. 116.6), are not fixed states; the psalmist does not pass from the first to the second as from one sphere to another. They are the poles of a constant tension: 'The death of his Hassidim is precious in the sight of the Lord' (v.15);[18] and

(d) this psalm is not a dogmatic expression of the resurrection, but rather the cultic actualization of the tension between death and life in the existence of Israel and every Israelite.

It is a question of being, therefore, and not of having. Pindar (imitated by F. Nietzsche) said: γενοίο οἷος ἐσσί, 'become what you can be'. That is, acquire as many virtues as you can, enrich your personality,

---

[15] Instead of 'final'. For us, the ultimate englobes the final.

[16] 'The symbol may become unavailable due to its contingent connotations (e.g., the swastika). It becomes utilizable again when it distanciates itself from these connotations.' (Paul Ricoeur in conversation.)

We believe that A. Bentzen is fundamentally in agreement with us when he says that Dan. 7 is the fruit of a remythologization (of Ps. 2, for example) because *mythological language no longer represented that much of a danger in Daniel's epoch.* (Cf. *King and Messiah*, pp. 74–5.)

[17] Based on the Pléiade translation. M. Dahood prefers 'Fields of Life' (III, pp. xlvii, 144, 148).

[18] Cf. Wisd. 15.2–5: 'For even if we sin, we are thine as we acknowledge thy power. But we will not sin, knowing that we are accounted thine . . . to acknowledge thy power is the very root of immortality' (cf. 3.4–9; etc.).

become a hero, a superman. Israel, on the contrary, says 'become what you are'.[19] The affirmation of the Resurrection in Israel is the affirmation of man's transcendent dimension, the affirmation of the existential tension between the σῶμα ψυχικὸν and the σῶμα πνευματικόν (1 Cor. 15.44; cf. the remainder of this chapter).

In Daniel's language, far from being a fact of nature, the resurrection is the transfiguration of the Israelite into the 'son of man'. As Enoch is identified with the son of man (Enoch 70; 71.14ff.), so too Daniel is specifically made the beneficiary of the resurrection (Dan. 12.13). It is certainly not by chance that the angel Michael, so closely associated with the figure of the 'son of man' in chapters 7—12, is the one who introduces the scene about the final resurrection.[20] Michael's inclusive character is underscored in one text from Qumran which, in our opinion, presents the message of the first part of chapter 12 in a condensed form:

'He has sent an eternal aid [cf. Dan. 10.13] to the company of his liberation thanks to the strength of the angel (whom) he has glorified, thanks to Michael's supremacy in the eternal light, to make resplendent in joy the Covenant of Israel peace and blessing for the company of God, to exalt over all divine (beings) the supremacy of Michael and the domination of Israel over all flesh.'[21]

We have demonstrated that the framework of the great vision of the 'son of man' in chapter 7 is constituted by the Feast of Succoth. In chapter 12 this liturgical computation is again present and it constitutes a supplementary element tying it to the book's central chapter. Twice in v.1 we find the expression 'in that time'. Its eschatological meaning is clear, but here once again it is not a question of a speculation about the 'end', but of a reflection on the 'ultimate'. 'That time' is the time of the reading of the 'book', a very old element of the Autumn Festival.[22] At that moment of the liturgical calendar is actualized the Last Judgement. Thus as H. Riesenfeld writes, 'the rites and motifs attached to the feast [of Succoth] nourish the hope in a resurrection of the dead.[23]

Within this perspective, the people's suffering also plays a cultic role, 'It will be a time of anxiety' (v.1), but it also introduces the supreme blessing. Already here we find a rough statement of the teaching of

---

[19] 'When I shall present myself before my sovereign Judge,' says Rabbi Sussya, 'he will not ask me why I did not become Moses, but why I did not become Sussya.'

[20] Re the priestly dimensions of such an inauguration by Michael, see *infra*. Notice also that the archangel is sometimes presented as the heavenly High Priest, see Test. of Levi 5; Test. of Dan 5–6; Ass. of Moses 10.1; 3 Baruch 10–15; the Rabbinic literature. What is more, when the archangel Michael appears, the son of man is never far away. In Dan. 12 we find in v.6: 'the man clothed in linen'.

[21] 1 QM 17.6–8.

[22] Its origin goes back to the tablets of fate from the Babylonian New Year Festival.

[23] *Jésus transfiguré*, p. 35.

Rabbinic Judaism which 'evolved from the old doctrine of the probationary and disciplinary value of adversity, sufferings and misfortunes are a divinely appointed means whereby the righteous man may *atone* for his sins here upon earth so that the judicial necessity for his receiving retribution for these sins in the hereafter is removed'.[24]

In Dan. 12.1–4, as in the calendar for the autumn festivals, Yom Kippur precedes Succoth.

Text 12. 1–4

(1) In that time Michael, the great Prince, will stand up, he who stands for the sons of your people. It will be a time of anxiety such as has never been since there was a nation until that time.

In that time, your people will escape, whoever will be found inscribed in the Book.
(2) The multitude of those who sleep in the land of dust will reawaken, these are for the eternal life, those for disgrace and the eternal horror.
(3) The thoughtful ones will be resplendent like the splendour of the firmament
and those who justified the multitude will be like the stars for ever onward.
(4) And you, Daniel, keep these words secret and seal this book until the time of the end.
The multitude will be perplexed but knowledge will increase.

Critical Notes 12. 1–4

V.1 ובעת ההיא: see 11.40. In chapter 11, we found many chronological expressions which have an eschatological significance (see 11.13, 14, 20, 24, 27, 29, 35, 45). None is exactly like this term in 12.1. These words in 12.1 are a prophetic way of 'attaching events of an eschatological order to historical acts which have just been described without any interval; see Isa. 7.14; Jer. 30.18; Ezek. 34.11' (L. Dennefeld, *La Sainte Bible*, ed. Pirot and Clamer, vol. vii, p. 693).—יעמוד: for יקום, see Dan. 11.17. LXX read: יעבור!—העמד על: this expression has two senses: (a) to lead as a chief (see LXX; cf. Num. 7.2); and (b) to protect or defend (see Esth. 8.11; 9.16; see Charles, p. 325; Montgomery, p. 472; O. Betz, *Der Paraklet* (1963), p. 64).

One also stands up to judge (see Deut. 19.17; Josh. 20.6; Isa. 50.8; Ezek. 44.24). Judicial functions are attributed to the angels in Zech. 1.12; 3; Prologue to Job; Jub. 17.15—18.12; Test. of Levi 5.6f.; Test. of Dan 6.1–5 (see G. W. E. Nickelsburg, op. cit., p. 13).—השר: prince, general (of the celestial army); see 10.13, 21; Josh.

[24] O. S. Rankin, *Israel's Wisdom Literature*, p. 115.

5.14f.; LXX, Θ: ἄγγελος ὁ μέγας, ὁ ἄρχων ὁ μέγας.—עת צרה: borrowed from Jer. 30.7, but also see Judg. 10.14; Ps. 37.39; Isa. 32.3; Jer. 14.8; 15.11; 1 Macc. 9.27; Ass. Mos. 8.1; Mark 13.19; Matt. 24.21; Rev. 16.18. 'The time of turmoil that precedes Israel's rescue and restoration into the community of the new covenant' (G. Nickelsburg, p. 15).—מהיות גוי: see Exod. 9.18, 24; Deut. 4.32; Joel 2.2.—ימלט ... כתוב בספר: see the parallel in 4 Q Dib Ham (published by M. Baillet, 'Un recueil liturgique de Qumrân, Grotte 4: "Les Paroles des Luminaires"', RB, 68 (1961), pp. 195–250):... כל הכתוב בספר חיים ... והצלה עמכם; cf. Exod. 32.32; Ezek. 13.19; Ps. 69.29; Enoch 104.1.

V.2 ורבים: see 8.25 and our commentary. Cf. Esth. 4.3; Matt. 20.28; 26.28.—מישני: 'to sleep' = to die; see 1 Sam. 28.15; Jer. 51.39, 57; Job 3.13; 14.12; Test. Zab. 10.4ff.; 4 Esdras 7.95; 2 Baruch 21.24; John 11.11; Acts 7.60; 1 Cor. 7.39; etc.—אדמת־עפר: see Charles, p. 327: 'in the land of dust' = sheol, see Dahood I, pp. 43, 140, 184, etc.: 'underworld'; see Ps. 7.6; 22.16; 30.10. עפר is not 'dust', he says, but 'mud' (ibid. III, pp. 28, 47). Cf. G. Nickelsburg, p. 18: sheol is a 'land' (ארץ = אדמה), see Isa. 26.19; 1 Q Isᵃ. = LXX, A, Θ, Σ, Targ. Daniel expands upon Isa. 26. Cf. Job 2.8; 20.11; 30.19; Ps. 22.30; etc.—יקיצו: see Ps. 3.6; 73.20; 35.23; etc. M. Dahood understands the term קץ here, as well as in Isa. 26.19, and in the Psalter, as meaning 'the awakening at resurrection' (see Introduction to Vol. II of his A.B. commentary on Psalms).—לחיי עולם: live for ever; see Wisd. 5.15. לעולם may be hyperbolic (see Moore II, p. 297, n. 6).—לדראון: here and in Isa. 66.24; decomposition of the cadavers of the wicked. Perhaps לחרפות is an explicative gloss on this rare word. LXX: διασπορά, corruption of διαφθορά (see Mgr Alfrink, Biblica (1959), p. 367).—The LXX here insists on the resurrection of the dead (see LXX Job 42.17; 19.25; 1 Sam. 2.6; 2 Kings 5.7).

V.3 The LXX understood מחזיקי הדברים instead of מצדיקי הרבים.—יזהירו: is only found elsewhere in its nominal form (Ezek. 8.2).—משכילים: see Dan. 9.22; 1 QS 9.19, 20; 1 QH 7.26. As a title, see Dan. 11.33; 1 QS 3.13; 9.12–14 (texts cited by Nickelsburg).—מצדיקים: see CD 20.18 (Schechter) = BII.18 (Dupont-Sommer).

V.4 ישטטו: LXX: ἕως ἂν ἀπομανῶσιν οἱ πολλοί. שט׳ט signifies 'to wander to and fro', see Amos 8.12 (cf. 2 Thess. 2.10–12). A. Bentzen, citing E. J. Young, says: '(Menschen) ... suchen Weisheit, wo sie nicht zu finden ist' (p. 85) = Rashi = Plöger = Heaton = Montgomery, etc. Behrmann, following Schleusner, proposes ישטו, see Ps. 40.5, LXX μανίας (ψευδεῖς) = fools. Here the meaning would be 'to become renegades, apostates'.—ותרבה הדעת: LXX presupposes the reading הרעה, see 1 Macc. 1.9, not so in Θ, Pesh., Vul.; cf. 1 Qp

Hab 9.1–2; Test. of Levi 18.5 (vv.3 and 4 are interesting for the context of Dan. 12.4).—עד עת קץ: = 11.35b.

Commentary

Paul Volz[25] has also been struck by the resemblance between the themes in chapters 7 and 12. Here Michael (v.1), there the Son of man ('*der Mensch*'), he says. But he then goes astray by affirming that it is a question of 'two independent traditions. Even the difference in the names of the saving personages (in 7.13, the man; in 12.1, Michael) demonstrates that these materials were originally foreign to each other and adopted in part by the final redactor.'[26] In fact, as we have seen repeatedly, the figure of the 'son of man' is an inclusive one and the angel Michael is one of its aspects.[27]

Michael's apparition on the stage of history is endowed with a military character. He is the general of the heavenly armies come to wipe out the enemies of God and his People (see our critical notes). But what comes next shows that the judicial aspect is also closely linked to him (cf. Josh. 5; Exod. 23.20ff.; Isa. 63.9). Like the 'son of man' in chapter 7, Michael combines the functions of priest, judge, and king. Here as there, it is a question of YHWH's enthronement within the liturgical framework of Succoth.[28] At the time of the final combat between God's chief and hero (מלך or שר)[29] on the one hand, and the powers of chaos (demythologized into universal powers) on the other hand, the amount of suffering is unprecedented, but the victory is certain. Better still, 'even suffering . . . is part of salvation; suffering is necessary, suffering is useful, suffering is the beginning of salvation, without suffering there is no salvation!'[30] Hence the greater the distress, the more imminent the victory. The triumph will be miraculous; it will even involve the resurrection of the dead.

For those who are inscribed in the Book 'will live even though they are dead'. This is what v.2, the central verse of this chapter, affirms.

---

[25] Op. cit.

[26] Ibid., p. 11.

[27] See Dan. 10.13ff.

[28] See *supra*. E. Heaton, op. cit., p. 241, writes: 'It is most important that these verses should be interpreted as presenting the establishment of God's rule as in ch. 7.'

[29] See 4 Esdras 13; cf. Or. Sib. III.633ff.

[30] P. Volz, op. cit., p. 128. O. Plöger invites us to compare our text with 1 Macc. 9.27 and to feel the difference of mentality between the two. For the Maccabean movement, heir of Chron., Antiochus' persecution is an historical event among others. Its exceptional character lies in the fact that there is no longer any prophet (non-eschatological conception). But, according to Dan. 12.1 there never were events like these of the second century BCE ever since man has lived on earth (eschatological conception). ('Reden und Gebete . . .' op. cit.)

Here once again Daniel is a pioneering work. It is true that W. Bousset[31] has seen Iranian influences behind this verse. Whatever the case may be, a good-sized amount of literature was inspired by Dan. 12.2, especially the Apocrypha[32] and the New Testament.[33] Indeed, this is the most precise text concerning the resurrection of (some of) the dead in the Hebrew Scriptures. The ancient historian Porphyry undoubtedly errs here because of his historicism. For him, Dan. 12.2 'is in no way an allusion to the resurrection of sinners and the elect. The pseudo-Daniel was here simply describing Israel's situation on the day after Antiochus' defeat and his death in Persia. The Jews who up until then had been buried under trials and miseries as though in a sepulchre, arise in jubilation at an unexpected victory while the traitors to the Law, Antiochus' partisans, are doomed to everlasting shame.'[34] In fact, however, it seems as if Plöger is correct when he says that the Author is reusing Ezek. 37 in an individual sense, at least if he did not know Isa. 26.19.[35] This latter text, from a late but uncertain date, presents indisputable ideological and linguistic parallels to Dan. 12. In any case, the influence of the Book of Isaiah is manifest here.[36] The term דראון is found only here and in Isa. 66.24 (see our critical notes). Furthermore, H. L. Ginsberg is certainly correct in seeing in Dan. 12.2–3 one important element of our Author's midrashic reuse of Isa. 52.13—53.12. Like the 'Servant of the Lord', the 'Thoughtful People' will shine like the stars in the sky (Dan. 12.3; cf. Isa. 52.13). And like the Servant, the *rabbim* were ill, but will be healed (Dan. 12.2; cf. Isa. 53.10–11; like him, the *maskilim* justify the multitude (Dan. 12.3; cf. Isa. 53.11); etc. It seems to us that these parallels allow us to see in Isa. 66.23–4 quoted above one valuable indication of our Author's intention in this verse. Isaiah, in effect, clearly says that the traitors will not come to life again for 'their worm will not die and their fire will not be extinguished'. B. J. Alfring[37] is convincing when he sees in the double אלה in our text

---

[31] W. Bousset, *Die Religion des Judentums* (1904)², pp. 540ff., (1926)³, pp. 510ff. But see *infra* the opposition of Paul Volz. Similarly, W. Eichrodt, *Theology of the O.T.* (OTL), Vol. II, p. 516, invites us to use prudence. '*There are clearly great difficulties in assuming extra-Israelite influence* [his italics] . . . the divergences between Persian and Jewish resurrection beliefs are too great to make mutual influence probable.'
[32] See Ass. of Moses 10.2; Enoch 20.5; 103.4; etc.
[33] Beyond the extraordinary development of this notion in the foundation documents of Christianity, it should be noticed that the presentation of the resurrection in Dan. 12.2 combines three registers found also in the N.T.: (a) the awakening of the dead from their sleep; (b) entering into eternal life; (c) glorification.
   On the motif of the suffering associated with transfiguration, see Heb. 1.3; 2.9f.; 5.7–9; 12.1–11.
[34] Pierre de Labriolle, *La Réaction Païenne* (Paris 1942), p. 267, quoting Porphyry, Fragment 43 W.
[35] Op. cit., ad loc.   [36] See G. W. E. Nickelsburg, op. cit., p. 20.
[37] 'L'idée de Résurrection d'après Dan. XII, 1.2', *Biblica* (1959), pp. 355–71.

two distinct groups as, for example, also in 2 Sam. 2.13. 'Thus (in v.2) the preceding generations who have already fallen asleep [in opposition to the generation who will not die envisaged in v.1], are divided into two categories: those who will return to life and those for whom the resurrection is not intended' (p. 365). The second אלה therefore must be understood as referring to those who will not be saved from death, not being inscribed in the Book, those who will remain for ever in the tomb where their corpses will rot (see our critical notes).

Who will come to life again? The elements of the text agree unanimously: Israel alone is envisaged, and even the faithful Israel, the *rabbim*.[38] This is God's triumphant response to the persecutor's jubilation—the martyrs for the faith, the Hassidim led by their Teachers, *Maskilim* and *Matsdiqim*, will be rewarded after death, they are living 'even though they are dead'.[39] 'By the resurrection', says R. H. Charles (p. 326), 'the righteous individual was to be raised to a higher communion (a) with God and (b) to be restored to communion with the righteous community. Thus the communion of the righteous individual with God was not temporally conditioned, because it was unbroken by death.' This mind-set is typically Israelite and Paul Volz concludes from it that there is a purely Israelite origin to the notion of the resurrection here since it is not born 'of anthropological representations, but from a religious necessity'.[40] Consequently, he continues, an influence from Parsism[41] must be considered but with caution. Yet the next motif of the transfigured righteous ones' shining forth 'like the splendour of the firmament' or 'like the stars' (v.3) may have its origin in an astral religion. Here again this theme was exploited by post-biblical Judaism.[42] In the

[38] The apologetic concern is evident in the affirmation by the Jewish commentators in the Middle Ages that it is here a question of all of Israel (see Saadia, Redaq, Ibn Ezra, Maimonides). In the same sense, E. F. Sutcliffe, *The O.T. and the Future Life* (London 1946), pp. 138–40. Let us note, however, W. Eichrodt's judgement (op. cit., I, pp. 470–1): 'This extension of the prophetic picture of judgement (to the dead)— at least where it obtains in full force—means that the distinction between Israel and the heathen becomes almost meaningless . . . and thus comes close to the universalism of the early expectation of doom.'

[39] Recall this moving speech by R. Eleazar (in the name of R. Hanina): 'When a righteous man dies, it is only for his generation that he is dead. With him it is like someone who loses a pearl. Wherever it may be, it remains a pearl, it is only lost for its owner' (*Meg.* 15a).

Re the problem posed by the martyrdom of men of faith in the second century BCE, see 2 Macc. 7. Tertullian's words on this topic are widely known: 'The martyrs' blood was the seed of immortality.' Ernest Renan supports this sentiment: 'Martyrdom was the veritable creator of the belief in a second life'; and A. Causse properly concludes: 'The real ferment of the belief in the resurrection was the persecution in the time of Antiochus Epiphanes.'

[40] Op. cit., p. 232.

[41] See W. Bousset's contrary opinion, *supra*.

[42] See Enoch 104ff.; 4 Esdras 7.97, 125; 2 Baruch 51; 2 Enoch 66.7; Wisd. 3.7; Enoch 51.5; 108.11ff.; Ps. of Sol. 3. 12; Matt. 13.48 (texts cited by R. Martin-Achard,

words of Jean Steinmann:[43] 'The deification of the Elect is expressed by the divine light with which they are irradiated, a light resembling that of the firmament, which is to say the stars, the symbols for the angels in the apocalypses[44] after having once been stellar gods in Babylonian paganism.'[45]

Several elements are worth noting in this quotation from Steinmann. The first concerns the 'Elect'. Without necessarily accepting O. S. Rankin's opinion[46] that, in this verse, 'the thoughtful ones' are distinguished from the *rabbim* as the former only rise to inherit heavenly abodes, whereas the latter are merely received in *terrestrial* spheres, we agree that the sages are distinguished from the multitude. Collectively they are what the Servant of the Lord represented in Isaiah's songs. As with him, their martyrdom has an expiatory value (see Isa. 53.11; Dan. 11.33), the *rabbim* benefiting from their sacrifice.

As for the stellar brilliance of these blessed ones, important conclusions are to be drawn from the biblical texts which inspired this image, texts such as maybe Isa. 26.19 which speaks of 'a dew of light'. Above all we need to consider two texts built around the same theme: Isa. 14.12ff. and Ezek. 28.12ff. These two prophets exploit the ancient myth of the Primordial Man with regard to the 'king of Babel' and the 'king of Tyre'. They are the models used by Dan. 12.3 and with them, we find ourselves right within a royal[47] and Adamic[48] ideology. In short, here too we

---

De la Mort . . ., p. 114, n. 1). In the literature from Qumran, see CD 3.20 (Adam's glory); 1 QS 4.8 (the luminous glory of the Firmament); etc.

[43] Op. cit., pp. 156–7.

[44] See, for example, Enoch 104.2, 4, 6; 4 Esdras 7.97, 125; 2 Enoch 1.5; 2 Baruch 51.3; Matt. 13.43 . . . and Dan. 8.10.

[45] Cf. Eric Burrows, 'Some Cosmological Patterns', *The Labyrinth*, pp. 66ff. He thinks the idea of an astral immortality was probably born in the sixth (fifth?) century among the Persians due to their contact with the Chaldeans. As for T. H. Gaster (*I.D.B.*, vol. IV, pp. 42–3), he turns his eyes in another direction: (The belief in) 'the location of the dead in the stars was a common idea in Greco-Roman paganism. . . . (It) may be traced even further to the Egyptian Book of the Dead and the Pyramid texts.'

The 'stellarization', process of 'angelization', uncovers, here again, a context of merger between heavens and earth as we spoke about especially in the commentary on Dan. 7. W. Eichrodt, op. cit., II, p. 514, is forcefully opposed to any notion of an astral religion in Daniel.

[46] Op. cit., p. 137.

[47] In the beautiful text from Wisd. 3.7–8, the ancient martyrs are God's appointed rulers. They *judge* and *govern* the nations, running to and fro 'like sparks through the stubble'.

Re the light attributed to the Saints, see Enoch 38.4; 2 Baruch 51.3, 5; Enoch 46.7; 43; 4 Macc. 17.5; Ps. of Sol. 18.9ff.; Jub. 19.25; Ass. of Moses 10.9; etc. (texts cited by Paul Volz, op. cit., pp. 398ff.).

[48] The Rabbis taught that Adam's original appearance was extremely bright, brighter than the sun. For the Tannaim, Adam's heel was brighter than the sun, implying that his face was all the more so. See *Tanḥ. B, ḥuqot* 17 (57b) Simon ben Menasya. Cf. 2 Cor. 4.6.

encounter elements which are familiar to us from chapter 7. There, God was fire and light and the 'son of man' participated in his brilliance along with the People of the Saints (vv.9ff.; Dan. 10.6; 8.10). Daniel, who himself is a 'member of the body' of the 'son of man' (see *supra* and 12.13) is moreover a representative of the Saints who benefit from the Light (see 5.14). Here, as in chapter 7, the colouration of the text is plainly messianic. The stellar splendour belongs to the Messiah, that is God's light as reflected by his Anointed, or in Daniel's language, by the 'son of man'.[49]

While awaiting this glorious end, Daniel—the sixth century prophet— is given the order to seal his book since its message is not for his generation (v.4). This is a direct parallel to 8.26 (see ad loc. and also *infra*, 12.9). The seal assures the inviolability of the writing (cf. Isa. 29.11).[50]

The end of v.4 is more uncertain (see our critical notes). The Masoretic Text, however, is to be conserved since it contains a reference to Amos 8.12 where it is a question of the People running here and there seeking the Word of the Lord but not finding it. Daniel adds, however, that 'knowledge will increase'. For the Author, salvation is linked to knowledge of mysteries, to the comprehension of God's plan in history (see v.10b; cf. 8.16ff.; 9.23ff.; 10.12ff.; 11.12). God's final word, therefore, is one of salvation.

The book could very well end here. Basing his argument on the introduction into the next verses of a plurality of angels as in chapter 8, H. L. Ginsberg[51] believes that in any case v.4 constitutes the finale of the vision in chapters 10—12. We will adopt the judgement of J. A. Montgomery that vv.5ff. constitute an epilogue or appendix, but they are authentic as our commentary will try to demonstrate.

Text 12. 5–13

(5) And I, Daniel, I looked and behold two others were standing there, one on one bank of the river and the other on the other bank. (6) He said to the man clothed in linen who was above the waters of the river: 'When will the end of these wondrous things come?' (7) And I heard the man clothed in linen who was above the waters of the river; he lifted his right hand and his left hand toward heaven and he swore by He-Who-Lives-For-Ever: 'This will be for one period, some periods, and a half (period); when the dismemberment of the power of the holy people is ended, all these things will come to an end.' (8) I heard but did not understand, and I said: 'My lord, what will be

---

[49] See W. Eichrodt, op. cit., II, pp. 513–14: 'Once again we may detect the transfer to the faithful of a distinction originally proper to the Messiah, for . . . in later Judaism the Messiah is the possessor of the divine glory.' See also pp. 510–11.

[50] Cf. Rev. 22.10 where the time of the end has arrived.

[51] *Studies* . . ., pp. 30–1. A. Bentzen, p. 85, rejects this opinion.

the issue of these things?' (9) He said: 'Go, Daniel, for these words are kept secret and sealed until the time of the end. (10) A multitude will be purified, whitened, and refined. The wicked will act wickedly. None of the wicked will understand, but the thoughtful ones will understand. (11) From the time when the regular offering ends and the setting up of the devastating abomination, there will be twelve hundred and ninety days. (12) Blessed is he who waits and comes to thirteen hundred and thirty-five days. (13) You, go until the end. You will have rest and you will arise to receive your lot in the end of the days.'

Critical Notes 12. 6–13

V.6 ויאמד: LXX, Vss. of Θ, Vul.: ואמר (first person). See Dan. 8.13.

V.7 בחי העולם: see 4.31 (cf. Rev. 10.6).—למועד וכו″: see 7.25 (cf. 8.14); 9.27).—וככלות: the LXX read 'when will stop (וְכָלוֹת) the hand of him who crushes (נופץ; or, see Bevan: נפץ יד instead of נפץ יד; see Judg. 7.19; Jer. 51.20; [Ps. 71.9]; Charles, p. 335) the holy people'. H. L. Ginsberg thinks here too of a poor Hebrew translation of an original Aramaic (restored we would have a text which could be translated as: 'and when the strength of him who profanes a holy people fails him . . .').—עם קדש: see 7.18, 25, 27; 8.24.

V.8 ולא אבין: see 8.27.—אדני: see 10.16.—מה אחרית אלה: like Charles (pp. 335–6), H. L. Ginsberg (p. 55) assumes that the original Aramaic text was: מה אחוית אלין (= מה פשר אלה, see 5.12; cf. Job 13.17). The LXX has, in effect: τίς ἡ λύσις τοῦ λόγου τούτου. But some mss. of the LXX add: καὶ τίνες αἱ παραβολαὶ αὗται, which makes one suspect that another reading of אחרית was אחידה as in 5.12 (ואחוית אחידן). Pesh. and Vul. read אחרי: 'What will come *after* these things?'. אחרית: with the same sense of result, see Dan. 2.18; 10.14.

V.11 הוסר התמיד: for the importance of the restoration of the regular offering, see Neh. 10.33ff.; Dan. 8.11; 11.31.—שקוץ שמם: see 8.13; 9.27; 11.31 (see in particular our commentary on 9.27).

V.12 אשרי המחכה: see Ps. Sol. 18.7; Θ: μακάριος ὁ ὑπομένων (LXX: ἐμμένων).—1335: repeated by Ass. Isa. 4.12.

V.13 לקץ: *del.* in Θ and LXX. Perhaps a gloss by assimilation with the end of the verse (see M. Delcor, ad loc.).— Θ and LXX add: 'for there are still days and seasons for the accomplishment of the end (and you will rest, etc.)'.—ותנוח: for R. H. Charles, it is a question of a repose of the spirit, not the tomb as in Isa. 57.2 (or in Sheol as in Job 3.17). We are following Montgomery (p. 478), however, and see in the remainder of the verse an allusion to the resurrection. Montgomery too refers to Wisd. 4.7; Rev. 10.13; etc.—ותעמד: is unique in the sense of 'to resuscitate'. But in 8.22

and 12.1 (cf. 11.17), it is used for קוּם. LXX and Θ have ἀναστήσῃ (Briggs, cited by Montgomery, p. 478, appeals to Ps. 1.5).— לְקֵץ הַיָּמִים: cf. עֵת קֵץ in Dan. 12.4. Paul Volz, p. 164, refers to 2 Baruch 29.8; 19.5; 59.4 (*finis temporis*); etc. R. H. Charles refers to Dan. 1.5, 15, 18 in Heb. and 4.31 in Aramaic: the expression in Daniel only represents the end of a determined period. But the *interpolator* responsible for this final verse of Daniel did not see this and attributed an eschatological meaning to this expression which it did not have.—לְגֹרָלְךָ: see Montgomery, ad loc.: the spiritual sense of the term also occurs in Jer. 13.25; Mic. 2.5; Ps. 125.3; Col. 1.12.

Commentary

The epilogue to the Book of Daniel begins in v.5. As the great vision was introduced by vv.1–3 of chapter 10, so it now ends with a finale in the same surroundings of the 'great river which is the Tigris' (10.4 and 12.5).[52] Yet we may also think of the Ulai which appeared in chapter 8 for we are here in a similar context with a similar import.[53] We understand that it involves Gabriel and the 'son of man' clothed in linen like the High Priest (12.6) as in 10.5 (see ad loc.; cf. 7; 8.15–16; 10.16).[54] The former speaks to the 'son of man' being himself ignorant of so great a mystery (v.6).[55]

There is a problem as to what meaning should be given to the Hebrew word translated as 'these wondrous things'. We might agree with R. H. Charles and think of what had been prophesied in 11.31–6 and 12.1, but our own preference leans more to the interpretation of M. Delcor: 'the actions of Antiochus IV (see 8.24; 11.36)', for in both texts referred to we find the same term without any equivocation.

The response (v.7) is given with a double assurance: The Man-priest lifts his two hands toward heaven to call upon 'The-One-who-Lives-For-Ever' who with the other angel and Daniel then becomes a witness to the vow.[56] The people will be totally humiliated but the end will be

[52] The term יְאוֹר which designates the river in question in ch. 10 and also here, properly signifies the Nile before 200 BCE. The 'great river' usually is the Euphrates. There is a third adaptation of the word since Dan. 10.4 says that we must understand the Tigris.

[53] See, for example, O. Plöger who invites us to read vv.5–13 in the light of 8.13–14, op. cit., p. 172.

[54] See Chary, op. cit., p. 36, n. 2: 'The term *bad* is exclusively reserved for sacred vestments. Outside of P, see also 1 Sam. 2.18; 22.18; 2 Sam. 16.14; 1 Chron. 15.27; Ezek. 9.2; Dan. 12.6.' Cf. Riesenfeld, op. cit., pp. 122–3.

Notice the text's insistence on the term 'man' (vv.6, 7). The same situation is found in the parallel text, Ezek. 9.2–3, which is Daniel's inspiration here.

[55] But see our critical notes.

[56] See Deut. 19.15. Usually one hand was lifted up (see Gen. 14.22; Exod. 6.8; Deut. 32.40; Rev. 10.5).

glorious (see *supra* concerning v.4, and *passim*). As in 7.25, the tribulation will last three and a half years, the time corresponding to the second half of the week mentioned in 9.27,[57] or 1,260 days (if each month has 30 days, see *infra*)—a figure to be kept in mind for interpreting vv.11–12.

Daniel's incomprehension (v.8) probably has to do with the time indicated by the 'son of man'.[58] The seer has understood the words but not their meaning which is expressed by the term אחרית (see our critical notes). This term is richer in meaning than is 'the end' in v.6 and it designates history's direction and ultimate significance. This is the stumbling block which hampers Daniel's comprehension. Why must history attain this end?

The heavenly response (v.9) is not a refusal of Daniel's petition. It stands in parallel with v.4 *supra*, cf. 8.17, 26. Daniel receives the order not to reveal these things (in the sixth century) before the time of the end comes (in the second century BCE). The end of the verse refers back to 11.35. The same thing holds for the next verse, v.10. What had been said about the 'thoughtful ones' is now extended to the whole 'multitude'. As G. von Rad puts it: 'indeed, their very death [the *maskilim*] has a purifying and cleansing effect, reminding one of the atoning function of the Servant (Isa. 53.11)'.[59] The use of the hithpael for the verbs in the first part of the verse indicates 'the martyrs' acceptance of their suffering'.[60] As for the wicked, they are confirmed in their wickedness.[61] M. Delcor draws attention to the intransitive causative use of the verb 'act with impiety'. He translates it as 'the wicked will persist in doing evil'.[62]

With v.10, we reach the second conclusion to the Book of Daniel. Vv.11–13 are a later addition, or, more exactly, two successive glosses (v.11 and vv. 12–13) designed to prolong the delay of the 1,150 days from Dan. 8.14.[63] In fact, the book gives four cyphers for the time of the End:

(a) 'three and a half years' in 7.25 and 12.17, a symbolic number designating what is doomed to fail (half of seven, the figure for totality);

[57] W. Eichrodt, op. cit., II, p. 306, blames apocalyptic impatience, constrained as it was by its own system always to calculate anew the date of the coming of the Kingdom. Paul Volz, op. cit., p. 10, sees here a positive sign of the assurance that these events will be accomplished according to God's express purpose. Illuminated by the End, every event will reveal its ultimate meaning (see p. 128).

[58] See LXX: παρ' αὐτὸν τὸν καιρόν. Or else, if we accept the lesson of some LXX mss. (see Critical Notes *ad* v.8), Daniel is puzzled by 'parables'. Then, only the angel of v.7 is able to solve those enigmas. But, v.10, Daniel receives the assurance that 'the thoughtful ones', i.e., the apocalyptic sages of his time, will understand these secrets, *like the angels*. Cf. Hans-Peter Müller: 'Der Begriff "Rätsel" im A.T.', *VT* 20 (1970), p. 475.

[59] *Old Testament Theology*, II, p. 315.   [60] M. Delcor, p. 258.

[61] See R. H. Charles, p. 337.   [62] P. 258.

[63] See H. Gunkel, *Schöpfung*, p. 269, followed by Montgomery, A. Bentzen, Rinaldi, M. Delcor, etc.

(b) 1,150 days, '2,300 evenings and mornings' in 8.14. They probably represent an exact calculation, and are not symbolic as in the preceding instance, of the period during which the cultus was interrupted in Jerusalem (Autumn 167 to 14 December, 164);

(c) 1,290 days in 12.11. For Rev. 11.2–3, the three and a half years have 30 days and a year equals 360 days. Therefore 1,290 days = three and a half years plus one month. It may be that this extra month represents the period of the composition of the great vision in Dan. 10—12;[64]

(d) '1,335 days' in Dan. 12.12 adding another month and a half to the preceding figure. We may see here the delay before the final publication of the Book of Daniel in its entirety (= two and a half months after the purification of the Temple on 12 December, 164, or February 163).[65]

V. 13 applies to Daniel personally the promise from Isa. 26.19 as it had been developed in the first verses of Dan. 12. But the import of the text is not limited to this, it is also an exhortation and promise to its readers.

[64] Others believe it is a question of Antiochus IV's death (summer 164), or the supplementary month of Adar II added in 167. The complicated numerical interpretation offered by C. Schedl, *BZ*, n.s. 8 (1964), p. 104, fails to take into account the symbolism of numbers in Daniel.
[65] We were greatly assisted by Professor P. Grelot in formulating these reflections on the chronological indications in Daniel.

Concluding Remarks

In another work presently under way,[1] we propose to draw some exhaustive conclusions from the Jewish apocalyptic texts from the second century BCE. Therefore we will limit ourselves here to a few remarks. Coming after the great prophets of the Exile as their successor and epigone, Daniel sees himself constrained to account for the objective fact that the announcement of the coming of the Messianic Era seems belied by ever more dramatic events. The extreme tension between the promises of a Second Isaiah or a Jeremiah, on the one hand, and the Hellenistic persecutions, on the other, overwhelms him. According to the 'books', the present should be a blessed time, a new era should have opened when God is universally recognized as 'God Most-High', the master of heaven and earth. For if the Word of God makes sense, it ought to be manifest here and now. If the promise of the Kingdom is to be verified, today is the time. Contrary to the prophet, the apocalypticist does not appeal to the past since it belongs to a completed epoch of the holy history. Nor does he evoke the future for we have arrived at the 'Day of the Lord' beyond which there are no more days to come. Time is telescoped into the lived moment. For the first time in biblical literature with a historical dimension we find no more mention of the Exodus, the Sinai Covenant, or the Davidic promise. The instant fills the whole horizon. Consequently it lacks historical roots, and therefore must be cyclically interpreted beginning from itself to return to itself. This is no longer the attentive work of a prophet who sees the צמח, the Branch[2] maturing in events. The apocalypticist has recourse to mysticism, even to myth. Jeremiah appears calm and steady alongside these hypersensitive apocalypticists. A decisive turn has been taken: a new world *has to* come, God's world. All of modernity's impatience appears in the second century BCE! To the cry 'God is dead' contained in events, the apocalypticists respond with a cry sprung from their martyred hearts. They demonstrate nothing, they do not preach or bear witness, they do not really recall a received tradition. They cry 'No!' Against tyrants, against themselves, against all evidence, they proclaim the impossibility of the death of God. They see The-One-Who-Endures triumphant, judging the world, attaining his ends just at the precise moment when men think he is 'out of breath'. Faith takes on a new

---

[1] *Daniel in His Times, A Study of the Jewish Apocalyptic Movement in the Second Century BCE.*

[2] See Isa. 4.2; Jer. 23.3–5; 33.14–26; Zech. 3.8; 6.9–15. Cf. J. G. Baldwin, 'Semah as a Technical Term in the Prophets', *VT*, 14:1 (1964), pp. 93–7.

signification. It is no longer simply faithfulness, firm assurance, certitude, hope, but a mystical vision, an affirmation unto death of God's truth *against* men's lies. From this time on, faith is no longer 'to do the truth'[3] *in* and *with* creation, but the proclamation of Truth, uncreated in spite of creation, divine in spite of the human, transcendent in spite of the immanence of our perception. A *dualistic* conception of the universe and of history thus becomes inevitable. It reaches, as is well known, an extreme form at Qumran. Yet as it appears in Daniel it is tolerable for it is not yet a system or reflective affirmation, but rather a largely unforeseen and even unconscious consequence of a message whose point lies elsewhere.[4]

Apocalyptic is not an academic exercise,[5] but the fruit of unbearable suffering. The wicked, the 'Hitlers' of the day were triumphant and went so far as to 'throw down some of the stars of heaven' (see Dan. 8.10). The righteous 'are slaughtered all the day long' (Ps. 44.23). It was a total impasse. Extraordinary conclusions had to be drawn from that extraordinary situation. Since one could not turn either to the right or the left, could not go forward or backward, God must be driving us into a corner where the only place to look is on high, as in the days of the נחשתן (the bronze serpent) set up by Moses in the desert (Num. 21.8–9). In the sixth century BCE, in the days of Nebuchadnezzar, the Israelites believed that everything was finished, that they were abandoned by God and men. At that very moment arose Israel's greatest prophets who transformed distress into hope, catastrophe into victory, the impasse into an avenue (see Isa. 40.3; 43.16). In the second century, the Book of Daniel placed its reader into these same Babylonian circumstances because contemporary events were at least as grave as had been those of the Exile. Then God had intervened in strength, today God is going to come in glory. The lesson of the Exile had been that the people's dereliction was a theophany at the same time—גלות signifying both exile *and* revelation ('To whom has the arm of the Lord been גלה?' Isa. 53.1). When the Kingdom seems farthest off—it is closest.

[3] See Ezek. 18.9; I QS 1.5, 6; John 3.21; I John 1.6.
[4] The partial resurrection belongs to this same 'dual' perspective. Humanity is divided into two groups, the one living 'for nothing', the other for eternal life.
[5] 'It appears increasingly clear that all the apocalyptic literature of the Second Commonwealth was not, as once assumed, the literature of the man on the street, but rather the esoteric Midrash of the intellectual élite' (S. W. Baron, *A Social and Religious . . .*, vol. II, p. 314).

Bibliography

Baumgartner, W., *Das Buch Daniel*. Giessen 1926.

Bentzen, A., *Daniel* (coll. HAT). Tübingen 1952².

—— *King and Messiah*. London 1955. (= *Messias, Moses Redivivus, Menschensohn*. Zurich 1948.)

Bevan, A. A., *A Short Commentary on the Book of Daniel*. Cambridge 1892.

Bickerman, Elias, *From Ezra to the Last of the Maccabees*. New York 1974.

—— *The Maccabees*. New York 1947.

Borsch, F. H., *The Son of Man in Myth and History*. London 1967.

Caquot, André, 'Les Quatre Bêtes et le Fils de l'Homme (Daniel 7)' (*Semitica* XVII, 1967).

—— 'Les Songes et leur interprétation' (*Sources Orientales*, no. 2, Paris 1959).

Carmignac, Jean, *La Règle de la Guerre des Fils de Lumière contre les Fils des Ténèbres*. Paris 1958.

—— and P. Guilbert, *Les Textes de Qumran traduits et annotés*. vol. 1. Paris 1961.

—— E. Cothener and H. Lignée, ibid., vol. 2. Paris 1963.

Charles, R. H., ed., *Apocrypha and Pseudepigrapha*. 2 vols., Oxford 1913, reprinted 1963.

—— *A Critical and Exegetical Commentary on the Book of Daniel*. Oxford 1929.

—— *Eschatology: A Critical History*. New York 1963.

Collins, John J., 'Apocalyptic Eschatology as the Transcendence of Death' (*CBQ* XXXVI:1, January 1974), pp. 21–43.

—— 'The Son of Man and the Saints of the Most High in the Book of Daniel' (*JBL* 93, no. 1, March 1974), pp. 50–66.

—— 'The Symbolism of Transcendence in Jewish Apocalyptic' (*Bibl. Res.* XIX, 1974), pp. 5–22.

Colpe, C., 'Ho huios tou anthropou' (*TWNT* 8, 1972), pp. 400–77.

Coppens, J., 'La Vision daniélique du Fils de l'Homme' (*VT* 19, 1969), pp. 171–82.

—— 'Le Fils de l'Homme daniélique et les relectures de Dan. VII, 13 dans les apocryphes et les écrits du N.T.' (*ETL* 37, 1961), pp. 5–7.

Cross, F. M., *The Ancient Library of Qumran*. London–New York 1958.

—— *Canaanite Myth and Hebrew Epic, Essays in the History of the Religion of Israel*. Cambridge, Mass., 1973.

Cross, F. M., 'The Council of YHWH in Second Isaiah' (*JNES* 12, 1953), pp. 274–8.

Dahood, Mitchell, *Psalms* (Anchor Bible) 3 vols. New York 1965–70.

Delcor, Marcel, *Le Livre de Daniel*. Paris 1977.

—— 'Les Sources du Chapitre 7 de Daniel' (*VT* XVIII/3, 1968), pp. 290ff.

Dequeker, L., 'Daniel 7 et les Saints du Très Haut' (*ETL* 36, 1960).

Dupont-Sommer, A., 'Le Livre des Hymnes découvert près de la Mer Morte (1 QH)', *Semitica* VII. Paris 1957.

—— *Les Écrits Esséniens découverts près de la Mer Morte*. Paris 1959. (ET, *The Essene Writings from Qumran*. Oxford 1961.)

Emerton, J. A., 'The Origin of the Son of Man Imagery' (*JTS* n.s. IX, pt. 2, October 1953), pp. 225ff.

Feuillet, A., 'Le Fils de l'Homme de Daniel et la tradition biblique' (*RB* 60, 1953), pp. 170ff., 321ff.

Frost, S. B., 'Eschatology and Myth' (*VT* 2, 1952), pp. 70–80.

—— *Old Testament Apocalyptic, Its Origin and Growth*. London 1952.

von Gall, A., *Die Einheitlichkeit des Buches Daniel*. Giessen 1895.

Ginsberg, H. Louis, 'The Composition of the Book of Daniel' (*VT* IV/3, 1954), pp. 264ff.

—— *Studies in Daniel*. New York 1948.

—— 'The Oldest Interpretation of the Suffering Servant' (*VT* III/4, 1953), pp. 400ff.

Grelot, P. and A. Lacocque, *Daniel* ('Traduction Oecuménique de la Bible [*T.O.B.*]). Paris 1975.

Gressman, H., *Der Messias* (FRLANT, vol. 43). Göttingen 1929.

Guillaume, A., *Prophecy and Divination*. New York–London 1938.

Gunkel, H., *Schöpfung und Chaos in Urzeit und Endzeit*. Göttingen 1895.

Hammer, Raymond, *The Book of Daniel*. Cambridge 1976.

Heaton, E. W., *Daniel* ('Twentieth Century Bible Comm.'). London 1956.

Hippolyte, *Commentaire sur Daniel*. ed. Bardy et Lefèvre. Paris 1947.

Hölscher, G., 'Die Entstehung des Buches Daniel' (*T.S.K.*, 92, 1919), pp. 113ff.

—— *Die Ursprünge der jüdischen Eschatologie*. Giessen 1925.

Jaubert, Annie, *La Notion d'Alliance dans le Judaïsme aux Abords de l'Ere Chrétienne* ('Patristica Sorboniensia', no. 6). Paris 1963.

Jeffery, A., *Daniel* ('The Interpreter's Bible', vol. 6). Nashville 1956.

Jepsen, A., 'Bemerkungen zum Danielbuch' (*VT* XI, 1961), pp. 386–91.

Kaufmann, Y., *Toldot ha-emunah ha-ysraelit*, 8 vols. Tel-Aviv 1956³. (ET and summ. Moshe Greenberg: *The Religion of Israel*, 1 vol. Chicago 1960.)

Kraeling, C. H., *Anthropos and Son of Man*. New York 1927.

McNamara, M., 'Daniel' (*A New Catholic Commentary on Holy Scripture*, new and fully rev. edn. London 1969), pp. 650–75.

Manson, T. W., 'Some reflections on Apocalyptic' (*Aux sources de la tradition chrétienne* [Mélanges offerts à M. Goguel] Paris 1950), pp. 139–45.

—— 'The Son of Man in Daniel, Enoch and the Gospels' (*BJRL* 32, no. 2, 1950), pp. 171–93.

—— *The Teaching of Jesus*. Cambridge 1935².

Martin-Achard, R., *De la mort à la Résurrection d'après l'A.T.* Neuchâtel-Paris 1956.

Menasce, Jean de, *Daniel* ('Bible de Jérusalem'). Paris 1954.

Michaeli, F., *Daniel* ('Bible de la Pléiade': vol. II). Paris 1959.

Miller, D. Patrick, *The Divine Warrior in Early Israel*. Cambridge, Mass. 1975.

Montgomery, James A., *The Book of Daniel* (ICC). New York–Edinburgh 1927.

Moore, G. F., *Judaism in the First Centuries of the Christian Era*. 3 vols. Cambridge, Mass. 1927–30.

Mowinckel, S., *He That Cometh*, ET, G. W. Anderson. Oxford 1955.

Müller, U., *Messias und Menschensohn in jüdischen Apokalypsen und in der Offenbarung Johannes*. Gütersloh 1972.

Plöger, O., *Theokratie und Eschatologie*. Göttingen 1959. (ET, S. Rudman, *Theocracy and Eschatology*. Richmond, Va. 1968.)

—— *Das Buch Daniel* (*KAT* vol. XVIII). Gütersloh 1965.

Porteous, Norman W., *Daniel* (*ATD*, 23). Göttingen 1962. (ET, *Daniel: A Commentary*. 'The O.T. Library'. Philadelphia 1965.)

Rowley, H. H., 'The Bilingual Problem of Daniel' (*ZAW*, N.F. IX, 1932), pp. 256–68.

—— *Darius the Mede and the Four World Empires in the Book of Daniel*. Cardiff 1959.

—— 'The Historicity of the Fifth Chapter of Daniel' (*JTS* XXXII, 1930–1), pp. 12–31.

—— *Jewish Apocalyptic and the Dead Sea Scrolls*. London 1957.

—— *The Relevance of Apocalyptic*. London 1944.

—— 'Some Problems of the Book of Daniel' (*E.T.* XLVII, 1935–6), pp. 216–20.

—— 'The Unity of the book of Daniel' (*HUCA* XXIII, pt. 1, 1951), pp. 233–73.

Russell, D. S., *The Method and Message of Jewish Apocalyptic 200 B.C.–A.D. 100*. London 1964.

Schmidt, N., 'The Son of Man in the Book of Daniel' (*JBL* XIX, 1900), pp. 22–8.

BIBLIOGRAPHY

Schmithals, Walter, *Die Apokalyptik: Einführung und Deutung*. Göttingen 1973. (ET, John E. Steely, *The Apocalyptic Movement: Introduction and Interpretation*. Nashville 1975.)

Schürer, E., *Geschichte des jüdischen Volkes im Zeitalter Jesu Christi*. vols. 1–3. Giessen 1885. (ET, J. Macpherson, S. Taylor and P. Christie, *A History of the Jewish People in the Time of J.C.* 5 vols. Edinburgh 1890; New York 1961.)

Sjöberg, E., בן אדם *und* בר אנש *im Hebräischen und Aramäischen* (*Acta Orientalia*, 21). 1953.

Slotki, Judah J., *Daniel, Ezra, Nehemiah* ('Soncino Books of the Bible'). London 1951.

Steinmann, J., *Daniel*. Paris–Bruges 1961.

Tcherikover, Victor, *Hellenistic Civilization and the Jews*. ET, S. Applebaum. Philadelphia 1959; New York 1970.

Vermès, Géza, Appendix E on the Son of Man in: Matthew Black: *An Aramaic Approach to the Gospels and Acts*. Oxford 1968³.

Virolleaud, Ch., *Textes en Cunéiformes Alphabétiques des Archives est, ouest et centrale* (vol. II, *Le Palais Royal d'Ugarit*). Paris 1957 (= *C.T.A.*).

Volz, P., *Die Eschatologie der jüdischen Gemeinde im N.T.en Zeitalter*. Tübingen 1934.

—— *Jüdische Eschatologie von Daniel bis Akiba*. Tübingen 1903.

Ziegler, J., ed., Septuaginta . . . (vol. XVI pars 2, Susanna. Daniel. Bel et Draco). Göttingen 1954.

1 Index of Subjects

abomination of desolation 58, 75, 191, 199, 229

Adam (adamic ideology) xx, 48, 50, 80, 86, 128n, 133n, 147, 164n, 168, 194, 245, *see also* son of man

angel 7, 65–7, 78–9, 81, 87, 118, 126–7, 133, 151, 162, 168, 190, 200, 204, 209, 211, 214, 240; as 'Watcher' 78–9, 81; as prince 162, 171–2, 194, 210n, 212–13, 240, 242; as star 243–5, 252; Gabriel 168, 172–3, 190, 200, 204, 206, 209, 211–12, 215–16, 248; Michael 133–4, 162, 190n, 200, 206n, 209n, 213, 215–16, 235, 239, 242, *see also* saints, elect

animal symbolism, 86, 113, 115, 119, 139–40, 157, 208; four animals 1, 24, 150, 156, 208; bestiality 76, 86–7; lycanthropy 74, 80, 86, *see also* kingdoms

Antiochus IV Epiphanes xvi, xviii, 7–10, 15, 18–19, 54, 57–60, 70, 74, 83–4, 86, 92, 94, 106–7, 112–13, 119, 123–4, 129, 132, 141, 144, 152–3, 156, 161–4, 169, 171, 177–8, 186, 189n, 190, 197–8, 205, 214, 226–9, 231–2, 243, 244n, 248, *see also* evil

apocrypha xviiin, xx, 3n, 4

Baal Shamem xx, 107, 137, 143, 146n, 147n, 153, 159, 164, 198–9, 231n

Babylon, destruction of 93, 103–4, 109

book(s) 143–4, 163, 212, 239, 246, 251; of Destinies 204, 235, 242, 244; of life 144, 180, 200–1, 235; of magic 27–8; as scriptures 179, of Truth 200

Chaldeans *see* magicians

clairvoyance, significance of xxv, 26, *see also* wisdom

clouds, as accompaniment to theophany 126, 137, 146

confession *see* piety

corporate personality *see* holy community

Council of Yahweh 129, 131–2, *see also* angel

Covenant 127n, 176, 178, 182, 184, 186–7, 198, 226–7, 237, 239, 251

cryptograms 102–3

Darius the Mede 24, 51n, 109, 111, 119

determinism xxiv–v, 81, 104

dreams, premonitory in tradition 32, *see also* Nebuchadnezzar, visions of Daniel

Elect (Thoughtful Ones) 235, 243–5, 249, *see also* Saints, angel

eschatology 5–6, 45, 81, 123; as priestly 194–5; 'realized' 51, 131–2; Messianic features 52; eschatological character of Daniel 192, 216, 232, community, Israel as eschatological 127–8, Exodus 177, victory 130, *see also* secret

Essenes 10–11, 31, 131

evil, nature of 94–5, ineffectiveness of 121, Epiphanes quintessence of 129, 141

faith *see* wisdom

fasting *see* piety

festivals: Yom Kippur (Day of Atonement) 192, 205, 209, 240; Passover 205, 209; Succoth 239–40, 242; New year Babylonian 50, 59n, 92, 239n, Jewish 59

fire as accompaniment to theophany 60, 66, 143, 246

food, clean *see* piety

freedom 11, 76, 81, 89, 105, 116, 119

God, titles of 42ff, 53, 68, 76, 82, 83–4, 87–8, 118, 142, 151, 152; enthronement of 153n, 242; intervention of 36, 48, 68–9, 95, 108, 118–19, 185; power of 63, 68–9, questioning of 63; sovereignty of 43, 78, 84, 86, 89, 101; as revealer of secrets 42ff, victory over chaos 142n, 144; divine plan 21, 40, 246

hand writing on wall 94–5, 101

Hassidim xx, xxiv, 11, 131, 193, 229–30, 234, 238, 244, *see also* martyrdom, resistance

history, divisions of 5–6, 48–9; meaning of 2, 101, 249; philosophy of 10, 81; Daniel as universal 214; goal of 114, 121,

2 Index of Authors

3 Old and New Testaments

4 Apocrypha and Pseudepigrapha

5 Rabbinic Literature

RABBINIC LITERATURE

6 Qumran Literature

7 Other Ancient Texts